MW00387143

Arkansas in Modern America

For Murphy—
with best
wishes
Ben Johnson
9 Dec 2000

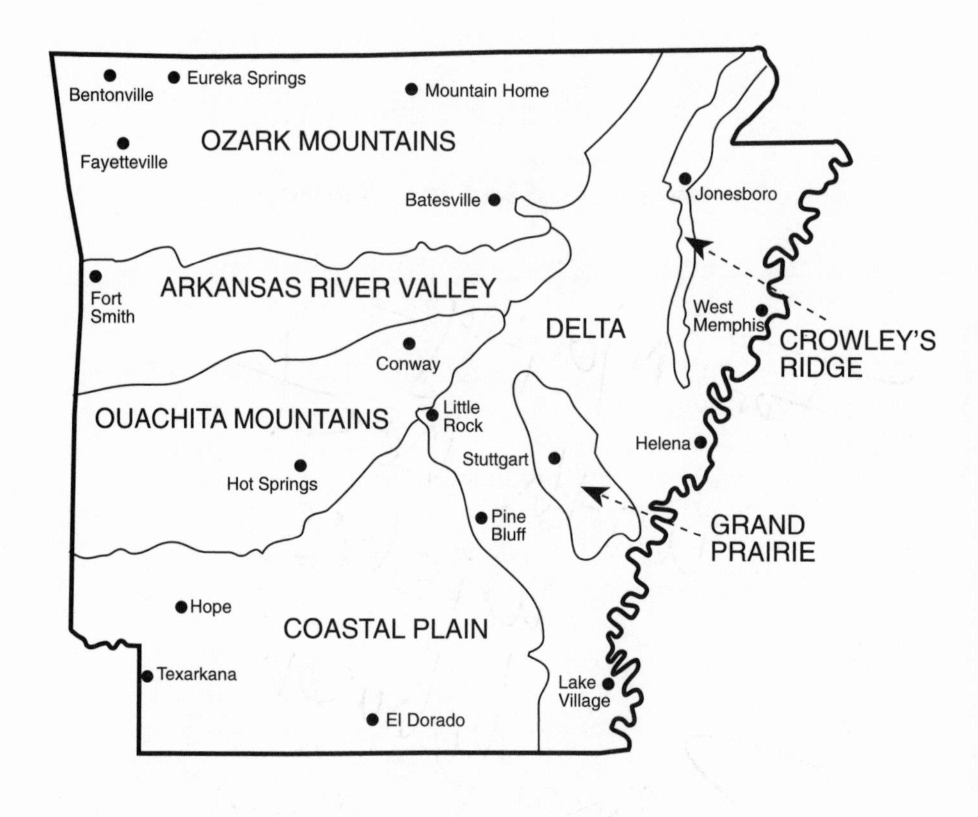

Histories of Arkansas

Elliott West, general editor

Arkansas in Modern America 1930–1999

BEN F. JOHNSON, III

The University of Arkansas Press
Fayetteville
2000

04 03 02 01 00 5 4 3 2 1

Designed by Liz Lester

♾ The paper used in this publication meets the minimum requirements of the American National Standard for Permanence of Paper for Printed Library Materials Z39.48–1984.

Library of Congress Cataloging-in-Publication Data

Johnson, Ben F., 1953–
Arkansas in modern American : 1930–1999 / Ben F. Johnson III.
p. cm. — (Histories of Arkansas series)
ISBN 1-55728-617-5 (alk. paper) — ISBN 1-55728-618-3 (pbk. : alk. paper)
1. Arkansas—History—1865– I. Title. II. Series.
F411 .J64 2000
976.7′053—dc21 00-009325

This project is supported in part by a grant from the Arkansas Humanities Council and the National Endowment for the Humanities.

For Sherrel

In Memory of
Stayton Wood II

Acknowledgments

This book would not have been completed without the generous help and advice from friends and colleagues.

Bettie H. Mahony skillfully edited the initial drafts of the manuscript. Elliott West gave encouragement and a fine critique. Ernest Dumas, Willard Gatewood, Roy Reed, Martha Rimmer, William R. Wilson, and Bill Worthen offered critical revisions and insightful suggestions. Kevin Brock was a superb editor in preparing the manuscript for publication. I am also grateful for the comments from the University of Arkansas Press's anonymous reviewer as well as those from Ted Ownby. These readers deserve much credit for the book's strengths, but I will answer for its faults.

Although cited in the bibliographical essay, I must extend profoundest appreciation to those who submitted to formal interviews: Dale Bumpers, Marcus Halbrook, Brownie Ledbetter, Sydney S. McMath, Emon Mahony, Sheffield Nelson, David Pryor, and Henry Woods.

Robert Brown and Rex Nelson kindly took time to answer my questions about recent developments. Jodie Mahony continues to provide a first-class political education. I am in debt to those who provided suggestions and documents in the course of my research: Curtis Sykes, Steve Wilson, Stephen Renken, Keith Sutton, Donny Harris, Alan Hughes, Becky Thompson, S. Charles Bolton, Bonnie Johnson, Susan Young, Mary McFarland, Charles Venus, Joe David Rice, Lee Zachery, Steve Jones, Greg M. Joslin, Max Brantley, Wendy Richter, and Donald Tatman. Michael Dabrishus and the staff of Special Collections, University of Arkansas, Fayetteville, kindly and effectively responded to my requests for help. Linda Pine of the Archives and Special Collections, University of Arkansas, Little Rock; Lynn Ewbank at the Arkansas History Commission; and Bob Besom at the Shiloh Museum provided crucial help in securing photographs. Margo Pierson at the Southern Arkansas University Library navigated me to relevant sources. With admirable patience and professionalism, Phillip Arndt, Joyce Adams, and Ellen McGowan at the South Arkansas Community College Library took in stride my numerous requests for materials and interlibrary loan volumes.

Out of my family of long-standing Texans, my cousin Ethel Johnson Wood and I had the good fortune to marry Arkansans. Beyond offering gracious encouragement, Sherrel kept the book on track with remarkable ideas that cleared away narrative roadblocks.

Contents

Foreword

In this splendid new history of Arkansas, Ben Johnson has taken on a formidable task. It would be hard enough to tell the story of any state during the extraordinary seven decades from 1930 to the end of the century. But Arkansas—there's a real challenge. Two complications immediately come to mind: The depth and breadth of change here has arguably been greater than in almost any other part of the nation. In addition, perhaps no state has been more afflicted with clichés and popular imagery that threaten to turn its complexities into caricatures. Johnson has more than met the challenge, and by doing so he has opened our eyes to a truly remarkable American experience.

Johnson's story begins with Arkansas devastated by the nation's most wrenching economic calamity. The promise described in Carl Moneyhon's preceding volume in the series, *Arkansas and the New South, 1874–1929*, has been dashed. Forces of change were not wholly blunted, however. New Deal programs, though a mixed legacy, began to gnaw at some of the worst and most persistent poverty. Literally and figuratively, the lights began to come on for more Arkansans. As with all Americans, World War II and postwar affluence quickened the pace of change still more. The move out of the countryside, begun after the Civil War, accelerated, and by the early 1960s Arkansas was officially urban, with more than half its people living in larger towns and cities.

Just as these changes seemed to be drawing the state into the national mainstream, Arkansas was indelibly stamped by what was by most measures its defining event of the century—Little Rock's Central High School crisis of 1957. The violence, nastiness, and heroism of those months produced heroes and goats, changed the contours of politics, twisted the course of race relations, and altered Arkansas's future in countless other ways. Certainly, nothing has come close to the influence of the Central High episode in painting Arkansas's portrait for the rest of the world.

Ben Johnson's impressive contribution here is to give that event its due while never allowing it to dominate the state's true history. He shows us so much more that was happening during these years, not the least of which was the startlingly diverse story of civil rights and desegregation before and after Central High. We also see economic transformations, the first flexing of industry, great shifts of population and the continuing stresses among the state's various regions, the birth of an environmental movement and the attraction of tourists and retirees, educational and political reforms (as well as their limits and frustrations), and the rise of prominent figures of public life, including two men whose names would be quickly recognized anywhere in the world.

The Arkansas we discover here is as difficult to categorize and sum up simply as any other part of our bewildering nation. Reminding us of that, Ben Johnson has taken an important step toward a fuller and more mature understanding of this understudied state.

The Histories of Arkansas Series is meant to give readers the means to explore our long legacy. Like the previous two volumes by S. Charles Bolton and Carl Moneyhon, Johnson's provides a careful, critical, yet respectful portrait. "She's awful hard to love sometimes," a friend once commented about Arkansas, but as this fine book shows us, the Land of Opportunity is also a place of remarkable and unexpected possibilities, both in the neglected study of its past and what we can expect in the coming century.

Elliott West
University of Arkansas, Fayetteville

Introduction

Between the grim years of the Great Depression and the advent of a new century, Arkansas completed a long struggle to merge with modern America. The fusion, however, left remnants of the state's older economy and society in place.

At critical points in the past, the state stood on the brink of opportunity before civil war and economic cataclysm doomed hopes. After World War II changes in national markets heralded the restructuring of the traditional agrarian economy while an expanding federal government buttressed rising incomes. Within Arkansas, business leaders overrode regional factionalism and rural skepticism to expand manufacturing statewide. They agreed with reformers that a professionally managed state government aided stable and responsible progress. The unfolding of an Arkansas cultural identity accompanied the state's economic and political integration into the nation. The inauguration of an Arkansan as president of the United States confirmed the state's hard-won achievement.

Before Bill Clinton's victory in the 1992 presidential election, the 1957 Little Rock desegregation crisis was the most studied and publicly recognized occurrence in recent Arkansas history. The drama revolving around the official and the popular resistance to the enrollment of nine African-American students at Central High School obscured the roots of the crisis and its consequences. The truncated story of civil rights in Arkansas began and ended at the schoolhouse door. As a whole, popular appraisals of the modern era became debates over the meaning of the 1957 conflict. Many Arkansans believed the televised images from Little Rock annulled a budding prosperity, and they welcomed subsequent advancements as rehabilitating the state's lost reputation. Scholarship confirmed their preoccupation. The large number of serious studies on the school crisis contrasted sharply with the scarcity of examinations of other topics. Clinton launched his campaign for the White House from a state known for one searing, angry episode.

Published without footnotes or references to historiographical debates, this book is intended as a general overview. I have aimed for a comprehensive portrait that does not sacrifice narrative coherence. Readers will note that several themes recur throughout the text. The crusade for economic modernization bound state politicians, federal officials, and business notables in shifting, sometimes uneasy, coalitions. Waning political localism lessened public corruption while state services were expanded to advance general prosperity. Changes in the state's economy spurred gradual urbanization and a widening consumer market. Even as their daily experiences more closely resembled those of other Americans, Arkansans supported events and institutions that presented a unique state heritage. As in the rest of the South, the struggle for racial justice proceeded from antisegregation activism to grappling with questions of power and opportunity. Observances of the Little Rock Crisis became civic history lessons to present a vision of a future liberated from crippling divisions.

A state is a political entity, but its citizens also come to see themselves as part of a community. The history of Arkansas breathes through the lives of its people. I will admit to considerable enthusiasm for the subject and to the ambition that this work will encourage others to look freshly and honestly at modern Arkansas.

General overview

Depression Arkansas: A Season without Rain

By 1930 the collapse of the international industrial and financial system registered only as a faint echo in Arkansas. Sara White Ragsdale recalled a childhood in which hard times were traced by burrowing cracks in the dry earth. "Swirling dust boils up from gravel roadbed, enveloping the trees and hollyhocks. Everything is the same monochromatic tan: people, trees, flowers and dogs. The choking, gasping heat of south Arkansas fills your throat. Why do I only remember the summertime? Later years and better years have winter, spring, and fall. But for me the summer and Depression are synonymous."

Eighty percent of Arkansans lived on farms or villages. For them the 1930 drought withered livelihoods, and it revived the old scourge of famine. The rains returned, but falling crop prices thwarted recovery. Unimaginably, one of the poorest states in America plunged deeper into poverty, and the long hot season of flattened hopes extended beyond the decade's first summer. Neither overburdened charitable organizations nor the sluggish turning of the business cycle restored home, work, or confidence. Arkansans in the past had received little from the national government, but a new Democratic administration and congressional majority intensified expectations.

In 1935 Ragsdale's mother, Mrs. J. Courtney White, worked for a federal relief agency in northern Arkansas. She and her children planned to join her husband in Tennessee, where he earned a good salary with the Tennessee Valley Authority. Surveying clients who had requested commodity aid, Mrs. White found "people living under bridges, in shacks, crannies, and cracks of the White River Valley." The plight of the marble cutters was bitterly poignant. Able to remain in company housing after the quarries closed, the craftsmen and their families desperately cultivated small house gardens too small to fend off hunger.

Loss and displacement did at certain times and places provoke resistance to entrenched authority. Yet, the political and economic establishment was well practiced in weathering popular challenges. Isolated food riots, the organization crusades of the Southern Tenant Farmers' Union, and the Arkansas Negro Democratic Association's call for voting rights were quelled and turned aside. The deference of federal officials to local elites disillusioned insurgents who had thought activists in New Deal agencies would side with them. The state government remained insular and corrupt. The struggle to manage change went beyond battles over elections and property. Writers, artists, and reformers fought to preserve traditional customs and expression against the threat of popular culture. Folklore collection and historical research became tools to construct a new Arkansas identity.

Daily and persistently, Arkansans bravely grappled with forces upending their lives within a society resisting transformation.

Before the Flood

No single event brought the Depression to Arkansas. Instead a series of interlocking crises swept over the state before the 1929 Wall Street crash: cataclysmic natural disasters, plummeting commodity prices, and mounting public debt. These crises battered an economy that since 1900 had been steadily developing in a manner comparable to those of most other industrializing southern states. A sprawling web of railroad lines connected growing Arkansas towns. New manufacturing and processing plants raised the hopes of urban boosters that the state had finally embarked upon modern diversification and market integration. However, in the midst of the apparent national prosperity of the 1920s, the state began a long decline that prevented its people from sharing fully in the American abundance.

The state's geographic diversity forged regional specialization within the dominant agricultural economy. Throughout the 1920s newly minted business development groups, such as the Arkansas Advancement Association, and former governor Charles H. Brough on the Chautauqua circuit relentlessly cited the state's impressive rankings in the production of cotton, corn, rice, lumber, livestock, and fruits. Yet, the post–World War I decline of the Arkansas economy in conjunction with the falling cotton market revealed the hyperbole in these proud claims.

Cotton plantations worked by tenants had become the common economic unit in the Arkansas Delta, the familiar name for the state's Mississippi River Alluvial Plain. Between 1880 and 1930, volatile cotton prices along with the expensive land clearance projects had doubled the percentage of Arkansas tenant farmers. As cotton dropped to nineteen cents a pound by 1929, Arkansas planters ignored the pleas of University of Arkansas agricultural agents and continued to open new tracts for cultivation. Outside the South, a new cotton belt was emerging in Oklahoma and Texas, ensuring continued oversupply of the commodity.

The university agronomists had promoted rice cultivation in the clay subsoil of the Grand Prairie along the western edge of the Delta. But few cotton farmers were willing and able to invest in the expensive machinery characteristic of rice operations. In the early 1930s, an Arkansas cotton farmer owned $137 in equipment, whereas the average rice grower had a $2,281 capital investment in machinery. In response to the 1920s price crunch, rice farmers organized the Arkansas Rice Grower's Cooperative Association, which not only reduced planted acreage but also ventured into processing with the purchase of a rice-milling company in Stuttgart. Since 1915 north Arkansas farmers had also marketed their apples and peaches through a cooperative association, but this organization failed to shield its members from market instability. By the 1930s the expansion of large commercial fruit farms in regions with more suitable climates and the infestation of the Ozark apple trees with the codling moth restricted

Arkansas orchards to the northwest corner plateau, where favorable soils could support expanded operations.

Arkansas farmers perpetually faced a credit crisis, leaving them more vulnerable when markets tumbled. A 1925 analysis calculated that interest rates to Arkansas farmers exceeded the national average by 3–5 percent, accounting in part for the 150 percent rise in farmowner and tenant debt throughout the decade. The state constitution did impose a 10 percent usury limit, but a series of state supreme court decisions allowed creditors to circumvent the barrier by cloaking rising borrowing costs as fees and ancillary charges. In everyday life, expensive credit fell heaviest on tenants, whose food and supply bills rose with hefty surcharges at local stores and commissaries. The sources of credit in the Arkansas Delta were varied and exploitative. Tenants and small farmers secured their debt to storeowners and landlords with liens on their upcoming crop. Memphis and New Orleans merchants aggressively marketed loans to large landowners, usually with the stipulation that the money be used to grow cotton. By contrast, Arkansas banks were unwilling to invest substantially in the local farm economy. In 1925 the average bank loan per farm acre in Arkansas was no more than half that for holdings in Illinois and Missouri.

The first Arkansas industrial revolution unfolded in the opening decades of the twentieth century, when the number of manufacturing firms grew from 547 to 1,167. Late-nineteenth-century industries such as sawmills, coal mines, cottonseed processing, and railroad shops were complemented by new enterprises such as bauxite and zinc mining, automobile manufacturing, and oil refining. But manufacturing employment peaked in 1919 and would not regain the same levels until the World War II era. In 1930 over half of Arkansas workers were still employed in agricultural occupations compared to about one-fifth of American workers overall.

The leading Arkansas firms processed raw materials and felt the same whiplash from erratic demand as those who produced commodities. Sawmills that produced cut lumber employed four times as many workers as those in finished-wood manufacturing and ten times the number laboring in the nascent paper and printing industry. In addition, vast cutover tracts had replaced the state's virgin forests, and few companies followed the lead of the Dierks Lumber and Coal Company, which in

1925 set up a management plant for its holdings throughout the Ouachita National Forest. From their inception, Arkansas mines sent most zinc and bauxite ore to out-of-state smelters, and consolidation in the zinc industry by 1930 centered extraction at high-grade ore sites in Kansas and Oklahoma. While railroads could haul ore beyond state lines, the expense and difficulty of transporting petroleum encouraged the founding of at least nine small refineries in the booming south Arkansas oil fields. Nevertheless, technological barriers and lack of capital meant that wells did not penetrate beyond four thousand feet, and the initial discovery fields of 1921–22 were depleted by the end of the decade.

The economic doldrums fueled a mushrooming fiscal crisis for the state government, but the fundamental causes originated in the contours of Arkansas politics. In the late 1920s, the Arkansas state government rapidly accumulated a level of indebtedness that provoked comparisons with the Reconstruction era. The state's constitution, drafted in 1874 by Democratic officials who had ousted the Reconstruction Republicans, had been devised as a bulwark to excessive state taxation, spending, and borrowing. The framers also crafted articles to obstruct the revival of a statewide opposition party. They concentrated public authority in the hands of local officials. Within their jurisdictions, county judges exercised almost unchecked discretion over disbursement of funds, management of road projects, and purchasing decisions. In most counties, the legislative body, or quorum court, was of an unwieldy size and met infrequently. The constitutional guarantees that provided each county, regardless of size, a member in the state house of representatives stunted democracy and augmented the clout of county bosses. Localism in politics strengthened the supremacy of local economic elites.

During the late 1880s, the Democratic Party discovered that the constitutional provisions would not stave off all insurgent threats. In 1888 only open fraud and intimidation denied an alliance of farmers and Republicans the governor's office. After employing deadly violence against African-American voters to retain power, Democratic officials decided thereafter to wield the less blunt and more precise instrument of disfranchisement. Offered as a reform measure, an 1891 law mandated that precinct judges rather than friends or relatives supervise ticket marking.

Thousands of black Arkansans avoided the polls in 1892 rather than face white election officials. In that same year, the diminished electorate approved the collection of poll tax payments, the sole means of voter registration in Arkansas until 1965.

Democratic leaders tolerated African-American political rights until they witnessed black participation in a class-based assault. In 1906 Gov. Jeff Davis made disfranchisement a solid underpinning for white supremacy when he pushed the state party committee to establish the whites-only primary. The nineteenth-century argument that black exclusion ensured clean elections was replaced by the overtly racist rhetoric of who was fit for civic responsibility. The recent solidification of the labor system left eastern Arkansas planters wary of the racial demagoguery of Davis, who hailed from the Ozarks. With nearly three-quarters of African-American farmers mired in tenancy, landed elites could easily resort to the manipulation and coercion of a dependent labor force to suppress scattered Republican challenges. The economic subjugation of African Americans, even more effectively than political disabilities, insulated the magnates from dangerous agrarian protest. The original provocation for disfranchisement lost its urgency, but the value of racism as political currency grew among remaining white voters. Rural legislators introduced and passed urban segregation statutes in the decade following disfranchisement.

As the twentieth century opened, Arkansas's white Republicans sacrificed their black constituency and surrendered ambition for office but enjoyed the solace of federal patronage jobs. The "post office" Republicans' descent into political irrelevancy splintered the Democratic party organization into shifting personal factions. The expiration of formal partisanship in Arkansas drained the substance from Democratic identity. On the other hand, the decentralized character of Arkansas politics thwarted the formation of a permanent state political establishment. Ambitious white males could rise in the state political ranks if they effectively garnered the backing of key local elites. The death of partisanship and suppression of insurgent movements framed twentieth-century campaigns as dramas of personality rather than arenas of ideas.

The corresponding decline in white voting with the near elimination of the black franchise was only partially due to poll taxes and requirements that voters be registered months in advance of an election. Low voter turnout among whites persisted deep into the twentieth century. Between 1920 and 1946, less that one-third of eligible whites voted in gubernatorial primaries. Throughout this era Arkansans understood that elections were not competitions for the votes of citizens but a struggle for the favor of those who dictated which ballots were counted.

The most common method of fixing elections grew from the right of an individual to purchase poll tax receipts for others. With relatively little trouble, local political bosses could buy large blocs of receipts and vote them in bulk. In addition, voters who showed up at polling places did not have to present their receipts but merely indicated that they were the persons listed on the voting roll. Thus, they could cast ballots in as many boxes in a ward or precinct as time and energy permitted. Honest citizens faced formidable hurdles to cast an independent ballot. They knew that their choices were not immune to scrutiny by election officials because voters were required to sign their names on a numbered register at the polling site in order to receive a ballot bearing the same number. Once inside the voting booth they had to strike through all unwanted candidates rather than check their specific choices.

Despite its limited scope, state government fulfilled certain necessary obligations. Constitutionally weak and titular heads of a nonexistent party, governors retained advantages similar to those enjoyed by county judges. The governor oversaw patronage, awarded state contracts, and managed state relations with the federal government. A governor's dispersal of favors led many Arkansans mistakenly to identify each administration as "a machine." In truth, when a governor left office after the traditional two terms, his political capital was spent. The myth of a gubernatorial machine rested on the notorious scrambling for government appointments. White-collar jobs, whether clerical or managerial, were at a premium in the state's agrarian economy. By 1930 only 6.5 percent of employees worked in the largely urban wholesale and retail trades. Fewer than 4.5 percent of employees were recognized as professionals, of whom nearly half were poorly compensated female educators. However paltry the spoils, government posts offered opportunity for enrichment.

Arkansas governors in the 1920s entertained reforms reflecting the interests of the incrementally larger business and professional class. Urban leaders insisted that education and highways were state responsibilities requiring uniform management and standards. These influential spokesmen for efficiency argued that modern economic development demanded a reversal of the continued dispersal of government resources to local units.

The nearly five thousand school districts enjoyed considerable autonomy but were starved for revenue. A constitutional ceiling on local property tax millage, haphazard assessments, and small taxing districts contributed to a multitude of one-room schoolhouses operating six or fewer months each year. Nearly every Arkansas schoolteacher was licensed through a county examination, and few had attended college or completed four years of high school. Dependent upon the property tax for nearly all of its funds, the state allotted stipends to local districts based simply on the number of students. Under this system, impoverished rural districts had no hope of closing the gap with comparatively better-off town and urban schools. A significant proportion of state moneys for African-American schools originated with northern philanthropic foundations, and several counties refused to pass through funds intended for black education.

In 1929 Gov. Harvey Parnell's tax program confirmed the rifts between town and country. Arguing that property owners should not bear the full burden for supporting state services, Parnell pushed an income tax measure through the legislature that supplied revenues for school equalization and held the promise of a reduction in the property tax. Business leaders usually supported school improvements but mounted a campaign to revoke a measure they viewed as inimical to industrial recruitment. Rural voters defeated the repeal initiative in a statewide referendum, although final results were delayed until the most notorious of the machine counties determined how many votes the Parnell camp needed.

The state responded to the automobile age by allotting taxing and revenue-bond authority to privately formed local associations. A 1915 act permitted local commissions to form road improvement districts empowered to issue bonds for highway construction. Numbering over five hundred by the early 1920s, the overextended road districts could not offer a network of paved roads to counter creditable allegations of fraud. A 1927 reform law pledged new gasoline taxes to assume $70.5 million of road district debt and also authorized $13 million in bonds for future state highway construction. These obligations, along with a new offering of $14 million in bonds for Confederate pensions, gave the state its highest level of debt since Reconstruction. The payments accounted for half the state's annual budget.

The 1920s reform initiatives defined the good government agenda for the following decades. That agenda, however, rendered few immediate achievements. Until the 1950s, paved highways were an uncommon luxury. Owing to an extraordinarily high personal exemption in the income tax schedule, the only individuals subject to taxation were those earning the equivalent of 500 percent of the Arkansas per capita income. In 1948 a constitutional amendment lifted the ceiling on the local school tax millage, and an initiated act collapsed school districts with fewer than 350 students into larger districts. The state property tax was not abolished until 1958.

In an agricultural state, even politics was overshadowed by the weather. Strong rains in the Mississippi River Valley throughout the winter and spring of 1927 spawned a flood that exploded through the system of public and private levees south of Cairo, Illinois. Unable to empty into the raging Mississippi, swollen Arkansas rivers inundated 13 percent of the state's surface and caused the deaths of 127 people. U.S. Commerce Secretary Herbert Hoover oversaw a relief effort to assuage the immediate plight of refugees. Federal officials believed responsibility for the repair of mangled roads and breached levees rested with the state. Arkansas, of course, did not have the resources to refurbish the infrastructure. The American Red Cross distributed through landowners food for displaced farm tenants. The philanthropy of others resuscitated the fraying paternalism of the planters.

Herbert Hoover's celebrated direction of the 1927 flood relief efforts buoyed his successful campaign for the presidency the following year. In August 1930 President Hoover convened a conference of governors whose states were ensnared in another natural cataclysm. No rain fell that summer in the South while temperatures soared over 100 degrees day after day. Farm income shriveled along with the crops as parched gardens left family shelves empty. Hoover's antipathy toward federal government relief and preference for developmental loans were reinforced by growing unemployment and business closings throughout the nation. The president viewed the drought as intertwined with the Depression and feared that siphoning the federal treasury for desperate farmers would unleash a torrent of similar demands from cities. Sens. Joseph T. Robinson and Thaddeus Caraway of Arkansas regarded the drought as a natural catastrophe, much like a flood or windstorm, and did not anticipate a long-term government obligation. When Hoover proposed in December to provide twenty-five million dollars in loans for crop production but nothing for food aid to families, Robinson pungently observed that men could no longer claim parity with mules.

Hoover did not appoint a disaster czar in 1930, the role he filled during the flood recovery. As in 1927, the Red Cross was the presumed agency for immediate relief, but the organization's officials remembered plantation owners' earlier double-dealings and were wary of an immediate massive effort. The national office instructed local chapters to use their own stockpiles to feed the hungry through at least the end of the year. The twenty-nine chapters in Arkansas reported their supplies were far short of what was required to sustain the estimated 100,000–200,000 families without subsistence.

One Red Cross worker documented the stark images in eastern Arkansas tenant cabins: "barefoot and without decent clothes, no meal, no flour in the bin, ragged children crying from hunger . . . nothing but hunger and misery . . . far worse than the Mississippi flood." In 1930 Arkansas farmers harvested 40 percent fewer cotton bales than in the previous year, but the drop in production was matched by a 42 percent price decrease. Overextended planters did not apply for additional private credit to provision their tenants. When the state director of the Red Cross toured thirty-seven cabins in St. Francis County, he found none with coffee or butter and only two with milk. By October local Red Cross agents distributed turnip seeds, a reliable late fall crop. Lard, cornbread, and turnips were the famine staples of poor rural families. In December the national Red Cross office began to funnel money into the state, however, fewer than 10 percent of the needy benefited from this aid. In early January 1931 the national leadership finally agreed to start large-scale relief after headlines in *The New York Times* gave news of a "food riot" in England, Arkansas.

The drought crisis did not incite organized movements among angry farmers. The few reported violent episodes were spontaneous and directed against the usual targets of grievance and resentment. In August white farmers who demanded public jobs fired at a group of black road-construction workers near Lonoke. Dozens of people raided stores in Conway, Forth Smith, and Pine Bluff to seize foodstuffs. Lonoke County area farmers had passively accepted the local Red Cross agent's evasions until H. C. Conley stirred nearly fifty of them to clamber onto his truck for the trip to the England town grocery. Conley had followed the congressional debates on relief in the Kansas City newspaper and proved to be a natural spokesman. As the crowd of mostly white farmers grew to nearly five hundred, town leaders decided to avoid an onslaught by distributing supplies directly from the stores.

For national observers, the England gathering was a warning shot, either ill or good. Drought-stricken Arkansas became a metaphor for anxieties spawned by the Depression. An Indiana congressman's declaration that communist subversion was at work perplexed the England mayor, who could not recall sighting bolsheviks. The homespun pundit Will Rogers judged that the farmers had "hit the heart of America" and later toured Arkansas to raise money for drought aid through benefit performances. Conley's subsequent descriptions of the incident underscored its nonpolitical character; he emphasized that the farmers were driven to unusual measures to save their families. In his retelling, Conley only acted instinctively after a desperate mother asked him what was to become of her children who had not eaten in two days: "Lady, you wait here. I'm going to get some food." Still, Conley warned, farmers would organize if hunger and official unconcern persisted. "I'll tell you that there's sure going to be something tearing loose around here someday."

No more than the 1927 flood did the Arkansas drought destabilize the plantation system. Neither the Red Cross nor the federal government wished to incite a social revolution and thus accepted the planters as middlemen for dispensing aid. Tenants were accustomed to the rituals of dependency evident in the settling of accounts with the harvest or in the furnishing of basic supplies in the spring. Yet in the midst of famine, planter prerogative appeared to take on the grim trappings of power over life and death. Sporadic gatherings to demand food for survival were not mass insurgencies, but the outbreaks suggested that tenants expected planters to provide a basic livelihood.

Between January and March 1931, the American Red Cross provided over three million dollars to feed 180,000 Arkansas families. The organization set a basic relief allowance and mandated a work requirement in exchange for food, but local oversight accounted for variations throughout the state. In eastern Arkansas, planter-dominated committees balanced charity with labor management. One committee report revealed the familiar assumptions: "We do not believe we should give enough food to be comfortable for this would destroy the incentive of our negroes to work and might even ruin our labor force for years." The labor requirement in many counties subsidized the plantations. Tenants cleared land and made improvements on farms in return for Red Cross staples or for warrants to be redeemed at the plantation commissary. In Lincoln County, John I. Smith, director of work projects in his county, used Red Cross funds to pay his tenants $1.50 a day to construct a road from his farm to a new state highway. When he upbraided his workers for malingering on the project, they responded that they were being forced to work for money that had been donated by others to feed their families. For these tenants and others throughout the Delta, late spring rains returned them to the fields and to the old cycle of credit and debt.

As the Red Cross aid trickled to tenants and sharecroppers, the president and congressional critics reached a compromise on an agricultural loan program. The bill allowed landowners to secure the loans and assume responsibility for feeding their tenants. Urban representatives decried the rebuff to the industrial unemployed, but Senator Robinson was satisfied with a program of federal assistance that acknowledged the special role of the planter. Within two years loans for food would be replaced by direct assistance grants under the New Deal. The policies of the new Franklin D. Roosevelt administration initially posed a more formidable challenge to planter authority than those arising from flood and drought.

The Old Politics Survives the New Deal

The 1933 inauguration of the first Democratic president in sixteen years heartened Arkansans, who believed this most solid state of the solid

Democratic South would no longer suffer neglect in its time of great need. However, when the administration attached conditions to Washington dollars for state services, political leaders felt betrayed. Still, New Deal activism was checked by Franklin Roosevelt's wariness about undermining state authority as well as by the ample influence of the southern congressional delegation. Neither federal policies nor a state political crisis involving scandals surrounding Gov. Harvey Parnell stimulated meaningful reform.

Taking office in 1928, Parnell had raised taxes to improve public schools and to expand such institutions as the mental health hospital, the tuberculosis sanitarium, and the school for deaf children. In the 1930 primary Brooks Hays opposed the incumbent governor on the grounds that he had raided the state treasury on behalf of cronies and supporters. Hays backed expanded government services but disliked the excessive reliance on debt obligations. Beneficiaries of Parnell's largesse such as financier A. B. Banks certainly understood their duty as Hays's campaign gathered steam. The governor's men raised $350,000 for his campaign in an era when the usual amount for such elections was well under $100,000. Undoubtedly, much of the money was used to buy votes. Hays himself recalled visiting a small town in a subsequent election and noting about fifty men milling about a polling site. A local friend explained their purpose. "They are waiting for the courthouse crowd to send some more money out here for them. The amount passed out to them earlier in the day was less than expected for their votes, so they are waiting. The money will probably get here." If Parnell's victory suggested the limited popular appeal of government reform, his second term demonstrated that the state's political class would not tolerate corrupt practices that endangered the status quo.

A. B. Banks had consolidated his Arkansas financial empire into the American Exchange Trust Company, but it all fell apart when a Nashville firm holding a large proportion of the newly issued stock declared bankruptcy. The collapse of the American Exchange in November 1930 dragged sixty-six other banks in the state into receivership. In Arkansas the reviled A. B. Banks replaced the specter of impersonal economic forces as the source of people's misery. The financier was indicted for continuing to accept deposits when he knew his bank was insolvent. Carl Bailey, the ambitious Pulaski County prosecuting attorney, earned a reputation as a crusader by securing the conviction of Banks. Senator Robinson was Banks's defense attorney but suffered no political aftershocks. On the other hand, in 1932 Parnell plunged deeper into disgrace when he pardoned his old supporter.

To secure legislative approval in 1931 for yet another road bond issue, Parnell delivered on a campaign promise to appoint a highway audit commission to provide accountability. The following year the commission reported that while Arkansas roads were deteriorating, highway commissioners and contractors had prospered. Most of the U.S. highway mileage in the state remained graveled surface and numerous local roads were designated "impassable." According to the audit report, at least 11.5 percent of appropriated highway funds since 1927 had been skimmed, including $105,000 put into the personal accounts of the chair of the state highway commission. Parnell defied angry legislators who demanded the governor call a special session to oust the entire highway commission; restructuring of the highway commission would wait another twenty years. Parnell's unpopularity deflected attention from the obvious bankruptcy of the state's political system, forestalling serious reforms.

As drought and depression shaved government revenues, counties and school districts had followed the state's example in using debt instruments to maintain normal operations. By 1932 Arkansas staggered under $160 million in public debt, the highest in the nation on a per capita basis. The following year Arkansas became the only state in the era to default on bond payments. After Parnell left office, the state house of representatives underscored which phase of Arkansas history it intended to repeat when it denounced the former governor's administration as "the most corrupt since the days of Reconstruction." The political leadership determined that shrinking an already stunted government was the safest way to curtail graft.

If Parnell was the Arkansas Herbert Hoover, J. Marion Futrell was no Franklin Roosevelt. Governor Futrell in his first term slashed government spending by over 50 percent, undermined fiscal integrity by lowering taxes, and drafted amendments compounding existing constitutional barriers to sound financial policy. Bonded indebtedness loomed as a severe obstacle to the governor's economic program. To his credit, Futrell did not endorse debt repudiation, even though backbreaking interest payments consumed the largest share of the annual budget. Believing tax cuts were the best tonic to aid desperate citizens, the General Assembly during the 1933 session reduced vehicle license fees even as it authorized the conversion of all the original highway bonds to lower interest state bonds. Unhappy over the lost income, creditors filed suit and won before a special federal judicial panel. This decision limited Futrell's options. He convened a special 1934 legislative session that raised the gasoline tax to fund new bonds bearing the original interest rate but maturing later than the old obligations. Future governors devoted themselves to continued tinkering with refunding to take advantage of low Depression-era interest rates.

One of the two constitutional amendments offered by Futrell was a reaction to the "Parnell debt," while the other was provoked by the Parnell taxes. The first amendment required a referendum for general obligation bond issues and reflected the state's strong tradition for popular rule. The other proposed measure required approval by either a general referendum or a three-fourths vote in both chambers of the legislature to increase existing taxes. Amendment 19, the result of this second proposal, also compelled the General Assembly to muster a three-fourths majority to pass most appropriation bills. Both amendments garnered overwhelming majorities during the 1934 election. Futrell had restricted spending, improvident and otherwise, but an effective budget control and reporting system was not put into place until 1945.

An eastern Arkansas landowner and former judge, Futrell knew government revenues would rise if the property tax laws were enforced. Because the assessed valuation of property was based primarily upon the landowner's statement of its worth, chronic underpayment or nonpayment of taxes was the rule throughout the Delta. Tax evasion followed class lines. A 1934 agricultural experiment station report noted that the largest property holdings were assessed at about half the rate of smaller operations. In four northeastern Delta counties, taxes were not paid on two hundred thousand acres of land between 1931 and 1933. During the 1934 session, in which gasoline taxes were raised for debt refunding, the legislature passed a measure allowing owners who defaulted on their taxes between 1931 and 1933 to redeem their property by paying only the 1934 tax. A populist measure on its face, the act's primary beneficiaries were not smaller landowners.

This tax decrease by a state living on the edge of penury was also the final straw for Harry Hopkins, who headed the Federal Emergency Relief Administration (FERA). Established in the first month of the Roosevelt administration, the FERA channeled grants to the unemployed through state bureaucracies. The predicable struggle between federal officials who demanded an efficient and nonpolitical system of relief distribution and state political leaders who wanted to protect their autonomy began early in Arkansas. Governor Futrell won the first round when Hopkins acceded to his demand to name an Arkansan as state FERA director. William R. Dyess of Osceola moved quickly to organize the Arkansas FERA into seven divisions, and his preference for work relief rather than handouts satisfied both federal and state officials. However, with Arkansas unemployment rates well over a third of the workforce and salary cuts helping to reduce the state's per capita income to a near-national low of $152, food provisions were a necessary part of the FERA obligations. Dyess bent to the state's plantation model in rural areas by distributing commodities through countywide commissaries and local merchant subcommissaries. Hopkins and other FERA officials denounced the system as inefficient and humiliating for recipients, who were compelled to accept publicly their allotments at the central commissaries. The distribution system survived, but Hopkins did not back down over the issue of the state's contribution to relief efforts.

If the 15 percent of Arkansas families on the FERA rolls by the fall of 1933 was stark evidence of the state's plight, Hopkins worried that it also revealed the shirking of responsibility by public officials and private employers. In October 1933 the regional FERA director reported that Arkansas planters were not supplying their tenants as they prepared "to shove them off on us the coming winter." More galling to Hopkins was the increased willingness of Arkansas to support public education with relief funds. Public school expenditures in the state declined by 40 percent between 1929–30 and 1933–34, while the number of FERA-salaried teachers escalated. By the 1934–35 school year, one-third of Arkansas teachers were federally funded. Elsewhere in the nation, FERA employment of educational professionals generated loud cries of "boondoggle" at the same time that the Great Plains drought spurred relief numbers. Hopkins understood that the Arkansas legislature's 1934 property tax relief package threw local school districts deeper into arrears. Consequently, he informed the governor that he would halt all federal aid for Arkansas if the legislature in its regular 1935 session did not provide $1.5 million for public welfare and raise educational funding.

At the beginning of the session, Futrell hoped to afford increased support for schools by calculating state funding only on the numbers of students in grades one through eight. This proposal represented his belief that substituting machine technology with hand labor would solve the unemployment crisis. While the governor's recommendation generated little enthusiasm, recalcitrant legislators defiantly established the Department of Public Welfare without an appropriation. When Hopkins suspended funding in March, Futrell predicted starvation would instigate food riots. The legislature capitulated after a few days. Restrained by the new constitutional requirement to procure a supermajority to raise existing taxes, the assembly unearthed new sources of revenue. The repeal of state prohibition permitted a liquor excise tax while newly authorized parimutuel betting on dog racing at West Memphis and horse racing at Hot Springs extracted dollars from out-of-state gamblers. The 2 percent sales tax, which exempted food and medicine, was the primary engine for reinvigorating the general school fund. By mid-March, Hopkins reopened the federal spigots.

The episode was illustrative. From then on, the state's dependence on federal funds to maintain basic services circumscribed the political leadership's options. Futrell's nostalgia for agrarian simplicity aside, prominent Arkansans assumed industrial development required minimum education and infrastructure standards. To demand complete freedom from federal intervention at the expense of prosperity was no longer politically viable. On the other hand, Arkansas was not a helpless province. The Roosevelt administration had no ambition for a radical restructuring of the American federal system. The elevation in 1933 of Joseph T. Robinson to Senate majority leader emphasized the particular benefits conferred by the congressional seniority system. Finally, the liberal New Dealers' vision of basic equity and opportunity for citizens throughout the nation meant they could not neglect the impoverished in order to discipline state officials.

The adversity suffered by Arkansans during the Depression inspired no native champion to speak for the dispossessed. The fevered populist-style oratory that had once enlivened Gov. Jeff Davis's speeches only found echo in a whirlwind that swung across the border from Louisiana. By 1932 Sen. Huey Long had come to think well of Sen. Hattie Caraway, who sat next to him in the chamber and often voted along the same lines. Harvey Parnell had appointed Caraway to the U.S. Senate to replace her husband, Thaddeus, when he died suddenly in November 1931. The governor also persuaded the Democratic state committee to support her during the special January 1932 election. Parnell may have anticipated that the quiet, seemingly apolitical widow would not enter the lists for the August 1932 Democratic primary, clearing the way for him. When she unexpectedly announced her candidacy, Carraway's amateurish campaign organization and the strong field of opponents convinced observers to dismiss her gambit. In truth, her record in the Senate reflected her husband's popular stands, and she would in any circumstances have been a formidable candidate. Caraway's unprecedented statewide tour with Long in early August sealed her triumph.

With two massive sound trucks leapfrogging from community to community, the two senators over the course of seven days addressed around two hundred thousand people in thirty-seven towns. Long was the main attraction, and ardent listeners urged him "to pour it on" as he excoriated Wall Street and the trusts. By 1932 Long's earlier assaults against specific corporations and unfair practices had diffused into a vague redistributionist scheme labeled "Share Our Wealth." Long only indirectly targeted Arkansas economic interests through occasional jabs at Senator Robinson's utility ties. "The Republican leaders are skinning the people from the ankle up, and the Democratic leaders are taking off the hide from the ear down." The blitz extended the tenure of the first woman to be elected to the U.S. Senate, and it served as a rehearsal for Long's foray onto the national political stage. Long's road show did not, however, stir a popular movement or alter the direction of Arkansas politics.

Caraway's candidacy attracted noticeable female support throughout the campaign. Prominent women in Russellville and Glenwood took the lead in organizing special welcoming activities for the candidates. All of the Mount Ida city officials were women, and they sought to encourage

Caraway by the example of their recent reelection against an all-male slate. Following the election, Caraway credited the votes of women for the amassing of her majorities in sixty-eight of seventy-five counties. The more visible female influence in politics took shape within the confines of familiar gender boundaries. While the leading Russellville women entertained Caraway at a hotel luncheon, the men's-only Rotary Club listened to Long's poetry recitations.

Throughout her two terms in the U. S. Senate, Caraway introduced few bills. On the other hand, she shrewdly leveraged her support for the Roosevelt program into building projects and grants to aid her constituency. The creation by the New Deal of a national broker state to mediate among various interest groups did substantially influence Arkansas politics. In 1933 an anti-Futrell coalition led by Brooks Hays and Carl Bailey took shape as a reform alternative to the current establishment. In the ebullient opening days of the Roosevelt administration, these young dissenters became associated with New Deal liberalism, although they repeated the familiar Progressive-era mantra of efficient government and clean elections. Unlike Futrell, they appeared willing to embrace the federal welfare agenda. Before long, however, the welcoming of manna from Washington ceased to be the defining characteristic of an Arkansas liberal.

With a Democrat in the White House, Senator Robinson was now the high priest of federal patronage for Arkansas and the gatekeeper for arriving federal dollars. Typically, Arkansas members of the congressional delegation enjoyed limited influence in state politics because they were unable to promise significant numbers of jobs or public contracts. The New Deal shifted the balance of power. Robinson solidified his base of support in 1933 by superintending the appointment of former Pulaski County sheriff Homer M. Adkins to Arkansas commissioner of federal internal revenue. The Adkins-Robinson nexus became recognized as the "federal faction." Its cooperation with the Futrell clique materialized in September 1933 during a special primary election to fill the fifth congressional district seat, made vacant when the incumbent accepted a federal judgeship. Governor Futrell prodded the state party committee to appoint his nominee to run against a token Republican opponent. Bailey and Hays opposed the anointing of a congressman without benefit of a real race, and the committee authorized a primary election. Hays entered the contest, managing to force a run-off primary despite the opposition of Futrell and Adkins. The desperation of the anti-Hays alliance was measured by the degree to which voting fraud became overt. In Yell County, 2,454 votes were cast in the runoff to give Hays's opponent a three to one margin although only 1,651 registered voters lived in the county. His slim final margin of defeat in the district as a whole gave Hays little solace.

This latest electoral setback for Hays combined with Bailey's 1934 election as attorney general left one figure as the identifiable leader of the reform group. Bailey's political ascent illustrated how a patron-client system of promotion kept Arkansas politics from ossifying into a permanent establishment. As a young lawyer in Augusta, Bailey first attracted the attention of an officer in the Arkansas Cotton Growers Association who brought him to Little Rock. Bailey next gained the confidence of the Pulaski County prosecuting attorney and was named a deputy prosecutor. Elected in his own right as prosecuting attorney in 1930, Bailey's prosecution of the widely loathed A. B. Banks fixed his name in state headlines.

Carl Bailey's successful bid for governor in 1936 rested with the happy combination of Futrell's failure to settle on one candidate as his successor and the 1933 repeal of the runoff provision (which was subsequently restored). In the primary, Bailey garnered a 32 percent plurality over five challengers. Given this slight victory margin, the legislative enactment of much of Bailey's reform agenda during the 1937 session revealed he was not a raw outsider unfamiliar with the rules of the game. Among Bailey's accomplishments, Arkansas became the first southern state to establish a civil service system; the state welfare department was reorganized to more effectively distribute federal aid; a state workers' compensation amendment was submitted to the voters, who approved it in 1938; and funds for local school districts were more than doubled with the reenactment of an expanded sales tax that now included levies on groceries and medicine. Clearly, the law to replace patronage with a limited merit system struck at the core of political influence building.

Those who believed that the character of state politics had been altered by the birth of a little New Deal in Arkansas were soon disappointed. A product of Arkansas political culture, Bailey's loyalty to New

Deal liberalism was shallow. When Joseph T. Robinson's death in July 1937 presented the opportunity for advancement, the governor displayed the instincts of a factional warlord. The state party committee complied with Bailey's wishes to nominate him as the Democratic candidate for the October special election. In 1933 Bailey had denounced Futrell's attempt to engineer a nomination through bypassing a primary. Bailey's turnabout in pursuit of office and control of federal patronage provoked criticism in the Little Rock newspapers and deprived him of the reform mantle. Fighting for survival, Homer Adkins and the Futrell forces threw together a rump convention to nominate U.S. Representative John Miller as an independent candidate. Miller's drubbing of Bailey in the special election embittered the governor, who vowed to resuscitate old-fashion logrolling. "I know now what we are going to do. We are going to drive a wedge; we are going to get our share of the factions," he confided to a supporter.

Bailey recovered to win reelection in 1938, aided by the federal faction's preoccupation with Sen. Hattie Caraway's successful rebuff of U.S. Rep. John L. McClellan's challenge. Bailey's ideological turnaround was evident throughout the 1939 legislative session. He sought to undermine the state Works Progress Administration director, Floyd Sharp, through a hostile investigation of the Dyess Colony in Mississippi County, an early New Deal agricultural-community project. Impatient with civil service restrictions on his prerogatives, Bailey tacitly endorsed the repeal of the merit appointment system. He also denounced a federal initiative to grant job protection to state welfare workers who supervised distribution of federal funds. Eventually, Arkansas complied with the rule, but Bailey's sullen conviction that federal regulations strengthened his political foes sparked his outbursts of Futrell-like rhetoric. Bailey continued to raise alarms about federal meddling and tyranny when he attempted to block Homer Adkins's path to the governorship by running for an unprecedented third term.

Adkins's easy triumph in the 1940 primary did not forge a harmonious federal and state relationship. The new governor continued his predecessor's condemnations of federal intrusions even as he angled for federal grants. His complaints became shriller as national attention shifted to the practices of segregation. In the era before civil rights activism, twentieth-century white thought about the role of African Americans had arrived at a consensus in Arkansas: conspicuous racist brutality and gratuitous violence threatened the agricultural economy and hampered industrial development. Planters understood their dependence upon black sharecropper labor, and urban boosters were sensitive to the pall that lynchings cast over the state's reputation for stability.

The horrific 1927 murder of John Carter by a mob who thought him guilty of assaulting two white women had tested the strength of this consensus. Carter's bullet-riddled body was dragged behind an automobile through Little Rock's black neighborhoods before being set on fire atop a pile of wooden pews ripped from an African-American church. Editorialists and businessmen publicly characterized the lynching as unrepresentative of the capital's progressive white citizenry. The failure of the grand jury to return indictments earned less fanfare. The killing and official dereliction, however, persuaded Dr. John Marshall Robinson that a black political organization was necessary to compel influential whites to acknowledge African-American interests.

A graduate of Knoxville Medical College in Tennessee, Robinson stood somewhat apart from the black Little Rock elite because of his involvement with the NAACP, which commanded less influence within the black community than fraternal societies such as the Grand Mosaic Templars of America. Robinson's formation in 1928 of the Arkansas Negro Democratic Association (ANDA) reflected his pragmatic evaluation that black loyalty to the Republicans delivered few benefits and built no bridges to the dominant party. While Robinson's statements reiterated the accomodationist approach of Booker T. Washington, he also understood that asking for a seat at the Democratic table offered an opportunity to challenge the whites-only primary rule. Shortly after its founding, ANDA filed suit in a Pulaski County chancery court on the grounds that the primary exclusion rule violated constitutional protections of voting rights. In November the chancellor ruled that the Democratic Party as a private organization could establish its own membership qualifications. In 1929 the state supreme court upheld this decision, and the U.S. Supreme Court refused to hear the case on the grounds that no constitutional issues were at stake.

Although African-American participation in the Democratic primary was ANDA's principal goal, the judicial setbacks did not undo the organization. In the 1930s Robinson used the leverage of his Democratic loyalty to request that Arkansas blacks share in some New Deal programs. Still, his key accomplishment was ANDA's survival into the 1940s, when federal courts reversed course on voting rights challenges. The growing African-American urban population also expanded a constituency no longer dependent upon Delta landlords. Robinson's consideration of primarily black upper class interests, however, provoked the founding of new organizations to appeal broadly and democratically to concerns of the larger community.

Land and Labor

As was true throughout the nation, the triumphs of organized labor in Arkansas during the pre–World War I era were reversed in the face of 1920s antiunion campaigns. Contracts won by the United Mine Workers made Arkansas coal miners the most generously rewarded of the state's manufacturing workers, and the UMW strengthened the broader movement with the 1904 formation of the Arkansas State Federation of Labor. Prodded by the federation, the General Assembly over the next ten years passed an array of protective statutes, including the regulation of hours and wages for railroad workers and women in manufacturing plants, child labor restrictions, and the creation of a state bureau of labor statistics. The UMW lost public support after a violent 1914 strike incapacitated mines, and in 1925 mineowners broke agreements with the union and imposed open shop practices at Arkansas sites.

In 1933 UMW president John L. Lewis moved to take advantage of newly enacted federal protections for collective bargaining to reclaim benefits surrendered during the lean years of the 1920s. The 1933 National Industrial Recovery Act (NIRA) authorized the development of industry-wide codes to limit overproduction through maintaining price and wage levels. In Arkansas, as in the Appalachian coal mines, the UMW forced owners to accept the closed shop and to submit to rising wages under the union-influenced codes. In 1935 Lewis founded the Committee for Industrial Organization (CIO) after the American Federation of Labor (AFL) hesitated to launch an organization drive of the mass production industries following passage of the National Labor Relations, or Wagner, Act. Having recaptured power in the western Arkansas coal fields, the CIO in 1937 moved to organize locals in the diversified manufacturing plants of Fort Smith. Over five thousand workers were employed in 121 of the city's factories, which included 14 furniture plants; 3 glass works; and 3 zinc smelters as well as apparel, cutlery, and cottonseed firms. Within a year the United Furniture Workers negotiated contracts with a number of Fort Smith plants to emerge as a leading manufacturing union in the state. The CIO locals formed the Arkansas Industrial Council, publishing the *Labor Journal* from Fort Smith as an alternative to the AFL's Little Rock–based *Union Labor Bulletin.*

Labor organizers had never mounted successful incursions into the state's sawmills. Agricultural depressions supplemented the sawmill labor force with failed farmers and tenants yearning for steady income. Because sawmills were constructed in the heart of virgin forests far away from established communities, owners erected company towns to house workers and supply them with provisions and services. Schools, barbershops, boarding houses, and taverns gave sawmill centers the character of any other thriving village. While workers labored for low wages at dangerous jobs and depended upon the owners' self-interested paternalism, these company towns were less exploitative than the plantation. In some cases a monthly wage deduction paid for visits to the company physician. Mill owners encouraged employees to patronize the company commissary, an anticipated source of profit. Those workers who took advances on wages, which included the majority, were compelled to buy the higher-priced commissary merchandise because advances were allotted in either company scrip or brass tokens known as "brozine." Yet, regular pay periods and restrictions on borrowing against unearned wages prevented debt from rising to the levels that strangled farm tenants.

The early New Deal delivered unmistakable benefits to sawmill workers. With the collapse of the construction sector during the Depression, the Arkansas lumber industry clearly needed an economic tonic. State board-feet production dropped 80 percent between 1925 and 1932 while sawmill employment fell by 60 percent. The implementation of the NIRA lumber codes boosted mill laborers' incomes to unprecedented levels. The workers' flirtation with prosperity only deepened their resentment when, in 1935, the Supreme Court declared the NIRA unconstitutional. Confronted with salary cuts, workers went on strike at West Helena, Warren, and Crossett. None of these actions salvaged former wage scales. Nevertheless, at Crossett, fired strike leaders formed the Sawmill and Timber Workers union and successfully petitioned the National Labor Relations Board in 1938 to order their reinstatement. By 1940 the union had established locals at several sites, including Crossett, Warren, Sheridan, and Malvern, while the United Paperworkers International was the bargaining agent at the Camden and Crossett paper mills.

New Deal policies only opened the door for union organization in the lumber industry. Employer recalcitrance combined with a low-skilled workforce accustomed to rural traditions of deference and producer autonomy thwarted labor activism. Sawmills in general were more labor intensive than other industries, and southern sawmills struggled against the more highly efficient mechanized plants on the Pacific Coast. Race also likely quelled the formation of a unified worker coalition. Company proprietors in the Ouachita Mountain timberlands invariably confronted hostility from the largely white communities when they recruited African-American labor. The segregation of company housing did not always buy stability. In the lowland southern Arkansas pine woods, the composition of the mill workforce increasingly reflected the overall biracial demographics. By the end of the decade, some of the new timber union locals included both black and white members. Still, racial division weakened union solidarity during one of the most significant industry strikes.

In 1940 negotiations between the Sawmill and Timber Workers and the Crossett Lumber Company over a contract to replace the original 1938 agreement reached an impasse. The union demanded a closed shop, and the company retracted its earlier acceptance of a union-preferential hiring clause. When the subsequent strike closed the sawmill, the paper mill and the chemical wood division workers were involuntarily off the job because of the lack of materials. Since Crossett was a company town, management stopped all credit purchases at the commissary. Initially, the strikers enjoyed the backing from a community in which most of the population were company employees. As hardship spread, however, a young Baptist minister assumed the role of conciliator and persuaded many residents that the welfare of the community outweighed the special interest of the union.

When nonunion haulers began to deliver wood to the paper mill, members of the paperworkers union returned to work. Following the reopening of the paper mill, four hundred black workers asked the company to permit them to start up the lumber division plant. Within a week the black work contingent was joined by an equal number of whites. Nevertheless, union members denounced the company for pushing black workers to seize the jobs of whites. The shootings of two African-American workers led town police to post guards on the edges of Crossett's black neighborhoods. Deprived of community support and unable to shut down company operations, the union capitulated. The new contract provided an hourly raise but included no provisions for a closed shop or preferential employment. The sawmill workers union as well as the paperworkers' organization survived the setback.

The industrial unionization drives of the 1930s were accomplished with few violent confrontations or work stoppages. Arkansas labor leaders generally shunned militancy, preferring to take advantage of New Deal favors. Owners of firms that employed organized labor discovered that a union presence did not alter basic work discipline or threaten management discretion. Even with union victories, the wages of low-skilled Arkansas workers lingered at around 80 percent of the regional average. However, plant owners' adaptation to a mild shift in labor relations and in overt federal government support for workers vividly contrasted with the battle unfolding in the state's cotton fields.

The 1933 Agricultural Adjustment Act (AAA) was the New Deal answer to the chronic overproduction of commodities. Cotton prices had fallen to their lowest levels in forty years as attempts by southern states to organize a general planting moratorium fizzled. The AAA program of payments to withdraw acreage from production began memorably in the spring with the plowing up of about 26 percent of Delta cotton fields. In subsequent years, agreements were hammered out that specified payments for keeping land out of production. The AAA funds slowed the cycle of farm failures, yet the distribution of benefit payments through landlords combined with the failure to require that a portion of the federal money be given to wage laborers stimulated a new phase of dispossession.

Grim resignation, not festive release, had long marked harvest time in the cotton South. Landlords weighed the crop, transported it to the gin, and refused to show the sharecroppers the tickets specifying price and credit for seed. Years of arranging one-sided settlements prepared planters to take advantage of the AAA crop reduction program. Many landlords either withheld benefit funds from sharecroppers or turned them into laborers. The tenants' only recourse was to hit the road. The planters' frequent justification that the Depression had made everyone poor rang hollow for those with an uncertain future. A 1934 economic survey concluded that on average planters lived well, with an 8 percent return on investment and an income more generous than that enjoyed by any member of the Arkansas professional class.

The local supervision of AAA policies and benefits ensured that prominent landowners retained their preeminence. In each county the extension agent worked with a local agricultural committee to adjust allotments and to settle disputes. Tenants knew that filing protests with these officials was both futile and dangerous. One sharecropper pleaded for help to the AAA directly: "We cannit get results by replying to thim for they ar crooked the Bunch." Chester Davis, the national AAA administrator, reflected the agricultural department's habitual preference to accept the assessments of the county extension agents. However, a group of liberals in the department's legal section argued that the agents had done little to protect tenant livelihood. This split in the federal agency was a struggle between unequal forces. In 1935 Henry Wallace, the agricultural secretary, purged the liberals after they attempted to prohibit tenant evictions. The secretary charged that the dissidents were motivated by "social preconceptions."

Gardner Jackson, one of the fired department lawyers, continued to address tenant interests in Washington by lobbying on behalf of the Southern Tenant Farmers' Union (STFU). Organized in 1934, the STFU evolved from the grievances of Poinsett County tenants over being excluded from the Civil Works Administration jobs program. H. L. Mitchell, a dry cleaning proprietor, and Clay East, a service station owner and town constable, were two young white socialists in Tyronza who had formed a short-lived unemployment league to advocate the tenants' cases to federal officials. Having achieved their immediate goals, the two thought that a local socialist party organization was the long-term solution to rural poverty and dependency. Paradoxically, Norman Thomas, head of the national Socialist Party, suggested during a February 1934 visit that Democratic domination of Arkansas precluded a political remedy. Instead, Thomas advised that a union be started. In July, East and Mitchell met with black and white tenants at Sunnyside schoolhouse on a nearby plantation to form the STFU.

Participants at the first meeting decided that a biracial union rather than a segregated organization would stall the inevitable attempts by planters to incite white hysteria over black activism. Yet, as STFU chapters developed throughout the region, integration of membership depended largely on population balance and individual preferences. In Marked Tree, organizers formed separate locals, but the two groups met together in an African-American fraternal hall, the largest available building in the community. Mitchell and East, in developing their overall strategy, concluded that often white tenants would pay attention only to white organizers and that black sharecroppers would trust only black recruiters. A 1937 report documented that only eighteen of fifty-five STFU locals were biracial, and most of these had a clear preponderance of one race or the other. Still, the color line was repeatedly and intentionally breached. In 1934 armed plantation hirelings attacked an STFU meeting and spirited a black union leader off to the Crittenden County jail. The union employed a local attorney, who advised that only white union members attend the court hearing. When the prisoner was released to the attorney's custody, his white STFU brethren escorted him from the town square to a rally. The union's practice of integrated seating at its annual conventions caused the group's eviction in 1938 from a Little Rock auditorium.

Although Mitchell later argued that the STFU's interracial gatherings and shared leadership were a prelude to the civil rights campaigns, the STFU's leadership at that time would not permit questions of racial justice to compromise the class aims of the movement. A 1936 STFU document plainly stated that "most of the trouble arising between the races is directly rooted in the problem of bread and jobs and economic security. It is not primarily a problem of color." Yet landless blacks did not believe exploitation was colorblind. In 1937 a New Deal agency asked Jefferson County tenants on a survey form to identify which "class of people" were on the bottom rung of the ladder. Most of the whites responded by listing renters, sharecroppers, or common laborers. African-American tenants replied with "colored" or "colored people." Black laborers believed race could not be separated from class. In 1939 one man instructed a white interviewer on the social reality: "The landlord is landlord, the politician is landlord, the judge is landlord, the sheriff is landlord, everybody is landlord, and we ain't got nothing."

If confident in their theories, union leaders were pragmatic in trying to achieve their goals. They relied upon Gardner Jackson's lobbying for equitable distribution of federal aid, raised money from sympathetic liberal groups, and organized selective strikes on behalf of cotton wage earners. A September 1935 work stoppage by pickers to force a raise in compensation to one dollar per hundredweight was declared a victory when several landowners raised the rate to seventy-five cents. The following spring Mitchell announced that cotton choppers would not enter the fields for less than one dollar a day. Since 1934, Delta planters had directed riding bosses and law enforcement officers to attack and arrest union members, but violent assaults grew more numerous and brutal during the strike. In Crittenden County thirteen black tenants were seized by authorities and imprisoned indefinitely. With a mob on his heels, Sam Bennett fled to Chicago from the same county after quietly greeting with a shotgun an armed planter who approached his cabin. Outsiders were not immune to the official terror. A Pulitzer Prize–winning reporter from St. Louis was held without charges or bail in St. Francis County until her newspaper arranged a release. The strike failed, but planter recalcitrance publicized the union's cause.

Distressed by the violence and documentation of peonage in Arkansas, Roosevelt became increasingly skeptical of the Department of Agriculture's deference to local interests. Governor Futrell was also shaken by the turmoil and the attention fixed on what visiting journalists were describing as a benighted land almost without parallel in the world. Wary of a pending federal grand jury investigation into peonage, and concluding that the tenant system was now a deadweight on the state's economy, Futrell appointed the nation's first tenancy commission. At the initial commission meeting in Hot Springs, the STFU protested the absence of tenant representation and were rewarded with the seating of two of their members. In December 1936 the commission issued its final report, which characterized tenancy as "a serious menace to American institutions." It proposed to end the system by turning tenants into homesteaders. The federal government should purchase state lands and then offer tenants long-term, low-interest financing to establish farms on the reserved parcels. The commission argued that farm tenancy not only posed an economic threat but also maimed the character and discipline of the sharecroppers. The rebirth of the small family farm would furnish "healthy and strong citizens."

The commission's recommendations reflected the preferences of Delta tenants. A 1936 STFU poll of its rank-and-file members revealed that most respondents aspired to be independent farmers, while only a small number preferred to join a cooperative farming operation. Delegates at subsequent union conventions continued to approve unanimously resolutions calling for a national homestead program. In letters to H. L. Mitchell, tenants clarified that, more than income, they wanted the dignity and rights accompanying farm ownership. "I want to hand my on [own] cotton myself," a Widener sharecropper wrote. STFU leaders appreciated the tenants' hope for independence, but they deemed individual homesteads to be nostalgic anachronisms in the modern agricultural economy.

Mitchell and the planters saw eye-to-eye on the economic viability of large farms. Arkansas planters were beginning to purchase tractors and employ seasonal wage laborers to replace evicted tenant families. The STFU officers concluded that tenants would soon find themselves even more precariously placed unless they formed large cooperative agricultural communities. In these proposed cooperative operations, the former tenants could enjoy the advantages of mechanization, crop diversification, and group purchase contracts. They could also avail themselves of decent schools and medical care without depending upon planter benevolence. Elements of both the STFU goals and the homestead concept appeared in the 1937 Bankhead-Jones Act establishing the Farm Security Administration (FSA). Consolidating a number of earlier farm programs, the FSA oversaw rehabilitation loans to farmers, easy credit for better-off tenants to purchase farms, and construction of migratory labor camps. The centerpiece of the legislation in the eyes of the STFU was the community projects section.

In 1934 William Dyess had established the first resettlement community in Arkansas, dividing 17,500 acres of cutover timber land in Mississippi County into family plots and platting a complete town. The FSA eventually supervised sixteen resettlement projects throughout the state. Intending to stimulate tenant civic responsibility, the agency invited a member from client families to serve on a governing association in each community. The government leased public land and buildings to the associations, which in turn subleased farm sites to the families. After a five-year trial period, clients were eligible to acquire their farms through a forty-year payment schedule. Three resettlement communities included only African-American residents, while elsewhere white and black families lived in segregated sections of the same project. The FSA rehabilitation loans and individual land purchase programs offered more tangible benefits for black farmers, although the number of recipients was modest.

While critics accused the FSA of imposing radical farm collectivization on southern soil, the agency's aim was to foster widespread farm ownership among the rural poor. Before their dismantlement during World War II, the resettlement communities sustained and provided opportunities for thousands of southern farmers at a cost lower than that of direct relief. However, the FSA did not tame rural poverty in Arkansas or elsewhere. While many of the resettled 1,438 families in Arkansas achieved independence and repaid their government loans, they were a fraction of the tenant population. In the Delta, tenant poverty rose as planters lost their incentive to prop up the region's traditional labor surplus. Not only was the FSA attempting to recreate a small producers niche that had disappeared decades earlier, it was in effect trying to sustain the farm overpopulation. Tenants would have to look beyond the Delta for a better life.

The influence of the STFU diminished as the resettlement experiment stagnated. From the outset union leadership represented a rich, often contentious, mixture of ideologies—democratic socialism, Christian social reform, communism, and Garveyite black nationalism—yet the STFU was also a product of its locale. During the organizational phase, sermon-like exhortations and movement songs adapted from familiar hymns roused local STFU gatherings. By consciously appealing to farmers through familiar religious ritual and culture, the STFU also encouraged the involvement of rural women, the mainstays of country churches.

The union locals depended on female members to manage the records and accounts. Nevertheless, singers without victories grow silent, and by 1937 the STFU was battered and adrift.

The revitalization of organized labor under the Wagner Act prompted the STFU to affiliate with the United Cannery, Agricultural, Packing, and Allied Workers of America (UCAPAWA), a CIO union. This merger uncorked simmering ideological and racial tensions. The Communist Party membership of the UCAPAWA president emboldened the Communists within the STFU to attempt an ouster of socialist leaders such as Mitchell and president J. R. Butler. In a dramatic showdown at the 1939 Memphis convention, Mitchell and Butler rallied the membership to secede from the UCAPAWA. The triumph was brief. Deprived of many black members who remained loyal to the racially progressive CIO, a vestigial STFU held on in only two east Arkansas counties.

Even before 1939 white Communists and black union leaders had already begun to swerve from the Mitchell and Butler orbit in the STFU through cooperation with Commonwealth College. Established by utopian socialists in 1925 at Mena, Commonwealth responded to the arrival of the Depression by training union organizers and dispatching students to aid western Arkansas coal miners. Hamstrung by the January 1935 arrest of one of his best organizers, Mitchell asked college director Lucian Koch to supply reinforcements so his organization could inform sharecroppers of federal protections against eviction. The Commonwealth alliance with the STFU caught the attention of the Arkansas legislature.

During February hearings by a house investigative committee, college opponents denounced Commonwealth's labor radicalism but pursued more ardently rumors of atheism and free love. The scrutiny of the college provoked telegrams and letters of protest from sympathizers throughout the nation and even Europe. The final committee report in March of 1935 concluded that even though the college did not espouse violent revolution, certain of its "militant actions . . . are extremely radical and close to the border line." Nevertheless, the committee recommended no action beyond a "close check" on Commonwealth's endeavors. The reluctance of Arkansas lawmakers to launch an official red scare was also demonstrated by the state senate's defeat of two house-approved sedition acts. To counter the second measure, Koch brought a Commoner delegation to testify before the house judiciary committee. One of the student witnesses was an Arkansas native making his first trip to the state capital. Orval Faubus explained that he was neither a communist nor a victim of Marxist indoctrination at the college. Shortly afterward, the gregarious Faubus's nonalignment with internal factions at the college made him a compromise choice for student body president.

Mitchell and Butler attempted in 1937 to reorganize Commonwealth College to serve as a genuine training center for trade unionists, but the growing communist influence reoriented the institution toward doctrinal advocacy. In 1940 the local prosecuting attorney seized the college's assets after an instructor delivered a speech in a park without a permit. Commonwealth College closed with little notice, but its reputation endured. Anti-Communist investigators in Washington in the late 1940s continued to consider it a threat despite the school's demise.

The steady displacement of small farmholders into tenancy had generated agrarian movements since the late nineteenth century. The STFU was the final rural insurgency since tenancy itself began to ebb. In the 1940s discontent in the countryside could be calculated in the numbers of migrants leaving for California or for industrial cities. The union had pioneered interracial cooperation to aid equally impoverished black and white farmers. Future Arkansas biracial movements, though, would be devoted to securing primarily citizenship equality and opportunity for African Americans, and these groups were often urban and middle class. Likely, the STFU's notable achievement was to develop a model democratic movement shaped by ideological engagement and by the vital culture of the dispossessed tenants. A stream of memoirs and histories ensured that the model remained an inspiration.

The Quest for Tradition and Identity

In 1930 two professors of history, David Y. Thomas and J. H. Atkinson, attempted to revive the Arkansas Historical Association, which had been supplanted by the 1905 creation of the Arkansas History Commission. That their goal was only fulfilled in 1941 indicated that Arkansans in the

1930s self-consciously began to develop the outlines of a state identity. As in politics and the economy, the federal government was a catalyst in the construction of an Arkansas culture. Seeking to ease present dislocation through the refurbishment of tradition, the Roosevelt administration created innovative public rituals and observances to promote stability.

The Farm Security Administration's encouragement of the independent farmer owners was only one example of New Deal romanticism for a lost world of self-sufficiency and plain living. In Arkansas, as elsewhere in the South, agricultural extension service agents plied rural families with "Live At Home" bulletins. These pamphlets advised that those who kept a dairy cow and hens and also planted a vegetable garden and orchard would no longer be passive victims of the commodities markets. Federal and state relief efforts also advanced the complementary goals of encouraging client responsibility and promoting the traditional rural economy. The agencies subsidized the construction of over twelve hundred canning centers in Arkansas to preserve the harvest of family gardens as well as to offer employment. Taking for granted wives' control of household accounts and home production, the extension service often placed women as canning center supervisors and as home demonstration agents to visit clients in their houses. Dorothy Bickerstaff of Lee County served between 120 and 150 client families, each of whom she called upon at least once a month. The panoply of women's associations in towns was invigorated during the 1930s by Home Demonstration Clubs, which coordinated educational programs with the extension service.

The federally inspired redefinition of domestic crafts as economic activities duplicated the efforts of some women to earn money by combining homemaking with entrepreneurship. In White County, women who enjoyed reputations for baking the best "beaten biscuits," guarding an old recipe for legendary cottage cheese, or planting the most admired flower garden began to sell their renowned wares. In northwest Arkansas the public canning program ran headlong into resistence from commercial canning operations, which processed local fruits and vegetables. In 1933 Washington County canning factory owners bluntly refused to follow NRA wage code regulations. The firms declared that paying two-thirds below the NRA scale was appropriate because their young female workers were not the primary family wage earners. By 1935 the canning interests forced the closing of the local canning center. Employing thirty women who produced clothing for welfare recipients, a federally supported sewing center survived until the arrival of commercial textile plants. The city of Fayetteville had provided the building housing the sewing operations, but in 1940 it took back the facility to offer it rent-free to a private company.

A growing proportion of the fruit and vegetable production in the Ozarks originated in small five-to-twenty-acre plots cultivated by new "back-to-the-land" farmers. Between 1929 and 1932 nearly 184,000 displaced and unemployed persons throughout the state returned to family parcels or rented sufficient acreage for subsistence. Some back-to-landers thought the breakdown of the industrial economy was an opportunity for utopian experiments. In 1931 a group of out-of-work professionals and technicians homesteaded a cooperative farm on public land south of Eureka Springs. The organizers established a forum to determine group policy, distributed family titles for ten-to-fifty-acre sections, and agreed to assume mutual responsibility for the ill and injured. These neohomestead ventures faded, however, as the New Deal began promoting its own vision of cooperative economics.

By 1934 the ambition of Charlie May and Howard Simon to function as viable artists in an isolated corner of upland Perry County was also drawing to a close. Having built rustic "Possum Trot" in 1931, the married couple was abandoning it for New York so that Howard could market his prints and Charlie May could continue her promising career as a writer. In May they entertained the state's best-known literary figure as one of their final visitors at the cabin. John Gould Fletcher himself had fled Little Rock for London before World War I to seek recognition as a leader of the modern poetry vanguard in the company of fellow expatriates Ezra Pound and T. S. Eliot. By the 1930s, angry that his reputation had been eclipsed and suffering from intensifying bouts of depression, Fletcher thought of his childhood home as a refuge. He had only recently returned from Europe when he made the expedition to Possum Trot. His curiosity about life in backwoods Arkansas reflected the quest by many modernist artists to uncover authentic life in the vernacular crafts of peoples untainted by technology.

In 1930 the cosmopolitan Fletcher had contributed to the Nashville Agrarian manifesto *I'll Take My Stand,* in which leading regional writers had offered the antebellum South as a humane alternative to the blighted industrial north. Throughout the following decade, he set a number of his most fully realized poems in rural Arkansas and eventually published the finest and most popular history of the state. When Fletcher won the 1938 Pulitzer Prize for poetry, many Arkansans thought it testimony that the state was achieving cultural parity with its neighbors. Privately, Fletcher was restless with the lack of publishing outlets and an energetic literary community in his home state. Yet, he stayed because his new wife, Charlie May Simon, would not live elsewhere. Unhappy in New York with Howard, Simon had continued to correspond with the fierce older poet whose visit to Possum Trot had greatly impressed her. They were married in 1936.

Simon also took Arkansas as her subject, often without the grafts of romanticism and modernist anxiety that characterized her husband's treatment of the state. In *The Sharecropper* (1937) she composed a solicitous *roman à clef* about the rise of the STFU. Her fictionalized memoir of the years in Perry County proved a remarkable document from the back-to-the-land era. *Straw in the Sun* (1945) depicted, without traces of exotic primitivism, a worldly outsider's adaptation to a traditional community beginning to adjust to contemporary intrusions. Describing a gray season of dwindling provisions, Simon observed, "But I lived through the rest of that winter, knowing a kindness and a generosity I had never known before, when, in their poverty, they shared the little they had with me and among themselves."

John Gould Fletcher's identification as an Agrarian partisan seemed to reinforce his conservative credentials, but he readily accepted a 1935 invitation to lecture at radical Commonwealth College. During the trip to Mena, he visited a small cabin on the outskirts of town to hear a blind singer who seemed to know all the forgotten songs. Others followed, and the recordings of Emma Dusenbury's remarkable repertoire of folk ballads eventually were preserved in the Library of Congress. Sharing Fletcher's interest in folk culture, high-modernist poet T. S. Eliot published the Arkansas writer's account of Dusenbury in the influential English journal *The Criterion.* The desire to seek the solace to modern uncertainty in the simple past was part of the appeal of early-twentieth-century folklore studies. On the other hand, a few careful practitioners devoted themselves to applying the techniques of anthropological research in their fieldwork among American mountain communities. Fletcher was as well-meaning amateur collector, but he conferred frequently with Vance Randolph, whose books became the fountainhead of Ozark folklore studies.

At least three decades before the recognition of an Ozark way of life, middle-class social reformers fanned out through the southern Appalachians to uncover the unique culture seemingly insulated from modern invasion. These cultural preservationists organized folk festivals, ballad-singing clubs, and handicraft guilds to counter the effects of millwork, popular sheet music and records, and consumer goods. Of course, preservation altered the mountain culture, and folklore activities more frequently reflected the collectors' assumptions rather than actual traditions. By the 1920s and 1930s, some folk endeavors embodied the era's racist fears that immigrant and African-American influences steadily adulterated white mores. An organizer of the White Top Folk Festival in Virginia viewed the upland communities as the last redoubt of Anglo-Saxon purity.

That early Ozark ethnography largely escaped similar malignant strains owed much to Vance Randolph's lack of middle-class gentility. His observation of the lives of zinc miners in his hometown of Pittsburg, Kansas, converted Randolph to socialism. Although his ideological commitment waned, Randolph continued to admire the ignored and scorned, whose everyday lives defied mainstream conventions. His regard for marginal communities blended with his respect for scientific discipline. Randolph earned a graduate degree in psychology from Clark University, but he had failed to persuade the pioneer anthropologist Franz Boas at Columbia to approve his doctoral research in Ozark culture. Throughout his career Randolph moved outside the boundaries of academic recognition. Published by a press associated with socialist works, *The Ozarks: An American Survival of Primitive Society* (1931) was a debut reviewed favorably in *The New York Times* and *Saturday Review* but ignored by scholarly journals. Taking inconspicuous notes, Randolph pursued his folk-tale collecting throughout the 1930s, while his folk-song efforts were boosted in the 1940s when the Library of Congress provided him with recording equipment. The 1947 publication of *Ozark Superstitions* finally earned Randolph academic recognition and income enough to break away from hack writing. In that same year he moved permanently to Eureka Springs, which had become the center of an Ozark salon.

Described by folklore scholar Herbert Halpert as the "perfect observer-collector," Randolph treated rural Ozarkers as both neighbors and subjects, a balancing act that kept him from either rehabilitating or romanticizing them. Beginning with the publication of *The Ozarks,* some Ozark residents spied not realism but a perpetuation of a hillbilly stereotype that hurt economic progress and regional self-respect. Randolph used the setting of a 1934 folk festival in Eureka Springs to turn their argument on its head: "The professional Ozark boosters would do well to put more of this primitive stuff into their advertising, and not talk so much about our splendid highways and excellent new hotels. . . . [Tourists] come to see rugged mountain scenery and quaint log cabins and picturesque rail fences and romantic-looking mountaineers." Randolph shrewdly, though with ambivalence, understood that any survival of folk customs in the long run depended upon accompanying commercial benefits. That Randolph's assessment won out was verified in 1954 when the Ozark Playgrounds Association, a tourism outfit, commended the maverick folklorist for bringing national attention to "The Land of a Million Smiles."

Arkansans have had a longstanding preoccupation with their image, judging from their reading and responses to published travelers accounts and literary efforts. Throughout the nineteenth century, various outsider descriptions of the state portrayed it as a lightly settled frontier with outsized characters and eccentric habits. The wide distribution of copies of Edward Payton Washburn's depiction of "The Arkansas Traveler" tale and the notoriety of the "Arkansas toothpick," or bowie knife, etched the state's signature. Antebellum frontier humor deteriorated into hack works, such as Thomas Jackson's *On a Slow Train through Arkansaw* (1903), in which the state became the almost irrelevant punch line for jokes conforming to vaudeville conventions. Northern readers of the joke books as well as the more creditable local-color works would find little to distinguish Arkansas from other states subject to similar treatments. The modernist revolt against literary formalism during the World War I era did not reach Arkansas, but it did kill off the genres that had exploited the state as a topic.

While depictions of the state had emphasized the prevailing "backwoods" environment, this feature had not been exclusively centered in the northern uplands. As the criticism of Vance Randolph's works suggest, state promoters in the 1930s increasingly assumed that descriptions of hill dialect, entertainments, and livelihood were slights that reflected upon Arkansas's reputation as a whole. However, a remarkable, if unintentional, cultural revisionism was at work. Both native and emigrant writers created a formidable canon dedicated to the richness of decidedly homogenous mountain communities: Charles J. Finger, *Ozark Fantasia* (1927); Charles Morrow Wilson, *Acres in the Sky* (1930); Wayman Hogue [Charlie May Simon's father], *Back Yonder: An Ozark Chronicle* (1932); Otto Ernest Rayburn, *Ozark Country* (1941); and Marguerite Lyon, *Take to the Hills: A Chronicle of the Ozarks* (1941). Supported by a Works Progress Administration commission, Louis Freund captured in his paintings the region's vernacular architecture, from cabins to mills. Freund and his wife, Elsie, later started an artist's cooperative in Eureka Springs. The Ozark heritage movement was beginning to define the elements representing traditional Arkansas.

Rural mountain society also stood for the state as a whole in the popular mass entertainment medium of radio. Once again Arkansans themselves shaped the message. In 1931 two Mena residents, Chester Lauck and Norris Goff, signed a contract with NBC to go national with a comedy program that had earned an enthusiastic Hot Springs radio audience. Lauck and Goff were the creators of Lum Edwards and Abner Peabody, proprietors of the Jot 'Em Down Store in Pine Ridge, a fictional town based on the Ouachita Mountain community of Waters. *Lum and Abner* continued on the air for twenty-four years, and the homespun storekeepers appeared in seven RKO movies. A 1936 audience poll identified the program as among the nation's most popular comedy shows, trailing only Jack Benny, Eddie Cantor, and Burns and Allen. Another Arkansas native who translated a radio career into movie roles was Bob Burns. He first appeared in 1934 on Bing Crosby's *Kraft Music Hall* and later began a run with his own CBS program. Burns was essentially a stage comedian who told jokes about life in Arkansas and enlivened his act by blowing a homemade musical horn he dubbed the "bazooka," the name later bestowed upon the World War II antitank weapon.

Generally, Arkansas listeners thought that Lum and Abner were salutary representations of rural Arkansas, while they censured Burns for peopling his tales with dimwitted hillbillies. A 1936 advertisement in a state newspaper contained a drawing of two businessmen commiserating, "All those stories that Bob Burns tells on Bing Crosby aren't true." Although noting the similarities between the comedians, Bob Lancaster, a journalist and historian, has convincingly observed that in the case of Burns "the rusticity of the characters was the *point* of the comedy—rather than the *flavoring* of the humor, as was the case with Lum and Abner." Responding to the Lum and Abner fans unable to find Pine Ridge on the map, the town of Waters changed its name to the fictional locale. Sensing what Vance Randolph suggested about the marketability of folk color, the owner of the Waters general store declared the state was squandering valuable tourist dollars by not erecting bridges over the creek crossings leading to the town.

Commemorated with a national radio broadcast from the capitol steps, the christening of Pine Ridge, Arkansas, in April 1936 was incorporated into the state's celebration of its centennial. The observance of the state's birth culminated with a visit in June by Franklin and Eleanor Roosevelt to Hot Springs and Little Rock. In the capital the president delivered a speech at the state fair grounds. While touring Hot Springs, the First Couple viewed a five-minute school pageant depicting the state's history, visited with one hundred flag-waving orphan children at Our Lady of Charity Convent, and lunched at utility tycoon Harvey Couch's estate; earlier, the president's secretary informed STFU leaders that Roosevelt's tight schedule precluded a meeting with a union delegation. The centennial prompted a variety of dramatic and literary homages to the state's history, including John Gould Fletcher's massive centennial ode commissioned by the *Arkansas Gazette.* The federal government, rather than private interests, underwrote these festivities.

Using history to promote civic unity and tourism was not lost on community boosters. Town and county festivals devoted to either historical or local resource themes became more common. These community gatherings were also linked to national goals through funding and support by New Deal agencies. Federal initiatives even reoriented traditional agricultural fairs. The state extension service and Home Demonstration Clubs revived the White County Fair and solidified it as an annual event. The Civilian Conservation Corps (CCC) during the decade sent selected enrollees from the young male contingents at the agency camps to organize local forestry festivals publicizing conservation efforts and resource development. A 1939 festival program in Sheridan included a speech by Governor Bailey; checker contests; sawing, a nail driving, chopping competition; various foot races; animal imitations; and a forestry motion picture.

Organized in April 1933, the Arkansas district office of the CCC oversaw the two-hundred-man camps, which numbered sixty-four at one point. The CCC in Arkansas encouraged rational management of the state's most plentiful resource by planting nearly twenty million seedlings, constructing 133 firewatch towers, and devoting 167, 227 enrollee days to battling forest fires. Significantly, the CCC also demonstrated that woodlands were not simply timber resources. Before 1933 Arkansas had three neglected sites designated as state parks—Petit Jean, Mt. Nebo, and Arkansas Post—but no park system. Prodded by federal officials, the state established a parks commission to acquire land and seek technical expertise from the National Park Service. After the CCC workers developed a park and constructed visitor facilities, the agency transferred operations to the state commission. The state generally did not appropriate money for purchasing acreage for future parks, rather it offered tax-forfeited property, as in the case of Devil's Den park, or depended upon donated parcels, as was done with the Lake Catherine park. The CCC also advanced future developments in outdoor recreation with the construction of the White River Migratory Waterfowl Refuge on ninety-five thousand acres spanning four Delta counties.

Just as cotton planters coveted crop allotment checks, Arkansas towns vied with one another for the location of CCC camps in their vicinity. Local contractors could bid for camp construction, merchants looked forward to selling supplies, and cafe and movie theater owners relished the prospect of CCC boys on weekend furloughs. Mena burghers estimated that their nearby camp infused about five thousand dollars a month into the town economy. Municipal rivalry, however, dissolved when it came to the placement of African-American camps. In the southern states, the CCC appeased powerful congressmen by creating a dual camp system. Notwithstanding this deference to segregation statutes, Arkansas officials refused to assign more than a handful of young black men to CCC projects. Eventually, African-American companies were stationed at Crossett, Strong, Charlotte, DeWitt, and Forrest City. Warren leaders deplored a plan to locate a black company in place of a white one, and Hamburg relinquished the opportunity for a camp since it would house black enrollees.

The presence of the state's black higher education institution in Pine Bluff encouraged the location in the city of one of only five National Youth Administration camps nationally for young black women. Named for Mary McLeod Bethune, the director of the NYA Negro Division, the camp not only provided classes in the liberal arts and vocational training but also gave the students a taste of outdoor life and organized lectures emphasizing individual self-worth. Supervised by Hattie Rutherford Watson, whose husband was the president of Agricultural, Mechanical, and Normal College, Camp Bethune closed in 1938 after two years in operation.

Another source for work as well as for promotion of historical identity was the Works Progress Administration (WPA). Enacted in 1935, this wide-ranging federal jobs program enrolled over thirty thousand Arkansans by the end of the first year. The state was the first in the South to employ every eligible woman, 75 percent of whom were assigned to the 123 sewing projects. Before its 1943 liquidation the WPA sponsored over three thousand construction projects in Arkansas, including bridge and road construction, schools and municipal buildings, and parks and public auditoriums. In addition, the WPA funded 138 nonconstruction projects, notably the Writers' Project. The state director of the writers' program was Bernie Babcock, whose 1919 novel, *The Soul of Ann Rutledge,* had earned a national audience entranced by the brief life of the putative first love of Abraham Lincoln. In 1936 the national director approved Babcock's proposal to compile a volume on Arkansas black history as long as African-American writers were employed on the project. Babcock argued that no Arkansas blacks on relief were qualified for the task and offered to write the book herself.

Her opposition continued after exemptions were granted black writers otherwise ineligible for relief, but the national office held firm. Under the auspices of the Little Rock Urban League, the project compensated six African-American researchers, who collected data later compiled by J. Harvey Kerns and Samuel S. Taylor to complete *The Social and Economic Life of the Negro in Greater Little Rock* (1941).

Taylor of Little Rock and Parnella Anderson of El Dorado were the two black participants among sixteen white women and two white men who interviewed former slaves and other observers of the peculiar institution. The 800 Arkansas accounts comprised the largest portion of the total 2,194 documented interviews conducted as part of the federal Writers' Project collection of slave narratives. Taylor, singled out by noted authority John W. Blassingame as "the most skillful of the WPA interviewers," discovered that many of the 129 people he visited were fearful of reprisals if they gave unvarnished descriptions. Nevertheless, Taylor's interviews were distinguished by their vivid rendering of treatment, work conditions, freedom from the potted dialect infecting the transcripts of white collectors. While the oral histories of slavery disappeared for decades into archival shadows, the WPA's valuable *Arkansas: A Guide to the State* found a place on the shelves of the state's libraries.

Awareness of the African-American past, however, was growing within the Little Rock black community during the 1930s. This cultural renaissance unfolded within the walls of the three-story Paul Laurence Dunbar High School. Dedicated in 1930, the school's "beauty, and modernity, and size" fulfilled the hopes of its community. In 1935 the composer Florence Price returned to her native Little Rock to present a benefit concert of her works at the Dunbar auditorium. Price and William Grant Still, who was educated in Little Rock public schools, pioneered the integration of African-American vernacular music—folk blues, spirituals, and jazz—into the symphonic form. Although Price's Symphony in E-minor was famously appraised by critic Alain Locke as "universal music" with meager ethnic influences, later analysis traced within its distinctive rhythmic elements echoes of the traditional "patting juba," a slapping of the hands, legs, and body that originally accompanied a dance developd by American slaves.

Another notable Dunbar visitor was the historian Carter G. Woodson, founder of the Association for the Study of Negro Life and History. In 1936 Gwendolyn McConico Floyd, a Dunbar teacher educated at Fisk University, began offering what was probably the first black history course in a southern urban high school. Woodson knew that the popular course used his study *The Negro in Our History* as the textbook, and his unannounced visit during a 1938 trip to the state attracted a roomful of students to hear his two-hour presentation. In the daily lessons the course stimulated realization that segregation was a constructed institution rather than the result of impersonal social forces and traditions. Floyd recalled that the students "were aware that we were being manipulated; that there were certain jobs we could not get; that we lived in an isolated society." This study of a buried history engendered a new defiant outlook, particularly among the young men who witnessed the trappings of privilege at the downtown hotels and businesses where they worked.

Taylor and Floyd wanted to burrow through the romantic and patrician veneer of official history to recover silenced voices and interdicted movements. The WPA and other New Deal initiatives aided the search for an undistorted past. Yet, as had the political and economic interests, determined local cultural agents also secured and deployed federal funds to memorialize the heroic ancestry of contemporary elite families. A descendent of the last Arkansas territorial governor, Louise Loughborough had long brooded that the late-nineteenth-century Little Rock red-light district had disfigured a hallowed city block. By 1938 the site had become a residential slum, and the city was preparing to raze a row of the dilapidated houses. Loughborough, a member of the Mt. Vernon Ladies Association, knew that several of the endangered structures dated from the territorial period and set out to counter the "slow train" image by saving remnants of Arkansas's brave origins. Relying on incomplete sources, she declared that the founding fathers of Arkansas had lived and governed on the site. She persuaded the legislature to create what became the state's first history museum, entreated prominent families to donate money, and pressed the state WPA administrator to adopt the renovation project. Completed in 1941, the Arkansas Territorial Restoration displayed errant characteristics of colonial British America as well as that of frontier Arkansas. No reminders of the old brothels survived: Mrs. Loughborough had made certain of that.

When Electricity Came to Arkansas

The largest picnic recorded in Arkansas was celebrated not at a camp meeting nor at a political rally but at an Arkansas Power and Light company (AP&L) stockholders gathering. On 24 July 1930 the families of small shareholders had journeyed from throughout the state to the building site of the utility's second of three planned hydroelectric projects. Congregating in the shadow of the unfinished Carpenter Dam near Hot Springs, the three thousand people were entertained by the AP&L orchestra while being served barbecue from long, custom-made tables. The company officers awarded electrical appliances as prizes to families with the oldest, youngest, and most stockowners. The conclave appeared to demonstrate that Arkansas was marching into a brilliant modern era without displacing the personal relationships that anchored rural heritage.

The company was inseparable from the personality and outlook of Harvey Couch, its founder and president. Couch was the first big man of twentieth-century Arkansas. Speaking to the stockholders that day, Couch noted that sixteen years earlier the state's only transmission line extended twenty-two miles between Arkadelphia and Malvern, whereas now three thousand miles of lines electrified most of the towns and cities. Couch did not need to remind his audience that he was responsible for the first Arkansas radio broadcast station nor that his company was a major retailer of radio sets. Arkansans were accustomed to accepting nature's devastation, but Couch's hydroelectric projects, beginning with the 1924 Remmel Dam completion, seemed to transform natural forces into agents of prosperity and convenience. Little wonder that Couch was placed in charge of state emergency operations during the 1927 flood and again during the crisis of the 1930 drought.

His prestige grew not simply from his reputation as the prophet of technological wonders but for his campaigns to expand the state's industrial and manufacturing sector. Couch calculated that his utility would stagnate without new industrial customers or the additional workers living in the already wired urban centers. Accepting the reality of the state's foundation in agriculture, he believed that Arkansas modernization required the encouragement of small industries that could process raw materials into finished goods. Couch had struggled throughout his career from lack of local investment credit, dependent on New York financial firms before his 1926 merger with the giant Electric Bond and Share Company. Rather than seek the relocation of large-scale manufacturing firms to the state, Couch angled for outside capital to underwrite native operations. Arranging motorcycle police escorts, Couch transported financiers across bumpy roads to Couchwood, his sprawling log house retreat on Lake Catherine. He believed that the rustic and verdant setting best advertised the state's capacity for development.

Couch also contemplated boosting farm income and rural electrical customers by touting investment in poultry and egg processing plants. In 1934 AP&L established a rural marketing department to support the state extension agents' attempts to persuade farmers to supplement row-crop revenue with egg and dairy production. The utility also proposed overcoming the high initial cost of wiring farm homes by offering inexpensive, long-term financing that could be repaid in part through signing on to company construction crews. Before 1934 neither AP&L nor the other four major electric companies doing business in Arkansas were aggressively extending lines into the countryside. The May 1933 enactment of the Tennessee Valley Authority (TVA) introduced a new player into the electric power market.

Although Couch claimed that AP&L strategy was not influenced by the possibility of the TVA's entering Arkansas, he took steps to bar the introduction of public projects to his domain. Brooks Hays observed that Sen. Joseph T. Robinson, the utility's legal counsel, registered strong opposition to Franklin Roosevelt's preparations to establish a federal power system for the Arkansas River Valley. Couch, on the other hand, discerned that a federal partnership with investor-owned utilities could bring lights to Arkansas farmers. He had served as a director for the Reconstruction Finance Corporation, created by the Hoover administration to fight the Depression through low-cost business loans, and wanted his old agency to underwrite AP&L's rural electrification costs. Nevertheless, Congress and the Roosevelt administration in the 1937 Rural Electrification Act (REA) favored nonprofit associations over utilities.

Still trolling for federal subsidies to fund corporate initiatives, Couch proffered what he termed the "Arkansas Plan": newly formed electrical cooperatives would secure REA loans and then transfer the money to AP&L, which would build and operate the rural systems. Federal officials were able to spurn this proposal from an influential figure because Couch faced opposition from a formidable agricultural coalition headed by the Farm Bureau and the university agricultural extension service. Years of utility reluctance to string wire to distant farms had heightened rancor. REA advocate Clyde Ellis recalled that John Hobbs of Rudy had unsuccessfully implored the utility to extend a nearby line to his house for the comfort of his desperately ill wife. Hobbs "used to get so angry and frustrated talking about the power company that tears would stream down his face."

By the end of 1937, the Farm Bureau incorporated seven electrical cooperatives whose customers were also members. The cooperatives did not have to construct costly generating plants once the state utilities department ordered AP&L to sell them electricity at wholesale rates. Demonstrating more flexibility than utility heads elsewhere, Couch acceded to REA requirements for universal service and low rates to secure agency loans for new AP&L service areas. The electrical cooperatives multiplied throughout the 1940s, but the cold war with AP&L continued, punctuated by open battles.

Couch, raised on a small Columbia County farm, was committed to rural modernization through expansion of electric service. However, he wanted to direct and oversee rural electrification with the same measure of independence that he enjoyed in running his own company. Couch possessed a broader vision and greater sense of public obligation than most of the state's political and business leaders. Still, his policies exhibited little recognition that the interest of Arkansas Power and Light and the interest of Arkansas citizens were not invariably the same.

Rural electrification delivered the industrial revolution to the countryside. Ellis remembered one woman's exclaiming: "I just turned on the light and kept looking at pa. It was the first time I'd ever really seen him after dark." A 1941 *Arkansas Democrat* piece extolled that the REA program eased domestic labor through electrical appliances and the distraction of a radio, powered the electric pump that provided water for new indoor plumbing, and strengthened farm income with the opportunity to raise chickens in heated incubators and brooders.

Unfortunately, the electric millennium flickered beyond the reach of most farm families for another decade; the 1950 census was the first to disclose that a majority of Arkansas homes had electric power. By the end of the 1930s, transmission lines extended to only 8 percent of Arkansas farms. Still, Harvey Couch's marketing efforts had at least persuaded Arkansans that radios were a necessity. In nearly 40 percent of farm homes, families could listen to *Lum and Abner* and Bob Burns, although apparently on antiquated battery models.

Flood, drought, and depression did not drive Arkansans off the land. During the 1930s the rural proportion of the population fell by only two percentage points. Since the beginning of the century, Arkansans in increasing numbers had left the state, though this steady rise slowed during the 1930s. Although around 213,000 emigrated during the decade, this was only about 75 percent of the total who had migrated out of the state duringthe 1920s. The Depression did not launch a grand exodus of Arkansas travelers bound for the golden west.

The most significant population shift in the 1930s was the almost 25 percent decline statewide in tenant farmer numbers and the accompanying dramatic reduction in the number of black farmers living in the Delta counties. Bolstered by federal crop subsidy checks, planters located near urban labor markets tentatively began to replace sharecroppers with tractors and wage hands. Trucks carrying hundreds of laborers to Delta farms became a familiar sight on the Mississippi River bridge at Memphis. Escalating investment in the region by national insurance companies may have accelerated the shift to a hired work force. Firms such as Prudential acquired large parcels of mortgaged property. Nevertheless, the nearly 60 percent rise in the state's gross farm income between 1933 and 1940 was due more to federal agricultural policies than to new operating efficiencies.

Only ten thousand tractors were chugging through Delta fields by 1940 (compared to over forty thousand ten years later), and the machines did not supplant labor-intensive jobs such as weeding, planting, and harvesting. Overall, the value of implements and machinery used by the state's farmowners did not noticeably increase from 1930 to 1940, and Arkansas inched only from a forty-sixth to a forty-fifth ranking when compared to other states. The 1930s was the first decade since Reconstruction in which the number of farms declined, but the surviving operations were not notably larger. In fact, the average tenant-holding in Arkansas expanded during the 1930s at a rate three times greater than the growth of owner-held farms; large-scale consolidation of farm ownership was to be a post–World War II development. The small one-crop farms worked by muscle and despair weathered the Depression, and their survival remained the bulwark of rural poverty.

Proportionately, fewer African Americans moved from Arkansas during the Depression than white migrants. Depression-wracked American cities attracted few newcomers, and opportunity seemed as likely in nearby places. The first stop for many black tenants who left the farm was the sawmill. The percentage of millworkers within the African-American labor force rose during the decade from 3.8 to 5.7 percent. Those who moved into town were excluded from the better-paying manufacturing and transportation occupations. Most black families rented small two- or three-room houses, only one-third of which had electricity and only one-fourth had running water. The percentage of African-American workers in the wholesale and retail trades doubled, though remaining under 5 percent of all black employed.

Black women had always been more likely than white women to work for wages, although during the Depression the rising proportion of white females on the job contrasted with the declining percentage of employed African-American women. In general, occupations were linked to both gender and racial identity. Working white women punched the clock as sales clerks, telephone operators, apparel mill operatives, and government employees, whereas black female workers were more often domestic servants and agricultural workers. Women of both races held the majority of public school-teaching posts.

In *I Know Why the Caged Bird Sings,* Maya Angelou portrayed the authority and influence of two women in Stamps's black community: her grandmother, the owner of a bustling general store with a steady clientele, and Buelah Flowers, the aristocratic literature teacher whose manner and learning gave lie to racist cant. Flowers's husband, Alonzo, had managed his savings from his job as a timekeeper at the local sawmill to become an insurance agent and to build an undertaking parlor. While

Mrs. Annie Henderson instructed her granddaughter on how to retain purpose and dignity while negotiating the treacherous shores of segregation, Mrs. Flowers demonstrated how language both liberated the spirit and nourished the appetite for better, distant worlds. The dreams for ambitious African Americans in 1930s Arkansas were best pursued elsewhere. William Harold Flowers, Mrs. Flowers's son, left in 1937 to study law in Washington D.C., but the memory of a terrible image drew him back to set up practice in Pine Bluff: as a teenager Flowers had witnessed the burning of John Carter in Little Rock. Shortly after his return to Arkansas, Flowers became increasingly frustrated by the inaction of the older black leadership in the state and by the refusal of the national NAACP office to contribute resources for civil rights cases.

In March 1940 Flowers established the Committee on Negro Organizations at a meeting of two hundred people at the Buchanan Baptist Church in Stamps. Flowers spoke for his generation when he declared that the state's first mass civil rights organization would "revolutionize the thinking of the people of Arkansas." This bold confidence, which once would have been reckless and delusional, was certainly of the moment. The Depression was fading in the gathering wartime boom and with it the old order that had gripped the state since Reconstruction.

The dry season was ending.

Chapter Two

Wartime Arkansas: Eroding Barriers

In 1941, as Vance Randolph was preserving Ozark folks songs with equipment borrowed from the Library of Congress, collectors Alan Lomax and John Work from the library were searching for Robert Johnson in the Mississippi Delta. They soon learned that all that remained were ominous legends and a series of blues recordings the guitarist cut in Texas studios in 1936 and 1937. When Johnson drained a poisoned whiskey served by a jealous husband, the manner of his dying deepened the legend that his talent had demonic origins. As critic Robert Palmer observed, Johnson's records were a bridge between the acoustic folk blues and the amplified riffs that eventually swept north to Chicago.

In Helena the distillation of the rural blues was continued by the likes of harmonica player Sonny Boy Williamson (Rice Miller) and guitarist Robert Jr. Lockwood, the stepson of Robert Johnson. Evictions and want in the 1930s had driven many black workers to the Mississippi port city for jobs on the docks or in cotton-processing plants. The combination of cash wages and all the people in one place charged Saturday night with an electricity that never crackled in the countryside's empty spaces. Unlike white taverns centered opposite the levee along Cherry Street, black juke joints flourished in enclaves scattered throughout Helena. The blues performances were background music to the real business of gambling.

Williamson and Lockwood had larger ambitions. In November 1941, when they heard that businessman Sam Anderson was opening Helena's first radio station, they persuaded food distributor Max Moore to sponsor them in exchange for promoting his King Biscuit Flour. The two white men were familiar with the music and knew it had an audience. Soon afterward, the King Biscuit Time's fifteen-minute live broadcast began each day at noon on KFFA and quickly made the two bluesmen celebrities. Moore soon began to hawk "Sonny Boy Corn Mill" along with the flour. This initial popular response ensured that the vernacular blues sought out by Lomax and Work was about to be as irretrievable as Robert Johnson himself. Many aspiring musicians throughout the Delta heard their first electric guitar when listening to Lockwood on KFFA. Lockwood himself was paying close attention to jazz performances on urban radio stations, and his impatience with the strict blues format of the King Biscuit Time led him to develop his own show.

By 1947 Lockwood was in West Memphis, a new destination for many Helena musicians attracted by jobs and blues scene along Beale Street across the river. Lockwood had learned his craft from Robert Johnson, and he willingly tutored guitarists who would come to define the modern blues, including both Muddy Waters and B. B. King. In 1950 Lockwood joined the great migration to Chicago, where he took his place among an expatriate class of blues aristocrats recording for Chess Records. At Chess the Delta sound flowed into rhythm and blues, and then Bo Diddley and Chuck Berry navigated it across racial boundaries into rock and roll. Surviving founding fathers like Lockwood hibernated and later resumed their careers in the 1970s, when a blues revival commanded a new, largely white audience.

If the small outmigration of Arkansans in the 1930s was disproportionately white, the massive exodus during the 1940s bore away about 20 percent of Arkansas whites and nearly one-third of the state's African-American population. The overall Arkansas white population grew slightly, but the number of black Arkansans declined 11.5 percent. These figures reveal little, however, about the experience of those like Robert Jr. Lockwood who moved from rural places to Arkansas towns before leaving for the anticipated promised land. And, of course, a significant number of African Americans did not venture outside the state once they moved from the countryside. During the 1940s, rural Arkansas's depopulation was based on the one-fourth drop in its black population, while the number of African Americans living in the state's urban areas grew by one-third. (The U.S. Census Bureau defines urban centers as places with twenty-five hundred or more residents.)

Both federal policies and federal largesse during World War II galvanized social tensions and stimulated economic opportunities. The widespread protests against the construction of Japanese-American internment camps in east Arkansas contrasted with the welcoming of prisoners-of-war as a nostrum for the shortage of agricultural labor. As was the case throughout the nation, Arkansas women found work in defense plants. The influx of new migrants into Arkansas towns and changes in gender roles, among other things, raised alarms with some who believed these resulted in a shredding of the state's moral fabric when, in fact, early marriages and frequent divorces were long-term patterns rather than wartime aberrations.

Urbanization enlarged the congregations of the state's major religious denominations while encouraging clergy and lay leaders to define their responsibilities more broadly. No one felt greater anxiety over the shape of postwar Arkansas than Hamilton Moses of Arkansas Power & Light. AP&L organized a statewide industrial recruitment campaign to compensate for the expected loss of jobs from the government's reconversion of its military production sites. By 1950 manufacturing gained a foothold in Arkansas just as the antiunion movement enacted its aims into law. The gradual shift to a diversified economy provoked little turmoil. However, the issues for future conflict came to be articulated by a new generation of civil rights leaders, made hopeful by favorable federal court rulings.

Questions of Loyalty

The eruption of World War II in Asia and Europe prompted the same mixture of responses in Arkansas as throughout the nation. While the neo-isolationist America First Committee had vocal and organized support in the state, prominent leaders rallied around the Democratic

President Roosevelt, who was steering the nation into open cooperation with the besieged Allies. Newspapers throughout Arkansas praised the Lend-Lease Act, introduced in January 1941 to allow war-material shipments to Britain and China. The influential statewide *Arkansas Gazette* had staked out a more aggressive anti-Axis position the previous June when it advocated American entrance into the war to avert an eventual stateside invasion.

In May 1940 Gov. Carl Bailey stoked apprehensions that Arkansas was being penetrated by enemy agents when he ordered the state police to investigate foreign subversion. That summer, when small parachutes were dropped over Cabot to promote a new business, residents fled into the surrounding woods and storm cellars to escape a perceived German aerial assault. Shortly afterward, a Danville pharmacist crushed the skull of a German immigrant who argued that not all of his former countrymen were Nazis. Following Pearl Harbor and the U.S. war declaration, random anti-German rhetoric and violence were turned against those deemed unpatriotic. In January 1942 El Dorado Veterans of Foreign Wars members fell upon and forced from the town a group proselytizing for the Jehovah's Witnesses, a sect whose antiwar views and unwillingness to salute the national flag were viewed as no less subversive than espionage. In September pipeline construction workers shot and severely beat Witnesses who had journeyed to Little Rock for an annual meeting. Police arrested and charged the victims of the attack with disturbing the peace.

Vigilance against subversive activities was a national crusade early in the war, and the Arkansas reaction was not unique. Most of those incarcerated in federal prisons for refusal to serve in the military were Witnesses. If Arkansans were no harsher to "dangerous elements" than other Americans, their reaction was conditioned by local experience and culture. When the national government established camps in the state for conscientious objectors, Japanese-American internees, and prisoners of war, it exacerbated anxieties over labor and race.

Most registered pacifists during World War II agreed to fill noncombat roles in the armed services. Others who held that even indirect support for the war compromised their principles were placed in camps reminiscent of the quasimilitary CCC centers. The only Civilian Public

Service conscientious objector camp in Arkansas was located near the Third District A&M College in Magnolia. The inmates, nearly all from out-of-state, labored on soil conservation projects but also took on charitable tasks such as toy repair to maintain goodwill with the local community. The only reported confrontation between conscientious objectors and residents occurred in nearby McNeil. Enjoying a brief leave, three camp members hitchhiked to the small town, where they passed the time reading, writing, and sketching. Discovering who the strangers were, a crowd gathered about the men and accused the artist of making drawings for enemy consumption. The threatening murmurs grew when the artist protested that nothing in the area was of military value. "That's just where you're wrong, Bub. It's little towns like McNeil that's the backbone of the country, and Hitler knows it," asserted one man. Soon a Magnolia city police officer arrived to extricate the three and return them unharmed to the camp.

Few Arkansans knew of the presence of the conscientious objector installation, but the forced evacuation of West Coast Japanese-Americans in 1943 to camps at Jerome in Drew County and Rohwer in Desha County ignited official and citizen protests. In the previous year the federal War Relocation Authority (WRA) had designated the two undeveloped Farm Security Administration (FSA) parcels in the Arkansas Delta as among the ten sites to house the seventy-nine thousand citizens of Japanese ancestry and thirty-one thousand Japan immigrants legally barred from applying for citizenship. These natives and long-standing resident aliens were singled out for detainment because of their small and concentrated numbers, their absence from vital war industries, and their Asian background.

Arkansas governor Homer Adkins demanded that the federal government erect sentry towers around the camps' barbed-wire perimeters and post only white guards. Southeastern Arkansas farmers speculated that the California fruit and vegetable growers had maneuvered the eviction of formidable competitors, who would, in turn, resettle in Arkansas. In 1943 the Arkansas legislature approved by nearly unanimous margins a measure prohibiting property ownership by any person of Japanese descent; the state attorney general's opinion that the law was in conflict with the Arkansas constitution left it unenforceable. Other anti-internee bills introduced during the session originated more specifically in racial hysteria. The Camden author of a measure to deny Asian students enrollment in white public schools explained, "I know none of you gentleman think Negroes are as good as your children, and I don't think any member of the yellow race is as good as my children or yours either." The bill failed as opponents cited the virtues of Chinese storeowners in such towns as Marianna and the fact that China was an American ally invaded by Japanese troops.

The two internment camps in effect became the last federally organized and constructed agricultural communities in Arkansas. Rohwer and Jerome each encompassed over ten thousand acres and held nearly eighty-five hundred internees apiece at one point. The mandatory labor requirement for all adult Japanese-Americans was filled primarily with tasks to complete the projects left unfinished by government contractors: repairing residential barracks, clearing acreage, and digging sewage trenches. The families also chopped firewood from the surrounding swamps to heat the tarpapered barracks, and their cultivation of over six hundred acres of vegetable fields in each camp decreased the WRA food expenses. The families' industriousness did not silence the criticism from surrounding communities that the authorities were "pampering" the camp residents. In all the camps, the internees organized cooperatives to purchase items and offer services not included in government rations. Leasing the WRA buildings, the cooperatives pooled the internees' Spartan wages to organize barber and beauty shops, shoe and watch repair businesses, and clothing and dry goods outlets. The WRA camp schools were conducted in unrenovated barrack spaces that bore little resemblance to classrooms. The WRA failed to maintain a full instructional staff because of the rudimentary conditions and more lucrative employment opportunities outside education.

The Japanese-American families left Arkansas after the relocation program ended with the November 1945 closure of Rohwer. Already, in June 1944, the internees had been transferred from Jerome, which was refurbished as the state's third German prisoner of war (POW) camp. German POWs began entering the state in 1943 after the victorious Allied campaign in North Africa. Eventually four thousand German prisoners were incarcerated at Fort Chaffee outside of Fort Smith while ten thousand were kept at Camp Robinson near Little Rock. Seven thousand officers and dedicated Nazi enlistees were dispatched to Camp Dermott, the former Jerome center. By the end of 1944, nearly two thousand Italian prisoners, primarily officers, were held at Camp Monticello. Apparently, most Arkansans took little notice of the POWs, many of whom were held within existing military installations. East Arkansas planters, however, spied a new labor pool.

As the war progressed, employers loudly warned about a shortage of workers. Yet, Governor Adkins sternly denied requests that had been forwarded to him through the War Relocation Authority to employ Japanese-Americans on projects outside the camps. On the other hand, Adkins diligently lobbied the federal War Manpower Commission (WMC) and the War Food Administration (WFA) to authorize the use of POWs in the Delta's cotton and grain fields. Under the international Geneva Convention agreement, enlisted POWs, but not officers, could be assigned work that was unrelated to war production and not dangerous.

Apprehensive about the effect of the wartime boom on their labor force, planters had been rethinking their growing reliance on wage labor and were using a variety of methods to lock tenants into long-term contracts. They were outraged in 1942 when the WMC and FSA officially identified the Delta as a labor-surplus area, a designation that permitted workers to be transported to other agricultural regions when not engaged in planting and harvesting. Once more the planters relied on the American Farm Bureau Federation to persuade Congress in 1943 to transfer authority over farm labor to the more accommodating U.S. Department of Agriculture. Nestled within the USDA, the WFA placated influential landowners, who communicated their demands through county extension agents. The federal agency readily changed course and demarcated the cotton regions as areas in need of outside labor. This decision insulated planters from market conditions favoring higher wages. Government favoritism also undermined the attenuated Southern Tenant Farmers' Union.

Although largely confined to the upper delta following their partition, the STFU still claimed forty thousand members. In 1943 the STFU could enforce a $3 wage for every one hundred pounds of harvested cotton because the pickers were primarily women who lived in Memphis and received checks from husbands in military service. By February 1944 the WMC gave its blessings to the distribution of German POWs to thirty branch work-camps, all but four located in the Delta. The WMC required that farmers compensate the government at a rate of $2.50 for two hundred pounds of picked cotton, a figure falling well below the STFU's demand. Whereas the Germans were content with familiar tasks such as hay cultivation, they resisted the distasteful chores of cotton chopping and picking through slowdowns and sabotage. One later explained, "It was, so to say, a continuation of the war on a lower level." Planters agreed that they endured the German prisoners' lamentable efforts in 1944 because the crop otherwise would have rotted in the fields. Union allies retorted that the planters preferred incompetent labor to paying experienced workers a living wage.

Not content to rely on POW labor, the planters in 1945 maneuvered the U.S. agriculture secretary to permit wage ceilings on cotton harvesting. The STFU responded to the Arkansas limit of $2.05 per hundredweight with another labor boycott, and planters groaned that by December, 30–40 percent of the crop stood unharvested. Continued STFU activism and the May 1945 defeat of Nazi Germany prodded the planters to develop new strategies. In the face of southern congressional entreaties, the Truman administration kept the POWs in the labor camps for nearly a year following the fall of Berlin. Within a few months after the Germans returned home, Mexican laborers under the auspices of the federal bracero program shouldered their sacks for the 1946 cotton harvest. H. L. Mitchell appealed in vain for native workers to be provided the same wage and housing protections that the U.S. government promised Mexico in exchange for transporting its citizens north. The STFU discovered once more that it did not have the strength to breach the united front of the farm interest groups, the Department of Agriculture bureaucrats, and old-line political leaders. However, any battles won against these adversaries could not change the reality that Mitchell's vision of economic justice was rendered increasingly irrelevant by the lure of out-of-state jobs and the mechanization of cotton agriculture.

Mobilization: Changes at Home and Work

Nearly two hundred thousand Arkansans, or about 10 percent of the population, served in the armed forces during World War II. That the state's service percentage slightly trailed the national rate owed much to the fact that a greater proportion of Arkansans were rejected for induction than those from any other state except South Carolina. The inability of young Arkansans to meet the selective service education requirements and to pass the medical exams was a direct outgrowth of poorly funded school districts and the scarcity of doctors and nurses to tend the rural population.

A notable exception to this pattern was the 206th Coast Artillery Regiment of the Arkansas National Guard, composed primarily of college students. Members had originally enlisted to make additional income and indulge a taste for adventure, but none had anticipated that their call to federal service in January 1941 would lead to a two-year posting in the Aleutian Islands. With relatively little fighting in the Aleutians, some regiment members were relieved that they had escaped the bloody struggles elsewhere in the Pacific, although nearly all complained of the tedium and discomfort in a cold, bleak environment. One soldier concluded, "Only a very young man with a pretty stable mind could have stayed as long as we did without going nuts." Still, most recognized that they had discovered at a formative phase of their lives the value of camaraderie, cooperation to a common end, and adaptation to different personalities. John W. Weese summarized: "I grew up and matured a lot. Learned how to deal with people—both enlisted men and officers."

Enlisting the civilian population in the war effort, the federal government encouraged the formation of new associations to blend with the activities of traditional community organizations. The parades and public displays of support for the National Recovery Administration's battle against the Depression during the 1930s were refashioned into war bond drives. The federal government shrewdly marketed the bonds to appeal to small investors' fears about a postwar depression and to hatred of the Japanese. As along Main Streets across the nation, downtown shopowners in Arkansas signed up for the American Legion Auxiliary's National Defense Window Contest. The Jonesboro American Legion granted membership in the "Slap-A-Jap" club to those who pledged a weekly defense stamp purchase. The combination of patriotism and organized competition also bolstered the collection of scrap and discarded waste for recycling as war material. Martha Newsome of Newport was recognized by the Victory Service League for setting a national record when she accumulated twenty-six hundred pairs of women's hose.

In communities located near military installations, chapters of the United Service Organization (USO) and existing women's service clubs organized entertainments, dinners in homes, and concerts to give the personnel the sense that hometown amenities were around the corner. The Searcy Girls' Service League arranged dances at the local American Legion hut for trainees stationed at the Newport Airfield. As in many similar instances, the local youth also benefited from the endeavor because the base supplied the orchestra for the dances. In Little Rock the City Recreation Council set up an elaborate downtown center with game areas, classrooms, and reading rooms for white soldiers from Camp Robinson and for workers at the Jacksonville and Maumelle ordnance plants. A separate USO club for African-American personnel was located in the former Taborian Temple on Ninth Street, the commercial heart of black Little Rock. The Little Rock Council of Jewish Women provided food for Sabbath services at Camp Robinson, and Reform and Orthodox members invited servicemen to their homes for religious holidays.

Urban leaders who anticipated a quick jolt to local economies from the placement of nearby military bases and new defense industries were not disappointed. The coming of the Southwestern Proving Grounds, an artillery-testing site, boosted Hope's population from 7,475 in 1940 to 15,475 in 1942, and about 25,000 people flooded into Little Rock during the last six months of 1940. Farmers who strongly protested the government's sixfold expansion of Camp Joseph T. Robinson through the leasing of private property rather than outright purchase did not gain a sympathetic hearing from Little Rock business and political figures. Congressman David Terry asserted that the potential contribution through camp personnel of four million dollars a year to the area's income outweighed the claims of aggrieved landowners. The farmers insisted that any land returned to them by the government would hold considerably less value and that the lease payments were inadequate in an inflated housing market. The development of the 71,115-acre Camp Chaffee southeast of Fort Smith prompted similar complaints from those resisting the forced sale of their land. The district's congressional representative unsuccessfully urged the USDA to supply alternative government-owned facilities for the displaced families.

The sudden influx into Arkansas towns and cities set off a housing crisis that persisted throughout the war and forced many hopeful job seekers to accommodate themselves in warehouses, tents, and wooden sheds. By 1945 the state's federal housing administrator reported that Little Rock was more densely populated than any other southern city. In 1937 the sight of Depression-era shanties in the capital had provoked the General Assembly to authorize the municipal government to establish a housing authority that could pursue funds under the Wagner Act. The enabling legislation defined the housing authority's main goals as slum eradication and "the provision of decent, safe, and sanitary dwellings for families of low income." The wartime boom, however, altered the aims of the program, and only military personnel, government workers, and veterans were accepted for residency in the three 1940s public housing projects. Sunset Terrace and Highland Park, the first two completed complexes with a total of 150 apartments, housed white tenants, while the 100 apartments in the Tuxedo Courts were reserved for African-American families. Venturesome investors spotted the profits in catering to the housing needs of more affluent transits. Wiley Dan Cammack procured the backing of the Federal Housing Authority to construct one hundred homes according to four basic floor plans and to rent them through federal agencies to the families of military officers. Incorporated in 1943, Cammack Village was perched just beyond the city's northwestern boundary, an outpost signaling the direction of future urban growth.

The rural migration did not impose a new traditionalism in the urban settings. The workweek for both Camp Robinson soldiers and the ordnance plant workers extended Monday through Saturday, turning the once-placid Sunday streets into bustling avenues. The ample shopping crowds persuaded Little Rock police officers that enforcing the ordinances prohibiting Sunday sales, known as the blue laws, would be futile and troublesome. Yet, the consumer demand for convenience was not the only chink in the moral order. Higher wages and newcomers' escape from family strictures widened the cultural distance between town and village. John Fergus Ryan recalled that on Saturday nights farmers, plant operators, railroad men, and their families promenaded along North Little Rock's Washington Avenue, which was off-limits to those stationed at Camp Robinson. Located along the street were small cafes, each separating black and white patrons with a board partition; grocers selling the pigs ears and feet that served as seasoning substitutes for the rationed salt pork; and the three movie theaters, ranging from the respectable Rialto to the shadowy Liberty, which ran such features as *Nadine, Queen of the Sun Bathers.* The enviable prosperity of those who worked in the Missouri Pacific Railroad shops was incarnate in their regal bearing and wardrobe: new dark brown wingtips polished to a brilliant orange hue and exotic hand-painted neckties set off with steel-sprung collar points. "Flashier dressers held their collar points down with little fake rubies backed with tiny spikes."

This Delta evacuation also swept into eastern Arkansas towns favored with military installations. In the summer of 1942, the U.S. Army Corps of Engineers completed the Blytheville Army Air Field, which was also served by four nearby auxiliary bases. Having reveled in the Saturday excursions to Blytheville from his family's tenant farm, a young B. C. Hall welcomed the decision to move to the town's rapidly expanding section of small houses inhabited by other white migrants. This neighborhood, known as the West End District, proved an economic transition ground between two worlds of rural and urban life. Hall's father continued to cultivate land he rented near town, but during the off-season older children hired on at the shirt factory or in a downtown five-and-dime. Living in Blytheville not only meant the luxury of an extra movie on Saturday, but it also presented Hall with new boundaries and opportunities for transgressing them. He formed a close friendship with Sam Lum, whose Chinese parents owned a store on Ash Street, Blytheville's black mercantile and entertainment center. In the company of this friend, Hall could maneuver through the proscribed sector that whites "had to pretend did not even exist." Unable to sidle into the popular Club Frolic, the two boys perched on a side alley fire escape to hear the blues players and jazzmen who played the club circuit from Kansas City to New Orleans. "Sometimes all that music and dancing spilled out into the alley and halfway up to Main Street. It gave me a spiny chill and made me feel I was missing out on something."

The rapidity of social changes during the war led Arkansans, as it did other Americans, to exaggerate the extent of these changes. Nationwide, both the marriage and childbirth rates escalated by 20–25 percent in the first years of the decade, a return to pre-Depression growth patterns. In actuality, the baby-boom generation originated in the pre–Pearl Harbor year of 1940. Undoubtedly, the strains of war and the desire to preserve a family identity against the chance of battlefield death profoundly shaped couples' decisions. The doubling of the U.S. divorce rate between 1940 and 1946 was consistent with a long-term development but also accelerated by long separations and the inherent awkwardness of any soldier's homecoming.

While a number of Arkansans saw ill-advised nuptials and rising divorces as evidence of moral decay let loose by the war, these phenomena were abetted by existing state laws. Brides as young as fourteen years old and grooms having reached sixteen could get a marriage license without a waiting period or health certificate. Intending to boost revenue for county governments, the legislature in 1931 had altered the divorce statutes to permit nonresidents to establish residency and obtain a final decree within ninety days. The improving economy leading up to World War II enhanced the attractiveness of Arkansas border towns and resort areas for estranged couples. In 1940 Hot Springs recorded 112 divorces by out-of-staters, an unprecedented tally surpassed by the 1941 total of 532. These statistics raised controversy among politicians, clergy, and social workers because they were linked to the other publicly cited ills of youth crime, child abandonment, and a venereal disease epidemic.

The public lamentations emerged from anxieties about the effect of the war on the status of the family. The chairwoman for the Youth Advisory Association of the Arkansas Council for Social Agencies declared, "This war is directly responsible for the boom in badness because children's fathers go off to war and their mothers go to work, and thus the interest of parents is diverted from the home and their children." In the new sociological vernacular, teenage pathology was categorized into male juvenile delinquents who committed various property crimes and female "Victory

Girls," or prostitutes, profiting from the boredom and loneliness of soldiers. Without question, newly arrived rural families confronted unfamiliar challenges in turbulent urban centers. The martial virtues touted in war propaganda overrode earlier homilies about patience and the need to resolve differences. Youth disorder increased, but it was not a tidal wave of degeneracy. The numbers of juvenile cases filed in Little Rock courts between 1939 and 1942 grew no faster than the city's population, and the rise in the state reformatory population derived from fewer foster families' taking in troubled boys and girls.

The efforts by civic reformers, religious leaders, and police authorities to extend community regulation of personal behavior ran aground against old-fashioned Arkansas political localism. The Little Rock City Council rebuffed demands to impose a curfew on adolescents as a usurpation of parental control. To preserve the license fee boondoggle, the Association of Country Clerks and Treasurers vigorously opposed bills introduced in the 1941 legislative session to revamp marriage and divorce laws. A proposal to require a one-year residency for those seeking a divorce was not even brought to a vote. Companion measures to mandate a venereal disease examination before granting couples marriage licenses fell victim to racist demagoguery. The Blytheville state senator asserted that "only Negroes have syphilis," while the Prescott lawmaker declared that requiring a blood test amounted to "an insult of the white women of the state." Higher divorce rates and the enrollment of attorneys into the reform coalition obliged the 1945 General Assembly to enact a modest revision that dictated a three-day waiting period before applicants gained a marriage license. Since county officials could waive the waiting period at their discretion, the law was a minor inconvenience to impatient couples.

The rising membership in Arkansas's churches during the 1940s afforded denominations new political leverage; however, involvement by noted church figures rather than institutional commitment was the rule during the marriage reform crusades. Of the largest white religious bodies in the state—the Methodist Episcopal Church South, Southern Baptist Convention, Missionary Baptist Association, and Roman Catholic Church—only the Catholic parishes had grown, albeit slowly, during the Depression era. In the following decade, Roman Catholic membership continued to expand at the same rate to include 2–3 percent of the state's population; the Missionary Baptist growth stagnated; the 1939 union of the three national Methodist groups prompted an upward shift in adherents; and the Southern Baptists quickly burgeoned to displace the Methodists as the state's largest denomination. Quite likely, 1940s urban growth was the primary force behind the blossoming church rolls. For town dwellers, church attendance became easier and more appealing because of the urban amenities of a full-time clergy and ancillary outreach programs. In 1922, 10 percent of Baptist churches were located in towns with a population of over one thousand, while 63.5 percent were classified as open country; by 1946 nearly 19 percent were in urban areas and 44.4 percent were found in the countryside. More significantly, by 1951 nearly half of all Baptists were members of urban congregations, although only a third of the state's residents lived in towns and cities. In the midst of the noisy fulmination about the breakdown of hearth and propriety, Arkansans became steadier churchgoers.

Both increasing prosperity and the new urban surroundings introduced greater uniformity into the order of worship, even among the most rigorously congregational Baptists. The Southern Baptist Convention's 1940 publication of the *Broadman Hymnal* not only standardized church services but also encouraged a fuller integration of congregational singing, calls to worship, and responsive readings. Members' demands during the 1940s for printed orders of service and the delivery of the benediction by noon each Sunday reflected new values of efficiency, individualism, and predictability. While Baptists shared the era's general anxiety over the wayward adolescents, they eschewed lobbying for new laws in favor of organizing sports leagues and youth camps. The move to the city had not altered the traditional Baptist skepticism toward the secular reform efforts associated with the social gospel movement, though. The preeminent exception was the Convention's unreconstructed opposition to the 1930s repeal of prohibition. In 1942 the denomination's Committee on Prohibition and Social Service participated in the successful campaign to pass an initiated act lowering the percentage of voters who could petition for an election to vote a precinct "wet or dry" from 35 to 15 percent. Undoubtedly, the increasing Baptist presence throughout the state fortified the prohibitionists' victories in thirty-two of the forty local-option elections held the following year.

If the major white Arkansas denominations generally refused to be identified with sustained political or social activism, they still would react to specific crises or incidents. In November 1938 Bishop John B. Morris of the Arkansas Catholic Diocese and the Rev. J. K. Cooper of the Pulaski Heights Methodist Church, along with Governor Bailey, addressed a Little Rock rally to protest *Kristallnacht,* the Nazi sack of Jewish property in Germany. Public lynchings of African Americans provoked statements of regret and pleas for reconciliation, though no support of antilynching legislation. In 1948 the Arkansas Southern Baptists continued to insist that an apolitical approach was the best answer to the growing demand for equal citizenship rights: "In the midst of agitated political issues dealing with the Negro problem in our Southland[,] . . . we recommend to the churches in our convention that we hold to the one guiding New Testament principle of Love as the surest way of two racial groups solving the problems incurred in a Christian democracy."

The white churches' relations with the black religious community were governed by particular institutional structures. The all-white Southern Baptist Convention contributed monetary support to the National Baptist Convention, although the hard-pressed Southern Baptists halted subsidies to the black religious body during the Depression. With the Methodist unification, the African-American members of the northern Methodist church were included as a separate jurisdiction within the overall Arkansas union. Most black Methodists, however, belonged to the African Methodist Episcopal Church (AME) and the Colored Methodist Episcopal Church (CME), which had been organized as independent bodies during the nineteenth century. The Methodist Union called greater attention to the notable efforts of Little Rock lay leader Joy Bates, who had cooperated in joint educational workshops and conferences with CME ministers since the mid-1930s. In 1939 Bates organized interracial gatherings of female members from the Miles Chapel CME and the Pulaski Heights Methodist Church. In subsequent decades, she extended her support of biracial associations through involvement in the founding of the Little Rock Urban League and the Arkansas Council of Human Relations.

In contrast to the two largest white Protestant denominations, neither a separate African-American Catholic Church nor any recognized black-led jurisdiction within the diocese existed. Instead, the small number of black Roman Catholics belonged to nine racially identifiable parishes served by religious orders such as the Franciscans and Holy Ghost Fathers. Primarily, Catholic ties to black Arkansans were established within the context of the church's mission and social service objectives In 1931 Bishop Morris established an orphanage for black youth on a 582-acre farm southeast of Pine Bluff. However, the reluctance of families to place children under the supervision of white clergy from an unfamiliar church doomed the center. The starting of a small number of African-American parochial schools in the 1940s offered an alternative to poorly funded public operations while also serving as the only contemporary educational institutions in which white instructors taught black students.

World War II profoundly altered the outlook of the Arkansas followers of one religious faith on a significant modern political issue. Before the war, the Arkansas Jewish community reacted tepidly to the call for the establishment of a homeland in Palestine, but reports of Nazi atrocities inspired a strengthened commitment to Zionism. Fearing internal conflict, the Arkansas Jewish Assembly in 1935 had refused to affiliate with the American Jewish Congress because of the national group's Zionist advocacy. By 1944 Dorothy Goldberg and Sarah Scrinopski organized a Little Rock chapter of Hadassah, the national women's league dedicated to the creation of a Jewish state. The liberation of the death camps the following year and the realization of the horror that had befallen European Jewry reinforced the belief that survival of the faith demanded solidarity and activism. Army medical corpsman Nathan Steppach of Little Rock described in a letter to his wife what he had seen when he entered Dachau: "If every person in the whole wide world would be made to march single file around the area where we are now, the German race would be wiped off the map to the last man. . . . The Pharaohs, the Czars, and the other madmen in history were pikers compared to these sons-of-bitches." In 1947 the Arkansas assembly sent two delegates to the American Jewish Conference, which convened to rally popular support for the establishment of Israel.

While each of these major denominations and faiths depended upon active women's groups to fulfill the churches' proselytizing, social duties, and charitable obligations, only the Methodists in the 1940s had a female member of the clergy, albeit inadvertently. Mrs. W. S. Mooty had served as associate pastor of her husband's Paragould Methodist Protestant Church, and the merger of this smaller organization with the two larger Methodist bodies in 1939 permitted her to enter the United Methodist Conference with full ministerial privileges. Subsequently, women were not admitted into the Methodist ministry until 1956, when the conference adopted a provision recognizing female pastors. This enlargement of women's religious service evolved from wartime opportunities. A Methodist woman in the 1943 annual Arkansas conference report questioned whether a return to peacetime traditions was salutary: "Your magazines are full of articles giving new feats in fields never before open to women. When the war is over, these channels may be closed. Let's be ready so they won't. We must study to know how to keep what we have gained." In 1950 women within the North Arkansas Division of the Methodist Church requested greater representation on boards and conferences.

As early as 1927 the Arkansas Southern Baptist Convention had created a Committee on Woman's Work, which delivered a final report that justified an enhanced station for women in church and family. Citing passages in the Gospel of St. Matthew, the committee observed that Jesus Christ's teachings did not require "woman's subordination or inferiority to man." The committee report insisted that a misguided emphasis of Old Testament strictures on female deference had "forced upon Christian women a struggle for liberty which is unmatched for heroism in all annals." In the following years Baptist women gained additional appointments to permanent boards and committees, though no greater authority over church governance. They were disproportionately concentrated on the Orphan's Home and Sunday School Committees as well as the board of all-female, two-year Central College (which was closed in 1950 and the campus sold to the Missionary Baptist Association). While women filled leadership positions in areas of education such as the Baptist Student Union, they were excluded from the governing Executive Board until a 1969 amendment allowed a restricted representation on that panel.

Throughout America the necessity and willingness to question female status originated in the changing character of women at work. Simply put, more women earned wages, more women earned those wages in industrial jobs, and wage-earning women were married and older. These well-known facts, however, have produced certain false impressions. While American women made up 38 percent of all factory workers by 1945, they occupied only about 4 percent of the better-paid skilled jobs. Without available day care, working mothers were forced to put in a second shift at home. However, these burdens also explain why the increase in married women who entered the factories were those with older children; only 12 percent of mothers in the labor force had children younger than six years of age.

About one-fifth of the Arkansas work force during the war was female, compared to around one-third for the nation as a whole. Defense manufacturing openings expanded the definitions of suitable female labor. Plant supervisors justified the hiring of women in three-quarters of the thirteen thousand jobs at the Arkansas Ordnance Works in Jacksonville by claiming that their superior dexterity was an asset in assembling detonators and loading primer mixture. Women were also called on to operate small businesses and farms as male family members left for military service. This temporary changing of the guard was evident at a number of the state's radio broadcast stations. When her husband joined the Army Air Corps, Veda Beard became the new manager of KBTM-Paragould and was the second woman in the nation to be granted FCC authorization to act in the absence of a station's assigned licensee. Dorothy Weise was program director for Little Rock's KGHI until she took to heart her own public service announcements and joined the Women's Army Corps. The shift of some women from farm to town did not escape the notice of local boosters. After 1942 the Searcy Chamber of Commerce began touting the rising female population as an available source of inexpensive labor for potential industries.

At war's end Arkansas hewed to the national pattern as its working-women left the labor market or reverted to old jobs. In 1945 Veda Beard surrendered her managerial position to once again take up the station's bookkeeping tasks. Most women exchanged paid work for homemaking. Yet, for those women who had held challenging and higher-waged jobs, the experience revised their ambitions and self-perceptions and encouraged them to respond differently in the future to changing personal and family circumstances. Born in 1922 in the Ozark village of Aurora, Irene Jackson Hunter quit school at the age of fifteen when she began processing tomatoes in a canning factory. Moving to California during the war, she was an electrician and riveter at Douglas Aircraft; women trained in Arkansas as aircraft metalworkers had to migrate west since no airplane manufacturing plants were located in the state. In 1945 Irene returned to her native Madison County to marry Olaf Hunter, who was disabled from his wartime service. Although a military pension supplemented their cattle-raising operation, Irene signed on with the U.S. Forest Service in 1954 and eventually became the first female forestry technician assigned to the Ozark National Forest. She later observed to an interviewer: "Sure, I believe in equal rights. I think you can do anything if you want to."

In the United States, female employment began to recover by the end of the decade, climbing once again to 30 percent of the labor force. Arkansas employment figures reflected the trend. The number of employed adult females in the state rose from 14.2 percent in 1940 to 19.8 percent in 1950. In addition, wartime job opportunities did not completely dissipate as women continued to escape from certain traditional low-wage posts. The percentage of workingwomen in manufacturing escalated between 1940 and 1950 from 4.5 percent to 10.2 percent, compared to the more modest increase for men of 11 percent to 14.8 percent. Throughout the decade proportionately fewer women labored as agricultural workers and household servants. Still, the new economic forces only marginally improved female income and chances for advancement. By 1950 less than 1 percent of wage-earning women were included in the more highly skilled manufacturing positions of foremen and craftsmen, and nearly three-fourths of female manufacturing workers labored in the lower-paying non-durable goods sectors of food processing and apparel.

The absence of women in heavy industrial concerns was due in part to the absence of those plants in Arkansas. If employees in furniture and lumber mills are not considered, durable-goods manufacturing firms such as metal industries hired less than 2 percent of all workers at the end of the decade. Federal wartime investment did not launch a new phase of Arkansas industrialization. As was the case throughout the South, a greater share of federal revenues went for the operation of military installations in the state than for the construction of manufacturing sites and infrastructure. In addition, Arkansas tied with Mississippi for the lowest total investment in private war-related operations. Yet, the war production plants at Jacksonville,

Maumelle, Camden, Pine Bluff, and El Dorado; the Nimrod and Norfork dam construction projects; and civilian employment at the two major army training installations at Fort Chaffee and Camp Robinson as well as the five air-training bases, provided higher than average compensation for tens of thousands of Arkansans. After the war the U.S. government continued to maintain several installations while transferring to localities airfields that could be converted into municipal airports.

The development of the aluminum industry fulfilled the long-cherished vision of processing native raw materials within the state. However, the unique conditions bringing these new factories to Arkansas were unlikely to be replicated in peacetime. The curtailment of foreign aluminum supplies and swelling aircraft construction justified the construction of expensive refining and reduction facilities to process the state's low-grade bauxite ore; Arkansas had supplied the bulk of this critical war material. The government funded the construction of the Jones Mill and Hurricane Creek plants and leased them to the Aluminum Company of America. Employment at the bauxite mines in Saline County rocketed from three hundred to five thousand. Despite the proximity of Lake Catherine, the Arkansas Power and Light hydroelectric dam could not generate sufficient power to run the Jones Mill plant, which required as much wattage as consumed by all the state's residential customers. The pooling of electricity from several utilities and federal construction of a steam generating plant rectified the shortage.

The same federal agencies that had overseen war mobilization also supervised the reconversion campaign to manage the transition to a peacetime economy. During the war a conservative Congress killed off New Deal agencies such as the Farm Security Administration and the Works Progress Administration, and reconversion proved to be the *coup de grâce* to liberal hopes that government resources would be distributed to benefit small enterprises. Federal officials solidified business consolidation by favoring corporate acquisition of government-built facilities at bargain basement prices. The Reynolds Metals Company first leased and then purchased the two aluminum plants in Arkansas as well as plants in Illinois and Oregon for about 38 percent of the government investment in the facilities. Arkansas political and business leaders were relieved that the Saline County plants did not fold with the end of the war, but they also were apprehensive that the well-paid, unionized work force would generate higher labor costs and worker autonomy. This ambivalence influenced the postwar industrial recruitment efforts.

Industrialization without Revolution

In 1943 Hamilton Moses of Arkansas Power and Light could not anticipate the direction of federal reconversion and worried that a rapid shutdown of war industries would disrupt electricity demand. The author of the state's first utility regulatory act, Moses in 1919 had caught the attention of Harvey Couch, who made the young attorney his company's counsel: "I need a front man; a man who can stand before a crowd and interpret the things which are in my mind, as I envision the possibilities of the future." While Couch was the gregarious industrialist who birthed a corporation from a patchy telephone system, a man whose favorite food was hot dogs, Moses was the smooth political gamesman, addressing audiences as if he were harvesting votes and cultivating government officials through friendship and favors. While still serving as the AP&L counsel, Moses in 1926 solidified the utility's alliance with its man in Washington when he formed a law partnership with Sen. Joseph T. Robinson. By early summer 1941 Couch was dying of heart disease at Couchwood. Reporters kept vigil outside the home, agreeing out of deference to family wishes not to reveal the severity of the illness. If the tableau resembled a royal deathwatch, there was little doubt as to the identity of the successor.

Overcoming Couch's best efforts, public utilities had entered his Arkansas realm. In 1941 the Rural Electrification Administration oversaw seventeen electric cooperative serving districts throughout the state. Moses's apprehension about a postwar energy glut was not based on his company's generating capacity, which remained underdeveloped during the war, but on the obstacles to market domination. The cooperatives deprived AP&L of customers, and Moses fought tenaciously throughout the era to prevent any additional hemorrhaging. In 1952 he personally appeared on the front lines when Jackson County conducted a referendum on whether to leave the AP&L fold and become an REA district.

The utility president conducted a radio talkathon over the Newport radio station, declaring that the residents were faced with the most important issue to come their way since Reconstruction. The media campaign ended in an AP&L ballot triumph.

In 1944 the U.S. Army Corps of Engineers' Norfork Dam on the White River opened a new era when it began generating electricity. In contrast to his predecessor, Moses was not unremittingly hostile to public hydroelectric projects, calculating that purchasing power at beneficial rates from federal facilities was more sensible than sinking investment capital into large-scale dam construction. Yet to his disappointment, Congress in 1944 created the Southwestern Power Administration to market hydroelectric power from Corps dams to a preferred customer base of rural cooperatives, municipal utilities, and military installations in Arkansas, Missouri, Oklahoma, and Texas. Fearing that Southwestern would tilt the balance in favor of the cooperatives, Moses initially opposed pending Corps plans for such developments as the navigation of the Arkansas River. Eventually, AP&L became a steady customer of electricity from Norfork and Bull Shoals Dams, while the cooperatives in 1949 formed the Arkansas Electric Cooperative Corporation to generate and transmit the power for their system.

At the close of the war, the cooperatives pointed to the small number of wired farms as the critical utility issue facing Arkansas rather than any power surplus. The REA redoubled its efforts, and by 1950 64 percent of farms had lights. Meanwhile, AP&L acted upon its claim that a basic overcapacity demanded a replacement of war production industries with new manufacturing plants. In March 1943 Moses convened a summit of state business leaders that evolved into the Arkansas Economic Council (AEC). While the federal government made electric service nearly universal in Arkansas, AP&L established an industrial recruitment model for the state that endured until the end of the century.

The AEC revived Harvey Couch's promotional term "The Arkansas Plan," but it altered the late utility magnate's development goals. Whereas Couch had sought to lure external capital to underwrite native enterprises, the new plan emphasized the solicitation of national firms to locate plants in the state. Nevertheless, Couch's skepticism about consolidating large factories in the state's few urban centers endured because AP&L was best served by a diffusion of industrial customers throughout its service regions. Confidently, the council determined that small localities would more likely break the old dependence upon agriculture if the towns themselves restructured their institutions to meet manufacturers' demands. Moses led the speaking tours, which pressed the basic message that "communities must develop their own assets rather than look to others to do the job." Combining the fervor of a camp revival meeting with new management techniques, the AEC outlined how towns should evaluate themselves through "community clinics." Groups of residents were urged to categorize their town's attributes as either constructive or unhelpful, vote on improvement projects, and then sign cards promising to devote themselves to civic betterment. In addition, by 1950 AP&L and allied groups began to sponsor annual "Community Accomplishment" contests akin to the competitions that once plumped war bond sales.

AP&L's far-flung local operations expedited the development campaigns, but the utility also delegated tasks to allied groups. In 1945 the AEC merged with the state chamber of commerce, which served as junior partner and the administrative arm for industrial recruitment. Moses also addressed the General Assembly that year to call for the creation of a state economic agency. Although the utility head depicted the speech as an unprecedented opportunity for a businessman to set the politicians straight, the performance was part of the general public relations effort directed at the state's citizens. AP&L dominated the legislature by keeping the members who were attorneys on retainer rather than relying upon the eloquence of its president. With full support by the governor, the assembly merged a host of nominal economic agencies into the Arkansas Resources and Development Commission. The commission, in conjunction with AP&L and other business groups, organized week-long bivouacs in northern metropolitan hotels to introduce corporate managers to Arkansas opportunities.

In 1945 the legislature, at the behest of the AEC, also expanded the University of Arkansas's mission by creating the Bureau of Business and Economic Research, a counterpart to the university's federally supported Agricultural Experiment Station. In 1955 the university established the

Industrial Research and Extension Center, which operated as the Little Rock branch of the university's business development program. That same year marked the dissolution of the university's Institute of Science and Technology, a progeny of the World War II military research grants that had brightened many American university balance sheets. The federal government had introduced the benefits of applied research, but private business leaders after the war enlisted university specialists to make the case for Arkansas as a promising manufacturing frontier.

The blending of public and private interests as well as the links between local and state institutions framed an industrial development structure resembling the agricultural coalition of university county agents, the Farm Bureau, and powerful local landowners. Arkansas Power and Light's authorship of the economic crusade evolved from its status as the first private entity to have statewide interests. While recognizing that a modernized Arkansas economy prospered his company, Hamilton Moses, like Couch, genuinely believed that his efforts and vision would distribute widespread benefits. And, like Couch, Moses failed to comprehend that corporate and public interests could diverge in fundamental ways. With its substantial resources and local ties, AP&L's sway over the legislature challenged the traditional latitude of the county elites and the governor. In 1948 Moses called upon gubernatorial hopeful Sid McMath, who was locked in a run-off battle with Jack Holt. After a half-hour interview, Moses pronounced the election irrelevant because the next governor would not accomplish anything.

The Arkansas manufacturing boom did take off following the creation of the Arkansas Economic Council and accelerated during the 1950s. Between 1946 and 1959 the state's manufacturing employment rose by 44 percent in comparison to the 11 percent rise throughout the nation. This jump was accompanied by a profound shift in the character of Arkansas manufacturing. As sawmill workforce numbers plummeted, Arkansans took jobs in factories once found exclusively in the northeastern United States. Both business leaders and university economists boasted that the organized industrial development campaigns were responsible for diversifying the state's economy.

Nevertheless, the celebrated shoe and apparel industries were already opening in small communities just as the AEC was beginning to muster its government and chamber of commerce phalanx. The state's first shoe factory started up in Pocahontas in 1945, and Searcy negotiators were in St. Louis on the day Japan surrendered to complete an agreement with the International Shoe Company. By 1950 fourteen shoe plants operated in communities along the rim of the northern uplands and upper Delta, including Piggot, Beebe, Bald Knob, and Russellville. Although textile manufacturing in Arkansas had never matched its importance elsewhere in the South, apparel production gained a foothold and proliferated quickly during the 1940s. In 1949 thirty plants, also concentrated in the northern half of the state, shipped hosiery, work clothes, and children's garments. Arkansas was attracting industries falling by the wayside in their former home states: leather and apparel manufacturing employment in the state rose 740 percent and 246 percent respectively between 1946 and 1959 while declining 8 percent and increasing 8 percent on the national level.

Despite this growth, the combined numbers of shoe and apparel workers by 1959 fell short of those employed in another rising industry, one that followed the old pattern of native resource processing. As of 1950 about five hundred food manufacturing plants were producing margarine, meat and cheese items, and preserved fruits and vegetables in largely the same locations as the shoe and clothing factories. The firm names were familiar labels in the new postwar kitchens: Kraft, Pet Milk, Swift, Swanson, and Welch's Grape Juice. The eventual success of native companies competing against these established national concerns was a striking reversal of the old colonial economic pattern.

As they had with the Delta cotton economy, federal agricultural and developmental programs nurtured northwest Arkansas broiler production during the 1930s. National Recovery Administration codes forced the state to develop a poultry inspection program, the agricultural extension agents pressured hill farmers to diversify operations by building brooder houses, and the Works Progress Administration built Highway 71 to Kansas City to give the northwestern region access to national markets. The necessity for live hauls and the small shipments by scattered growers made truck transportation more feasible than rail. Growers sold their birds to independent truckers such as John Tyson who would in turn unload the cargo through urban commission houses. Tyson first hauled chickens to Kansas City and St. Louis, but his 1936 nonstop trek to Chicago established a direct link to a lucrative market. During World War II the national government exempted chicken from rationing limits and included the product in the Lend-Lease food export program. These federal policies soon rendered poultry the second largest source of agricultural income in the state. National annual consumption of chicken increased from 16.8 pounds in 1938 to 30.5 pounds in 1943.

Even with an expanding market, the ten thousand commercial poultry farmers in Arkansas were attached to an industry with critical inherent weaknesses. The intensive segmentation associated with independent feed operators, hatcheries, breeders, truckers, and processors heightened the burden of volatile prices. Unprotected by federal allotment limits extended to other commodities, broiler producers also suffered from the continuing reluctance of Arkansas bankers to issue agricultural loans. Consumer habits after the war also compelled growers to standardize the breeding process through careful management and additional investment. Shoppers at suburban supermarkets preferred oven-ready birds that were uniform in appearance and size. The surge in demand enticed national processors to construct plants in northwest Arkansas, and the A&P grocery chain sponsored the "Chicken-of-Tomorrow" contest to encourage the development of improved breeds.

The national corporations, however, were not the originators of a vertically integrated system in which one company kept ownership of the product from egg to dressed bird. In the early 1950s the first steps in this direction were taken by Harold Snyder of the Arkansas Valley Feed Mill in Russellville, Collier Wenderoth of OK Mills in Fort Smith, and John Tyson of Tyson Feed and Hatchery in Springdale as each negotiated feed and broiler purchase agreements with area farmers. In addition, outside corporate investment indirectly bred a formidable state political lobbying association. In 1952 prominent Arkansas producers used surplus funds from the Chicken-of-Tomorrow contests to underwrite the formation of the Arkansas Poultry Federation. Two years later the group threw its support and hefty campaign donations to gubernatorial contender Orval Faubus, who pledged to exempt feed from the states sales tax.

While northwest Arkansas agriculture entered the first stages of a new commercial economy, the Delta's cotton culture was continuing its long transition from labor-intensive plantation to mechanized agribusiness. In 1934 John and Mack Rust demonstrated in east Arkansas the cotton spindle picker, which John first developed in Texas during the 1920s. News of the Rust brothers' mechanism stirred apocalyptic warnings. The authors of the 1935 *The Collapse of Cotton Tenancy* delivered a grim prediction: "There is impending a violent revolution in cotton production as a result of the development of the mechanical cotton picker. . . . When it comes, it will automatically release hundreds of thousands of cotton workers particularly in the Southeast, creating a new range of social problems." A fear of disorder also gripped the Delta and Pine Land Plantation's business manager, who explained after witnessing a 1936 demonstration, "I hope it won't work, because it would upset our present system and Southern agriculture would be in turmoil in the future."

The Rust brothers themselves were socialists and shared H. L. Mitchell's apprehensions over the fate of tenant farmers. The Texans offered to market the device through the STFU, but the organization lacked the resources to enter into an agreement. The Rust Cotton Picking Company itself could not secure the credit to mass produce the prototypes and declared bankruptcy just as World War II induced the region's first modern labor shortage. The wartime metals scarcity also delayed the manufacture of a model that International Harvester developed in 1942; in 1948 the company opened a Memphis plant that rapidly produced hundreds of harvesters. In 1949 a Pine Bluff archery equipment firm employed John Rust as a consultant and began manufacturing Rust pickers.

Even with commercial marketing of the harvesters, Delta cotton mechanization proceeded erratically and was not fully realized until the 1960s. Hiring pickers remained a cheaper alternative to buying the machines until the mid-1950s, and even planters with the mechanical harvesters often preferred to use laborers to ensure a higher quality yield. In previous decades Delta landowners had skillfully adapted to changing conditions and federal intervention to retain control of their labor supply. When confronted with new forces rendering fieldwork obsolete, planters hesitated to step over the brink into unfamiliar territory. In contrast, small farmers and tenants, primarily African Americans, buried a decaying order by leaving for urban jobs in Arkansas and beyond. The nearly simultaneous phenomena of depopulation and mechanization during the 1950s have inspired the "push-pull" explanation for this movement: automatic cotton harvesters induced a labor surplus that was drained off by opportunities in postwar cities. Nevertheless, Donald Holley has demonstrated that planters only fully committed to mechanization after the grand migration left them without sufficient, affordable laborers. In addition, the early introduction of tractors and combines in soybean fields speeded the dethronement of "King Cotton." Landowners by the 1960s also could easily dismiss the overwrought prophecies that social revolution would accompany the machines. In truth, the civil rights movement persuaded planters that stability and order hinged on eliminating their reliance on a potentially militant class.

Delta landowners' continuing preoccupation with the labor question during the 1940s drove them to foment antiunion sentiment. Planters were no longer confident that local police power alone could cope with the continuing activism of the Southern Tenant Farmers' Union and the aggressive organizing campaign of agricultural workers by the CIO-affiliated Cannery, Agricultural, Packing, and Allied Workers (UCAPAWA). They championed the revision of Arkansas labor law, which had originated in the Progressive reform aims to protect vulnerable categories of workers and to ensure work-site peace. With the exception of lumber companies, Arkansas manufacturers were largely satisfied with the general tranquility on the labor front and were reluctant to endanger the status quo. The state's pioneering role in southern antilabor legislation predated the AP&L-led industrial development campaign. Antiunionism in Arkansas germinated within the stratified and paternalistic agricultural economy rather than in the expanding urban sector.

After the Christian American Association (CAA) of Houston successfully pressured the Texas legislature to adopt a strike restriction measure, the group mobilized to promote the law as a model for other southern states. Only Arkansas enacted the Texas "anti-violence" bill. Introduced during the 1943 session by state senator W. H. Abington of Beebe, the bill made it a felony offense to use or threaten force to obstruct anyone "from engaging in any legal vocation of their choice." Advocates of the antistrike proposal countered the arguments that it would "stir up strife and conflict" by explaining that only the dangerous CIO (rather than the responsible AFL) would suffer under the new law. Nevertheless, all labor organizations inveighed against the measure. An AFL leader from industrial Union County charged that the bill gained house passage only when "representatives of the Farm Bureau appeared at the legislature with little black grips."

The bill mattered little in the short term, given the continuing federal oversight of war production. In 1945, the Food, Tobacco, Agricultural, and Allied Workers (FTA) union, formerly UCAPAWA, asked the War Labor Board to authorize its organization of Little Rock cottonseed oil mills. Failing to act before the end of the war, the WLB washed its hands of the matter, and the FTA struck the plants. A black striker was killed when pickets at one of the plants were assaulted. Although a strikebreaker was arrested for the murder and released under a thousand-dollar bond, seven members of the FTA local were charged under the Abington law and placed under bonds ranging from one thousand to twenty-five hundred dollars.

Emboldened by the enactment of the antiviolence law, the CAA mounted a successful petition drive to place a right-to-work, or antiunion shop, amendment on the 1944 ballot. The organization's forty-seven thousand dollar advertising blitz reminded voters of an unpopular 1943 national coal mine strike by the United Mine Workers. Echoing the debate over the antiviolence measure, even business-friendly newspapers in Little Rock and Pine Bluff warned that the amendment was unnecessary and provocative. Amendment 34 garnered 54.5 percent of the ballots cast, linking Arkansas with Florida as the first southern states to establish right-to-work laws. These victories did not stint the antilabor fervor of eastern Arkansas farm and town leaders. In 1956 the Delta communities of Trumann, Marked Tree, Star City, Lepanto, DeWitt, and Harrisburg enacted ordinances imposing annual permit fees as high as one thousand dollars on unions. By the mid-1950s urban economic boosters incorporated the antilabor message into their recruitment arsenal. The Arkansas Industrial Development Agency reproduced the language of the right-to-work amendment in promotional materials dispatched to prospective industries.

Even as other southern states followed the Arkansas antiunion model, the state retained a higher than average percentage of organized workers within the region. Between 1939 and 1964, union membership rose 348 percent. The aluminum, paper, oil and chemical, and rubber products industries registered the highest percentage of union membership. In contrast, emerging industries largely withstood unionization. Among the nondurable goods manufacturers established in the state after World War II, only the shoe factories harbored a significant union presence, contrasting with the negligible membership among the apparel and food operatives. Throughout the state twice as many women as men worked in nondurable goods jobs, although in 1960 the median earnings for these female employees was 79 percent of what was paid to their male counterparts. Nearly 58 percent of the women working in the shoe, clothing, and poultry processing operations lived in rural areas. More than the laws or even the putative southern suspicion of labor unions, the recruitment of women from village and farmstead with little work experience or training insulated the new manufacturers from union forays.

In 1962 the University of Arkansas's Bureau of Industrial Research published a reassuring analysis for its business clientele: "A concentration of high-wage, highly organized industries in a labor surplus area does not raise the levels of wages and union organization for other manufacturing industries of the area." The report examined several industrial centers: the aluminum counties of Clark, Garland, Hot Spring, and Saline; the paper counties of Jefferson and Ouachita; and the petrochemical counties of Columbia and Union. Because the better-paying industries employed less than a third of the local manufacturing work force, the wages in these localities' nonunion plants and businesses did not exceed those paid elsewhere in the state.

The New South dream of late-nineteenth-century Arkansas movers and shakers was fulfilled by post–World War II industrialization. Delta planters overcame their reservations to prosper from the transition to heavily capitalized operations underwritten by federal crop subsidies and generous grants for irrigation districts. Landowners also evaded the indirect costs associated with the maintenance and pacification of year-round residential labor. Neither local governments nor charities offered services to replace the medical care and furnish what had once been paternalistic obligations. Even the growth of 1960s federal transfer payments did not stave off malnutrition and chronic medical infirmities. Mechanization and the migration of tenants stranded an even more abjectly impoverished population of seasonal laborers, small children, and elderly non–property owners. (Although the median age of African Americans in the state plummeted from 24.1 in 1950 to 20.5 in 1960, the proportion of black Arkansans over the age of 60 increased from 10.8 percent to 13.6 percent.)

The rise of manufacturing little disturbed either traditional labor relations or the rural social structure. Between 1947 and 1957 the number of strikes in Arkansas fell below the southern average, while 30 percent fewer workers in the state were idled by work stoppages than in the nation as a whole. Employees struck lumber mills more frequently than any other industry, but picket lines were an uncommon sight at most manufacturing plants. Rising industrial employment accompanied by declining farm laborers increased total personal income statewide by 81 percent between 1946 and 1959, but this improvement straggled behind the 116 percent national rise. The dispersal of leather, apparel, and food processing facilities to small communities muted the social consequences of industrialization. Employees' ability to return to their country homes after each factory workday helped to preserve the state's rural character and achieve the economic developers' goals of stable, predictable change.

If persistent ruralism weakened workers' organizations, urbanization stimulated new African-American movements, and during the wartime ferment a new generation of black leaders challenged the racial status quo. In contrast to their adaptability in the face of economic change, white business and political leaders responded to the emerging civil rights agenda with stubborn resistance.

Sounding the Trumpet: Early Civil Rights Struggles

As had J. M. Robinson's Arkansas Negro Democratic Association (ANDA), the Committee on Negro Organizations (CNO), founded in 1940 by W. Harold Flowers in his hometown of Stamps, called for the extension of voting rights to the state's African-American population. In contrast to ANDA's emphasis on an elite black political class tied to the Democratic

Party, the CNO asserted that broad-based, nonpartisan activism could best achieve social justice. In 1941 Flowers mobilized the generally untapped power of African-American civic and professional organizations throughout the state to spur the purchase of poll tax receipts, the only registration requirement in Arkansas elections. The campaign both increased the number of registered black voters and laid a foundation for grassroots coalitions.

ANDA's quest to participate in party primaries was stymied until the 1944 *Smith v. Allwright* Supreme Court decision. The court's voiding of the Texas whites-only primary as an unconstitutional abridgment of the Fifteenth Amendment knocked the props from under similar arrangements throughout the South. Robinson's ever-present optimism about the intentions of white officials was buoyed by conciliatory remarks from several Democratic officials; however, the head of the party in 1944 was the state's most overtly racist governor in the modern era. A former Ku Klux Klansman, Homer Adkins at first refused to compromise on altering the exclusionary language in the party constitution but then relented by authorizing changes that indirectly prevented black participation. The revisions permitted black electors to nominate federal but not state candidates, prevented African-American candidates from competing for office, and required all primary voters to uphold segregation statutes. Robinson strongly protested the obvious circumvention of the court ruling at the state party convention, declaring that the desire to exercise constitutional rights was not a demand for social equality.

The amended rules did not take effect for that year's primary contests. Robinson not only urged black Arkansans to go to the polls but attempted to mollify the unreconstructed Adkins by endorsing him in his bid for the U.S. Senate against the incumbent, Hattie Caraway, and factional adversary J. W. Fulbright. Adkins replied with a harsh affront: "If I cannot be nominated by the white voters of Arkansas, I do not want the office." Adkins delivered the snub as part of an attack on Fulbright as being sympathetic to black interests, charges that the Fayetteville congressman countered by denouncing the *Smith* decision. The election launched the long senatorial career of Fulbright. It also revealed that court decisions and federal policies had stimulated the revival of antiblack rhetoric even when no candidate questioned the consensus on segregation.

In September 1944 Secretary of State C. G. "Crip" Hall followed Adkins's insult of Robinson with a more striking display of intimidation. Hall announced that Robinson was disqualified from voting on the grounds of a 1911 manslaughter conviction. Believing incorrectly that he had been pardoned upon his release from prison, Robinson volunteered to resign from ANDA and cease his efforts promoting voting rights. The war against Robinson enfeebled ANDA and suppressed registration initiatives within the Little Rock black community. During its 1945 session the General Assembly buttressed the Democrats' new party rules by enacting a complicated double-primary system, limiting the choices of African-American voters to federal aspirants. Yet, the disorganized antisuffrage efforts in Arkansas suggested that voter exclusion was not a popular obsession. The double-primary system fell of its own weight after its implementation in the 1946 election entailed regular and runoff contests on four successive weeks. In addition, Democratic mandates requiring oaths of fealty to segregation were not enforced at the precinct levels. In 1950 the delegates to the state party convention repealed the provision limiting the vote to "white electors."

White leaders in counties with significant black population had not depended on a racially exclusive primary system to retain authority. A planter explained to V. O. Key why he was untroubled by court decisions: "We're going to follow the law, but I don't care if they vote or not. If they do, they'll vote the way I want 'em to." Seventeen percent of registered African-American voters in 1947 were primarily residents of Little Rock and Pine Bluff, although CNO's campaign had made incursions in other towns. The poll tax, which excited the ire of white reformers, was often seen as a false issue by urban black leaders such as Robinson, who perhaps was not strongly troubled by a device that fell heaviest on lower-income residents. In any case, observers agreed by the 1950s that the one-dollar annual tax, the lowest in the South, was not the principal impediment to voting. The protracted domination of state politics by local elites suppressed black political independence more effectively than did election regulations. Yet, the closed nature of the political system also left whites generally apathetic about questions of who could vote and who could not. The exodus of black Arkansans reinforced the relative indifference. Disfranchisement's slow death did not invoke a sweeping white backlash. The conflagrations of the future erupted over other matters.

The voting rights movement did not address discrimination associated with economic and social segregation. The inequities fostered by segregated institutions contradicted the system's "separate but equal" constitutional foundation and left southern governments vulnerable to court challenges from the National Association for the Advancement of Colored People. The NAACP's attempts in the 1940s to enforce the letter of the 1896 *Plessy v. Ferguson* decision revolved around two sets of cases: equalization of teachers' salaries and admission of African-American students to graduate and professional schools. Clearly, the NAACP intended for the suits over access to graduate programs to promote integration since dual systems of professional education were not practical. If closing the salary gap between teachers in black and white schools did not challenge segregation, the efforts confirmed the stake the African-American professional class had in struggles for equality.

In 1940 the Supreme Court ruled in *Alston v. School Board of the City of Norfolk* that racially identifiable salary differences for public school teachers failed the constitutional test. This case galvanized educators as the *Smith* decision later roused the hopes of Arkansas suffrage organizations. And, as in the *Smith* case, the strategy of public officials was simply to ignore the law until challenged by local residents, resist its implementation, and finally concoct elaborate evasions. In 1941 the Little Rock Classroom Teachers Association (CTA), a black professional group, compiled evidence of salary disparities prior to requesting adoption of a graduated equalization plan. Throughout the state, the average black teacher's salary of $367 foundered below the $625 white average, and the gap in the Little Rock district was only slightly narrower. The difference could not be justified by disparate levels of training. The state black teachers' median education level of 2.5 years of college virtually matched the whites educators' 2.6 years. After the Little Rock School Board in 1942 worsened the salary imbalance following a review of district compensation ranks, the CTA filed suit.

The NAACP for the first time took interest in an Arkansas discrimination case, and the organization's Thurgood Marshall assisted local attorney Scipio A. Jones in preparations for the October 1943 hearing. The lawyers settled on Sue Cowan Morris as the lead plaintiff. Morris's well-documented abilities in the classroom and her excellent grades in University of Chicago graduate courses showed her to be better qualified than the majority of white teachers in the district. Since a legal defense of discriminatory actions could not constitutionally rest on appeals to racism, the chief goal of the school district's attorneys was to cloak arguments for black inferiority in racially neutral language. While the lawyers for the defendants carefully ascribed different wage scales to "special training, ability, character," they could not always rely upon the discretion of their witnesses. A white primary-school supervisor declared that "regardless of college degrees and teaching experience no white teacher in Little Rock is inferior to the best Negro teacher." For their part, school administrators complemented their legal team's strategy with selective reprisals. Morris's contract was not renewed following the 1942–43 school year, the Dunbar High School principal who testified on her notable record was compelled to resign, and the head of the CTA was forced from his teaching post.

In January 1944 federal district judge Thomas C. Trimble decided in favor of the school board by discerning no merit in the plaintiff's charges that racial discrimination governed the pay differences of black and white teachers. It was left to the Eighth Circuit Court of Appeals in St. Louis to extend the protections of the *Alston* ruling to Arkansas teachers when it overturned Trimble's ruling. Even before this 1945 decision, the Little Rock School Board had already determined that the subjective criteria intoned by their lawyers in Trimble's court were shaky justification for its salary schedule. The district constructed a formal evaluation system, which led to immediate raises for some black faculty while retaining the fundamental inequities.

In February 1948 the enrollment of Silas Hunt as the first black student at the University of Arkansas law school demonstrated that compliance with court decisions preserved institutional credibility by avoiding clumsy subterfuges. For years southern states had preserved segregated professional and graduate schools by offering able African-American students tuition at out-of-state institutions. Although the Supreme Court in a 1938 Missouri case struck down the evasion in reference to law colleges, no black Arkansan before 1946 had directly applied for admission to the university law school. By 1945 about one hundred applicants had requested funds from the twenty-thousand-dollar fund the state Department of Education budgeted to provide out-of-state graduate training for black students. In 1946, as African Americans in Oklahoma and Texas brought suits in federal courts to gain a legal education at home, Clifford Davis submitted a formal application to the Arkansas School of Law. Dean Robert Leflar almost immediately instigated a calibrated lobbying effort to persuade university and state leaders that ultimately futile litigation to deny Davis or any other qualified African-American student admission would damage the institution's reputation. Leflar's initiative was supported by the absence of Arkansas statutes prohibiting integrated schools as well as a resolution of the original university board of trustees that declared "the institution open to all without regard to race, sex, or sect."

After consultation with Leflar, key trustees promised that the university board would not overrule his decision to enroll black law students. Apprehensively, Leflar then scheduled an audience with the governor, who could both halt the admission and stir up popular resentment against the university. In contrast to the reflexively bigoted Homer Adkins, Gov. Ben Laney had devoted considerable thought to the best methods to salvage segregation. Aware that the courts would soon shut down the tuition shell game, Laney mulled over the prospect of all-black southern regional professional schools. The idea soon fizzled in the face of opposition by Arkansas black leaders and the apathy of other state governors. Receiving Leflar in his office, Laney listened wordlessly, frequently gazing out the window, as the law dean explained that any alternative to accepting black applicants was expensive and divisive. At the end of their meeting, the governor accepted the logic of Leflar's analysis and agreed not to interfere in how the university handled the issue.

Emboldened by Leflar's coup, the president and board chair agreed that the UA Board of Trustees, during its January 1948 meeting, would formally approve a policy desegregating the graduate and professional schools. The board also stipulated in that meeting that black students would not sit with whites in lecture halls but receive instruction through undefined segregated arrangements. From the beginning Leflar had conceded nominal segregation within the law school to win support for black admission.

Davis, the original applicant, refused to enter the university under such provisions. Nevertheless, Harold Flowers on 2 February 1948 accompanied Silas Hunt and Wiley Branton, who wished to enroll in the undergraduate business school, to the Fayetteville campus. Branton did not protest when he was told that the new board policy applied only to graduate education, and Hunt enrolled in the law program without incident.

A wounded World War II veteran, Hunt took his classes in a special basement classroom, usually joined by three to five white students who were either sympathetic to his cause or eager for the more intensive instruction. By the summer of 1948, Hunt became so ill that he withdrew from the university, and he died from tuberculosis the following April. Hunt's battle wounds likely broke his health, which may have also been undermined by his isolation in the overwhelmingly white environment. Jackie L. Shropshire of Little Rock enrolled that fall and in 1951 became the first black law graduate. On his first class day, Shropshire was not consigned to the basement but seated behind a wooden rail in a corner of the class hall. Five law faculty complained to Leflar, who that night surreptitiously tore down the railing. Shropshire, however, remained in the segregated space for the remainder of the year. By 1950 Shropshire and fellow students Chris Mercer, Wiley Branton, and George Haley were free to choose any seat in the hall. These first graduates would follow in the footsteps of Harold Flowers as they later contested segregation throughout the state in Arkansas courtrooms.

John Kirk's perceptive studies have argued that the new postwar generation of African-American leaders were the heirs of Flowers rather than Robinson. If ANDA and the CTA entered into struggles that served narrow class interests, the emerging associations believed equality of condition demanded the definition and expression of African-American rights as a whole. In 1949 I. S. McClinton organized the Young Negro Democratic Association as an alternative to ANDA. Dismissive of the older organization's autocratic decision making and cultivation of white Democratic patronage, McClinton's group moved to establish chapters throughout the state to conduct voter education and articulate issues.

The 1927 lynching of John Carter in Little Rock had provoked Robinson's political activism, and the 1945 police murder of Sgt.

Thomas B. Foster elevated L. C. Bates to prominence as the state's most eloquent and thoughtful advocate for racial integration. A Mississippi native, Bates worked as a newspaperman before the Depression took its toll on African-American papers and forced him to turn to selling insurance. During his rounds in Arkansas, he met Daisy Gatson, a native of Huttig, and they moved to Little Rock shortly after they were married. A reluctant Daisy came to endorse L. C.'s decision to invest their savings in the establishment of the *Arkansas State Press,* which published its first issue in May 1941. L. C. Bates did not detach the realism of a journalist from the passion of an insurgent. In contrast to the more stolid *Southern Mediator Journal,* reflecting the outlook of the traditional Little Rock black leadership, the *State Press* publicized discrimination in defense-plant hiring practices during the war and the failure of trade unions to represent black employees. Subscriptions accumulated, and white business advertisers treated the *State Press* as the most efficient conduit to black consumers.

The Foster killing revealed that white patronage of the *State Press* did not assure leverage over the newspaper's editor. In March 1942, Sergeant Foster, a member of a black engineers battalion, intervened when Little Rock officers began beating an African-American soldier in custody of military policemen. The military police rebuffed Foster's attempt to investigate the rough treatment immediately, and he fought their subsequent moves to arrest him. As the confrontation in the black business district of West Ninth Street attracted a growing crowd, white city police surrounded and pummeled Foster with nightsticks. Finally, Officer Abner Hay shot the unconscious Foster five times and then stood smoking his pipe over the body until the ambulance arrived.

Three days later the city coroner officially closed the case as a justifiable homicide. The most comprehensive account of the shooting in Little Rock papers was published in the *State Press,* and Bates's pointed ridicule of the coroner's ruling compelled black leaders to form an investigatory committee. Based on extensive testimony from witnesses, the committee report was forwarded to both local and federal authorities. While dismissed by the state district prosecutor, the findings prompted the federal justice department to convene a grand jury hearing. In June 1942 the panel of twenty whites and three blacks heard Judge Thomas C. Trimble's instructions to take action only if it advanced a "useful purpose" before voting nineteen to four not to indict Hay. Anger over the verdict as well as the public remonstrances of military authorities pressured the city to appoint its first African-American police officers. The eight officers could only patrol the West Ninth Street area and had to waive the right to participate in the department's pension fund.

Neither an advertising boycott by white downtown merchants nor an offer of a bribe muffled Bates's coverage or cooled his impassioned editorials. The near doubling of circulation following the death of Sergeant Foster justified the editor's sense that vital issues could stoke African-American unity and clarified his status as part of the new leadership. Bates's evolving views also propelled the transition in civil rights strategy from one of claiming redress within a segregated system to a crusade to secure equal rights through desegregation.

Chapter Three

Arkansas at Midcentury: Manufacturing Opportunity

Hot Springs was a machine town like no other in Arkansas. The prince of this city-state was a flamboyant boss whose grandiose behavior represented the political organization's magnanimity and its self-assuredness. If Mayor Leo P. McLaughlin's riding breeches and red carnation boutonniere called to mind Mayor Jimmy Walker of New York, his occasional habit of gliding along Central Avenue in a buggy pulled by the smart-stepping horse Scotch and Soda was part of his own self-invented role. McLaughlin seized office in 1926 when he entrained from outlying towns two thousand voters whose fraudulent poll-tax receipts permitted them to cast ballots in the city's Second Ward. The election outcomes for twenty years afterward held few surprises.

Except during his brief marriages, McLaughlin lived with his mother and sisters in an imposing white house. Residents recalled that one sister enforced party discipline with steely facility: "Stella was his hatchet man. She would deliver the ultimatum; if you didn't vote for Leo, this would happen to you." Retaining the office of circuit judge was key to the machine's survival, for only that magistrate could impanel juries to examine election fraud. If McLaughlin's vote-getting methods were not unusual, the massive payoffs from the gambling operations brought profits beyond the aims or calculations of other Arkansas bosses. Gambling had flourished along with the bathing industry throughout the nineteenth century, but like an eager industrial development booster, McLaughlin recruited major gambling interests to invest in his town. The casinos and horse-race betting joints plied their trade openly and without the violent feuds that clouded the gaming climate in other cities.

Alfred "Hat" Abbott was a bookmaker who figured the odds, dispensed the payouts, and balanced the take while in the upstairs nerve center of the Southern Club. His daughter Shirley Abbott captured the feckless ostentation of the club—and of the city—in her elegant memoir of growing up among the players and political fixers.

> Known to the entire horse-playing nation, the great palace of the Southern Club was fronted with gleaming black marble trimmed in chrome. . . . Downstairs was a restaurant, the Southern Grill, fit for Sicilian gangsters from Chicago and New York, who indeed often lunched there. But up a flight of curvaceous marble stairs was the horse book, with mahogany counters and Prussian blue carpets with white roses woven into them and a domed ceiling embellished with a mob of radiant plaster cherubs frolicking among the swags . . . Bathed in the brilliant light, a roomful of gentleman studied their racing forms, chewed their cigars, and calculated their chances.

Not all residents were charmed by the resort's core industry, which was illegal under the state constitution. Periodic antivice campaigns sparked publicized raids on the clubs and book operations, which took the disruptions in stride. The gambling proprietors paid semimonthly fines to remain in business, which in 1946–47 amounted to over sixty thousand dollars. The machine used the take to spread good will through charitable donations, soft jobs, and supplements to the municipal budget. Hat Abbott's instruction of his daughter in practical civics was doubtlessly repeated in many Hot Springs households: a liberal was "wise and sophisticated and merciful toward human failings," while a reformer was "tight-fisted, sour, and punishing."

Like most rulers too long in power, McLaughlin began to confuse the realm with his palace and forgot to blend his self-aggrandizement with disinterested patronage. By the 1940s the criticisms from those who once tolerated the machine began to mount. Many were embarrassed when the city attempted to protect the gangster Lucky Luciano from extradition to New York; residents resented the mayor's decision to name the new airport after himself instead of as a memorial to World War II veterans; and a general outrage erupted when several downtown stores burned while firetrucks were parked at a political rally for a McLaughlin ally. The 1946 Sidney McMath–led "GI Revolt" reform slate only halted gambling for a few years, but it did bring an end to the McLaughlin regime. While the mayor escaped conviction on bribery and malfeasance charges, the grand jury investigation into his activities was sufficient to force him from office. When he died in 1958, looters ransacked the great house looking for hidden spoils, even probing his gravesite.

McLaughlin's town also soon disappeared. Beginning soon after the close of World War II, trainloads of visitors no longer came to seek cures at the spas for arthritis, rheumatism, and syphilis, and Bathhouse Row soon thereafter acquired a disheveled and forlorn countenance. The bathers were replaced by the tourists, who flocked to the region's only horsetrack at Oaklawn, indulged themselves at the shows and the slot machines in the Belvedere or the Vapors, or simply reclined on the airy verandah of the Arlington Hotel. The merchandising of Hot Springs was underway.

The Americanization of Arkansas also picked up speed. Voters approved the distancing of state commissions from direct political influence in order to improve the effectiveness of government services. Gov. Ben Laney's regard for business efficiency led to a rational process for the distribution of tax revenues while also encouraging a more responsible legislature. His successor, Sidney McMath, pursued a new progressive agenda of economic development, enhanced schools, and racial moderation. With the downturn of McMath's political fortunes, no other major figure embraced his full reform program. During the first Orval Faubus term, those who wished to maintain segregation at any cost formed the White Citizens Council.

The legislature continued to bolster industrial recruitment with a series of measures permitting local governments to entice new plants with tax-free financing and low-cost site development. The appetite for credit led to the era's most notable success story. Witt Stephens employed the profits from his bond business to purchase Arkansas and Louisiana Gas Company while parlaying his influence to dethrone Arkansas Power and Light from political supremacy. If Arkansas incomes did not rise enough to keep residents from leaving the state, budding prosperity did alter recreation and leisure. Traditional hunting and fishing were revamped by game management and the feverish construction of lakes. Victories on the gridiron elevated the University of Arkansas Razorbacks to a statewide phenomenon.

The state's movers and shakers took credit for moving Arkansas into a new economic era and assumed prosperity would prevent racial strife. The generally peaceful desegregation of schools in Charleston, Fayetteville, and Hoxie suggested that the state might evade the conflicts raging in the Deep South states.

The Managerial Reform of Government

The economic development campaign led by Arkansas Power and Light was accompanied by the gradual professionalization of state government. Previous populist crusades had shattered against the autonomy of local bosses, but economic modernization loosened the grip of county elites. Although a more efficiently managed government appealed primarily to urban business interests, voters in popular referendums approved the constitutional revisions curbing the latitude of elected officials.

Shortly after taking office in 1941, Gov. Homer Adkins purged the University of Arkansas Board of Trustees, which then fired university president J. William Fulbright. The deposed academic was the son of Roberta Fulbright, publisher of the Fayetteville *Northwest Arkansas Times* and an influential supporter of Adkins's *bête noire,* Carl Bailey. Adkins's blunt treatment of the university post as merely another chunk of patronage disturbed alumni and those anxious about the state's reputation. Robert A. Leflar drafted an initiated petition to insulate state boards from gubernatorial control, and the proposed amendment was approved during the 1942 general election. Amendment 33 thus set the terms of office for appointees to boards and commissions, prevented the governor from either decreasing or increasing the number of board members, and protected members from removal without demonstration of cause.

Both the gubernatorial and legislative prerogatives were pared in 1944 when the Arkansas Game and Fish Commission (G&FC) became the first of two constitutionally independent agencies. In 1915 the General Assembly established the G&FC to parry the endless demands for specific hunting and fishing statutes. Yet, the G&FC's mandate to develop and enforce game regulations was undermined by low funding and the legislature's continued enactment of local regulations. The 1923 session, for example, put thirty-two laws on the books that governed such matters as the use of nets to catch fish in Chicot County and the extent of quail season in Columbia County. The drive for professional, nonpolitical oversight of game populations originated with an urban interest group. In 1943 the Pulaski County chapter of the Arkansas Wildlife Federation wrote an amendment that vested in the G&FC exclusive authority over game and wildlife management and provided it an independent source of income from hunting and fishing license fees. Governors could not dismiss commission members, who were empowered to employ an executive director answerable to them. Overshadowed in 1944 by the controversial right-to-work amendment on the ballot, the G&FC initiative aroused little public opposition and garnered about a 61 percent majority of the ballots cast. The autonomy of the commission and its director grated upon the sensibilities of some legislative kingpins, who throughout the 1950s delayed commission appropriation measures.

Crippled by the bond default of the 1930s and the low priority for highway construction during World War II, the woeful road system was additionally burdened by the developing industrial pattern of widely dispersed factories. Seven county seats still had no paved outlet. Gov. Sidney S. McMath successfully lobbied the 1949 legislature to submit a twenty-eight-million-dollar general obligation bond issue to the voters for highway construction and maintenance. Opponents, who somberly recalled public insolvency during the Depression, were drowned out by the state's chambers of commerce, civic clubs, and the Farm Bureau. Voters sanctioned the bond issue by a four to one margin. Almost twenty-three-hundred highway miles were added during the McMath years, but the rapid and massive program exposed the governor to charges of bribery and featherbedding. A 1952 highway audit commission concluded that the administration had solicited campaign contributions from contractors and vendors and continued to distribute highway department posts as rewards for supporters.

Having won his credentials as reformer by vanquishing the McLaughlin machine, McMath fought back by noting the links between audit commission members and his political adversaries. The special counsel to the commission entered the primary race later that year in opposition to McMath's re-election. Nevertheless, the administration's reputation for probity suffered when executive secretary Henry Woods refused to supply campaign contribution records. Woods believed that the governor's enemies were attempting to discredit him by revealing that McMath backers included liquor dealers, labor, and African-American groups. The administration staunchly maintained that it followed a policy of favoring friends only when price and quality were equal to that of other bidders. While the two thousand pages of audit commission transcripts detailed influence peddling, the investigation produced no indictments of administration officials. Nevertheless, this practice of old school politics by a reform administration persuaded the voters in 1952 to approve another constitutional shift of authority from elected officials to long-term independent appointees.

Known as the Mack-Blackwell amendment after its legislative sponsors, Amendment 42 established a state highway commission of five members whose staggered ten-year terms were intended to encourage the development of long-term plans without the contamination of political pressures. As with the G&FC, the commission, rather than the governor, enjoyed the right to name a director to oversee the Highway Department. If the loosening of patronage bonds improved agency professionalism, the regional distribution of commissioners assured that completion of hometown projects took precedence over an integrated state road system. As one legislator explained, "I'd rather have a highway commissioner than a governor from Craighead County."

Touted as fostering honest government, the amendments also weakened the ability of the chief executive to manage a growing state bureaucracy. The restrictions on the appointive and supervisory powers of Arkansas governors became among the most binding in the nation. Yet, administrative and regulatory consolidation also stripped local governing bodies of long-held prerogatives. In the area of public education, postwar governors regained ground by taking an interest in fixing local schools.

Although Arkansas school districts had recovered slightly from the Depression years, when they were wards of the federal government, the 1940 educational revenues remained lower than those distributed to districts in 1931–32. The opportunities for wartime employment drew teachers from the profession and left behind overcrowded classrooms. By 1945 over half of those teaching before the war were no longer working in Arkansas schools, replaced by instructors possessing fewer college credit hours. The length of the average scholastic year was briefer than both the southern and national norms. This indisputable crisis provoked the first substantial education reform proposals since the 1920s. In 1948 the Arkansas Education Association (AEA), the professional organization of school administrators and teachers, led the campaign that persuaded voters to approve both an amendment removing the eighteen-mill limit on local school district taxes and an initiated act abolishing school districts enrolling fewer than 350 students.

While the number of school districts had declined from over 5,000 during the 1920s to 1,598 by 1948, nearly a third, serving 65,000 children, still did not offer high school classes. Black students in particular suffered from the survival of small rural districts. During the 1942–46 school year, 7 percent of all black students were enrolled in high school grades compared to 19 percent of whites; by 1950, the 5.6 median number of school years completed by African-American adults remained significantly lower than the 8.7 years achieved by whites. Yet, throughout the 1940s the gap in comparative outlays for black and white pupils narrowed. In 1950–51 the average per student expenditure for African Americans was 61 percent of that for whites, a notable gain from the consistent 40 percent proportion of the 1930s. These statistical improvements derived from the declining numbers of black students, migration of families to better-financed urban schools, and growing judicial scrutiny of southern segregation.

The impressive two-to-one popular vote for the 1948 school consolidation measure was the culmination of a movement dating from early in the century. The victory also reflected both the quest for economic modernization and the desire for uniform government services. Even though over 200 districts raised their millage rates following the abolition of the constitutional ceiling, Arkansas joined other industrializing southern states in funding schools primarily from state revenues rather than from local sources. In 1941 state moneys were only 43.5 percent of the combined state and local district contributions; in 1951 the state supplied 57.8 percent of the combined revenues. The increasing state responsibility was not accompanied by a significant upsurge of tax revenue, which hindered curriculum expansion and the replacement of dilapidated buildings. In addition, the consolidation amendment did not require districts that fell below 350 students in the future to merge with larger neighbors. By 1966, 116 of the state's 409 districts claimed fewer than 350 students, and none of the seventy-one high schools that taught fewer than 100 pupils had earned regional accreditation.

The perseverance of small school districts also sabotaged the state's attempt to establish the Minimum Foundation Program. The creation of the 1951 Arkansas program was consistent with the reform effort in other southern states to narrow the disparity among local districts through equitable distribution of state funds. At least three-quarters of the Arkansas minimum foundation funds were transferred to school districts to escalate faculty salaries, but the amount of money allotted to each district was based on the number of employed teachers rather than tied to the school population. In addition, the state did not reduce funding to rural schools, which continued to lose students. These provisions, in effect, gave declining districts a greater share of minimum foundation resources while growing districts were penalized with a decreasing proportion of money in relation to their expanding enrollment. The structural inequities continued until a 1981 state court decision declared that the state's funding formula violated Arkansas constitutional provisions ensuring equal protection and maintenance of a "general, suitable, and efficient" system of schools. The 1951 program's solicitude for country schools demonstrated that powerful rural interests had not quite succumbed to the industrial modernizers.

Efforts to modernize government services and to promote business expansion proved to be rare continuities between the postwar administrations of Govs. Ben Laney and Sid McMath. Laney was an unflagging fiscal conservative, suspicious of welfare expenditures and resolute in preserving segregation. McMath was sympathetic to organized labor, mindful of the impoverished, and thoughtful in seeking paths to peaceful desegregation. Their careers revealed the emergence of economic development as the priority for politicians of various stripes.

Worried that an unprecedented budget surplus would be squandered, Laney introduced the Revenue Stabilization Act as his major legislative proposal for the 1945 legislative session. Although Arkansas was constitutionally obligated to operate within a balanced budget, the allocation of specific taxes to separate state agencies left the fate of programs to the vagaries of tax collection rather than the priorities of elected officials. An agency in any given year could find itself flourishing while another was left indigent through an inadequate tax effort. Approved almost without dissent, the Revenue Stabilization Law placed most tax revenue in a general fund and established a mechanism for the legislature to incorporate unanticipated surpluses and downturns into budget priorities.

Wishing to apply business techniques to the lawmaking process, Laney in 1947 introduced a measure that shoved the General Assembly closer to the modern era. In effect, legislative sessions had long been biennial conventions in which delegates tended to business primarily at Little Rock's downtown Marion Hotel. Committees met infrequently, kept no minutes, and gave "do passes" to unread bills. The casual procedures were in part due to an overcrowded capitol building, which housed virtually all state agencies and afforded no committee rooms. In any case, the Marion was a more congenial setting for lawmakers. To protect hotel manager Ben Shelley from overextended solons, the state paid legislators a daily allowance rather than disbursing their per diem funds as a lump sum. At the close of each session the secretary of state covered the desks in the chambers with dust cloths and the General Assembly ceased to exist.

Pulitzer Prize–winning novelist Richard Ford, Shelley's grandson, lived part of his boyhood in the Marion, which represented an oasis of elegance and understood power:

> There was a curving marble fish pond in the lobby; a tranquil, bannistered mezzanine with *escritoires* and soft lights; a jet marble front desk; green leather couches, green carpets, bellboys with green twill uniforms and short memories. . . . Ladies from the Delta stayed in on

shopping trips. The Optimists and the Rotarians met. Assignations between state officials went on upstairs.

Using a Kansas law as the model, Laney in 1947 persuaded the legislature to organize the Bureau of Legislative Research and to approve the creation of the Legislative Council, which would review agency budget requests before each session. In 1951 bureau director Marcus Halbrook and his small staff took on bill-writing duties. Previously, either the attorney general or lawyers for private interest groups drafted nearly all the measures. Determining from the beginning that the bureau served only the legislature, Halbrook shocked lobbyists by refusing to divulge the contents of bills before they were introduced in the assembly. The influence of the structural reforms was augmented by a host of younger faces; the 1947 legislature included thirteen new senators and sixty-nine freshman representatives, some associated with the 1946 GI Revolt reform tickets.

By the end of his term, Laney's attention turned from the good government issues to the construction of a regional defense of segregation. In February 1948 Pres. Harry S. Truman placed before Congress a civil rights program that included elimination of the poll tax, an antilynching statute, creation of a federal fair employment committee, and the halting of segregation in interstate transportation. These relatively mild recommendations excited whelps of betrayal from southern political leaders stunned that these new carpetbaggers were from their own party. Carrying out a strategy developed during the March 1948 southern governor's conference, Laney chaired a States' Rights Democratic Committee to coordinate the opposition to Truman's renomination at that summer's party convention. In July Laney was briefly the Dixiecrat candidate for the party nomination, but the movement failed to sidetrack Truman or dislodge a civil rights plank from the Democratic platform. Regrouping their forces in Birmingham, the Dixiecrats launched a third party campaign, settling upon Gov. Strom Thurmond of South Carolina as their presidential candidate after Laney rejected the bid. The Arkansas governor continued to prefer that the states' righters subvert the national Democratic organization by seizing control of the party apparatus at the state level.

Laney's acquiescence to the desegregation of the university law school suggested his basic unwillingness to defy federal court authority openly.

He also advised his Dixiecrat brethren that white supremacy oratory was tactically less effective than denunciations of federal usurpation of state powers. Laney's crusade earned the support of business associations such as the planters' coalition, which had engineered the antiunion legislation, and the Arkansas Economic Council, which accused Truman of abetting communism. Still, racism was intertwined with the defense of segregation. When Laney embarked on a quixotic effort in 1950 to regain his old job from McMath, his candidacy attracted racial radicals who harped on miscegenation. The diminishment of Laney to spokesman for the "bitter-enders" was instructive. The continued erosion of segregation's constitutional status posed a dilemma for conservative proponents, who were reluctant to discard the rule of law. Attempts to keep Jim Crow on life support continually fell into the grasp of diehard elements demanding white solidarity.

Strom Thurmond in 1948 carried only the four southern states in which his name appeared on the ballot as a Democrat rather than as a third-party candidate. Despite the influence and hard work of Laney, Arkansas stood with Harry Truman, the official nominee of the party. The outgoing governor's maneuver to stage a Dixiecrat takeover of the September 1948 state party convention was short-circuited by Sid McMath, fresh from victory in the gubernatorial runoff primary.

A Marine veteran of Guadalcanal and the battle of the Solomons, McMath in 1945 established a law practice in his boyhood home of Hot Springs. The following year he organized other veterans into the Government Improvement League to run a slate of candidates against the McLaughlin organization. The GI Revolt, which broke out in other Arkansas political-machine counties and in surrounding states, targeted local corruption without instigating a full-scale reform campaign. In 1946 the Hot Springs GIs secured a federal court ruling purging the voting lists of sixteen hundred suspect poll-tax registrations and then ran successfully as independents in the general election. As the new prosecuting attorney, McMath devoted himself to putting Leo McLaughlin in jail and preparing for a 1948 run for governor. Despite securing a change of venue to the rural county seat of Mount Ida, McMath failed to nail down a conviction in McLaughlin's trial. Shirley Abbott recalled learning that the mayor's allies before the trial traversed Montgomery County to offer farmers startlingly high prices for their cattle.

Unburdened by previous political connections, McMath was a natural candidate whose striking looks and impressive war record fitted him for a statewide campaign. He also proved to be adept at navigating the murky depths of Arkansas factionalism. Aware of Homer Adkins's contempt for McLaughlin and of Carl Bailey's concern that the Hot Springs hero might threaten Senator Fulbright's re-election, McMath was able to draw the two bitter enemies into his gubernatorial caravan. He also enlisted notable young white liberals Harry Ashmore, Edwin Dunaway, and Henry Woods, who did not shy from plotting strategy with the reactionary Adkins. McMath entered office with the faith that a moderately progressive program was a better avenue to economic modernization than the business conservatism of Hamilton Moses.

The governor's 1949 highway bond program excited the business community, and he explicitly incorporated the road building initiatives into his own industrial recruitment pitch. When the Eastman Corporation considered a site near Texarkana, McMath promised to construct a four-lane highway between the prospective factory and the city. Yet, McMath also publicly questioned the wisdom of maintaining a low-paid labor force to placate the state's employers. McMath's attempts to raise minimum wages and toughen factory-safety regulations reinforced union support for the governor. In 1949 McMath prodded the General Assembly to approve construction of a teaching hospital to protect the accreditation of the university medical school. However, the legislature balked at appropriating the full authorized funding, and thus the medical center was not completed until 1957. Although improving schools was consistent with the goals of industrial developers, McMath's 1951 proposal to raise revenue through a higher income tax rather than the more regressive sales tax was considered by legislators too high a price for progress.

McMath's conviction that education, decent labor conditions, and the pursuit of higher-wage plants was the best path to higher per capita income countered the assumptions of the AP&L boosters. This conflict played itself out dramatically in 1951, when the governor, over AP&L objections, sided with the Arkansas Electric Cooperative Corporation's (AECC) plan to build a steam generating plant. Viewing cheap power as an important incentive to new industry, McMath backed the Public Service Commission (PSC) when it approved the AECC generating station at Ozark, and he lobbied the Truman administration to facilitate REA loans for the project. Moses's suspicions of McMath had arisen earlier when the governor neglected to vet his PSC appointees through Moses. The Ozark imbroglio solidified his enmity. The hand of the AP&L president was evident in the appointments to the ad hoc highway audit commission, which issued the report damaging the McMath administration.

In contrast to these public battles, McMath believed that racial moderation could be pursued only indirectly. He prevailed upon party regulars to repulse the Dixiecrat coup attempted during the 1948 state convention out of loyalty to the national ticket rather than acceptance of the national civil rights program. McMath as a young man had seen the work of a lynch mob, but he was forced to defend his antilynching measure on the grounds that it guarded against federal interference. His lukewarm effort to repeal the poll tax was advanced as an initiative to clean up elections. He was the first governor to appoint African Americans to the state boards overseeing black institutions, and his 1949 doubling of the appropriation for Agricultural, Mechanical, and Normal in Pine Bluff gave the black college the means to achieve North Central Association accreditation. Neither the appointments nor the increase in funds for black education incited notable opposition. Apart from the motives, a moderate program to offset decades of discrimination produced the same results as a segregationist strategy to make separate institutions somewhat more equal. McMath aggressively bolstered funding for black public schools, but he was accelerating a trend that had been developed under conservative predecessors.

However circumspect, McMath's tolerance and recognition of the bitter fruit of inequality was a fresh breeze in the incendiary atmosphere of racist demagoguery. His assimilation of racial moderation within a modernization program provided his successors a justification for official compliance with future desegregation court decisions. The conflagration of 1957 revealed that the state's leaders did not take the lesson to heart.

The leverage of AP&L and the proliferating business associations altered the nature of state factionalism. Acquiring statewide office was no longer simply a matter of appeasing a sufficient number of county elites. The business interest groups counted on allies and employees throughout the state to sway local legislators. The isolated pockets of organized factories left most lawmakers with no labor constituency, but the unions' ability to deliver a mass of votes in a general primary caught the attention of candidates for governor. In addition, the growing federal contribution to the state budget and subsidies for private interests drew congressional officeholders into the complex web of rivalries. Although depopulation reduced the size of the state's delegation in the U.S. House of Representatives from seven in 1940 to four after 1960, the Arkansas influence in Congress expanded as long-serving members ascended to the summit of powerful committees. The U.S. Senate careers of J. William Fulbright (1945–75) and John L. McClellan (1943–77) demonstrated how personality and ideology molded differing concepts of congressional responsibility.

The intellectual character of Fulbright, the junior senator, reflected his classical liberal outlook. Fulbright's belief in free markets complemented a skepticism toward government ventures intended to shape individual and social behavior. His internationalism began as a Rhodes scholar at Oxford and deepened with the emergence of the new American globalism in the early Cold War years. Yet Fulbright's conviction that nations developed in accord with their particular cultural institutions and with little regard for outside intervention provoked his growing criticism of the American containment policy toward Communist states. His dissent culminated during the Lyndon Johnson phase of the Vietnam War. This same wariness of government social reform governed his civil rights record.

As a member of the House of Representatives, and continuing after he entered the Senate in 1945, Fulbright acted on his belief that federal grants and projects could lay the foundation for Arkansas prosperity. At the same time, he denounced the Truman civil rights program as an unconstitutional assertion of national authority. Declining to add his name to the Dixiecrat roster, Fulbright in 1948 believed himself a moderate in the mold of McMath. The senator quietly endorsed as a compromise to the Truman civil rights initiative a proposal to outlaw vigilantism and disfranchisement that did not extend desegregation and fair employment protections. Fulbright assumed that segregation was imbedded in the social fabric of the South rather than serving as a political and economic instrument to preserve white supremacy. Throughout the 1950s racial moderates shifted to support outright desegregation, but Fulbright stood firm with southern colleagues in filibustering and voting against civil rights acts.

By the 1960s the remnants of Fulbright's moderate reputation rested with his unwillingness to stir popular hatreds. While critics dismissed as political opportunism the incongruity of the Vietnam War critic upholding southern sovereignty, Fulbright was conscious of a philosophical consistency. Shortly after voting against the 1964 Civil Rights Bill, he complained to a State Department official that invitations for blacks to attend social functions at the U.S. embassy in Pretoria offended the apartheid government of South Africa: "It does seem to me that we should be guided in the main by the practices of foreign countries in which we have embassies and that we should not try to impose upon them our particular ideas of morality."

For many Arkansans of a certain class, the urbane and professorial Fulbright was a bracing repudiation of the stock hillbilly image, which they assumed was how the larger world saw the state. The senior senator, by contrast, seemed in the mold of the careerist southern officeholder who amassed favors and brought home the bacon. In actuality, Fulbright assiduously represented major corporate Arkansas interests, but he generally deferred to John L. McClellan to corral the big-ticket federal projects and dispense patronage. However, McClellan was not simply a provincial mossback. If Fulbright mapped the byways of international diplomacy, McClellan relished the investigatory powers of the Senate and authored major revisions of the federal criminal code. As the long-time chair of the Senate Permanent Investigations Committee, he conducted over three hundred investigations and widened the powers of federal prosecutors through his drafting of the 1970 Organized Crime Act. Washington columnist Mary McCrory famously observed that McClellan's questioning of witnesses sounded like "the voice of doom."

A strident campaigner, given to racist invective in his early contests, McClellan was a fiscal conservative whose voting record mirrored his white constituency's opposition to civil rights, organized labor, and federal social spending. Ideological commitments did not drive his actions. A 1972 profile by a consumer advocacy group offered a widely accepted description: "Some colleagues consider him capable and decorous, although none are really close to him personally. The adjectives most commonly used to describe him by ally and opponents alike are grim, dour, unsmiling, temperamental, hardworking, and tough, very tough." While his intelligence and diligence won the loyalty of aides, McClellan was merciless against politicians he considered unreliable.

A rousing speaker, McClellan was not closely identified with the existing party factions in 1938 when he took on Sen. Hattie Caraway and the Homer Adkins federal group. Following his defeat, he established a lucrative law practice in Camden before running in 1942 for an open U.S. Senate seat. Locked in a bitter runoff primary, McClellan's lack of a political base left him short of funds and on the verge of withdrawing from the race. The encouragement and influence of Ouachita County sheriff Edgar Pryor revived the confidence and finances of the melancholic McClellan. He won the election with a remarkable 61.6 percent margin. The new senator became readily identified with AP&L, an alignment that played a part in an acrimonious rivalry with Governor McMath.

With barely a nod toward customary neutrality, McClellan pitched in to help Francis Cherry derail McMath's bid for a third term in 1952. Two years later McMath failed to even the score when he mounted a barebones senatorial campaign against an entrenched incumbent now accommodated by utilities, timber companies, bankers, and planters. McClellan would not face serious opposition until 1972, when he was forced into a runoff by Congressman David Pryor, the son of the Camden official who had helped salvage his 1942 effort. As in the earlier race, McClellan despaired over his prospects and was persuaded not to bow out during a meeting of leading businessmen, who delivered sufficient cash to revitalize his campaign. In a televised debate, McClellan characterized the Pryor campaign's war chest as a union-stocked "cookie jar," and this antilabor strategy carried McClellan to an upset victory.

In the 1954 senatorial contest, McMath fruitlessly raised the issue of McClellan's ties to AP&L, which in May had received a steep and unpopular rate increase. Orval Faubus exploited the issue more tellingly against Gov. Francis Cherry. Only the second twentieth-century incumbent denied more than one term, Cherry was one of the least politically adroit governors. His foe was one of the best.

A Jonesboro chancery judge when he entered the 1952 governor's race, Cherry overcame his low name recognition and nonexistent political connections by fielding questions from listeners during twenty radio talkathons. Having won office by appealing directly to voters through the media, Cherry summarily rebuffed political bosses who paid courtesy calls on the new governor. He assumed that establishing sound government procedures counted for more than a hard-nosed political organization. Cherry organized the Department of Finance and Administration to supervise the state budget, advocated a property-tax equalization amendment, and stiffened welfare requirements. This last policy change immediately expelled about twenty-three hundred people from the rolls. The Cherry program revealed the limited appetite in Arkansas for authentic fiscal conservatism.

The property tax proposal would have ended wildly divergent assessments, but it precipitously increased the tax on agricultural and timber holdings. Most welfare recipients in the 1950s were elderly and white, and many voters considered them the deserving poor rather than "deadheads," as characterized by Cherry. The governor's industrial program was in harmony with his frugal outlook, but the northwest Arkansas poultry companies forecast ruin arising from his veto of a feed and seed sales tax exemption. Conventional wisdom argued against a cakewalk for this governor's re-election.

In 1954 Faubus broke early from the pack of Cherry's challengers. A Madison County newspaper publisher and McMath highway director, Faubus had an instinct for speaking the minds of his listeners. Cherry was a diffident campaigner, more comfortable making a pitch from a broadcast booth. At a boisterous Perryville rally, Faubus worked the crowds while Cherry waited in his car listening to a baseball game before materializing to deliver his scheduled speech. Pushed into an August runoff, the staid Cherry understood that attempts to tie his opponent to the earlier highway scandals had fallen flat. Cherry was already on record as promising adherence to court desegregation rulings and thus made little of the

May *Brown v. Board of Education of Topeka* decision that held school segregation to be unconstitutional. For his part Faubus did not pillory Cherry's subdued reaction, although the hill country politico had opened his campaign by denouncing race mixing in the classroom. Rather than race, Cherry determined to hinge his fortunes on redbaiting. On 2 August he went on statewide television and radio to detail Faubus's enrollment and leadership of the student body at radical Commonwealth College.

Cherry had once again shown a poor sense of timing. By 1954 the excesses of Joseph McCarthy were dampening the postwar "Red Scare." John McClellan, the ranking minority member on the McCarthy committee, had a year earlier led a Democratic walkout and returned only when he was allowed to replace the baleful committee counsel, Roy Cohn, with Robert F. Kennedy. Faubus supporters decried the slander against a decorated veteran who fought bravely during the battle of the Bulge. The candidate himself intoned his defense in every address: he had remained at Commonwealth a few days as an unenrolled student, never attended classes, and left after the radicalism and atheism of the staff were made evident to him. These were lies, of course, but frequent repetition elevated them to serviceable facts. The Faubus victory also rested on tried and true methods. On election night the Garland County votes remained unreported well into the early morning hours. There the Hot Springs machine, under new management, was fiddling with the vote totals to help out Cherry against the former McMath associate. Finally, Homer Adkins placed a call from Faubus headquarters, explaining that he had a sufficient number of north Arkansas boxes in reserve to counter anything coming out of Hot Springs. The Garland County crowd blinked, and it was over.

Later described by McMath as "the most liberal member of my administration," Orval Faubus buttressed his progressive reputation by withstanding the McCarthyite assault. Yet neither his father's socialism nor the brief stint at Commonwealth College had deflected his preference for mainstream politics. Roy Reed has explained that while an inclination for compromise grew in reaction to Sam Faubus's dogmatism, young Orval also learned from listening to his father and friends that politics greatly mattered to a people living in a poor state. Politics also conveyed status and respect, qualities craved after by the young man from Greasy Creek.

The first Faubus legislative session followed the postwar model of modestly expanding and professionalizing government services while banking on the arrival of new industries to lift the state from its chronically low economic rankings. Familiar with the activities of the Ozark Playground Association, Faubus established a publicity and parks department to promote tourism, although the upgrading and expansion of the state parks were deferred for another era. His veto of an anti-striker bill and sponsorship of a bill to delay the implementation of utility rate increases were not surprising given both his background and appreciation for REA ventures to electrify Ozark cabins. Faubus, however, also eagerly collaborated with AP&L and the state chamber of commerce to reorganize the state resources commission as the Arkansas Industrial Development Commission (AIDC). Faubus's coaxing of Winthrop Rockefeller from his Petit Jean hilltop retreat to lead the AIDC cheered business leaders. In 1953 Rockefeller had moved to Arkansas to start afresh, following a well-publicized divorce, and to establish a legacy apart from his notable brothers. State boosters anticipated that even the prodigal scion of America's first family of capitalism could offer uncommon access to New York offices.

The governor did give his blessings to a project championed by state senator Max Howell. Arkansas was among the last states to house developmentally disabled children with the general population of the state mental hospital. Faubus made the creation of a separate residential center, or children's colony, an administrative measure, and the bill was approved early in the session. The new director and board chairman of the colony rejected the traditional construction of large dormitory complexes in favor of a village-like arrangement of cottages housing up to eight children each. Completed in 1959, the Arkansas colony was identified by leading mental health officials as "one of the best" of its kind, and the center served as a national model.

A veteran from Little Rock who first entered the legislature as part of the GI Revolt, Howell also sidetracked a 1955 bill to mandate school segregation: "Just because Alabama or some other dyed-in-the-wool Southern state jumped in haste to preserve something doesn't mean Arkansas should." Faubus did not enter the fray over the bill, just as he declined to intervene that summer when opposition mounted against the desegregation of the small eastern school district of Hoxie. In the wake of *Brown,* Faubus detected little political gain from brazen defiance and concluded that occasional segregationist rhetoric would placate the white majority. Conscious of an emerging voting bloc, the governor made the first appointment of African Americans to the state Democratic committee. While few could fault Faubus's reading that most white Arkansans were quiescent segregationists, he did not reckon on the ability of virtuoso insurrectionists to mobilize the racial extremist minority.

James Johnson was a Marine veteran from Crossett whose ambitions had propelled him to the state senate by the time he was twenty-six years old. In contrast to other politicians such as Faubus, Johnson believed he could ride the tiger of race to statewide office. In 1955 he founded the White Citizens Council of Arkansas and soon led rallies attacking the Hoxie school board for voluntarily integrating the district. Council leaders attempted to kindle local resistance with racist taunts and violent rhetoric. The arch-segregationists' crudity and appeal to disorder appalled conservative whites. The sheriff of southeastern Lincoln County explained in October that he canceled a citizens council rally because "we're getting along fine without anybody stirring up trouble."

Citizens council members laid most of the blame for the enrollment of black students in Hoxie's white schools at the door of the governor's mansion. In the pages of the segregationist paper *Arkansas Faith,* the inaction of "Awful Faubus" was explained by his confusion over whether he had been trained at "communist Commonwealth College or a mule barn." Johnson, for either personal or strategic motives, channeled the anti-integration crusade into a political campaign organization. Not wanting to be written off as a rabble-rouser, he sought respectability through public appearances with former Governor Laney and by arguing that the state could veto the *Brown* decision through the device of "interposition." In 1956 Johnson proposed an interposition amendment to the Arkansas constitution to require "nullification" of "dangerous invasions" of state sovereignty. The amendment became Johnson's platform for his run for the governorship.

In the 1956 campaign Faubus assured voters he could preserve segregation without radical measures or the hooliganism still associated with Johnson. Not even the governor was immune to the angry men bellowing threats from the edges of the crowds during his south Arkansas stops. Faubus countered the rabid chorus by summoning a former antiunion tough to patrol the audience with club in hand. In his speeches Faubus advocated his voluntary pupil-assignment proposal as an effective and legal method to frustrate school desegregation rulings. Not only was Faubus confident that this evasion would win over ordinary voters, but he presumed that the east Arkansas county elites saw Johnson's fire-eaters as a greater threat to the status quo than the distant federal government. Indeed, Faubus's 58.1 percent statewide victory was reinforced by a 67.7 percent margin in machine-controlled Crittenden County, a Delta province of the sort that had represented Johnson's best hope. However, Johnson's defeat was accompanied by the approval of his interposition amendment. Defiance had a constituency, but the lesson was lost on Faubus. His reelection seemed to justify his assumptions that desegregation was amenable to the usual techniques of compromise and catering to factional leaders. Faubus was a moderate by default. He never troubled to develop a politically viable strategy for compliance that asserted that order and economic development required obedience of the law.

The postwar reforms of Arkansas government weakened local factionalism without erasing election corruption, interest group influence promoted statewide economic development without overhauling issueless politics, and increasing professionalization significantly improved government services to citizens without instigating meaningful popular control of officials. By the mid-1950s this firm political consensus appeared unassailable, but its most formidable test was on the horizon.

Land of Opportunity

Called variously "The Bear State," "The Wonder State," and "The Toothpick State" (in homage to the bowie knife), Arkansas was officially christened "The Land of Opportunity" by the 1953 General Assembly. If the resolution suggested that urban boosterism had supplanted the celebration of rural traditions, it also represented an anxiety that the 1940s industrialization boom was subsiding.

Before 1955, private groups associated with the Arkansas Economic Council marketed the benefits of a surplus labor force and compliant local governments to prospective industries. However, federal minimum wage laws prevented Arkansas from offering a labor-cost incentive lower than that of other southern states, which, in turn, were aggressively extending subsidies to new manufacturers. Even more troublesome to Arkansas business leaders was that the continued outflow of population endangered the availability of low-wage workers. The conservatism of Arkansas bankers and the state's shaky reputation in capital markets forced the political and industrial leaders to turn to public financing of private development.

Act 404 of 1955, which created the AIDC, also authorized the creation of local industrial development corporations. These organizations were able to raise local funds through stock sales, purchase industrial sites, and issue tax-free bonds. A number of communities immediately jumped on the bandwagon: Searcy developed an industrial site and extended a railroad siding for a Frostyaire Frozen Foods warehouse, later raising five hundred thousand dollars to acquire a ten acre parcel for a California business-machine manufacturer; the Morrilton Industrial Corporation leased a building to the Oberman company, which employed two hundred people to produce men's slacks; the El Dorado corporation arranged for two hundred thousand dollars in financing to entice Jess Merkle to locate J-M Poultry in Arkansas rather than in Ruston, Louisiana.

By 1957 the statutory limits on yields undermined the marketability of the local Act 404 instruments. Created by the legislature that year and capitalized with an investment of over nine hundred thousand dollars from forty-three utility companies, the First Arkansas Development Finance Corporation was empowered to issue the type of long-term business loans shunned by banks. The General Assembly also in 1957 referred to the voters a constitutional amendment permitting local counties and municipalities to issue industrial development bonds with interest exempted from both state and federal taxes. Even with the approval of Amendment 49, the legislature in 1960 passed Act 9, which made it even easier for local governments to finance the purchase of property that could be leased to industries.

In 1966, 151 Arkansas communities boasted at least one economic development organization, 136 of which had organized an industrial development corporation. In this era Arkansas, along with five other southern states, issued 87 percent of the industrial bonds in the entire nation. Congressional representatives from states that did not resort to municipal financing incentives charged that the federal treasury was being looted to entice industries to relocate from one region to another. Bills to curtail the bond issues disappeared into oblivion in the House Ways and Means Committee, chaired by Wilbur Mills of Arkansas. For the most part, companies did not close factories in northern states and relocate the operations in the South; yet southern communities held a particular attraction for wage-sensitive, highly competitive industries. Although corporate executives' claims that they were not swayed by local subsidies warrant skepticism, southern industrialization was primarily sustained by cheap labor, a growing regional market, and an improving transportation system. These factors were largely outside the compass of the development enterprises.

In general, new manufacturing plants were built in areas of white surplus labor rather than in regions with a significant or predominant African-American population. This selective pattern owed to the reluctance of eastern planters to see their remaining farm workers siphoned off into other occupations, to the strategies of industrial promoters who believed jobs for whites garnered better publicity and political good will, and to the hesitation of unions to open their ranks to black workers. The construction of the J-M Poultry plant demonstrated how even entry-level manufacturing jobs altered the labor markets. African-American women won positions on the processing line in sufficient numbers to make Jess Merkle a much-reviled figure in upper-class El Dorado households accustomed to inexpensive domestic workers. The plant was also one of the few poultry operations to be quickly organized.

By 1960 over 25 percent of Arkansas black workers were classified as agricultural labors, 20 percent earned wages in private households, and well over half of the 15 percent employed in manufacturing worked in lumber and wood products occupations. While black income grew during the 1950s, the practices and policies confining African-American workers to arduous and poorly paid work solidified economic inequities. Throughout the decade black per capita income stagnated at 42–43 percent of that of whites.

Even those who boasted that the state could live off its own resources if walled off from the rest of the world had to acknowledge that the fundamental Arkansas scarcity was capital. That one of the dominant figures during the latter half of the century amassed a fortune trading bonds rather than selling timber or cultivating Delta soil defied historical prediction. Wilton (Witt) R. Stephens borrowed fifteen thousand dollars in 1933 to organize his own investment company and purchase depressed municipal, school, and levee bonds for as low as ten cents on the dollar. With his profits from reselling the debt instruments at nearly face value, Stephens eventually bought an interest in thirty-seven banks through which he could market his bonds. In 1946 he made his younger brother, Jack, a partner in what became Stephens Incorporated, and the firm began to underwrite bond issues rather than simply buy and sell them. The firm's presence in the state was critical to the evolution of native enterprises. Stephens, Inc., was the principal underwriter for the initial public offerings of stock for Wal-Mart, Tyson, and Systematics.

Doing business in Arkansas required intimate and active attention to politics, particularly for one worried about the credit worthiness of local governments and schools. Witt Stephens devoted money and influence to have the voters see things his way, as in 1948 when Arkansans approved lifting the school millage ceiling. Eventually, the Stephens firm and another allied bond house managed the sale of 70 percent of the school bonds in the state. Unerringly flexible, Stephens insinuated himself with Governors Adkins, McMath, and Cherry. It required only one day after the 1954 election for Stephens to shake off the dust of Cherry's defeat and be accorded an honorable reception into the Faubus camp. That transfer of loyalties foreshadowed a continental shift in the Arkansas political landscape.

Shortly before the election, the Stephens' interests purchased the ailing Arkansas Louisiana Gas Company (Arkla), and the following year they secured two rate increases from the Faubus appointees on the Public Service Commission. The favorable decisions escalated Arkla's stock value well above the Stephens's purchase price while hitting particularly hard the natural gas company's largest consumer, Arkansas Power and Light.

The AP&L men and their industrial customers pressed the new governor for relief, but Faubus had not forged close ties with the electric utility and refused to injure his new patron. AP&L then turned to the courts to reverse the commission's adoption of a pricing structure that Stephens had put forward to ensure himself high returns. In February 1957 the state supreme court sided with AP&L. The following day lawmakers introduced bills to enact the Stephens rate system, known as the Fair Field Price Law. The overwhelming votes in favor of the measure revealed that Stephens had supplanted AP&L to become the new sovereign of the General Assembly.

It required little imagination to show gratitude to citizen legislators who were attorneys, business proprietors, or landowners. Members who were insurance agents soon provided coverage for Arkla's operations, a service station owner fueled Arkla vehicles, and others went into the banking business with Stephens or found him a reliable lender for farm purchases. The natural gas mogul also extended legislators a viable explanation for favoring his utility. Indicting AP&L for reducing industrial electric rates on the backs of residential customers, Stephens declared that Arkla stood with the "biscuit cookers." Cultivating the image of the country boy who made good through hustle and native wit, Stephens became widely known as "Mr. Witt." Nevertheless, Stephens, unlike Couch or Moses, never underwrote industrial development campaigns or took up issues that did not directly touch upon his interests. Throughout his life he was a wealthy and powerful man who continued an indefatigable pursuit of wealth and power: "It's a game with me. That's how they score the game."

State promoters claimed that the financial and corporate achievements of the folksy Stephens symbolized a more worldly Arkansas that continued to value personal ties and disdain affectation. The image was not altogether at variance with reality. Most Arkansans remained rural, but the larger urban areas—particularly the cities of Little Rock, North Little Rock, and Fort Smith—grew faster between 1950 and 1960 than the national rate, while the smaller towns and rural areas continued to lose residents. Beyond census designations, the boundary between town and country was etched by the ownership of consumer appliances. Unlike farm households, most urban residents in 1960 were warmed by natural gas rather than wood fuel, cleaned the laundry in automatic washers, placed telephone calls from their homes, and enjoyed the convenience of indoor bathtubs and flush toilets. However, life in the country did not impose cultural isolation. Television sets flickered in about 75 percent of Arkansas homes. The proportion of rural families able to watch Milton Berle, *Playhouse 90,* and *Ozark Jubilee* with Red Foley was only slightly lower than that of their urban counterparts.

Expanding consumer demand in Arkansas, stimulated by commercials for national products, actually preserved an old economic pattern by drawing the state into the national market. Even though the value added by manufacturing to Arkansas products had increased by fifteen times since 1935, by 1960 the value of the goods and services the state imported still outstripped its exports. If the industrialization of the state had wrested it from the quagmire of basic processing of natural resources, the higher-priced items purchased by Arkansans were still generally made elsewhere. The one area of a positive balance of payments was in federal spending. In 1958 the state received about $113 million more from the U.S. government than it sent to Washington in taxes and fees. Although the net receipts declined to about $79 million by 1963, federal funds remained an important source of outside capital for state development.

The state's most dramatic net loss was its people. Economic diversification within the state had not absorbed the flood of Arkansans abandoning farm and village. An exodus of 371,000 between 1950–58 forced a 6.5 percent drop in the state's population during the 1950s. Although a reduction in the surplus labor force had the potential to lift wage and income levels, the exit of young adults possessing the information, wherewithal, and ambition to embark on a long-distance move likely deprived Arkansas of highly productive employees. As in the 1940s, African Americans were more likely to relocate than whites, although the rate of black migration slowed. The youth of the migrants altered the state's demographics, increasing the number of Arkansans who depended on income other than wages. After 1960 the 10.6 percent of Arkansans over sixty-five years of age and 32 percent younger than fourteen were greater than the national proportions.

The state attracted few immigrants as permanent residents, but more visitors arrived as vacationers. Out-of-state tourist spending doubled between 1948 and 1959, with most of the dollars circulating through Hot Springs and the Ozark region. Organized in 1919 to promote the uplands of southwestern Missouri and northwestern Arkansas, the Ozark Playgrounds Association incorporated the U.S. Corps of Engineers' construction of Norfork (1944), Bull Shoals (1951), Greers Ferry (1962), and Beaver (1963) Lakes into its marketing strategy. Rather than simply lauding scenery and historic sites, the association more commonly highlighted water sports and country music entertainment at resort centers. In 1945 thirteen camps and hotels offered overnight lodging in the vicinity of Baxter County; by 1971, following the creation of Norfork and Bull Shoals Lakes, about three hundred businesses had space to serve over eight thousand visitors. Soon, the listing of weekly cabin rentals was supplanted by publicity about retirement communities. In 1955 John C. Cooper, an east Arkansas attorney and farmer, summoned first-term governor Faubus to the dedication of Cherokee Village, his four hundred acres of subdivided housing tracts in Sharp County. Having intended to promote Cherokee Village as a second-home development, Cooper by 1960 offered expense-paid tours of his community to those seeking a permanent retirement residence. Cooper later purchased the older Benton County resort of Bella Vista and also constructed Hot Springs Village near the shores of Lake Ouachita, a Corps project created by the 1955 completion of the Blakely Mountain Dam.

The formation of lakes throughout the state was the most apparent reconstruction of the Arkansas landscape in the latter half of the twentieth century. The restoration of the white-tailed deer herd was another environmental modification that redefined leisure. Critical to Arkansas's first economy, hunting gave rise to the narratives and images defining the state's early identity. Beginning in the 1950s, the efficacy of the Game and Fish Commission's wildlife management policies enabled hundreds of thousands of Arkansas hunters to revive a forgotten tradition as modern sport.

During the 1927 flood, deer fled for safety to the top of levees, where they were easily slaughtered. Although it was thought that the flood had destroyed the deer population in the state, the commission recorded about five hundred animals by 1930. While game laws limited the number of bucks killed and prohibited outright the taking of does, habitat destruction and the stubborn use of dogs by mountain hunters to run down game depressed the numbers. Realizing that regulations did not solve the problem of habitat recovery, the G&FC by 1934 developed twelve wildlife refuges throughout the state, and in 1939 they restructured one in Howard County as a "deer farm."

When the modern, autonomous G&FC came into existence with the approval of Amendment 35, the benefits of the refuge policy could be measured by population count and the increase in the legal deer harvest from 203 in 1938 to 1,606 in 1944. The commission cooperated with federal forest agency officials to trap deer from overstocked herds in the Ozark National Forest and distribute them to the state refuges. Predictably, news of the deer surplus in the national forest became common knowledge, and in 1949 FBI agents and the state police were called in to bolster game wardens' efforts to repulse marauding hunters. The transplanting of the animals led to the establishment of herds in sixty-six counties, and in 1950 the G&FC permitted hunting in several counties for the first time since the war.

In 1943 Alvin Bates saw his first deer when it crossed a Drew County road: "I didn't know what it was, thought it was a curious animal." In 1947 even long-time residents of Augusta believed that the first deer to inhabit the area were those released that year near the wildlife management refuge bordering White and Woodruff Counties. When hunting was authorized locally in 1952, prominent townsmen set up a camp on a bend of the White River. Having no experience in bagging deer, the camp members during the first hunt lined themselves besides trees a few hundred yards apart and waited as another person drove the game toward them. Soon they adopted the common approach of constructing stands up in large trees.

Herbert Lunday of the Buckeye Camp recalled that G&FC-scheduled deer seasons became integrated into the rhythm of community life. "Many citizens of Augusta have enjoyed the excitement of the deer hunts with us. They've wished us safety and good fortune and watched eagerly for us to return to town with our bounty. I especially remember the excellent pies, cakes, and other food sent to us by the women of the community." Within a few years in Arkansas, this contemporary recreation, a product of scientific management techniques, became a tradition complete with ritual, folklore, and special knowledge to be passed from father to son (a 1998 survey indicated that only about 6 percent of those holding hunting licenses were women, who were more likely than men to hunt with family members). The commission's absolute prohibition against the taking of does became so imbedded in the evolving hunting culture that it became difficult to persuade future generations to reverse course when the imbalance of female to male threatened herd size and health.

The white-tailed deer began to displace squirrel as the game of choice for hunters. Nevertheless, the annual deer harvest did not exceed ten thousand until 1959, although the numbers killed accelerated afterward and surpassed one hundred thousand by 1987. The sale of Arkansas hunting licenses rose steadily after World War II, increasing about 65 percent between 1946 and 1956. With few women taking up the sport, the 209,400 resident licenses in 1960 represented 42.3 percent of the male population in the state between the ages of fourteen and sixty-four.

This hunting boom, however, was dwarfed by the 216.5 percent jump in the issuance of fishing licenses in 1946–56. Wherever the Corps of Engineers went, the fishermen were not far behind. One wildlife historian has explained why new equipment rendered Arkansas river fishing obsolete: "Any up-to-date fisherman in the 1930s and 1940s wanted a rod and reel instead of a pole; plugs and flies instead of minnows and worms; as well as a good-sized boat, preferably one with an outboard motor. Few persons were content anymore to sit on a stump and dangle a line in the water waiting for a fish to bite." In addition to the federal dam-building boom in the 1950s, the G&FC began its own lake development program in 1951 with the construction of the sixty-seven-hundred-acre Lake Conway.

Tuning into broadcasts of the University of Arkansas football games was another new fall pastime of the 1950s that ripened into tradition. The only non-Texas member of the Southwest Conference, Arkansas for decades fielded teams that rarely achieved winning seasons. The program, which had adopted the Razorback mascot by 1916, drew primarily upon northwest Arkansas fans before World War II; before the McMath highway program, the Fayetteville campus was an eight-hour journey from Little Rock. Yet, some boosters elsewhere in the state did follow the teams' up and down fortunes. Scrambling for programming, Col. T. H. Barton in 1935 set up a rudimentary sports network by broadcasting both home and out-of-state games on his radio stations in Little Rock, El Dorado, and Jonesboro. For the away games, the chief engineer hired local carpenters to build a temporary booth in exchange for the lumber used in the construction. Dale Alford, a young ophthalmology student and later a key figure in the segregationist movement, was the game announcer as well as moderator for the *Pigskin Parade.*

In 1945 the UA Board of Trustees hired the well-regarded coach John Barnhill from Tennessee to salvage a barely competitive and tepidly supported program. As academics questioned the expense and merit of big-time football, prominent urban businessmen and influential alumni encouraged the Razorbacks with determination equal to their fervor for new industry. Tight-fisted Ben Laney loosened the purse strings to push a measure during the 1947 session that authorized a bond issue to construct a stadium in Little Rock. In September 1948 at the inaugural clash in War Memorial Stadium, Arkansas thumped Abilene Christian 40-6 before twenty-seven thousand fans, the largest crowd ever to view a football game in the state. The Barnhill era also marked the emergence of statewide broadcasts of the games on the Razorback Network. John F. Wells, newspaper publisher and political gadfly, anchored the network with his North Little Rock radio station and persuaded recently arrived Reynolds Metals to make a good impression by sponsoring the broadcasts. Virtually every home in the state was within earshot of George Mooney's play-by-play descriptions. Following game days, comprehensive accounts engorged the Sunday *Arkansas Gazette,* which had upgraded its coverage through the persistent coaxing of its gifted sportswriter Orville Henry.

Although Barnhill's first team won the 1946 conference championship, the 1954 "25 Little Pigs" became the watershed that both institutionalized and mythologized the Razorbacks. Inexperienced and boasting little depth, Bowden Wyatt's squad easily outdistanced dire predictions with a 7-0 start that propelled it to a number four national ranking. The play that came to represent the miracle season was a sixty-six-yard fourth quarter touchdown pass from Buddy Bob Benson to Preston Carpenter that booted offensive juggernaut Ole Miss from the unbeaten ranks. Four years later Frank Broyles began his nineteen-year stint as head football coach with a below .500 season, but this was followed by successive conference titles between 1959 and 1961. The habitual top ten rankings and postseason bowl invitations culminated with the recognition of the 1964 team as national champions. The compatibility of politics and sport was on display at the university's most celebrated game, the 1969 shoot-out between number two Arkansas and the top-ranked University of Texas. With Pres. Richard Nixon in attendance at Fayetteville, the Razorbacks' early two-touchdown lead did not stand, and they fell in a 15-14 heartbreaker. If promotion and corporate regard forged the program into a business-like enterprise, hard-fought battles by underdog squads turned the Razorbacks into a symbol of the state's perseverance against the odds.

In October 1960 a devoted fan was driving through central Arkansas, unhappy that business kept him from watching the regional television broadcast of the contest against the arch-rival University of Texas. The game faded in and out over his car radio, and he arrived in Malvern without hearing the final minutes. He recalled entering a ghost town: "It looked deserted. Nobody on the streets, nothing. Then it just exploded, like everybody in town yelled at once, and some came running out on the sidewalks. I knew Arkansas had won, but I had no idea how. I felt like the loneliest and least informed man on earth." Such extraordinary zeal waned during the 1990s, when a series of overmatched teams began competing with melancholy results in the powerful Southeastern Conference. Appearances in premier postseason bowl games at the end of the decade, however, revived enthusiasm. Football also ceased to monopolize fan loyalty due to the rising national reputation of the basketball program under Nolan Richardson, the university's first African-American head coach.

The assembling of the Razorback Network went against the grain of the revolution that swept away local radio current-affairs programs and live musical broadcasts in favor of a standard top-forty music playlist. In 1955 KVLC–Little Rock became the state's first station to install the new popular music format, which also introduced rock and roll music to the airwaves. Working as a salesman for a competitor that thought big-band swing would outlast the rock fad, Ray Poindexter assured business owners that the new music appealed only to kids with little spending money.

When a middle-aged beauty shop customer interrupted his pitch to the proprietor one day with the declaration, "I like 'Rock around the Clock'!" Poindexter bowed to the inevitable.

The antecedents of rock, if not the music itself, shook the rafters in a number of locales, but no place with more ardor and fire than in Sam Phillips's Memphis Recording Service studio. In 1950 Phillips built his studio from scratch in order to get on record the stunning array of black musicians heard in Memphis clubs and on Rufus Thomas's WDIA radio program. Regularly, he sent the recording masters for such artists as B. B. King, Ike Turner, and Howling Wolf to Chicago, where they were pressed under the Chess or Modern labels. Phillips first heard the primal, deep roar of Wolf (Chester Burnett) on a West Memphis radio station, and he went on to sign for his own Sun Records a number of other artists working in West Memphis: James Cotton, Little Junior Parker, and Auburn "Pat" Hare. Believing the vitality of rhythm and blues could remake American music, Phillips with considerable regret saw these musicians instigate the revolution by joining the continued exodus to the north.

Phillips had little choice but to unearth the less-apparent white talent, though he preferred a sound more soulful than the "weeping steel guitars and cornstalk fiddle" of country music. He cast about for young whites who had lived across the tracks from genteel neighborhoods and within earshot of black clubs. Phillips later boasted: "I knocked the shit out of the color line." Elvis Presley showed up on Phillips's doorstep to cut a record for his mother's birthday and then made history with a jam session of Arthur "Big Boy" Crudup's blues hit "That's All Right, Mama." When RCA in 1955 gave Philips forty thousand dollars to release Presley from his contract, the Memphis producer finally had the assets to snare other whites whose voices had a blues edge. Johnny Cash, reared on gospel in the Dyess resettlement community, remained steadfastly country, but the rise of "Cry, Cry, Cry" and "I Walk the Line" in the charts helped Phillips advance pet projects like wild man Jerry Lee Lewis.

Lewis came to Phillips's attention when he played piano on Billy Lee Riley's regional favorite "Flying Saucers Rock and Roll." A native of Pocahontas, Riley grew up in the blanched world of Delta poverty and learned to play guitar from an area bluesman. Riley soon broke with

Phillips after accusing the Sun owner of abandoning his rave-up single "Red Hot" to push Lewis's records. Charlie Rich spent his childhood in Colt, Arkansas, listening to the *Grand Ole Opry* while also being tutored by a sharecropper in blues piano phrasing. His 1960 release "Lonely Weekends" was a rare Phillips's hit that made waves beyond the South. Eventually, Rich, like Helena's Conway Twitty (Harold Jenkins), threw over rockabilly for greener pastures as a straight country artist.

Outside the Delta, an explosive mix of styles was delivered by musicians in central Arkansas dives, who wished only to get through a set without angering volatile audiences. A popular band among juke-joint patrons was Ronnie Hawkins and the Hawks, a white outfit that adopted James Brown's "Shout" as their signature performance (the Hawks later moved to Canada and achieved fame as The Band). In 1956 KKOY, the first radio station with an exclusive format of r&b and gospel, went on the air in Little Rock. Around 1960 fifteen-year-old Robert Palmer began playing saxophone with the only other white students at Hall High School, who doted on artists such as Ray Charles and Cannonball Adderly. While his two fellow enthusiasts had played in black venues along Ninth Street, Palmer performed his first gig with the duo at a white joint far into the country and way beyond the law. Too green to structure a proper set, Palmer's group innocently brewed a new world music, "stirring Dixieland and surf music, rockabilly and r&b, pseudojazz and honky-tonk country and western into a big gumbo." Of course, the same home cooking was going on all across Arkansas and the South.

Palmer not only continued to play in bands but also became the nation's most notable and sagacious popular-music critic and historian. Reflecting on rock and roll's birth, he observed that the music's diverse genealogy broke through cultural barriers just as segregationists were rallying for a final stand. "The first racially integrated public functions in many American cities and towns (including Little Rock, where I grew up) were not church services or school board meetings; they were rock and roll concerts." Outraged defenders of the status quo wailed that the mass popularity of a music arising from African-American experience and culture challenged the assumptions of the caste system. Basically, they were right.

The Springtime of Moderation: Early School Desegregation

Following the May 1954 *Brown* decision, two northwest Arkansas school systems, with the beginning of the fall term, became the first desegregated districts in the former Confederate states. Charleston, a small Franklin County community near Fort Smith, and Fayetteville each had consolidated all black students through the junior high grades into a single, separate school. Both systems transported African-American high school students to other districts.

As attorney for the Charleston School Board, Dale Bumpers argued that the district should not uphold a judicially suspect arrangement by repairing the deteriorating building reserved for black students. The board voted in July to bring all of the thirteen black students into the five-hundred-member white student body. The superintendent won over town business leaders, detailed transition plans with black parents, and persuaded the Fort Smith newspapers to withhold lengthy coverage. The opening day of the semester unfolded without incident or outside notice. During the year, black students suffered verbal harassment from other students and dismissive treatment from some teachers, but they also formed white friendships and participated in extracurricular organizations.

By 1954 the five-thousand-dollar annual cost of providing board and tuition at distant high schools for its black students gnawed through the Fayetteville district's financial balance. One school board member acknowledged that the *Brown* decision "pulled us out of the hole." In truth, the Supreme Court in its 1954 decision had deferred ruling on the matter of implementation, and districts such as Charleston and Fayetteville were acting under financial exigencies rather than legal sanction. Still, most southern school districts grappled with similar artificial expenses and chose to continue to pay the bills rather than dismantle a costly dual system. The school board in the south Arkansas district of Sheridan voted to save four thousand dollars by integrating twenty-one black students into the high school. A mass protest meeting provoked the resignation of four board members and capitulation to the heated segregationist sentiment. The presence of the university in Fayetteville created a core white constituency for integration that complemented a secure financial and merchant elite whose interests had not rested upon an unskilled black labor force. About 2 percent of the town's eighteen thousand residents were African American.

Four days following the *Brown* decision, the Fayetteville School Board agreed to enroll for the upcoming year the seven African-American students ready for high school and to desegregate the junior high grades over the course of the following three years. The official policy of quiet compliance was ensured by Hal Douglas. A member of the school board, Douglas was also publisher of the local *Northwest Arkansas Times,* which his mother-in-law, Roberta Fulbright, had transferred to him. If the board decision had the markings of a cautious business decision, private efforts transformed bureaucratic procedure into biracial cooperation. White parishioners from the major Protestant denominations, excepting the Southern Baptists, and a small delegation of black women formed the United Church Women to encourage white teenagers to discuss racial questions openly. Several of the organization's leaders also joined the Arkansas Council on Human Relations, established in late 1954 to assist school boards preparing to desegregate. More critical than the good intentions of community associations was the active collaboration of Minnie B. Dawkins, the principal of the black Lincoln school, and Louise Bell, the principal of the white senior high school. Both women advised students and faculty, arranged tours of the white school for black students, and addressed the apprehensions of patrons and parents.

In the wake of the 1957 Little Rock Crisis, the Fayetteville School Board suspended its desegregation schedule, and the elementary schools remained racially separate until the advent of a new community movement. Witnessing the 1960s civil rights victories, African Americans formed the Community Concerns on Equality, which in conjunction with interracial groups pressured school leaders to resume desegregation. In 1965 the Lincoln school was shuttered and eventually razed, its instructors reassigned within the district, and its students enrolled in the nearest white elementary schools.

Charleston and Fayetteville in the Ozarks were inconvenient destinations for Delta racial extremists. By contrast, Hoxie was an east Arkansas community within a day's drive of Mississippi, and local leaders could not coax cooperation from the national reporters on the scene. Nevertheless, like other districts, the Hoxie School Board by June 1955 begrudged the financial burden of segregation and was certain that the relative dearth of black students would stem a white backlash. *Life* magazine documented the tranquil first day of the 1955 school term with photos of African-American and white children playing and studying together. This montage of a peaceable kingdom goaded Jim Johnson and Little Rock attorney Amis Guthridge to muster forces to buttress the hastily assembled Hoxie chapter of the White Citizens Council.

The school board parried segregationist harassment by gaining an injunction prohibiting council disruption of school operations. Defeat at Hoxie galvanized the various radical segregationist factions to consolidate in 1956 as the Association of Citizens Councils of Arkansas. Johnson, Guthridge, and other leaders came to understand that boisterous rallies and relentless badgering of school officials extended the influence of the council well beyond its numbers. If the Arkansas citizens council was formidable compared to other state chapters in the upper South, its several hundred members did not approach the burgeoning council brigades in Mississippi and Alabama. The Arkansas group was also unique in that class considerations stoked the fervor of its members. Unlike the organizations elsewhere, neither the leaders nor the rank and file of the Arkansas council hailed from the business or civic elite. Through council direct action, lower-status whites exercised rare influence within their communities. Yet, the radical segregationists of the council did not constitute a populist movement: they were too few to be representative, offered no program beyond white supremacy, and followed charismatic leaders rather than built participatory organizations.

The citizens council failed to sidetrack integration in Hoxie because school board members and administrators developed the program and intended to see it through. Whether or not they accepted the principle of integration, the Hoxie officials were dedicated to stability, community reputation, and the rule of law. Commitment to these obligations was sufficient to ward off the vehement outsiders.

By 1957 about 940 African-American students out of a total black student population of 102,000 were attending integrated public schools in Arkansas. While Governor Faubus had declared school integration to be a local matter, neither had he impeded the desegregation of state-funded higher education. All seven of the predominately white colleges accepted black students: Arkansas State in Jonesboro, Arkansas Polytechnic in Russellville, Henderson State Teachers in Arkadelphia, Southern State in Magnolia, Arkansas A&M in Monticello, Arkansas State Teachers in Conway, and the University of Arkansas in Fayetteville. The McMath-era building program at Arkansas Agricultural, Mechanical, and Normal in Pine Bluff, the land-grant college for African-American students, had ended, and the college would not see significant capital improvements until after the segregationist moment had dissipated. None of the private white colleges admitted African-American students until the 1960s.

If Hot Springs was in many ways an anomaly among Arkansas towns and cities, the same patterns and habits of segregation coursed through its public life. Desegregation at the high school by 1957 went no further than one auto mechanics class that enrolled ten students. Yet in the matter of pleasure and games, Hot Springs whites occasionally demonstrated flexibility if not open tolerance. In 1953 the Hot Springs Bathers, a Class C team in the Cotton States Baseball League, announced that it had signed Jim and Leander Tugerson, stars from the Negro American League. For the Bathers' owners, just as it had been for strapped school superintendents, money was the basic issue. The Bathers had closed the 1952 season last in the league standings and last in attendance. With four of its eight teams in Mississippi, the Cotton States League was one of only two of the twenty-five professional leagues to prohibit black athletes. Unwilling to change the exclusionary policy, a majority of team owners in April 1953 voted to evict the Bathers from the league.

In response, the Hot Springs Junior Chamber of Commerce sent the league president a telegram censuring the "arbitrary, unjust, undemocratic, un-American, and un-Christian" action. More eloquently, the Tugersons issued a joint statement: "Are we fit to work in your homes and fields only? We can talk for you and help elect you when it is time for voting. . . . Now we're the forgotten ones. You haven't been fair to us in the South. We don't want to, as Negroes, stay with you or eat with you. All we want to do is play baseball for a living."

Although Jackie Robinson had entered major league baseball six years earlier, league officials had issued no standing policy on integration. In response to an appeal from the Bathers' management, the national director of the minor leagues announced a precedent: "The employment of Negro players has never been, nor is now, prohibited by any provision in the major-minor league agreement." On 20 May 1953 the crackerbox Hot Springs Park was filled with eighteen hundred fans, including three hundred black spectators consigned to bleachers along the first-base line. They had come to see Jim Tugerson pitch against the Senators from Jackson, Mississippi. The eruption of cheers when Tugerson took the mound soon turned to boos and catcalls as umpires declared the game forfeited. The Cotton States League had not relented and had instructed the umpires beforehand to designate Tugerson as an ineligible player.

The following season the league opened the door for black players, but it folded in 1955 as television upended another small-town southern tradition. Jim Tugerson continued to play baseball, although he never donned a major league uniform before his retirement. In Hot Springs Leo McLaughlin was dead, but the gambling casinos flourished with a new clientele who camped at the rows of slot machines. Embarked on her career as an editor and writer in New York, Shirley Abbott on a visit toured the refurbished Southern Club: "The crowds didn't arrive in tailor-made suits anymore, didn't squint knowingly at the boards while savoring a good cigar, didn't know how blackjack was dealt, couldn't make their way through the racing form."

Shortly after taking office, Orval Faubus announced that law enforcement, like school desegregation, was best left to the discretion of local officials. Throughout his administration, the governor continued to wink at gambling while casino owners regularly ferried cash packets to Little Rock. On the other hand, Faubus revised his policy on desegregation.

An Ozark client of the federal Rural Rehabilitation program, August 1935. The New Deal promoted the practice of traditional crafts such as spinning to encourage small farmers to remain self-sufficient. *FSA-OWI Collection, Library of Congress.*

Faulkner County farmers seeking aid. Periodic agricultural crises took a severe toll in overwhelmingly rural Arkansas. In the 1930s the federal government assumed relief obligations formerly carried out by private organizations. *Arkansas History Commission.*

A resident at the Lake Dick Farm Resettlement Project near Altheimer prepares dinner on a wood-burning stove in late 1930s. Amenities such as a hot-water boiler did not prevent families from abandoning the model federal cooperative by 1942. Throughout the 1940s increasing numbers of rural Arkansans enjoyed electric lights, even though wood-burning stoves and outside water pumps remained the rule. *Arkansas History Commission.*

Sen. Joe T. Robinson examines the business end of a "bazooka" horn held by radio comedian Bob Burns about 1935. The two men were among the best-known Arkansans of the era. Robinson exercised legendary influence as a congressional leader, while Burns entertained audiences with hillbilly sketches resented by many in his native state. *Harlan Hobbs Papers, Special Collections Division, University of Arkansas Libraries, Fayetteville.*

Arkansas Power and Light founder, Harvey P. Couch, seated *(left center)* on the steps of Couchwood with visiting businessmen about 1930. Couch launched the modern phase of Arkansas industrial recruitment by hosting business prospects as well as Herbert Hoover and Franklin Roosevelt at his log retreat. Couchwood overlooked Lake Catherine, created in 1924 when AP&L constructed Remmel Dam to generate electricity. *Entergy Arkansas.*

Sonny Boy Williamson and Robert Jr. Lockwood, along with announcer Sam Anderson, promote "King Biscuit Time" on KFFA in Helena during the 1940s. Williamson became recognized as one of the finest blues harmonica players after he began recording for Chess Records in Chicago. Lockwood was an important figure who bridged the acoustic guitar tradition of Robert Johnson and the electric blues of Muddy Waters and B. B. King. *Special Collections Division, University of Arkansas Libraries, Fayetteville.*

Ben Laney, Guy E. Williams, J. William Fulbright, and Carl Bailey at Lake Chicot in August 1944. Laney won the Democratic nomination for governor that month after his opponent withdrew from the primary run-off election. Bailey had helped Fulbright gain the nomination for U.S. senator over the former governor's old rival Homer Adkins. Attorney General Williams aided Fulbright during a subsequent senate investigation into whether voting fraud determined election results. *Bailey Collection, University of Arkansas at Little Rock Archives.*

Sidney McMath leads a parade in Little Rock. McMath launched his career as a reformer and fresh face, but old-fashioned campaign skills made him governor. The crumpled hat became a familiar prop. *Larry Obsitnik Collection, Special Collections Division, University of Arkansas Libraries, Fayetteville.*

A biology class at Dunbar High School in Little Rock in 1947. For over two decades the city's only African-American high school was noted for its strong educational program as well as hosting significant speakers and performers. Nevertheless, crowded classrooms and lack of equipment revealed the effects of segregation. *National Dunbar Alumni Association Collection, University of Arkansas at Little Rock Archives.*

A successful duck hunt at the Bayou Meto Wildlife Management Area near Stuttgart in the early 1950s. In 1948 the Arkansas Game and Fish Commission began acquiring Bayou Meto tracts for a combined public hunting area and refuge. The agency's game management practices established hunting and fishing as the state's most popular recreations. *Arkansas Game and Fish Commission.*

Gov. Orval Faubus meets the press at the state capitol, 2 October 1957. The Little Rock crisis offered American viewers the first television images from the front lines of the new struggle for civil rights. National reporters were not above resorting to stereotypes. A *Time* magazine article referred to Faubus as a "slightly sophisticated hillbilly."
Larry Obsitnik Collection, Special Collections Division, University of Arkansas Libraries, Fayetteville.

Little Rock police detectives look on as Daisy and L. C. Bates inspect remnants of a burned cross outside their home in 1957. Years of experience as activists prepared the two civil rights leaders to sustain their commitment to desegregation in the face of unrelenting harassment during the school crisis. *Daisy Bates Papers, Special Collections Division, University of Arkansas Libraries, Fayetteville.*

Main Street, Little Rock, Christmas 1960. Although Blass and other department stores continued to anchor the downtown retail district, crowded traffic conditions stimulated the opening of shopping centers in the western section of the city.
Gene Hull Photograph Collection, Butler Center for Arkansas Studies, Central Arkansas Library System.

A sit-in demonstration at Woolworth's in Little Rock, 7 November 1962. Unlike the sit-in movements elsewhere, the Little Rock effort did not yield immediate results. However, downtown Little Rock stores were desegregated before the passage of the 1964 Civil Rights Act. *J. N. Heiskell Collection, University of Arkansas at Little Rock Archives.*

Supreme Court Justice William O. Douglas fishes in the Buffalo River, May 1962. Advocates for preserving the river had gained the support of key state journalists, but Douglas's three-day canoe trip attracted national attention. Environmental leader Neil Compton observed that with the justice's visit "we knew that we had a cause not to be denied." *Neil Compton Collection, Special Collections Division, University of Arkansas Libraries, Fayetteville.*

Gov. Winthrop Rockefeller at a memorial service to Martin Luther King Jr. on the steps of the state capitol, 7 April 1968. The only southern governor to publicly honor the civil rights leader after his assassination, Rockefeller wished to include African Americans in a Republican coalition to challenge Democratic dominance. *Winthrop Rockefeller Collection, University of Arkansas at Little Rock Archives.*

Dale Bumpers makes a point. Regarded by scholars as the state's most effective governor, Bumpers was an exceptional orator, whose appeal came through on television. Bumpers and his successor, David Pryor, were rare examples of Arkansas governors who went on to notable second careers in the U.S. senate. *Larry Obsitnik Collection, Special Collections Division, University of Arkansas Libraries, Fayetteville.*

Working on the line at the Tyson chicken processing plant in Springdale in 1978. Women were a significant portion of the new Arkansas manufacturing labor force after World War II. *Shiloh Museum of Ozark History, Springdale, Arkansas/Bob Besom, photographer.*

Fay Jones built tree houses while growing up in El Dorado. His design of structures such as Thorncrown Chapel near Eureka Springs and the Cooper Memorial Chapel in Bella Vista earned the architect worldwide recognition. *E. Fay Jones Collection, Special Collections Division, University of Arkansas Libraries, Fayetteville.*

President Bill Clinton, Gov. Mike Huckabee, and Hillary Clinton listen to Ernest Green's address at the fortieth anniversary observance of the Little Rock desegregation crisis, 25 September 1997. The legacy of both the crisis and the Clinton presidency continued to be debated as the century came to a close. *Aristotle Web Design.*

CHAPTER FOUR

Arkansas Divided

On 3 October 1963 Pres. John F. Kennedy, in his dedication of the Greers Ferry Dam in Cleburne County, observed how the project tied Arkansas to the national economy. The president predicted the massive federal structure would fatten local wallets and boost the demand for American-made consumer goods. Arkansas industrial and political leaders had been advancing the same argument since World War II to justify requests for federal revenues. However, the unraveling of the consensus that had sought growth without social change was evident on that bright autumn day.

In the planning stages for Greers Ferry, the U.S. Army Corps of Engineers was surprised that environmental objections to the hydroelectric project had arisen in congenitally dam-friendly Arkansas. A state game and fish commissioner, a newspaper writer, and a representative of a wildlife association demanded that the structure be redesigned to release water from the top of the lake as well as from the bottom. The critics knew that the flow of cold bottom-water into the Little Red River below the dam would extinguish the smallmouth bass population. Claiming that this modification would cost six million dollars, the Corps nearly abandoned the project. The controversy was settled when the Corps provided land to the U.S. Fish and Wildlife Service for a trout hatchery on the river. The outdoors interests were mollified, and by the late 1960s the Little Red, sans bass, was renowned among area trout fisherman.

The dam testified not only to the Corps's engineering prowess and bureaucratic savvy but also to the state's congressional clout. With the flower of Arkansas's political aristocracy arrayed behind him, Kennedy observed in his dedication that "pound for pound, the Arkansas delegation in the Congress of the United States wields more influence than any other delegation of any of the other forty-nine states." The House Ways and Means Committee chairman Wilbur Mills had just shepherded the president's major tax legislation into law. Nevertheless, Gov. Orval Faubus tailored his remarks for home-front consumption. The governor's use of state police power to resist the 1957 desegregation of Little Rock Central High School had given him an unprecedented tenure. Faubus's disparagement of the president's pending civil rights legislation was so apparent that it provoked a congratulatory call from his old nemesis, Jim Johnson.

The national forces of reaction, originating in the anti–New Deal backlash and nurtured by the McCarthyism of the second Red Scare, had been reinvigorated as bulwarks against the rising civil rights movement. While individual Arkansas figures participated in radical-right organizations, the movement did not reshape the state's political factionalism. Even so, Sen. J. William Fulbright was angered by ultraconservative leaders who denounced his internationalism as a variant of tea and sympathy for communists. As the two men traveled by car from Little Rock to Greers Ferry in early October, Fulbright urged Kennedy to cancel an upcoming trip: "Dallas is a very dangerous place. I wouldn't go there and don't you go."

In the early afternoon of 22 November 1963, the teacher of the advanced calculus class at Hot Springs High School told his students that President Kennedy had been shot while in Dallas. Phil Jamison recalled the reaction of his friend Bill Clinton after the instructor's announcement: "He was motionless. Not even a twitch on his face. Yet you could feel the anger building up inside him."

By 1957 the massive resistance campaigns to court-ordered integration that thundered throughout the Deep South began to resonate in Arkansas. Governor Faubus's tactic of posing as a responsible defender of segregation crumbled as more radical figures began to command public attention. The unwillingness of Little Rock's business leadership to support publicly any gradual desegregation persuaded Faubus that his political survival rested with defiance. The courage of the nine black students who entered Central High School and the stalwart commitment of Daisy and L. C. Bates eventually forced influential figures to confront the arch-segregationists.

White Little Rock's wish to avoid a public debacle similar to the riots at Central High School enabled civil rights strategists to push forward the desegregation of downtown stores. Yet the flow of retail centers and white residences westward dissipated these victories. Influential real estate developers allied with those who wanted to restrict school integration. In the wake of civil rights conflicts, new biracial coalitions formed that became the foundation for urban liberalism. In contrast to the old-fashioned business progressives, the new liberals advocated expansion of rights, aid to the poor, and accountable elected representation.

At the state level, the 1966 election of Winthrop Rockefeller to the governor's office led to a return of the moderate liberalism introduced by Sid McMath. The fading of segregation as a salient issue gave Gov. Dale Bumpers the opportunity to push through the century's most extensive reform agenda, which included a recognition of the growing environmental movement. The first clashes over the state's ecological future centered on preservation of river environs and later erupted over harvesting practices in the national forests.

Lines of Resistance: The Little Rock Crisis

When *Charlotte News* editor Harry S. Ashmore, in the spring of 1947, told his Boston-born wife about an offer to work for the *Arkansas Gazette,* she replied: "Little Rock? Little Rock? Why, it's not even on the way to anywhere." Soon the Ashmores themselves were on their way to Little Rock. John Netherland Heiskell, *Gazette* owner, had edited his newspaper for forty years and wished to transfer some of the daily editorial responsibilities to Ashmore. In 1927 Heiskell had denounced the lynching of John Carter in a front-page editorial, and he thought Ashmore's liberal credentials were in order and fully agreed with his own. Published since 1819, the *Gazette* enjoyed an ample lead in statewide circulation over the *Arkansas Democrat,* its afternoon rival, which had been directed since 1926 by K. A. Engel. While the *Democrat* championed scientific farming and inveighed against federal authority, Ashmore found the *Gazette* a congenial venue to launch broadsides against Gov. Ben Laney and the Dixiecrats. In 1951, when Gov. Sidney McMath invited him to address the Southern Governors' Conference in Hot Springs, Ashmore discomforted most of the chief executives by advocating gradual desegregation.

Ashmore's 1957 book, *An Epitaph for Dixie,* was a poignant meditation by a regional partisan who celebrated the South's distinctive history and traditions while admitting its failure to eradicate racial oppression. Arguing that segregation was an adaptation to post–Civil War emancipation, Ashmore explained that the system had been manipulated by those in power to foster discrimination. Though disagreeing with the *Brown v. Board of Education* decision's assumption that segregated facilities were inherently unequal, Ashmore praised the Supreme Court's willingness to allow school districts to fashion desegregation plans appropriate to local conditions. The editor regretted that since *Brown,* elected officials had rebuffed this judicial deference: "The South has always contended that given time it could work out its own problems; offered time by the Supreme Court the Southern leaders for the most part have so far refused to use it to make even a tentative start toward the accommodation all of them recognize must ultimately come." White recalcitrance, observed Ashmore, had driven many black southerners to the side of African-American leaders who demanded rapid, full-scale integration. Ashmore considered both those petitioning for immediate rights and those clinging to white supremacy to be obstructions to a peaceful resolution of a southern dilemma.

Beginning in the fall of 1957, Ashmore's brave editorial indictments of Faubus's policies pleaded for adherence to the law rather than for integration. Ashmore's desire to see segregation expire quietly and naturally contrasted with that of the white southern majority, who preferred the status quo. Ashmore did, however, share the assumption of segregationists that the pace of desegregation would be governed by the willingness of southern whites to adapt to new conditions. At the dawn of the civil rights era, he did not foresee the scope and force of black engagement against apartheid. Nevertheless, Ashmore would in the future document with admirable breadth and sensitivity the role of race in America without falling into the disillusionment that infected many white liberals of his generation.

In *Epitaph for Dixie,* Ashmore concluded that the new economic forces that had demolished the Old South would also foil vehement opposition to desegregation rulings. Shortly before the *Brown* decision, Ashmore chatted with Hamilton Moses, one of the architects of Arkansas industrialization. Moses clearly dreaded the demise of segregation but exploded when Ashmore suggested the possibility of white race riots. "One lynching and we've wasted $200,000 in magazine advertising. . . . Hell, what we've been selling is peace and order[,] . . . telling 'em that what we've got down here is stability—friendly politicians who are not going to gut a business with taxes, and workers who are grateful for a job and are not going to be stirring up trouble." Moses assured Ashmore that while he would not publicly urge compliance, he and his fellow business leaders would ward off mob violence.

A narrow professional and managerial elite governed the political and economic life of Little Rock. Elizabeth Jacoway has identified roughly thirty-two men who maintained interlocking leadership positions in municipal reform, industrial recruitment, and civic uplift associations. Reflecting an urban progressive outlook unaltered for fifty years, the Little Rock ruling class beat the drum for an efficient, nonpartisan local government and modern social amenities to win the hearts of corporate prospects. The biggest job coup during the 1950s rose from the cooperation between the local oligarchy and the state's congressional delegation to establish Little Rock Air Force Base on the site of the old Arkansas Ordnance Plant. Everett Tucker led a chamber of commerce campaign to raise the funds to purchase and donate over six thousand acres for the installation. The welcoming of a racially integrated military and workforce contingent was proffered as evidence that the city would not endanger jobs by permitting the sort of police brutality suffered by black soldiers stationed at Camp Robinson during World War II. At the same time, the urban managerial campaign was reinforcing older ad hoc policies that had produced racially divided neighborhoods.

In February 1949 Little Rock voters narrowly approved a bond issue to construct a park for black residents. The outcome attested to the growing political power of African-American leaders, who lobbied the city council to place the matter before the public. In addition, white voters may have accepted the arguments of Ashmore, who noted that neglecting recreational facilities for black citizens set the stage for integration. The African-American community was not unified on the matter. *State Press* editors L. C. and Daisy Bates opposed site development at the distant, inconvenient Gillam Park location. The city council delayed construction until it used the bond revenue as a stake to procure additional funds from the federal urban renewal program. A portion of the federal money was allotted for white neighborhoods while an African-American residential project was erected near Gillam Park. John Kirk has concluded that this marshaling of federal funds was the initial demarcation of Little Rock between a constricted black eastern section and an expanding white province to the west.

The election in 1952 of Daisy Bates as president of the Arkansas chapter of the NAACP resolved the conflict within the black political community in favor of the younger generation of African-American reformers. The older leadership had temporarily revived its dominance in 1949 by ousting W. Harold Flowers, the father of Arkansas black engagement, from the state presidency. Yet, Flowers's adherents were not stilled and continued to insist that the NAACP exploit the openings provided by federal court decisions. Daisy Bates's unshakable opposition to segregation was forged in part by her childhood in southern Arkansas. At eight years old she learned from a cousin that three white men had murdered her mother. Armed with this terrible knowledge, she thereafter carried on a private war against local whites. But when her dying stepfather called her to his bedside, an adolescent Daisy listened carefully to his advice: "Don't hate the white people just because they're white. If you hate, make it count for something." Her marriage to L. C. ushered her into activism. Even among his militant contemporaries, L. C. was distinguished by his uncompromising advocacy for thoroughgoing integration and disdain for the segregationist gratuities that substituted for fair access.

By 1955 Daisy and L. C. Bates took the lead in consistently assailing the gradual desegregation plan designed by Virgil Blossom, the Little Rock school superintendent. More than simply a matter of student assignments, Blossom's plan was a school placement strategy that mirrored the city fathers' blueprint for residential segregation. In 1956 the school district opened Horace Mann High School in the predominately African-American eastern ward and assigned to it an all-black faculty and staff. Students who once attended Dunbar High School were sent to Horace Mann, and the former black high school became a junior high. Before the beginning of the 1957 fall term, the district announced that the newly completed Hall High School in the western suburbs would enroll its first students that year.

While an early version of Blossom's plan included a minimal desegregation of all high schools, the process by 1956 provided only for the limited admission of black students to Central High School, located in the midst of adjacent white working class and black neighborhoods. Blossom told white patrons such as Sara Murphy that he was delaying integration of the elementary grades until new facilities could be constructed to ensure the effective survival of single-race schools. The superintendent did not believe that equity for the district's black students was his first responsibility: "Uncontrolled integration would lower the quality of schools."

In February 1956 Wiley Branton, a Flowers protégé from Pine Bluff, filed *Aaron v. Cooper* on behalf of thirty-three black students who had been denied admission to four all-white Little Rock schools the previous month. Sponsored by the state NAACP, the suit reflected the pragmatic calculation of Daisy and L. C. Bates to breach the segregation barrier with selected students rather than to demand compete integration. Federal Judge John E. Miller ruled, however, that the Blossom plan was a legally acceptable strategy that would "lead to effective and gradual adjustment of the problem." In April a federal appeals panel upheld Miller's endorsement of the school district plan while also confirming his stipulation that desegregation must begin with the 1957 fall term.

Having stymied the move for authentic desegregation, Blossom and the school board were confident that the token effort would not arouse white fervor. Their optimism was bolstered by the uneventful desegregation in April 1956 of public transportation in Little Rock, Hot Springs, Pine Bluff, and Fort Smith after municipal officials mistakenly assumed that a

Supreme Court decision immediately outlawed racial separation on city transit. The antisegregation bus boycotts in Baton Rouge, Tallahassee, and most famously, Montgomery were not replicated in Arkansas. Gradualism also seemed to be ratified by the voters when two supporters of the Blossom plan defeated open segregationists in the March 1957 Little Rock school board elections. The superintendent himself was certain that his scores of speeches to civic and education groups and his apprising the core elite on the plan's particulars would ensure a smooth transition. Blossom promised that compliance would not threaten business stability. In early 1957 chamber of commerce director Tucker gave the schoolman partial credit for landing an industrial prospect by alleviating the new corporation's apprehensions over desegregation.

Blossom cherished his plan as a model for southern education and believed that it accommodated all eventualities. Consequently, he advised the Little Rock mandarins of his intentions, but did not request their commitment to intervene if things began to fall apart. He rebuffed the involvement of the local Parent-Teacher Association and dismissed a proposal to form a biracial advisory committee. The black students slated to enroll at Central High were not included in the customary school tours afforded new students. The steps followed by Fayetteville leaders in 1954 to encompass the community in preparations for desegregation were disregarded in Little Rock. The shortcomings of Blossom's campaign were apparent to one business observer: "Blossom is a salesman selling his idea. He kept in the good graces of the power structure and sold rather than received ideas. He would accept no suggestions."

The governor of Arkansas was also a man who did not readily seek advice and kept his own counsel before taking action. Overcoming the usual political infirmity of second-term chief executives, Orval Faubus pushed through the 1957 legislature the first general tax increase since the Futrell administration. The twenty-two-million-dollar package included a one-cent increase in the sales tax, a boost of the severance tax on minerals, and a jump in income tax revenues by replacing the high personal exemption with a tax credit. The rise in collections fueled a 40 percent increase in overall education funding during the 1957–58 school year, underwriting an unprecedented eight-hundred-dollar increase in the average public schoolteacher's salary. A masterful political accomplishment, the progressive expansion of government was purchased with the governor's signature on four segregation measures. Among other things, the new laws required the NAACP to identify its members to state officials and authorized the establishment of a state sovereignty commission. Still certain that he could outflank segregationists and moderates, Faubus generally avoided enforcement of these laws, which had been a sop to east Arkansas legislators.

In 1956 Faubus's conviction that segregationist bluster defanged white extremists prompted his lobbying of moderate congressmen to sign the resolution known as the Southern Manifesto. Arkansas representatives Brooks Hays and James W. Trimble were wary of the document's pronouncements that the *Brown* decision was unconstitutional and that the signatories must oppose federal enforcement of the ruling. Hays recalled Faubus's telling both congressmen that the declaration was the sort of palliative necessary to stop "the Ku Klux Klan and the extreme Citizens Council groups from taking over the political life of the state." The two reluctantly joined ranks with the other members of the state delegation. With notable exceptions such as Lyndon Johnson of Texas and Albert Gore of Tennessee, a southern congressional bloc supported the manifesto. Southern moderates were abandoning the task of developing a strategy of compliance because they assumed that radicals were on the verge of capturing white majority opinion.

By 1957 the radical segregationists in Arkansas spoke loudly and with little hint of contradiction from mainstream white leaders. The Capital Citizens Council, the Little Rock chapter of the state organization, had around five hundred members. Led by Amis Guthridge and the Reverend Wesley Pruden, who had hosted the daily radio "Country Church" during the 1930s, the council inundated the governor's office with angry phone calls warning of a riot if black students entered Central High School. Understanding that he could no longer satisfy the segregationists by pleading lack of authority, Faubus decided to embrace the radicals as the base of support for a third-term election campaign. By July the governor assured Guthridge and Pruden that he would halt desegregation in Little Rock. If Faubus had abandoned moderation, he had not given up the politics of evasion. He cast about for a way to emerge as the state's chief opponent to integration without provoking a showdown with federal officials.

For a time Faubus thought Virgil Blossom would become a collaborator. Besieged as well with threatening phone calls, Blossom asked the governor whether he would take steps to keep order when school opened. Faubus thought that the clearly shaken superintendent and school board would welcome a maneuver to delay desegregation and relieve the pressure. In August the governor choreographed the filing of a suit in chancery court on behalf of the segregationist Mothers League of Central High that would enjoin the school's integration on the grounds that it violated the 1957 segregation statutes and risked civil disorder. Faubus knew the state laws were unconstitutional, but he hoped that federal hearings on the case would both postpone desegregation and prove that state authorities were powerless against the courts. Yet, the Little Rock school leaders balked at any more delays, a position Blossom confirmed when he testified at the hearing that he did not foresee trouble at Central High. When federal judge Ronald N. Davies threw out the Mothers League suit and ordered the Blossom plan carried out, Faubus was left with hard choices.

Winthrop Rockefeller, the AIDC chair, pressed Faubus to urge compliance publicly and to use the state guard to implement the desegregation order. However, Faubus was certain that he would be replaced by an archsegregationist such as Jim Johnson if he heeded Rockefeller's advice. In a late August visit, Marvin Griffin, the firebrand governor of Georgia, widened support for defiance by boasting that his state would never allow black students to enter white schools. The school leaders continued to fear that they would provoke segregationist fury if they publicly enlisted the community in support of desegregation. Congressional representatives and senators issued no statements. Most Protestant clergy implored their congregations to observe the law without defending the principles behind the judicial rulings. The recent decision by voters to replace the mayor-council form of government with a city manager deprived the lame-duck municipal officials of effective authority. The private interests that governed the city stood aloof from the school issue. An admirer of Sid McMath's racial moderation, Witt Stephens later explained his inaction by noting that he was on a foreign trip: "If I had been here, I couldn't have done anything about it. Faubus knew how I felt about it." The abdication of responsibility by powerful and influential whites was astounding in its completeness.

When Faubus announced on 2 September 1957 that the Arkansas National Guard had encircled Central High, neither the White Citizens Council nor the NAACP were certain whether the troops would enforce or prevent integration. The governor warned that the steps were necessary because of evidence that black youths were acquiring weapons and of reports that "caravans" of whites were descending upon the city. Judge Davies announced the following day that he would accept the governor's word that the troops were in place to keep the peace and told the parties to carry out the court ruling. Worried about the nine students' safety, Daisy Bates arranged to have them accompanied through the jeering whites to Central High by white and black ministers. The captain of the guard told the contingent that under orders of the governor they could not pass. Elizabeth Eckford's home did not have a telephone, and she was not told to rendezvous with the others before approaching the school. Turned away by the guard, she was forced to walk alone through a frenzied crowd threatening her life before Grace Lorch, a white leftist, escorted her to a city bus. Wearing a freshly starched school dress, the young black student's dignity and composure in the midst of convulsive bigotry was emblematic of similar scenes in the years to come.

While Faubus knew that his claim of a flurry of gun and knife sales in Little Rock was unsubstantiated, he may have been taken in by the segregationist callers who manufactured tales of the menacing caravans. Certainly, by the time the nine students would again attempt to enter Central High in about three weeks, the numbers of Delta white council members keeping vigil had grown to a menacing size. As the court battles unfolded during the interim, Brooks Hays arranged a meeting between Pres. Dwight Eisenhower and Faubus at Newport, Rhode Island. Hays believed that Faubus's native realism would make him amenable to compromise, but politically astute figures such as Henry Woods in Arkansas and Vice President Richard M. Nixon understood that the presidential negotiations actually elevated the governor's credibility. At Newport,

Eisenhower announced Faubus's agreement to adhere to *Brown* but was furious when the governor did not withdraw the troops upon his return to Arkansas. When Judge Davies almost a week later ordered the troops removed, Faubus complied and immediately left the state for a conference.

When the nine black students entered Central High on 23 September, most of the thousand whites surrounding the school broke through the undermanned police lines surrounding the building. The rioters, a majority of whom were local residents, differed from the all-male toughs seen by later audiences of television broadcasts from Birmingham and Selma. With members of the Mothers League encouraging the assault and berating officers, viewers had the impression of an entire community in revolt. The fire chief ignored Mayor Woodrow Mann's instructions to turn fire hoses on the crowd, and police officials panicked at the thought of a full-scale race war if the students were harmed or killed. Even after the students were removed covertly, the terror continued. That evening about one hundred cars rolled into the Bates's neighborhood, and police discovered explosives and arms when they stopped the vehicles short of their goal.

Eisenhower's own efforts to avoid desegregation controversies fell apart with the Arkansas defiance. The following day he federalized the state guard and sent the 101st Airborne Division to Little Rock to restore order and enforce the court rulings. On 24 September the nine students were waiting at the Bates home when an army officer came to the door: "Mrs. Bates we are ready for the children. We will return them to your home at three thirty o'clock." The army division remained stationed at Central High until November, and the National Guard continued to patrol the halls throughout the year.

The military presence did not halt an organized harassment campaign against the students: Melba Pattillo, Jefferson Thomas, Gloria Ray, Carlotta Walls, Minnijean Brown, Thelma Mothershed, Terrance Roberts, Elizabeth Eckford, and Ernest Green. Walls's legs were regularly bruised by blows from steel-tipped boots; Thomas was knocked unconscious from a punch that produced an egg-sized lump behind his ear; Ray was followed by a boy swinging a rope fashioned into a hangman's noose; Pattillo was tripped at the head of a flight of stairs; and Brown was doused with hot food and repeatedly kicked. Prudence and school regulations rather than theory warranted nonviolent responses to repeated provocation. The African-American students were not to assist each other if in trouble because doing so might spark a dangerous melee. White assailants were punished if an adult observed their attacks; firsthand reports from the black students were not credited as sufficient evidence for fear that white students would begin to fabricate charges. Brown was expelled in February after she retaliated against a final indignity, but she was soon placed at a first-rate high school in New York City.

Navigating uncharted territory, Daisy Bates made the students aware that public attention was both an intrusion and an opportunity to educate the audience beyond Little Rock. She coached the students before they spoke to reporters. She also treated these young people as embattled veterans suffering from wounds that few could comprehend. At the end of each school day, the students would meet in the basement of the Bates home to compare notes and uncork the anger that brewed during the long classroom hours. As the mentor for the students, Daisy Bates also became in the public's eye the primary leader of the civil rights movement in Little Rock. This status owed in part to her position as head of the state NAACP but also derived from her precise and eloquent expressions of the integrationist viewpoint to the media. Despite the pressure of constant terroristic threats, she successfully adhered to the overall strategy while remaining fiercely protective of the students' well-being. Her ability to balance the cause against the personal cost of daily battles placed her in the front rank of the era's combatants for social justice.

The recalcitrance of white Little Rock also was decisive in rallying the African-American community around the strong integrationist program of Daisy and L. C. Bates. Yet divisions persisted. Melba Pattillo recalled an impassioned debate at her grandmother's house among the women of her church as to whether the students were claiming their just due or bringing trouble to their neighbors. As part of the new generation, Bates also lacked the ties to the local white politicians cultivated by older black leaders for favors and patronage. Reportedly, she regarded only Edwin E. Dunaway as trustworthy. Dunaway was a well-respected white attorney and former state supreme court justice, but his liberalism reduced his influence with the white elite. And even Bates questioned the benefits of an alliance with upper-class progressives. She pointedly told Dunaway that Faubus's poor-boy resentments were directed at those who lived in old-monied Pulaski Heights: "He's against you and the people in the Heights, and I'm going to have to pay for it." Although white liberals such as Dunaway, Henry Woods, Harry Ashmore, and Fred Darragh enjoyed prominence in Little Rock, the core business movers and shakers were moderate segregationists whose support for Faubus's stand intensified with the introduction of the federal troops.

Even if they were not about to sponsor Capital Citizens Council insurrectionists for country club membership, the civic leadership permitted the radicals to seize control of public life because they too wanted segregation to endure. Without the acquiescence of the business leadership, the economic and legal sanctions against Faubus's opponents would have been less onerous. Spurred by state attorney general Bruce Bennett, North Little Rock and Little Rock city councils approved ordinances requiring membership lists from "certain organizations." The Reverend J. C. Crenshaw, the president of the Little Rock NAACP chapter, and Daisy Bates were arrested and forced to post bond when they refused to reveal members' names. Bennett, the most ardent segregationist among elected state officers, depleted NAACP resources and energy over the next seven months in pursuit of the group's records. Several parents of the nine black students at Central High were either dismissed or forced from their jobs. Major corporations such as Southwestern Bell Telephone, the Stephens-owned Arkansas Louisiana Gas Company, and Hamilton Moses's Arkansas Power and Light Company removed their advertising from the *State Press,* and by the end of 1959 the Bateses were forced to close the newspaper that was their livelihood and forum for new voices.

Ashmore's editorial condemnation of the governor's resistance subjected the *Arkansas Gazette* to reprisals that slashed circulation in 1957 by over 15 percent and lowered revenue by about 7 percent. The popularity of Orville Henry's coverage of the Arkansas Razorbacks and the refusal of major department stores to join the advertising boycott helped the newspaper continue to show a slight profit. Thriving from its rival's plight, the *Arkansas Democrat* kept editorially mum but became a ready conduit for Mothers League accusations through its news columns. The awarding of two Pulitzer Prizes for commentary and public service consoled *Gazette* owners and staff.

With Martin Luther King Jr., the head of the newly formed Southern Christian Leadership Conference, attending as the guest of his family, Ernest Green walked with the other graduates during the May 1958 Central High commencement ceremonies. The end of school did not mean victory for constitutional equity. In early 1958 the school board, in essence, abandoned the Blossom plan when it petitioned the courts for an extended delay in continuing desegregation. The board's action and the subsequent ruling by the federal district judge granting relief wrecked the moderate argument that segregation's demise was inevitable. Orval Faubus, however, knew that the *Brown* decision would not be rescinded and did not want to find himself again at risk of federal sanction. He determined to both shore up his popular support and entangle other branches of state government by drafting segregationist measures. After a late July 1958 primary victory ensured his third term, Faubus called the General Assembly into special session to arm him with the authority to interdict school integration.

The most formidable weapon among the array of laws rapidly approved by the legislature was Act 4. Under this measure, the governor could shut down schools facing desegregation orders and then have the local voters decide in a referendum whether to integrate the district or keep the schools closed. When the U.S. Supreme Court reconfirmed on 12 September 1958 that Little Rock must continue to desegregate, Faubus ordered the city's high schools to cease operations. As the governor set the date for the school-closure referendum, several of his moneyed supporters formed the Little Rock Private School Corporation to operate a white high school. The Capital Citizens Council aggressively solicited donations for the private T. J. Raney High School from fellow councilors scattered throughout the South. The margin of votes ratifying the Faubus school closure was likely widened by the fact that integration was the only alternative offered on the ballot. Different wording, however, would not have changed an outcome that reflected the aroused hostility of white voters. No established civic or school betterment organizations campaigned before the election for the reopening of the schools. In November the successful write-in candidacy of segregationist Dale Alford over incumbent congressman Brooks Hays, recently re-elected as president of the Southern Baptist Convention, sealed the ascendancy of the racial radicals.

In the long run, the majority would not cling to the doctrine of pure racial apartheid if the costs became too great. Founded by Adolphine Terry and Vivion Brewer, the Women's Emergency Committee To Open Our Schools (WEC) adroitly diminished the controversy over integration by emphasizing the growing extremism of the segregationists. No Arkansan boasted a more stately family genealogy than Terry, who was the sister of the poet John Gould Fletcher and whose reform activism had begun in the women's suffrage and antilynching crusades. Brewer's parents also were part of the Little Rock patrician set, but they atypically encouraged their daughter to enter law school following the customary sojourn at Smith College in Massachusetts. Both women married within their class, which continued to insulate them from economic and social coercion. Eventually, nearly fourteen hundred women joined the WEC, and Faubus's famous gibe that their movement was the "charge of the Cadillac Brigade" was not far off the mark. The income of the families of WEC members was about twice that of the Arkansas average, nearly all of them had attended college, and most were Methodist and Presbyterian rather than Baptist. Their education, confidence of position, and experience in clubs and associations also strengthened the independence of the members, who felt they had waited too long for male leaders to protect the interests of their children.

Mindful that her own racial liberalism exceeded that of most of her counterparts, Terry steered the WEC away from a broad program of inclusion and kept its membership all-white. Restricting the group's mission to saving the schools also advanced the basic strategy of prodding the business elite to reassert their authority. The members of the WEC, like those of the segregationist Mothers League, used their identity as women to popularize their cause while at the same time challenging traditional gender roles. Both groups highlighted their special responsibility for the welfare of children, marketed their message through mass advertising, demanded accountability from highly placed men, and gained support through telephone chains and canvassing door-to-door. Of course, the groups' differences in background and goals produced distinctive tactics.

The families of the roughly two hundred League members mirrored the lower-middle- and working-class backgrounds of the citizen councilors. With troops guarding Central High halls, League leaders strove to disrupt school operations throughout the year to demonstrate that integration was unworkable. Segregationist activism conferred a rare authority on a marginal class without the costs inflicted upon moderate and liberal partisans. Like Daisy Bates and the nine students, WEC leaders were plagued with telephone hate callers following a precise schedule. Irene Samuel, for example, parried menacing calls every fifteen minutes on Wednesday and Saturday nights.

When segregationists extended their harassment beyond black targets to include prominent whites, they became increasingly viewed as a source of instability. By 1959 the WEC was finding it easier to claim that a resumption of school operations was also a return to the status quo. The unstated corollary to the WEC argument was that reopened high schools would eventually be desegregated institutions. The message finally began to win over the business community. A February survey of Little Rock Chamber of Commerce members revealed an overwhelming majority would endorse a "controlled, minimal plan of integration acceptable to the Federal Courts" in order to return the students to the classrooms. The shift in opinion also reflected new chamber leadership. Previous presidents of the group had been executives of utilities subject to state regulation. Grainger Williams, who took over the post in January 1959, was a moderate oriented toward local interests. In May the overreach of the racial separatists dispelled the civic elite's benign neglect. Despite a walkout by moderate members to prevent a quorum, the rump segregationist faction on the Little Rock School Board voted to dismiss forty-four teachers and administrators who were viewed as sympathetic to integration.

Evolving from the PTA of a Pulaski Heights elementary school, Stop This Outrageous Purge (STOP) became the organizational vehicle for attorneys and businessmen to confront the archsegregationists. STOP unleashed a successful petition drive to submit the recall of the hard-line school board members to the voters. The Mothers League's counter-campaign to remove the moderate directors led to the formation of the Committee to Retain Our Segregated Schools (CROSS). Even thought the WEC had studiously avoided any identification with integration, STOP leaders believed the women's group too controversial to be more than a silent partner. Yet, the WEC's experience in the Brooks Hays congressional campaign and in egging supporters to attend public rallies made it the moderates' best hope in the weeks leading up to the recall election. Irene Samuel recalled visiting the STOP headquarters early on: "I sat there and those men were running around like chickens with their heads cut off. . . . [This minister] was standing there smoking his pipe, thanking everybody." Advised by Henry Woods, the WEC brought to bear unprecedented modern techniques of data gathering, precinct organization, and direct contact to prod sympathetic voters to cast ballots. The women of Little Rock introduced grass-roots, democratic electioneering into an Arkansas political culture long dominated by machine and boss.

The 26 May 1959 referendum results that ousted the segregationist school-board members and retained the moderates broke along class and racial lines. The moderates earned nearly three-fourths of the votes in both the upper-income white ward and predominately African-American precincts. On election day students from Philander Smith College, an AME institution, alerted black voters and organized automobile rides to the polls. STOP lost most decisively in the working-class white neighborhoods and fell short to a lesser extent in the middle-income sections. Still the antisegregationist campaign had not challenged apartheid mores. A few days before the election, white supporters of STOP attended a rally at Robinson Auditorium, while African Americans gathered at the Dunbar Community Center. If marked by caution, this campaign to recover the schools from segregationist control did engender a new progressive alignment in Little Rock. In the future, coalitions of elite white women, labor, and black leaders disregarded the traditional reform goals of economic modernization to address issues of equity and rights.

If the recall election signaled that Little Rock civic leaders had accepted desegregation as compatible with orderly development, the opening of the high schools in August 1959 indicated that they also had regained their nerve. Hall High School in the western section of the city peacefully enrolled three black female students. At Central High School, authorities used fire hoses to break up a phalanx of two hundred segregationists marching from a protest rally at the State Capitol. With mobs held in check, Jefferson Thomas and Carlotta Walls resumed their education at Central. On Labor Day three dynamite charges damaged city and school property. The five convicted of the bombing were linked to the Ku Klux Klan, and one of the culprits was a Capital Citizens Council board member; his sentence was commuted by the governor.

Orval Faubus recognized that the recall election marked the apex of strong segregationist influence, and he adjusted his politics accordingly. While the governor had openly commended the CROSS position, his aid to the segregationists was generally covert and dispensed through surrogates. The decline of the radical separatists did not hamper Faubus's maneuverability. In 1960 Attorney General Bruce Bennett mounted a primary election challenge by charging that Faubus had turned soft on integration. The governor's re-election demonstrated that his 1957 defiance continued to inspire loyalty among conservative whites. In a textbook display of *Realpolitik,* Faubus employed patronage to gain the regard of some well-placed black leaders. In 1960 and subsequent elections, the black majority votes for Faubus originated in his expansion of government services and the shortcomings of his opponents.

Faubus's unprecedented length of tenure in office generated an unprecedented gubernatorial political machine. Despite the authoritarian intent, neither the State Sovereignty Commission nor the 1958 law requiring that state employees reveal their organizational memberships provoked a statewide purge. On the other hand, the Criminal Investigation Division of the state police served as the governor's surveillance squad. The CID spied upon and harassed white liberals and civil rights leaders less for ideological reasons than for their identification as political enemies of Faubus. By 1960 Faubus had jettisoned his old hillbilly populism, and even his tolerant moderation, as he thundered reactionary bromides and consorted with far-right figures. In 1960 the National States' Rights Party, an invention of the southern citizen councils movement, selected the governor as its presidential candidate. Although Faubus belatedly turned down the nomination, he had clearly become a creature of the forces he had set loose in 1957.

Daisy Bates in *The Long Shadow of Little Rock* pronounced the crisis a fire bell in the night for white America and a catalyst for the civil rights crusade: "Little Rock gave the signal. Events in history occur when the time has ripened for them, but they need a spark. Little Rock was that spark at that stage of the struggle of the American Negro for justice." However, subsequent histories of that struggle have catalogued the confrontation at Central High as a spectacular eruption with little impact on the evolution of the organized movement. The denouement of Faubus's endgame with Eisenhower offered an ambivalent legacy. The deployment of federal troops persuaded moderate governors that token compliance was preferable to outright defiance, but the lesson was lost on chief executives in the Deep South. If the crisis introduced a liberal ideology of equity and rights into Arkansas politics, it also withered Faubus's inclinations to take up the restructuring of economic and political power begun under Sid McMath. Though not united, the African-American community showed greater strength of purpose and courage under fire than did white Little Rock. Even the most hardened racist had to recognize that stark intimidation was now a blunted weapon. However, the new militancy was not a product of the crisis. Black solidarity and organizational effectiveness had developed from the emergence of a more forceful leadership after World War II. While adopting supporting roles during the 1957 crisis, many long-term activists continued to agitate for social justice in the following years. Estranged from her husband and living elsewhere for an extended period, Daisy Bates herself would not be instrumental during the 1960s campaigns. The *State Press* remained silenced.

The Little Rock Crisis was a tragedy. While not a few individuals displayed integrity and social responsibility, the material and psychological toll exacted costs for many years. The promise of human rights was neither fulfilled nor hastened by the course of events. The failure to desegregate Central High School peacefully was the legacy of a political system dominated by personal opportunism and narrow economic self-interest.

Urban Reform, Urban Renewal

In the 1960s Arkansas was drawn into the campaigns of the civil rights movement, although without the acrid smoke of battle that hung over

Mississippi and Alabama. The experience of the school desegregation crisis encouraged Little Rock white leaders to accept peaceful resolutions when it appeared that recalcitrance threatened to attract national attention. New civil rights leaders emerged from the city's African-American professional class, but the campaigns to desegregate public services and accommodations also required the intervention of national activist organizations.

In March 1960 about fifty Philander Smith students took seats at the Woolworth's lunchcounter in downtown Little Rock. They remained seated when refused service, and five were arrested for not leaving after the lunchcounter abruptly closed. A month earlier students from North Carolina Agricultural and Technical College in Greensboro used the sit-in tactic to pressure that city's department stores to serve its black patrons at the counters alongside whites. Within a week this method of demonstration spread to other southern cities and by September about seventy thousand blacks and whites had quietly and politely endured taunts and assaults after requesting the right to order a sandwich and soft drink. By that time twenty-eight cities had opened the lunchcounters, but Little Rock was not one of them. Municipal authorities decided to suppress the demonstrations by wielding the 1958 segregation statutes to impose heavy fines and jail sentences on students convicted of "trespassing." Official intractability prodded the NAACP to declare a boycott of the downtown stores. The reluctance of older black leaders to foster direct action protest, however, killed the campaign within a week. When Philander Smith students picketed the stores in April, Daisy and L. C. Bates on behalf of the NAACP were nearly alone in praising the students' courage. The disapproval of community leaders and the summer college break halted the sit-in movement with no victories to its credit.

Raising no federal issues and kept out of the national headlines, the lunchcounter desegregation efforts in Little Rock posed no costs for white intransigence. The July 1961 arrival of a delegation of Freedom Riders raised a different challenge. Sponsored by the Congress of Racial Equality, organized interracial groups of travelers journeyed throughout the South, entering bus station waiting rooms and restaurants to test the enforcement of a 1960 Supreme Court ruling that desegregated interstate travel facilities. Not unexpectedly, the Freedom Riders in May 1961 aroused well-documented violence in Alabama, particularly in Montgomery, where a thousand whites bludgeoned the riders as well as a federal observer. Little Rock authorities resolved to garner no such infamy. Buffered by city police from a jeering crowd, the Freedom Riders confronted in the Little Rock bus terminal an example of segregationist ingenuity. One waiting area was designated as open to all black and white interstate passengers, while another was reserved for white intrastate travelers. Deciding that racial separation must be challenged in all of its forms, the riders entered the whites-only sitting area even though the station adhered to the letter of the law. They were almost immediately arrested.

Pronounced guilty in state court, the riders spurned the judge's offer to waive the jail sentence in return for agreeing not to continue their campaign into Louisiana. With the riders threatening a hunger strike in jail, Little Rock business chieftains took steps to make certain that the judge had a change of heart and that the activists departed the next morning. Influential whites were confident that desegregation could be managed so as to forestall federal intervention and dampen social upheaval.

The assuredness of the power brokers compelled African Americans to see the need for an umbrella organization that could articulate community interests more comprehensively than could individual figures with patronage ties to white officials. Several young physicians in 1961 convened representatives from African-American organizations to form the Council on Community Affairs (COCA). As COCA met with various white civic groups, its representatives explained that the endurance of segregation and failure to redress discriminatory practices made turmoil inevitable. COCA resorted to litigation when the city board rebuffed proposals to desegregate municipal parks and facilities. The direct action protests dreaded by white notables actually originated outside the groups in the COCA orbit.

In the fall of 1962, the interracial Arkansas Council on Human Relations (ACHR) asked the Student Nonviolent Coordinating Committee, a product of the southern sit-in movement, to dispatch an activist experienced in mobilization campaigns. Founded after the *Brown* decision, the ACHR set about to advance the peaceful implementation of desegregation plans through education and mediation. After 1960 the ACHR both increased its black membership and advocated that the pace and extent of integration be determined by African Americans rather than white acquiescence. In October 1962 William Hansen, a white veteran of the Freedom Rides and southern jails, arrived from SNCC's Atlanta headquarters and consulted with Philander Smith student Worth Long, who had attended SNCC conferences. Hansen detected that Little Rock whites on the whole did not recoil from casual racial interaction in public places, unlike what he had witnessed in Deep South locales. Knowing that the business community had been traumatized by the ignominy arising from the 1957 crisis, Hansen decided that negotiation in combination with selective protest actions could compel the integration of downtown stores.

Following brief sit-ins at the Woolworth's lunchcounter, the ad hoc Downtown Negotiating Committee, chaired by banker James Penick, opened talks with a team of two students joined by Philander Smith chaplain Negail Riley and ACHR leader and COCA director Ozell Sutton. The parley broke down when the business group outlined a desegregation process requiring years to complete. In December Hansen coordinated another round of sit-ins that expanded targeted stores beyond Woolworth's. The not unexpected arrests of protesters inspired over one hundred Philander Smith students to conduct a Main Street march. Penick then met successively with downtown store managers, using initial capitulations to pressure hold outs to end segregation practices. The January 1963 desegregation of lunchcounters proved to be the first domino as hotels, restaurants, and movie theaters fell into line. Relieved that discrimination against retail customers had faded without incident, municipal authorities abolished racial restrictions at Robinson Auditorium, the city zoo and arts center, and all public parks and golf courses. By the end of 1963, as southern congressmen continued to bottle up the Kennedy civil rights legislation, integrated public services were the rule in Little Rock.

The school board, on the other hand, cleaved to the minimal desegregation aims that had been the basis of the businessmen's successful STOP campaign. The Women's Emergency Committee was increasingly impatient with the gradualism of its former allies from the antipurge election. The school board circumvented federal desegregation rulings through the advice and court filings drawn up by a firm headed William Smith, who had served as Governor Faubus's trusted legal adviser. Mahaffey, Smith, &

Williams (later renamed Friday, Eldredge, & Clark) was retained by school districts throughout the state to craft obstructionist strategies that perpetuated school segregation more effectively than the bombast of the White Citizens Councils.

The failure of the citizens council in 1960 to prevent Delores Jean York from becoming the first black student to enter a Pine Bluff all-white elementary school demonstrated the group's faltering influence. The traditional entrepôt for the Delta, Pine Bluff was the home of a sizable African-American professional class and was served by a newspaper that had editorialized in favor of desegregation. Throughout east Arkansas, however, school officials made certain that nothing more than token integration was achieved. In 1966 an estimated 2 percent of black students attended schools with whites in Forrest City. That year African-American patrons of schools in Crittenden, Lee, Phillips, and St. Francis Counties reported that school buses remained segregated, black parents had been kept from attending school-board meetings, and federal funds had been used to expand a school that taught only black students.

In Little Rock the school board's evasions also reflected the influence of William F. Rector, a pugnacious insurance and real estate mogul who was putting his stamp on the city. One official mused upon Rector's death in 1975: "There will never be another Billy Rector. His leadership was a dictatorship. The king is dead." Although a segregationist, Rector was at cross-purposes with Faubus in 1957, when the unrest put at risk completion of his new shopping center in the western suburbs. As the crisis cooled, Rector renewed his labors to keep integration at bay. Overseeing the relocation of the city's retail center from downtown to the new hub at University Avenue and Markham Street, Rector was little concerned about the fate of Main Street lunchcounters. The school district was another matter. Comprehensive and authentic desegregation most certainly would compromise the all-white character of Rector's western developments. When Everett Tucker, a Rector ally and chamber of commerce official, faced a December 1962 challenge from a WEC member for his school-board seat, the business community exploited liberal divisions to stay the course.

Sara Murphy filed to oppose Tucker, who had been instrumental in the STOP campaign, while white progressive pediatrician John A. Harrel declared for an open seat. WEC leaders were disappointed when Dr. Maurice A. Jackson, one of the COCA founders, entered the race against Harrel. Jackson, however, judged his chances better against an opponent who shared his integrationist views. While WEC leaders hoped to form a biracial coalition to accelerate desegregation, Jackson launched his campaign for a different purpose: "I ran for the school board in order to help solidify the Negro community." COCA also was aware of the all-white membership of the WEC, which only admitted its first black member the following year. Racial identification indeed marked the outcome of the Harrel-Jackson contest; African-American voters pulled the Jackson lever, while Harrel won on the strength of white ballots.

The split of black votes in the Murphy-Tucker race kept the incumbent in office. Although she gained its endorsement, COCA's enthusiasm for Murphy was cooled by the WEC's opposition to Jackson. Her candidacy was also harmed by Tucker's bottomless campaign coffers, which financed the old-time practices of circulating campaign flyers to black church congregations and employing drivers to ferry African-American residents to the polls. While COCA eventually pared the ability of Little Rock white power-brokers to capture black voters, the group was new in 1962 and did not apparently join forces with the NAACP. During the crisis over the desegregation of downtown businesses, COCA, rather than NAACP leaders L. C. Bates and Dr. Jerry Jewell, took the lead in negotiations with white business representatives. Regardless, Bates's influence at the state level was enhanced with the passage of national civil rights measures that authorized the withdrawal of funds from states that continued discriminatory practices. In 1964 Bates reminded Faubus that the paltry number of black state employees endangered Arkansas's share of federal revenue. Acknowledging the point, the governor generally approved applicants forwarded by Bates even as the civil rights leader never stinted in his public criticism of Faubus.

Harrel's presence did not alter the Little Rock School Board's deliberate circumvention of desegregation rulings. By the mid-1960s the district pioneered the "freedom of choice" plan, which served as a prototype for those adopted by most schools districts throughout the state. While students had the right to attend a school of their choice, inexorable and well-designed residential segregation in Little Rock rendered it an empty option. By 1966 only 16.7 percent of black students sat in integrated classrooms while seven schools retained an all-white student body and twelve remained completely African American. In 1970 a federal district court applied recent Supreme Court rulings and ordered the district to develop a full-fledged student assignment plan. The busing of students throughout the district demolished the post-*Brown* tactics of relying on racial housing patterns to minimize integration. Throughout the 1970s white suburbanization infiltrated out-of-district communities perched on the rim of the metropolitan area. By 1976 black students comprised the majority in Little Rock schools, and in 1982 the proportion had grown to 70 percent. The district filed suit in federal court during 1982 based on the argument that it had suffered from segregationist state policies and real estate practices. The board requested the court provide relief by ordering the consolidation of the Little Rock, North Little Rock, and Pulaski County School Districts. Henry Woods, appointed a federal district judge in 1979, ruled in favor of the plaintiffs, but the reversal of his decision by the appeals court removed consolidation as a method of desegregation.

Their differences during the 1962 Little Rock school-board election did not create a permanent rupture between the white liberals of the WEC and the black leadership of COCA. After the WEC disbanded in 1963, a number of its members committed fully to interracialism with the formation of the Panel of American Women. Modeled after a Kansas City experiment, the panel formed discussion groups of Catholic, Jewish, white Protestant, and African-American women to relate their distinct experiences before community organizations throughout the state. The panels elicited audience comments to confront directly the assumptions underlying bigotry. During one session in Bryant a man asked the Jewish panelist if "Jews still practiced blood sacrifices." With the women's movement still in the future, the seminars examined discrimination exclusively in terms of race and religion and did not explore gender assumptions.

During the 1970s the panel began to develop human relations curriculum workshops for teachers in the Little Rock public schools, but eventually the group evolved into the activist Arkansas Public Policy Panel, which forged a network encompassing the state's environmental, civil rights, and workers' rights organizations. The transition had begun during the mid-1960s when Brownie Ledbetter and other white liberal women participated in COCA's organization of black Little Rock voters. In 1998 the panel, representing fifty grass-roots organizations, organized the Arkansas Citizens First Congress, which outlined a series of legislative goals. Rather than urban issues, the agenda of the congress emphasized environmental rehabilitation and even revived the vintage insurgent issue of saving the small family farm.

The Arkansas Community Organizations for Reform Now (ACORN) was another interracial umbrella group formed in 1970 by organizers from the Boston-based National Welfare Rights Organization. Although ACORN instituted direct antipoverty campaigns such as furniture collection for welfare families and expansion of school lunch services, its leaders believed that the combination of an impoverished majority and a weak political establishment made Arkansas fertile territory for citizen activism. The group's early political efforts revolved around the establishment of minimum utility rates for poor families and property-tax reform. As ACORN expanded into a national organization, its Arkansas operations centered on poorer and older Little Rock neighborhoods. While ACORN's spirited protest rallies garnered significant media coverage, the organization engaged in activist campaigns on several fronts. In 1994 the group gained funds from the federal Department of Housing and Urban Development to set up an ACORN Fair Housing subsidiary, which began filing antidiscrimination suits against real estate agencies and public entities. ACORN's presence aided the establishment of a Little Rock branch of the New Party, a grass-roots electoral organization formed in 1992 in Madison, Wisconsin. By 1999 the Little Rock New Party, which included 5 percent of the group's national membership, held four of the eleven director's seats on Little Rock's governing board.

The other segment of the emerging social justice coalition of white middle-class churchwomen, young volunteer activists, and African-American leaders emerged from the unlikely quarter of organized labor. J. Bill Becker, the president of the state AFL-CIO from 1964 until 1996, aligned the labor federation with a broad civil, political, and economic rights agenda generally ignored by union organizations in other southern states. Becker's convictions discomforted many rank-and-file members in Arkansas. Uncompromisingly tenacious, Becker successfully lobbied the legislature to raise unemployment benefits to among the highest in the nation as a percentage of state income, to strengthen the workers' compensation law, to replace the poll tax with a registration system, and to establish the state's first minimum-wage law.

Labor triumphs during the 1960s reflected the organizational clout of grass-roots organizations that could deliver votes in the twilight of the system of traditional Arkansas bosses. The mid-1970s proved to be the high tide of the state's labor movement, when over 15 percent of the state's workers were organized. By 1998 the proportion of union members had slipped to 6.2 percent, placing Arkansas ninth among thirteen southern states. Not coincidentally, in 1993 Becker failed to halt a business-friendly revision of the workers' compensation system that dramatically reduced the number of successful claims by injured workers.

With the exception of the Fayetteville university community, Arkansas liberalism in the civil rights era and beyond was a Little Rock phenomenon. Contemporary liberals adopted some principles of the earlier good-government reformers, but they advocated redistributionist policies rather than industrial recruitment. As a minority movement, liberalism generally met derision in the legislature. Yet the devotion of progressive adherents to full-time political grunt-work got them through the door of the governor's office and put them in control of the creaky machinery at the Democratic Party's state committee. Activists such as Becker and Ledbetter exercised surprising influence before losing ground during the administration of Gov. Bill Clinton.

In the 1970s, Little Rock urban reformers searched for methods to stall the flight of residents to suburbia. They charged that the structure of city government ensured the dominance of a business oligarchy that sacrificed neighborhood integrity for commercial development. Adopted in 1957, the city-manager system and election of at-large municipal directors had adulterated black and white working-class representation. Before the 1994 overhaul that reintroduced ward positions, about 85 percent of the board directors were male, 82 percent were white, and 68 percent hailed from the affluent Heights or western realms. However, the reformers were no longer confronting a united civic establishment. William Rector's death exposed dissension within elite ranks over the pace of westward expansion and the protection of heavy commercial investment in the downtown sector.

The decline of downtown retail outlets began with the automobile. The location of the only two Arkansas River car bridges in the downtown area created congestion, which only worsened after World War II. Attempts to ease traffic tie-ups with parking meters and one-way streets only inspired shoppers to look westward. The hopscotch of shopping centers during the 1960s and 1970s to the University and Markham axis, and then later along Rodney Parham Road, both preceded and delimited middle-class residential developments. This east-west orientation spurred municipal planners' quest for a crosstown freeway, an obsession thwarted by the inability of the city to fund the route. Although both the state highway department and the federal transportation agency concluded the project's expense outweighed its merit, Wilbur Mills in 1970 browbeat the bureaucrats to insert the expressway into the interstate highway system. Mills assured constituents that the freeway that eventually bore his name would lift downtown from the doldrums. This was an implicit admission that Mills's road would be filled with commuters traveling between their offices and suburban homes. The reconversion of a portion of Main Street into a pedestrian mall after 1970 hastened the departure of center-city anchors such as Blass and Pfeiffer Department Stores and engendered a financial district of towering bank headquarters. The last downtown movie theater gave up the ghost in 1973, and in 1980 the Marion Hotel, no longer a siren to the new political class, was imploded to make way for a convention center.

By the mid-1970s the downtown business interests agitated for tax relief on commercial property and special incentives for central-city development. Wary of this approach, the real estate heirs of the Rector dynasty ridiculed special taxes to burnish downtown. One developer stated flatly, "The future of Little Rock is up and down the freeways." Nevertheless, both business camps supported the marshaling of federal urban renewal funds to sweep aside older, low-income neighborhoods in favor of new retail centers and higher-priced housing. Originating in the Housing Act of 1949, urban renewal was to underwrite the razing of blighted properties and the selling of resulting cleared lots to private investors. Congress also authorized construction of over eight-hundred-thousand public-housing units in the measure, but subsequent appropriations fell well short of the promised numbers. Little Rock was among the first cities in the nation to start up the bulldozers. Before urban renewal's demise in the 1970s, black and interracial communities such as West Rock, located along Cantrell Road below the Heights, and University Park, near the burgeoning shopping malls, were the primary targets for destruction even though not all homes were substandard. At the same time, the Little Rock Housing Authority erected in the eastern section public-housing blocks reserved in practice for black tenants.

According to one estimate, over fifty-five-hundred families were relocated in Little Rock during fifteen years of urban renewal. Poor white and black residents in University Park were succeeded by middle-class African-American families; West Rock vanished into a retail strip; and the century-old black farming community of Longley was obliterated to pave the way for the Little Rock Industrial Park. The planning and construction of the east-west freeway undermined the African-American commercial center along Ninth Street with the same effectiveness of the formal urban renewal projects. The city's purchase of tracts along the proposed route and designation of Ninth Street as a one-way thoroughfare isolated black-owned businesses from African-American neighborhoods.

Across the Arkansas River in North Little Rock, Mayor Casey Laman and the city council provided fodder for critics who likened urban renewal to a scorched earth campaign. In 1960 a city planner announced that a 140-acre tract in the Military Heights section "would be cleared of most of its existing structures." When the city housing authority refused to administer the federal grant program, Mayor Laman secured a tailor-made bill from the state legislature that permitted him to form a separate urban renewal agency. The uprooting of black families led African-American leaders to observe that other areas of North Little Rock suffered from more evident blight than the targeted section, which was also home to nine churches. Opposition culminated in 1961 when thirty African

Americans filed suit in chancery court to prevent the disinterment of over seven hundred graves from the Odd Fellows Cemetery, which had been established in Military Heights in 1891. An unfavorable judicial decision paved the way for the destruction of the cemetery and the building of a hotel. In 1999 Curtis Sykes, a local historian, organized the dedication of a marker at the original burial site. During the event, the city of North Little Rock issued an apology for the condemnation of the cemetery. Continuing his research, Sykes was unable to determine whether the deceased from the Odd Fellows cemetery were actually relocated to a new resting place as promised by developers.

By 1963 North Little Rock identified two other sections as future urban renewal projects. Responding to objections from an African-American minister, the urban renewal director noted that the transplanted families from Military Heights were satisfied with their new residences, nearly all of which were outside the city. Between 1960 and 1970, the North Little Rock black population plummeted by over 25 percent.

Unable to halt Little Rock's elongation along the river, some critics of suburban blight turned to the creation of an alternative model. Throughout America, middle-class activists read Jane Jacobs's *The Death and Life of Great American Cities* (1961) and accepted the premises that preservation of older buildings, encouragement of population density, and allowance of a mix of retail, commercial, and residential uses nurtured a more humane civic environment. Incorporated in 1968, the Quapaw Quarter Association designated a downtown sector of nineteenth-century homes as the "quarter," hoping that middle-class professionals would resettle in the ascribed historic neighborhood. The passion to salvage Victorian bourgeoisie homes contrasted with the oblivion facing black communities.

The most far-reaching enterprise to recreate a past era centered on the old river-landing area. Masterminded by a prominent banker, a 1980 municipal bond issue financed the construction of a seventeen-acre landscaped sward, a convention center, and an adjacent hotel. In the late 1990s business advocates for downtown development sought to fulfill Jane Jacobs's vision by transforming a row of riverfront warehouses into shops, galleries, cafes, and loft apartments. Both neighborhood advocacy groups and civic improvement forces viewed the new River Market district as a gateway to compact walking neighborhoods and a business district built to foster gatherings of people. Jim Lynch, head of the New Party, hoped the new endeavors would redirect investment and jobs to the central core of the capital city, while Jimmy Moses, president of the Moses Nosari Tucker real estate firm, noted the need "to build a grassroots community." Even before the building of the Clinton Presidential Library near the River Market area, local officials boasted that offices and businesses were migrating downtown in anticipation of the boom in visitors.

The consensus on the future of downtown dissolved over whether or not city boundaries should continue to follow westward migration. The erection of new office buildings and national chain stores west of Shackleford Road during the 1990s laid the foundation for a second downtown to serve the burgeoning edge communities. Between 1980 and 1996 older Little Rock neighborhoods lost 21 percent of their residents, while the western enclaves welcomed 67 percent more people. Over the final forty years of the century, the city's population density dropped from forty-five hundred persons per square mile to fifteen hundred. In 1998 the Sierra Club concluded that Little Rock suffered from one of the worst cases of urban sprawl among small cities in the nation. The following year the New Party representatives on the city board opposed annexation of new western tracts without a comprehensive analysis of the cost in providing additional municipal services. The majority of city directors overrode these objections. Real estate developers argued that without continued annexation, Little Rock would be hemmed in by incorporated communities luring away tax-paying residents.

As population, wealth, and power discharged from the countryside following World War II, Arkansas public life revolved around Little Rock to an extent found in few other states. The city was the financial capital as well as the home of government. The only metropolitan hub, it also occupied the geographic center of the state. For decades the exclusive home of Arkansas business professionals, Little Rock by the end of the century trumpeted cultural amenities and a worldly upper class. The greater range of ideological opinion characterizing Little Rock politics stimulated a broader participation in policy debates than was evident in other Arkansas communities. The legacy of the Women's Emergency

Committee and the Council of Community Affairs continued through the leadership by women and African Americans of successor advocacy groups. The westward expansion, a manifestation of the civic elite's response to integration, generated new conflicts and political alignments. By 1999 Arkansas's one big town had become a completely American city.

Politics after Segregation

During his long tenure, Orval Faubus expanded educational, public welfare, and economic development services to raise the state's competitive standing in the race for industrial recruitment. These goals hastened the consolidation of political authority, which undermined the rural powerbrokers who had nourished Faubus's career. The governor's rote denouncements of civil rights may have outflanked radical segregationists, but it also demoralized moderates. At the end, the very public scandals during the last Faubus term prepared the way for reform governors who shifted public attention to the perils of corruption.

Federal action prompted cleaner Arkansas elections. In 1964 the nation ratified the anti–poll tax amendment to the United States Constitution, and the Supreme Court issued its "one man, one vote" decisions leading to reapportionment favoring urban centers. Unlike in other southern states, however, the official antagonism to outside intervention in Arkansas was half-hearted. Racial exclusion was not firmly imbedded in the electoral system, which was shaped more thoroughly by manipulation of ballot results. Faubus, himself, cultivated black votes through the tried-and-true techniques of retail electioneering and patronage.

Local caudillos in black majority counties, however, understood the threat from William Hansen's 1963 SNCC voter registration project in Pine Bluff, which was funded by the southern Voter Education Project, directed by Wiley Branton. The drives helped boost African-American registration from 34 to 49.3 percent between 1962 and 1964. The passage of the landmark Voting Rights Act of 1965 did not bring federal monitors to Arkansas because the state met the basic requirements through the registration of over half its adult voters and the lack of a literacy requirement. Still, significant barriers remained. A 1966 report by the state advisory committee to the U.S. Commission on Civil Rights concluded that voting irregularities in four east Arkansas counties arose from both intentional fraud and ignorance about new procedures. The committee noted reports that in one county African-American voters lined up at separate ballot boxes, clearly compromising secrecy and ballot integrity.

In November 1964, 56 percent of those voting approved a new voter registration amendment to replace the poll-tax system in state elections. Reform groups, newspaper editors, and party leaders—as well as both Faubus and his Republican opponent, Winthrop Rockefeller—backed the amendment. Opposition by the Farm Bureau and a number of county judges defeated the measure in the Delta counties, but the rural tally was no longer comparable to urban ballot numbers. The dwindling of rural clout continued the following year as federally mandated reapportionment consolidated depopulated legislative districts throughout the countryside. Although a few perennial solons exited the scene in 1966, a more thorough revamping of the General Assembly followed the 1970 election, which installed eleven new senators and thirty-one freshman representatives. Among the most consequential members of the new class was Nick Wilson of Pocahontas, who deftly accumulated influence and debts while surviving the initial displeasure of senate overlords Knox Nelson and Max Howell. The belief of Howell and Wilson that government should not shirk job creation and social welfare obligations complemented gubernatorial activism. A 1973 restructuring plan reduced the number of legislative committees and for the first time gave them an effective role in shaping laws. On the other hand, the continued allotment of committee assignments and chairmanships by seniority checked the ability of newcomers to reinvigorate the institution.

The debate over reapportionment did provoke the most notorious political oration in the modern era. First elected to the state house of representatives during the 1930s, Paul Van Dalsem of Perry County had distinguished himself for rank self-interest and bullying in a setting where opportunism and intimidation flourished. Van Dalsem's success in killing voting registration reform during the 1963 session exposed him to galling criticism from leaders of the American Association of University Women. In a speech that August to a Little Rock civic club, he assured his audience that when any Perry County woman began "poking around in something she doesn't know anything about . . . we get her pregnant and keep her barefoot." Van Dalsem's remarks sparked a public protest by seventy-five local women at the Perryville courthouse but proved no political danger to him until the redrawing of district lines removed his safe seat.

Van Dalsem's defeat in 1966 was viewed at the time as a triumph for good government rather than as a blow for women's rights. Nevertheless, when redistricting restored a rural bastion to Van Dalsem, he determined that he could best make amends by sponsoring the resolution for the ratification of the Equal Rights Amendment. In the 1973 session he diligently accumulated the votes necessary to gain victory in the house, but then his plan fell victim to the sort of personal, factional politics at which he had excelled for decades. Legislators sympathetic to the ERA but contemptuous of Van Dalsem delayed consideration of the resolution. The postponement enabled ERA opponents to mount phone campaigns and to bus to Little Rock conservative women to argue the amendment was not simply an uncontroversial gesture. The ERA and Van Dalsem's rehabilitation sank together. Although introduced in the next three regular sessions of the General Assembly, the ERA resolution never gained a roll-call vote.

The anchors of rural localism, county judges also forfeited power, although conniving in their own descent. Following the revamping of the election system, influential reformers held that fundamental constitutional restructuring would improve government more effectively than piecemeal initiatives. In May 1969 law professor Robert A. Leflar called to order the one hundred delegates elected to draft a new constitution. The convention expanded individual rights to include access to public documents, strengthened the governor through longer terms, and permitted the legislature to convene annual regular sessions. In November 1970 the voters rejected the proposed document by a 57.5 to 42.5 percent margin. The proposal had loomed as an oversized target for various groups that found specific sections inimical to their interests. Among the most notable of opponents, the county judges had objected to the prospect of more viable quorum courts, the local legislative bodies.

The original constitutional mandate requiring a justice of the peace for every two hundred voters in the county distended the quorum courts into bloated delegations that met annually to ratify without debate the judge's recommended budget. The 467-member Pulaski County Quorum Court was reportedly the largest legislative assembly in modern politics. However, the judges chafed at the five-thousand-dollar constitutional salary limitation. With the acquiescence of the county officials association, the legislature submitted to the voters in 1974 an amendment that stipulated the duties of the judges, invested genuine legislative powers in the quorum courts, and removed the fixed-salary ceiling. The enactment of Amendment 55 did not make the judges irrelevant but encouraged managerial skills foreign to the traditional potentates. Old practices were also discredited during the late 1970s by a four-year FBI probe that produced multiple indictments and convictions of long-time judges. The investigation revealed that kickbacks from vendors as well as the funneling of county-owned materials and labor for personal use were considered the privileges of office. An assistant U.S. attorney observed in 1982 that in the counties subject to the probe, "every transaction was illegal and over long periods of time. This was simply a way of life for these men."

In general, the decline of political localism, the evolution of a more representative legislature, and the unseemly twilight of the Faubus reign marked the most far-reaching reform phase since the Progressive era of the early twentieth century. The Faubus formula of expanding public services while denouncing liberal activism had eased public suspicion of a larger government. State expenditures, which had risen about 60 percent between 1947 and 1955, soared nearly 200 percent during the Faubus years. Although the governor had designated public education as the chief beneficiary of his 1957 tax program, the growth in the school fund slightly trailed the overall budgetary surge. Official petulance toward Washington edicts masked the deepening state reliance on national revenue as expenditures of federal funds bounced from nine million dollars in 1957–58 to forty-six million in 1966–67. If the twelve-year Faubus administration meant that patronage rather than professional expertise dominated the state bureaucracy, broader services and bigger budgets placed Arkansas within the ranks of New South governments. In the ten years following the Faubus era, state spending accelerated even more rapidly, although the public school fund's increase once again did not match the ascent of total expenditures.

His status as an entrenched incumbent did not prevent Faubus in 1964 from launching a class-based populist campaign against Republican challenger Winthrop Rockefeller. Recalling his tenure as first chairman of the Arkansas Industrial Development Commission, Rockefeller emphasized government's contribution to economic growth and did not crusade for lower taxes and diminished services. In contrast to the Democratic good-government advocates, the New York expatriate declared that only a viable two-party competition could permanently end cronyism and graft. However, civil rights remained the sole defining ideological issue for white candidates, and the 1964 campaign demonstrated its potential to outweigh party loyalty. Although Rockefeller publicly objected to the 1964 Civil Rights Act, Faubus played up his opponent's liberal reputation with the same relish that he pronounced him a playboy interloper. In the short term, Rockefeller's racial moderation brought him few African-American votes while alienating the state Republican leadership, who embraced the new conservatism of national standard-bearer Barry Goldwater. Goldwater had vanquished Rockefeller's brother Nelson for the Republican nomination, and the party platform bristled with anti-statist and cold war rhetoric. At the same time, Faubus was disgruntled by his own party's enlistment in the civil rights crusade, and he belatedly and tepidly endorsed the Lyndon Johnson ticket. In 1964 Johnson and Faubus registered almost identical winning margins in Arkansas.

Rockefeller's strategy ran against the current of his party's growing appeal to southern white voters. As Rockefeller harvested votes from urban centers and traditionally Republican northwest Arkansas, Goldwater attained majorities in Democratic south Arkansas. The urban-rural split also characterized black balloting in the gubernatorial contest. Rockefeller accumulated strong majorities in east Little Rock precincts while losing badly in black majority Delta districts. Two years later, with Faubus on the sidelines, the great majority of the state's African-American voters joined the Rockefeller coalition to repulse Jim Johnson's bid to ride rural white resentment into the governor's mansion.

As the first Democrat to lose a gubernatorial contest to a Republican since Reconstruction, Johnson compounded his political irrelevancy in 1968 when his challenge to Sen. J. William Fulbright fell short. The downfall of the state's leading segregationist and the moderation of the Rockefeller administration resurrected progressive candidates who had been unwilling to make the Faubusian bargain with racist sentiment. At the same time, Rockefeller's effort to base a black-white GOP alliance on the middle-of-the-road issues of jobs, schools, and fairer taxes limited his party's appeal to conservative white Democrats. Arkansas was the last of the Old Confederacy to abandon the Old Democracy.

The first Rockefeller term was buoyed by the revenue windfall derived from the beginning of income tax withholding and the public demands to rectify the scandals of the final Faubus years. Newly appointed directors of the insurance department and securities commission halted the chartering of transient companies that sold worthless policies or trafficked in fraudulent securities. In both the 1964 and 1966 campaigns, Rockefeller upbraided Faubus for abetting the survival of Hot Springs gambling. In 1967 the state police descended upon the casinos and delivered the confiscated slot machines to the local police. When the gambling devices reappeared in the clubs, the state troopers returned and burned the machines; Hot Springs gaming never recovered. A museum of celebrity wax figures eventually occupied the old Southern Club site.

Publication of shocking practices in Arkansas prisons forced the legislature in a 1968 special session to approve most of Rockefeller's penal-reform package. Since the abolition of the convict lease system in 1913, convicts worked the fields at the Tucker and Cummins prison farms to produce their own food and to return a profit for the state through the sale of the surplus. The system's self-sufficiency was abetted by the use of armed prisoners rather than employed guards to stand watch over inmates. Officials kept order through prolonged whippings and dialing the "Tucker telephone," a battery-powered device that sent an electrical current through wires attached to an inmate's genitals and toes. A 1966 state police investigation revealed odious housing conditions at the Tucker unit: "The mattresses were filthy and rotten and appeared to be badly discolored. . . . The commodes were stopped up or would not flush. The showers were pouring water from the leaks. . . . The entire barracks area smelled from filth." Meat was served only once a month, and eggs were a Christmas morning treat. Faubus had ordered the investigation of the prisons system, but the twilight of his administration had postponed meaningful changes until the arrival of the new governor.

The Rockefeller reforms established the Department of Corrections as well as an independent parole board to halt the rampant bribery accompanying the early release of prisoners. Even before the legislature acted on the administration proposals, Rockefeller in 1967 appointed Thomas Murton, an academic penologist from Illinois, first as superintendent of Tucker and then as overall director of prisons. Murton's knowledge and zeal seemed to fit him for the task, but his disdain for policy procedures and bent for dramatic public accusations tried the governor's patience. Rockefeller fired the mercurial Murton after the prison head insisted before television cameras that he had discovered the bodies of murdered prisoners in a forgotten graveyard near Tucker. A subsequent analysis of the corpses disproved Murton's assertions, but he repeated his charges during a U.S. Senate hearing and in a 1970 book. Improvements in treatment and facilities continued following Murton's departure. However, Rockefeller could not land a significant appropriation for the corrections department until a federal district judge in February 1970 declared the state's prison system unconstitutional. Describing Arkansas prisons as a "dark and evil world," Judge J. Smith Henley ordered that the prisoner trustees be disarmed.

Rockefeller's willingness to carry out authentic penal reform was both morally courageous and politically responsible. He was also ushering Arkansas into a post-segregation phase of politics. Political scientist and legislator Cal Ledbetter has argued that "probably his greatest accomplishment was to make racial toleration acceptable and respectable in Arkansas." Alone among southern governors, Rockefeller paid homage to Martin Luther King Jr. when he sang "We Shall Overcome" hand-in-hand with African-American leaders on the capitol steps three days after the assassination of the civil rights leader. Rockefeller appointed the first black members to selective service boards, named COCA leader Ozell Sutton to the newly formed human resources council, and made William "Sonny" Walker the only African-American state director in the South of a federal Office of Economic Opportunity.

Overall, Rockefeller displayed the mixture of forthrightness and hesitation to be expected from a leader attempting to mollify both black and white voters. He preferred noncompulsory eradication of barriers rather than aggressive civil rights enforcement. He was reluctant to prod state department heads to recruit black employees or develop procedures to ensure equal services. In 1969 his restrained response to unrest in Forrest City earned him criticism across the political spectrum. After the all-white school board fired a teacher active in civil rights efforts, Forrest City black leaders organized a store boycott and formed the Committee for Peaceful Coexistence. Angering white conservatives throughout the state, Rockefeller visited Forrest City, where he openly acknowledged the African-American group's grievances. At the same time, the governor also wished to persuade committee leaders to call off a planned march from Forrest City to Little Rock. In the end, a small group of protesters led by Lance Watson of the Invaders, a Memphis group whose militancy had soured Martin Luther King's 1968 operation on behalf of sanitation workers, trekked to the capital. Ignoring those within his party who demanded that he stop the protest, Rockefeller assigned a state police contingent to protect the marchers. Within a week, a large crowd of whites attacked seven blacks near the city hall in Forrest City, and Rockefeller sent fifty National Guard troops to pacify the divided town. This crisis festered as African-American leaders became increasingly troubled by Rockefeller's school integration stance, which veered from compliance to tacit support for the "freedom of choice" evasion. The governor's ambivalence weakened his biracial coalition and offered an opportunity for a moderate Democrat to recover black support.

Rockefeller's coalition held firm during his 1968 re-election bid, aided by the customary granting of a second gubernatorial term. In that year a majority of Arkansans at the polls also supported George Wallace's independent bid for president and Vietnam War–critic Fulbright's return to the U.S. Senate. Pundits at the time facilely linked the three races as proof of the engrained independence of the Arkansas voter. The results actually suggested that the politics of personalism and weak party organizations survived even as the state began to conform to broader regional trends. The Wallace plurality, Fulbright's defeat of Jim Johnson in the party primary, and Rockefeller's victory over Faubusite Marion Crank in November clarified a white preference for racial peace and expanded government services. At the same time, these voters continued to distrust national civil rights initiatives. As elsewhere, Arkansas was receptive to racial politics cloaked in the rhetoric of populist grievance against an elitist establishment. Rather than an aberration, Democratic presidential nominee Hubert Humphrey's 30.4 percent of the Arkansas vote was barely exceeded four years later by that of George McGovern, who finished far behind Richard Nixon. The GOP's successful co-option of the Wallace constituency transformed white Arkansas Democrats into presidential Republicans. At the state level, a revived Democratic Party, unburdened from segregation, emerged from the ashes of Rockefeller's second term. The legislature's repudiation in 1969 and 1970 of the governor's ambitious proposals to increase sales and income taxes owed as much to his political and managerial ineptness as to partisan rancor. Rockefeller's ineffectuality cost him progressive support even as he prepared for a third-term campaign.

Rockefeller launched his long-shot bid in 1970 partly in reaction to the entrance of Orval Faubus into the Democratic primary. While Rockefeller believed that Republican viability required him to hold onto the office, he was particularly galled by the prospect that his program would be discarded if the Old Guard returned to power. In the August balloting, Faubus led the eight-man primary field but was forced into a runoff with the dark-horse runner-up, Dale Bumpers. The Charleston attorney had considered running for governor in 1968 but feared that the Democratic Party was not yet prepared to nominate a racial moderate. In 1970 Bumpers effectively expanded the politics of personality to a new medium with a series of television spots that featured the candidate seated on a stool talking directly to the audience. Faubus's ties to rural conservatives had been frayed by his 1969 decision to jettison his wife of thirty-seven years and marry a thirty-year-old divorced mother of two young children. The former governor's runoff loss sealed the defeat of Rockefeller, who could no longer portray his candidacy as the one shield against resurgent corruption and intolerance.

Bumpers accomplished what his predecessor had been unable to manage: the enactment of the Rockefeller program. Using the previous administration's reorganization proposal as a blueprint, Bumpers collapsed about sixty state agencies into thirteen cabinet departments. Then, in an extraordinary demonstration of political adroitness and gritty work, Bumpers maneuvered through the legislature the first significant tax increases since 1957. Although a boost in the sales tax required only a majority vote, Bumpers opposed its regressive effect. Originally proposing to lift the top income-tax rate to 9 percent from the original 5-percent level set in 1929, he had to accept a 7-percent ceiling as he hammered together the necessary three-fourths majority. With the revision, income tax collections immediately climbed nearly 50 percent and approached the level of total sales-tax revenue. The retention of the twenty-five-thousand-dollar threshold for the top rate effectively permitted future tax revenue to rise along with inflation. While the income of only 4 percent of filers in 1971 was subject to the maximum rate, by the 1990s about two-thirds fell into this bracket. Even with the dilution of progressivity, the wealthiest 2 percent of taxpayers in 1990 accounted for over one-fourth of personal income tax revenues. However, tax increases following the Bumpers's administration targeted consumer sales, and local and state taxes combined continued to claim a greater share of the income of the poorest Arkansans when compared to better-off groups.

The income-tax hike subsidized programs and services for Arkansans that residents in other states had long taken for granted. Bumpers pushed the legislature to adopt most of his educational agenda, including increases in teacher's salaries and retirement, state support for kindergartens, and free textbooks for high school students. While impressive, the boost in public school appropriations did not match the accelerated funding for higher education, corrections, and social welfare. The state assumed the operational funding for community colleges, launched a major construction program on college campuses, replaced the unconstitutional prison facilities, expanded services for the physically and developmentally disabled, and promoted childhood immunization and rural health care. Bumpers had been the first candidate for statewide office to incorporate newly awakened environmental concerns into his campaign. In 1971 he declared the twenty-seven state parks an "embarrassment," and the General Assembly, with little dissent, awarded the parks system an unprecedented $22.5 million for capital refurbishment and expansion.

Bumpers continued Rockefeller's policy of expanding African-American appointments to state commissions and agencies. And as had

Rockefeller during the Forrest City confrontation, Bumpers was forced to intervene in another east Arkansas community convulsed by post-segregation issues of power and opportunity. In late 1971 the Farm Bureau and county judges' association demanded that Bumpers withdraw state approval of a federal antipoverty health center in Lee County. The plagues of poverty—gum disease, anemia, skin infection, arrested physical development, intestinal parasites—were epidemic in the county. As throughout the Delta, the plight of low-income sharecroppers had been supplanted by the misery of unemployment. Nearly three-quarters of population of Lee County fell below the poverty line, but only 15 percent of its residents received federal welfare payments. The school lunch program for children broke the monotony of daily meals of beans, bread, and potatoes, a common diet for those relying almost exclusively on food stamps.

The Lee County establishment believed federal moneys were bankrolling social revolution. Neighborhood councils selected low-income representatives to serve as directors of the Marianna Medical Center, where two Volunteers in Service to America (VISTA) physicians saw about fifty patients a day. In contrast to Delta attitudes, VISTA projects among the white poor in Arkansas mountain counties had not aroused local government hostility. After placating state rural interests with a study of the Lee County VISTA operations, Bumpers announced in April 1972 the authorization of a $1.2 million federal grant to construct a permanent clinic building. Federally funded health care began to correct the imbalance in who lived and died in the county. Between 1970 and 1975 the death rate among black infants dropped 50 percent. Nevertheless, the governor's decision flared into an issue during the May 1972 primary as his opponents rehashed accounts of the year of racial turmoil that had splintered Marianna.

Sparked by the arrest of an African-American school employee who refused to accept and pay for a pizza she did not order, the black community in June 1971 began a year-long boycott of Marianna's white-owned businesses. This community action was broadened in January after high school students staged a sit-down strike to protest the calling off of an assembly to honor Martin Luther King. Class officer Rodney Slater recalled attending a meeting in the principal's office to mediate the dispute when he saw fire hoses directed at students already braving near-freezing temperatures. "All of a sudden we see kids running by the window with this blast of water, in some instances, knocking kids over, picking them up off the ground. It was just bad." The arrest of two hundred students led Slater and fellow black students to stay out of school for the remainder of the year.

Although the VISTA volunteers were ostensibly neutral, clinic director Olly Neal covertly rallied local residents to stand fast with the business boycott. Neal symbolized a new African-American leadership in his evolution from nonviolent civil disobedience to a willingness to counter white terrorists on their own terms. He later explained that the bomb threats against the clinic never materialized because of his frequent public declarations as to the certain fate of the bombers. "I promised that if someone messed around—and was slow about it—I would get him with my shotgun. If he was fast, I would tear him up with the 30-06." Neal later completed law school, challenged the Lee County Democratic establishment through Republican Party activism, and became prosecuting attorney for the district. The business boycott ended in July 1972 when demands for increased private and public employment of African Americans were largely met. Yet job opportunities dried up with the closing of most of Marianna's stores. The boycott had accelerated the transition to the commonplace Delta scene of a town square embroidered with empty storefronts.

In 1974 Bumpers was nearing the end of his second term with solid popular support and a list of accomplishments that persuaded future scholars to judge him the state's finest twentieth-century governor. Bumpers also knew voters were by habit unkind to those scrambling for third terms, and he had never shaken his long-held Washington ambitions. When in March he announced his candidacy for the U.S. Senate, he acknowledged that his views largely mirrored those of the incumbent, J. William Fulbright. Rather than the sterile persistence of issueless politics, this unanimity spoke to the new moderate consensus on race and the federal government's role in moving Arkansas up the economic ladder.

While Fulbright had moved to win the allegiance of labor and African Americans with support for a minimum-wage boost and sponsorship of a jobs program, Bumpers's progressive reputation appealed to voters loath to overlook the senator's anti–civil rights record. Bumpers's early polls indicated that he enjoyed a nearly 20 percent advantage. Fulbright fell back on time-honored methods by enlisting the aid of Witt Stephens and William E. Darby, the kingmakers who had pressured state oligarchs two years earlier to salvage John McClellan's floundering race against David Pryor. Both Bumpers and Fulbright in past campaigns had depended on the urban middle class, and it was this group of voters who agonized over the choice between the urbane and eloquent candidates. "It is a contest that has divided families, marriages, business partners, and old friends," noted one newspaper columnist. Bumpers's 65 to 35 percent margin in the May primary not only indicated his capture of Fulbright's constituency but also suggested a promising future for centrist Democrats whose reform programs centered upon education and job creation.

After 1980 the most potent challenge to Democratic preeminence in Arkansas and elsewhere emerged from the Right rather than from impatient liberals. The New Right's suspicion of elites and elevation of moral credos over business efficiency distinguished the movement from the traditional conservatism once associated with southern Democrats. Flourishing in a southern and western tier of states that became known as the Sunbelt, the New Right advance was set in motion by the president of a small sectarian college in Arkansas.

In 1941 a theological dispute within the Churches of Christ threatened the financial health of Harding College in Searcy. Taking a road that would become familiar to Arkansas industrial recruiters, George S. Benson traveled to New York to supplicate corporate heads for contributions to keep his school afloat. In May, Benson's stock with business leaders rose when he advocated the dismantling of New Deal agencies before the House Ways and Means Committee. While a missionary in China during the 1920s, Benson's confrontations with Marxist cadres had merged anticommunism and Christian piety in his mind. On the eve of World War II, laissez-faire capitalism completed his ideological trinity. He institutionalized the funneling of corporate donations to Harding and the promulgation of his views with the founding of the National Education Program (NEP).

Benson throughout the 1940s delivered about two hundred speeches annually, an exhausting schedule made possible by Beech Aircraft's donation of an airplane. In 1949 the NEP used the backing of the Advertising

Council, a coalition of marketing firms, to organize the Freedom Forums. Benson intended these workshops on the Harding campus to give the participants the tools to become instructors in Americanism. During the next fifteen years, over thirty-six hundred corporate executives attended the forums and subsequently circulated among their employees literature intended to convey "the facts about our economic system, our constitutional government, and our spiritual heritage." By one estimate, the forum's instructional materials reached about nine million people. Among the most steadfast of corporate supporters were Boeing and General Electric, which depended heavily upon cold war–era defense contracts.

The success of the conferences bankrolled the NEP's media program, which was in full swing throughout the 1950s and early 1960s. Among the over fifty films the organization distributed to television stations, *Communism on the Map* excited the profoundest outrage with its assertion that Western European socialist democracies were essentially communist states. Benson had not significantly intervened in Arkansas political wars as he forged a national conservative network. Yet, the use of NEP materials by U.S. military commanders to indoctrinate troops and to warn citizens in base communities of communist subversion brought the crusade to the state. In 1961 a Harding vice-president shocked the audience at an army citizens' education conference in Fort Smith when he declared that the U.S. Rep. James W. Trimble had "voted eighty-nine percent of the time to aid and abet the Communist party." Following the conference, a local bank became the headquarters of a group that suggested that "twenty card-carrying communists" lurked within the city. Sen. J. William Fulbright complained to the U.S. defense secretary that military officers were igniting a new McCarthyism, and a subsequent congressional investigation revealed the NEP seminars had aided military intrusion into civilian politics.

Barry Goldwater's capture of the 1964 Republican presidential nomination prompted national journalists to search out the building blocks of the movement that had nurtured the conservative Arizona senator. In the columns of *The New York Times, Newsweek,* and *Time,* Harding was identified as the "academic capital of ultra-conservatism." Benson protested that the NEP was nonpartisan and not affiliated with extremist groups such as the John Birch Society. Certainly, Benson had not advocated a draconian razing of government, nor had the NEP echoed the racism of the citizens councils. On the other hand, notable radical-right orators such as Billy Ray Hargis addressed NEP forums. Wherever one draws the line between moderate and ultraconservatives, Benson molded the coalition and refined the issues that first undergirded Goldwater's nomination and then the 1980s New Right ascendancy. In 1978 Ronald Reagan phoned Benson on his eightieth birthday to acknowledge the debt that he and other conservative activists owed the Harding leader. Anticipating a presidential run, Reagan recalled his own long years on the speaker's circuit, carrying forth Benson's mission of "talking about the evils of big government, the conspiracy against this freedom of ours, both from without and from within."

Many Rivers to Cross: The New Environmentalism

The shift from rank exploitation to the managed development of natural resources left its mark on the face of twentieth-century Arkansas. The Theodore Roosevelt administration created the Ouachita and Ozark National Forests, the largest federal landholdings in the state, to ensure a perpetual source of timber for harvest. In contrast to the attitudes toward the far west, aesthetics and wilderness preservation did not figure into the plans of early government conservationists for Arkansas. Hot Springs stood as the state's only national park. Only with the 1930s expansion of state parks through the Civilian Conservation Corps program were natural environments showcased as tourist destinations. As Arkansas Power & Light's objections to federal dam construction faded, elected officials scrambled to welcome U.S. Army Corps of Engineers' flood control, irrigation, and navigation projects. If the Arkansas congressional delegation regarded warily those federal officials charged with enforcing labor and civil rights regulations, they cultivated those who could straighten rivers and manufacture lakes. The first stirrings of resistance within the state to the Corps of Engineers' endeavors predated the late 1960s national environmental movement and revolved around individual crusaders. Early on, Arkansas preservationists aspired to identify a natural legacy for the state that would counter the popular appeal of the economic development model.

The 1927 flood had awakened the Corps to the necessity and opportunities of flood control projects throughout the Lower Mississippi River Valley. In 1941 Sen. Hattie Caraway and Rep. Clyde T. Ellis, the champion of the electrical cooperatives, cosponsored a bill to establish an Arkansas River Valley Authority. The proposed authority would have overseen an area seven times larger than that administered by the Tennessee Valley Authority. The bill was eventually supplanted by a narrower measure authored by AP&L-ally John L. McClellan. The McClellan plan authorized the Corps to offer hydroelectric power generated from dams on the Arkansas to the wholesale market. Congress included the project in the 1946 Rivers and Harbors Act, but significant appropriations were delayed for a decade. In 1956 Senate public works chairman Robert S. Kerr of Oklahoma leveraged Dwight Eisenhower's ambition for an interstate highway system to secure the Arkansas River project.

The problems that dogged this largest Corps civil project to date required the constant attention of the state's congressional dynasty. In 1963 *Life* magazine published a blistering critique in which an anonymous Corps engineer exclaimed that "the Arkansas is the most godawful, cantankerous river in the county." Governor Faubus retorted that the magazine targeted Arkansas because its citizens were "too decent, honest, God-fearing and patriotic." When the Corps determined that several railroad and automobile bridges across the river would need to be modified to accommodate new barge traffic, McClellan compelled the federal government to absorb nearly all of the thirty-six million dollars required to replace or alter the bridges serving cars.

On 5 June 1971 Pres. Richard M. Nixon, in a ceremony at the Catoosa port in Oklahoma, dedicated the McClellan-Kerr Arkansas River Navigation System. Nixon echoed John F. Kennedy's Greers Ferry observations eight years earlier by proclaiming that the project would boost agriculture and stem rural migration through regional industrialization. Throughout its first two decades of operation, the waterway was a transportation alternative for farm products and raw resources but not a conduit for industrial jobs. The most common freight was sand and gravel used in the maintenance of the waterway itself, although the proportion of steel, scrap metal, coal, and wood-product shipments rose. The McClellan-Kerr was the most spectacular of the navigation projects that altered the course of rivers throughout the state. In the mid-1990s Arkansas ranked sixth among states with miles of navigable rivers. However, the charges of critics that such projects reflected congressional clout rather than real economic development were bolstered by Arkansas's thirty-sixth ranking among the states in waterborne tonnage.

In stabilizing the banks and current flow, the Corps gladdened sport fishermen by producing a cleaner river. Regular channel dredging revived bird populations inhabiting the newly created sandbars. Unfortunately, the loss of wetlands along the river eradicated plant species, and new reservoirs covered several archeological sites. The absence of environmental controversy reflected the Arkansas River's historic status as a transportation artery. In contrast, the green and leafy Ozarks were seen as a last bastion of authentic Arkansas landscape.

By the mid-1950s the Corps of Engineers' White River Basin project had underwritten north Arkansas tourism through the creation of Norfork and Bull Shoals Lakes. Local boosters also expected the planned Beaver Dam reservoir to be a magnet for visitors. The first public alert that dam building threatened the integrity of the Ozark landscape was issued by state game and fish commission biologist Harold Alexander in a series of 1956 *Arkansas Gazette* articles. Alexander's essays troubled Bentonville physician Neil Compton, who was drawn home after World War II by memories of the region's unspoiled beauty. Compton's apprehensions were deepened by the Corps' intention to dam sections of the Buffalo River and flood the picturesque Lost Valley in Newton County. In 1961 Compton founded the Ozark Society, although he often grew impatient with the fractious group's inability to settle upon a common strategy.

Compton's solid Republican and civic leadership credentials gave his crusade a mainstream cast, but his sharp instinct for publicity opportunities proved even more decisive. In 1962 the antidam movement achieved a public relations coup when Supreme Court Justice William O. Douglas made a canoe trip down the Buffalo River under the watchful eyes of national reporters. The environmental case was continually aired thanks to sympathetic articles by journalists writing for the *Arkansas Democrat* and the *Pine Bluff Commercial.* The Ozark Society was complemented by established organizations such as the Audubon Society, the League of Women Voters, and the Arkansas Wildlife Federation. An unlikely ally of the preservationists, the Ozarks Playground Association feared Buffalo River dams would divert the tourists already flocking to Corps lakes along the White River. The river supporters kept their distance from the national Sierra Club, which they saw as more oriented toward western issues.

The Corps refused to strike its colors when faced with citizen mobilization. Eager for federal largesse, U.S. Rep. James W. Trimble continually steadied the agency's resolve, as did the pro-development Buffalo River Improvement Association (BRIA), led by Marshall newspaper editor John Tudor. BRIA insisted the new dams would ensure affordable electricity for rural customers, a reliable source of drinking water, and welcomed dollars from visitors. In 1965 Orval Faubus decided the issue when he expressed his opposition to damming the Buffalo in a florid letter to the chief of engineers for the Corps: "In so many places, the giant power-driven machines of man are flattening the hedges, fence rows, and nooks, where the song birds nested[,] . . . leveling the forests where once roamed the wild deer; scarring the mountains and pushing down the lofty crags where perched the eagles." The Corps had long followed a policy of never undertaking a project in a state over the objections of a governor. The Republican John Paul Hammerschmidt's victory over Trimble in the 1966 general election marked the final demise of the dam projects and accelerated the movement to designate the Buffalo a national river. This prospect of a national reserve stimulated the imagination of some developers, who broached such schemes as an Ozarkland theme park and the resuscitation of an old zinc mining boomtown into a tourist center. While these speculative ventures came to nothing, the 1972 law that turned the Buffalo River over to the National Park Service (NPS) did refashion the area.

Stretching for 135 miles across three counties, the Buffalo River park's limestone bluffs and clear water lured nearly one million visitors annually by the 1990s. A fraction of those coming to the park floated the river by canoe, while most made their way along the trails or swam off the banks. Unlike advocates for mountain folk culture, Compton had not insisted that wilderness ranges would be cash machines for local economies. And indeed, twenty years after the establishment of the park, the Buffalo River counties were poorer and less populated than those encompassed by the giant White River reservoirs. Over ten times the tourist revenue entered the lake counties as compared to that in the Buffalo localities.

The Buffalo River legislation not only compelled the park service to maintain the river but also to keep fixed in the nineteenth century the community of Boxley, located in the Newton County section of the park. Town residents thereafter had to gain authorization from the NPS to make property improvements. Long-time Boxley dwellers were divided over the restrictions, and newcomers committed to the preservationist movement began to occupy the old homesites. One refugee from the outside world who settled in the village observed in 1998: "Boxley is actually an experiment. It's a social experiment as well as a cultural and environmental experiment, and it will take a generation or two to see how things turn out."

Outside the northern uplands, questions of natural aesthetics and cultural authenticity figured less in the arguments of Corps of Engineers opponents than concern over degradation of hunting, fishing, and recreational boating opportunities. Like the Arkansas River, the Ouachita River was among the earliest of the Corps' projects in the Lower Mississippi River Valley. Importuned by the local Ouachita River Valley Association (ORVA) and persistent congressmen, the Corps by 1925 gouged a shallow navigation channel north from the river's mouth in Louisiana to Camden. During World War II, channel maintenance and river traffic dwindled and the Corps moved to abandon the Ouachita. The intercession of U.S. Rep. Oren Harris and Senator McClellan, the titan of river development, forced a timely bureaucratic reconsideration. A 1949 *Harpers* essay identified a formidable "Rivers and Harbors Bloc" in the U.S. Congress linked to the National Rivers and Harbors Congress, "an organization dedicated to the principle that no stream is too small for a federal handout, no levee tall enough, no channel deep enough." McClellan was the president of the organization.

By 1950 Harris secured authorization for dredging a nine-foot channel to permit increased barge traffic up to the Camden port. Conflicts between the ORVA and wildlife advocates over land acquisition bottled up the project until McClellan broke the impasse in 1970 with legislation that included funding for a wildlife refuge to accompany the construction of two dams.

The uneasy alliance between the two interests ruptured in 1981 when local conservationists summoned the Arkansas Wildlife Federation, Audubon Society, and Ozark Society to protest Corps plans to redirect the river course through twenty-five bend cuts. The Corps accepted eight cuts as a necessary compromise, and the ORVA's old dream of the Ouachita as a busy thoroughfare seemed assured with the 1985 completion of the dams. In truth, the project drew south Arkansas hunters, fishermen, and ski-boaters but few commercial shippers.

By 1988 environmentalists and outdoors enthusiasts charged that even eight bend cuts endangered the river's recreational attractions. Although a few opponents of the Corps wanted the river returned to its nineteenth-century condition, most river patrons understood the perils of a free-flowing river, which would run dangerously low during the summer and in droughts. The grass-roots preference that the Corps maintain the river primarily to serve recreational interests contributed to the 1992 defeat of incumbent U.S. Rep. Beryl Anthony, a proponent of barge shipping. Its stewardship marked primarily by dredging operations, the Corps ensured that recreational boaters would be free of the inconveniences of a natural river.

While the proliferation of lakes was the most dramatic change in the Arkansas landscape in the second half of the twentieth century, the eradication of the east Arkansas bottomland forests, the fabled Great Swamp, had been the hallmark of the first half. Even after World War II, the toppling of King Cotton in the midst of a skyrocketing soybean market also prodded landowners to petition for expanded flood control initiatives to bring marginal land under production. Senator McClellan's patronage of water projects spanned the spectrum from the mighty Arkansas River to humble Delta drainage improvement districts. In 1970 he and U.S. Rep. Bill Alexander pushed through Congress a measure to channelize the Cache River Basin, which extends from near the Missouri "bootheel" to the Cache's confluence with the White River at Clarendon. The agricultural Delta seemed to be one of the last redoubts against environmental challenges to Corps of Engineers handiwork; then migratory ducks became the unexpected wild card.

Shrinking winter habitats throughout the Mississippi Flyway since

1950 had not been the first threat to the North American duck population. Mallards, in particular, had long alighted along east Arkansas rivers, and since the 1920s they had also flocked to the harvested rice fields and irrigation impoundments surrounding Stuttgart. While the 1930 drought aroused fears that ducks would go the way of the passenger pigeon, the population quickly recovered. By 1947 a St. Louis reporter described a season in which the migrating waterfowl turned the sky dark: "I watched mallards sitting in vast and solid rafts on the Arkansas reservoirs quacking raucously and happily, and at dusk, saw them start for the rice fields. They took off in successive roars like fleets of miniature B-29s."

For a variety of reasons—the emphasis on marksmanship, the necessity for trained dogs, the advantage of securing a leased site—duck hunting held special appeal for wealthy individuals. Organized into shooting clubs or paying duck-camp fees, hunters had generally observed bag limits and restricted the killing of hens prior to the setting of public game regulations. This informal tradition of game management influenced Rex Hancock, a Stuttgart dentist and duck hunter, to form the Citizens Committee to Save the Cache River Basin. As in the unfolding of the Buffalo and Ouachita River battles, well-regarded local figures formed alliances with established environmental organizations, lobbied sympathetic federal agencies, and relied upon friendly media coverage. During the controversy, the *Arkansas Gazette* ran an editorial entitled "The Rape of the Cache," and *Gazette* cartoonist George Fisher fixed the image of Corps bureaucrats as befuddled men in Bermuda shorts and pith helmets sporting badges reading "Keep Busy." The Corps engineers almost lived up to the Fisher parody when they defended the Cache River project in a 1974 environmental impact statement that attacked their critics for having "an exaggerated view of the Cache River basin as a mallard wintering area."

McClellan's death in 1977 and a subsequent government study establishing the importance of Cache River flooding for waterfowl habitat buried full-scale channelization. In 1980 the U.S. Fish and Wildlife Service outlined the boundaries of a national wildlife refuge in the middle section of the basin, but the new administration of Ronald Reagan opposed the necessary appropriations to purchase land. Plummeting agricultural prices by the mid-1980s provided an opening for the Nature Conservancy, an environmental group with unusually deep pockets, to buy up depressed farm acreage. In 1986 the fish and wildlife service began to purchase what the Conservancy held in reserve. Seven years later Senator Bumpers induced Potlatch Corporation to transfer its substantial holdings of Delta wetlands to the fish and wildlife service in exchange for federal forest acreage in Idaho. The land swap expanded both the White River and the Cache River wildlife refuges and gave hope to area naturalists that a substantial remnant of the big woods of east Arkansas would outlast the twentieth century.

If it did not reach the levels of earlier decades, the duck population continued to climb during the 1990s, and the hunting season steadily increased from thirty days in 1990 to sixty by 1997. The revival of a sport popular with the well heeled offered a grand opportunity for mixing business with pleasure. Over forty commercial hunting clubs around Stuttgart alone allowed corporations to entertain out-of-state clients with a good shoot and a fine dinner at a well-appointed lodge. As one club proprietor explained: "It's one of the few hunting sports where you can get a group of people in a blind. They have a captive audience with their customers." As in past decades, important national business leaders thought of Arkansas first as a hunters' paradise.

As the Corps of Engineers in the 1980s began to seek accommodation with its critics, the new federal *bête noire* for Arkansas environmentalists became the U.S. Forest Service. Beginning in 1967, the forest service shifted from single-tree harvesting to even-aged management, or clear-cutting, in the Ouachita Forest; by the mid-1980s all harvested acreage was clear-cut. A coalition of preservationists, hunters, and birders formed the Ouachita Watch League (OWL) to file objections to the agency's long-term management plan, which would expand even-aged cutting practices and favor pine tree growth. Although opponents of the forest service failed to make their case in federal courts, the service in the 1990s sharply reduced the level of clear-cutting, which occurred only on designated research plots.

To the north the Sierra Club and Newton County Wildlife Association in the 1990s resorted to direct confrontation and lawsuits to halt logging in the Buffalo River watershed of the Ozark National Forest.

Rebuffed in federal courts, the environmentalists continued to argue that forest-service plans would endanger aquatic life in the Buffalo National River through erosion and silting. Agency officials insisted that harvesting would restore the less thickly forested landscape of the previous century as well as combat disease. Throughout the decade, environmentalists also worried that the spread of poultry and hog farms would leave Ozark rivers polluted. In 1998 the U.S. Geological Survey released a study that noted that the region's streams contained increased nutrients from animal waste, but these levels were far from toxic, and overall water quality ranked among the best in the nation.

If often fragmented, Arkansas environmental activists skillfully won public approval for those goals that could be linked to popular traditions. In a state still half-covered by forests and largely rural, outdoor pursuits, whether shooting mallards or sighting songbirds, was an unquestioned part of everyday life. While environmentalism, like other reforms, required the growth of an urban professional class, city dwellers did not have to venture far beyond the suburbs to locate rivers and deep woods. The new ecological awareness was also tapped in the state's quest for capital and jobs. In the early 1970s the parks and tourism department contracted with a marketing firm to develop a slogan that could be used for out-of-state advertising campaigns. The phrase "Arkansas is a Natural" caught on, and in 1995 the legislature replaced the "Land of Opportunity" motto with "The Natural State" as the official state nickname. The factory-less green spaces were recognized as a unique resource for an economy built around tourists and retirees. This new industry did not require a skilled work force, disrupt community patterns, or command significant state government outlays. Tourism became the meeting ground between the new environmentalism and New South boosterism.

Chapter Five

An American State

In the spring of 1981, Berton Roueché, a writer for the *New Yorker,* spent nearly a month in Hope gathering material to be included in a book of essays on American small towns. Visiting seven communities, he moved easily in unfamiliar locales, and his sympathetic interest encouraged candor from residents. When the magazine published his profile of Hope, copies quickly disappeared from local news racks, and reprints of the article circulated widely. The enthusiasm seemed warranted by the Edenic introduction: "The sun shone every day of my stay but one, and the nights were mild, and many of them were moonlit, and almost every night I fell asleep to the long, slow, faraway whistle of a freight train."

Sketching the town's origins as a railroad terminus, Roueché noted that all residents calculated a delay or two at a track crossing into their daily schedule. He praised the downtown Crescent Drug as a "beguiling relic of the long-gone days when the corner drugstore was a social center." Yet the comments of townspeople revealed that even in Hope, the old soda fountain was a quaint reminder of an unrecoverable past. Confirming both the importance of broiler production to the local economy and the ebbing of home-cooked meals, one man observed: "We love chicken here in Hope. We've got Colonel Sanders and Chicken Country both." Residents shopped the national grocery chain store, but its selections were tailored to the hometown palate. The butcher explained to the visitor: "We don't carry veal or any kind of lamb. Folks here just won't eat it." Along with mass-interest magazines, the newsstand offered *Gun Times, Gun Journal, Gun World,* and *Guns & Ammo* for the patrons of Hope's three firearms shops.

As throughout the nation, local preferences smoothly blended into a standardized consumer economy without fanfare. Yet, Arkansas had only recently begun to look like the rest of America, and debates over the gains and losses were far from silenced. The owner of a men's clothing store welcomed assimilation into the mainstream: "We're not all barefooted hillbillies settin' on the front porch and spittin' tobacco juice. We're the Sun Belt now. We've got more new people coming into town than you would believe possible." The mayor was more skeptical about the consequences of the economic development campaigns: "There's a trend these days toward thinking what's good for business is good for Arkansas. I don't agree. This is still an unspoiled state, and Hope is an unspoiled town. We have a good industrial base. It's clean and pleasant. It accepts the environment." The most significant remnant of the old society was Hope's status as a "dry" community, or one that prohibited the sale of alcohol. In southwest Arkansas, liquor could be had only in larger, industrial towns such as Texarkana, Camden, and El Dorado or at lightly settled outposts where local-option elections had created bonanzas for package store-owners. Divisions over prohibition followed sectarian lines. The Baptist majority made it unlikely that Hope would ever see a "wet" future.

Roueché had not been in town long before learning he was in "the watermelon capital of the world." Hempstead County's light, sandy soil enticed farmers early in the century to plant fruit as a buffer to the vagaries of the cotton market. In the 1920s a seed salesman began to offer prizes to farmers' producing the largest watermelon. The contest evolved into a festival that coincided with the August harvest. Both the prizes and the festival were intended to boost product marketing rather than improve the fruit; gargantuan watermelons could not be commercially shipped and were not particularly tasty. The watermelon crop survived the 1930 drought but the festival did not. When revived in 1977, the festival's rationale had shifted to the promotion of Hope itself, and its success was measured by the number of visitors.

The Hope event was not an isolated phenomenon. Dozens of communities tapped the tourism market through the organization of festivals. Most of these weekend events self-consciously evoked particular local traditions either through an agricultural commodity (Warren Pink Tomato Festival, Emerson Purple Hull Pea Festival, Atkins Picklefest), an older industry (Malvern Brickfest, Smackover Oil Town Festival, Fordyce on the Cotton Belt), or folk arts and games (Rison Pioneer Craft Festival, Mena Lum and Abner Days, Harrison Bluegrass Festival). A town no longer required a lake or mountain scenery to promote its cultural identity as a product in the growing leisure industry.

In 1999 the watermelon capital was known for other reasons. Native sons were simultaneously governor of Arkansas and president of the United States.

Bill Clinton's climb to the presidency would have been steeper if Arkansas had not achieved political reform, diversified its economy, and evolved into a more equitable society. In a twist upon the old notion that the state was a colonial pawn of northern capitalists, Arkansas entrepreneurs such as Walton, Tyson, and Dillard became familiar names to shoppers throughout the nation. The thriving urban centers on the state's northwest boundary challenged the accustomed preeminence of Little Rock while adapting to the arrival of much-needed Latino workers. As Arkansans came to resemble more closely other Americans, they flocked to centers dedicated to sustaining distinct folk customs. Native writers and artists produced works with a rich blending of tradition and modern awareness that kept them far from the shoals of nostalgia.

Despite its strengthened cultural identity, Arkansas during the Clinton presidency endured condescending treatment in national publications. The popularity of the Republican governor at century's end demonstrated that the state's political system was more fluid than acknowledged in media thumbnail sketches. Government in Arkansas was larger and generally more professional, developments arising from the constant demands by economic development boosters for an educated labor force and reliable services. Summing up Arkansas was not a simple matter.

C. Vann Woodward, in his magisterial histories of the South, located a regional identity in the burdens of poverty, neglect, and loss. Woodward's instruction on understanding the South would have served well journalists visiting his native Arkansas: "the key would seem to lie in the history, the collective experience of the Southern people of all colors."

Uneven Progress

Once in the decade before the Civil War and again in the period before the 1920s agricultural collapse, the state had reached the brink of prosperity before catastrophe descended to destroy the fine hopes. By contrast, the foundation of a modern economy characterized by rising manufacturing and shrinking agricultural sectors was in place by the 1950s and was not wrecked by the 1957 Little Rock Crisis or by the early 1980s recession. After 1970 most Arkansans lived in towns, were wealthier than at any other point in the twentieth century, and were thoroughly American consumers. Business and government leaders had based the great leap forward on industrial recruitment and gloated as manufacturing employment indices rose higher and higher. By the end of the century, however, the state remained fixed at the bottom of the national personal income rankings and in the comparative rates of poverty. The tried-and-true development strategy of touting inexpensive labor costs and low taxes threatened future growth in a global economy that rewarded technologically sophisticated production and services. How to expand public investment in education and infrastructure while retaining low taxes was an old question surviving into the new millennium.

The importance of manufacturing in the Arkansas resurgence contrasted with its diminishing significance after 1970 in the national economy. While manufacturing production increased by nearly 50 percent in the United States between 1967 and 1980, it soared by over 300 percent in Arkansas. At the same time, agriculture continued to exert a considerable influence on the state's well-being. During the same period, cash receipts from farming rose by 350 percent in the state, which outpaced the national advance of less than 250 percent. Escalating crop prices in the inflationary 1970s helped explain why the decade was the state's most prosperous in the twentieth century. Per capita income peaked in 1978 at 78.3 percent of that for the United States generally, having risen from 61.5 percent in 1956. This singular good fortune during the 1970s produced a remarkable demographic result. For the first time since the nineteenth century, more people moved to Arkansas than left.

The surplus of new residents was also a measure of the industrial decline in the Midwestern cities that had commonly offered Arkansans hope for a better life. Misery elsewhere and a booming state economy kept people home. Arkansas's defiance of national economic trends in the 1970s continued during the following decade, to the state's detriment, when it did not join the national recovery from the 1982 recession. Arkansas's twenty-year failure to regain the late 1970s plateau originated in both the persistence of the traditional economy and the weaknesses in the new manufacturing sector.

The displacement of cotton by soybeans and broilers did not cushion Arkansas against volatile agricultural markets. In 1979 the Federal Reserve System embarked upon a tight money policy to combat inflation. Farmers, who had overextended themselves during the agricultural boom, were casualties of that decision. The heat wave and drought that struck Arkansas in 1980 approached the apocalyptic years of 1930 and 1954, fostering losses within the state of about $1 billion and directly causing the deaths of over 130 residents. Not only were the crop fields parched, but also millions of chickens succumbed to the heat. The golden year of 1978, marked by a net income per farm of $29,451, was a bitter memory by 1983, when the average income languished at $5,386. The postwar trend of fewer farms continued after 1970, although the rate varied in conjunction with agricultural income. The precipitous decline in the number of operations during the 1980s was reversed in the next decade as the market value of agricultural products sold increased by about one-third. Overall, between 1954 and 1997, the number of farms shrank from 145,076 to 45,142, while those that remained increased in size from 124 to 318 acres.

The upsurge of bank closures accompanying the agricultural collapse was largely coincidental. The inveterate caution of Arkansas bankers had limited their exposure to shaky farm loans. More so than in nearly every state, Arkansas farmers had been forced to look to the federal Farmers Home Administration, a traditional lender of last resort. Banks regained their equilibrium by mid-decade just as the Sunbelt-wide real estate bust upended Arkansas savings and loan institutions. The Federal Reserve's anti-inflation strategy of boosting interest rates had encouraged savings and loans to offer attractive returns to depositors. Reassured by federal insurance protection against default, Arkansans moved their funds into these financial institutions. Between 1983 and 1986 the number of S&L accounts rose by almost one-third. Soaring land development values seduced S&L executives desperate to make loans that would return a profit on accounts paying rates exceeding 10 percent. When Congress repealed generous federal tax incentives for commercial real estate purchases, speculative frenzy turned to panic. In Arkansas federal regulators closed and assumed the obligations for thrifts ranging from large entities such as FirstSouth in Pine Bluff and Savers in Little Rock to the smaller Madison Guaranty. After 1986 a plunge in the total accounts in savings associations revealed that surviving S&L's were either merging with or reorganizing themselves into banks.

The financial turmoil of the 1980s demonstrated that the contemporary Arkansas economy was influenced by factors extending beyond commodity prices. The nationwide 1990s merger movement expanded the customary out-of-state ownership of Arkansas land and resources into financial markets. No more than three bank mergers were consummated in any one year between 1988 and 1994, but sixteen were completed in 1995 and eleven the following year. In 1994 the three largest banks were metropolitan Arkansas institutions that had already embarked on takeovers of other state banks: Worthen (Little Rock, established in 1877), First Commercial (Little Rock, 1934), and Twin City (North Little Rock, 1904). By 1999, those names no longer graced the front of any building. In 1995 Boatmen's of St. Louis acquired Worthen, and then two years later Boatmen's was absorbed by Nations of Charlotte; also in 1995 Twin City was added to the rapidly growing empire of Mercantile Bancorporation of St. Louis, which in turn fell into the possession of Firstar of Milwaukee; and in 1998 Regions of Birmingham added First Commercial to its holdings. Consolidation cost hundreds of employees their jobs, and the largest state-owned banking companies were headquartered outside of Little Rock, the state's financial hub since the territorial era; El Dorado found itself the new home of the state's largest Arkansas-based bank holding company.

Not only were farms and banks chilled by recession and dislocation, but manufacturing, the engine of the postwar Arkansas economy, stalled as well. The state's manufacturing employment crested in 1979 before entering a slump that kept the factory job numbers from returning to an equivalent level until 1987. Yet evidence abounded that the hard times were a gestation for modernization. State economic leaders confidently pointed to the expansion of plants turning out electric motors, refrigerators, automobile tires, power tools, and fabricated metals. By 1984 employment in the electrical-equipment industry surpassed that in lumber and wood products, the century's perennial top job producer among manufacturers of durable goods. In 1987 an American steel concern and a Japanese steel company built the Nucor-Yamato plant adjacent to cotton fields in Mississippi County, and in 1992 the Nucor firm constructed near the first factory a rolling mill that produced I-beams. More intensively mechanized than the shuttered mills in the Midwest and operating without union contracts, the Delta steel works directly employed about 1,200 workers, who earned incomes several times greater than the state average. The new steel jobs partially offset the demise of an older metal industry. In 1981 Alcoa closed the Saline County bauxite-mining operations it had operated for over a century, and employment at its nearby aluminum plant dropped from 1,800 in the 1970s to 450 by 1999.

Nevertheless, restructuring within the labor-intensive nondurable goods sector represented the most notable manufacturing trend. Always sensitive to price swings and labor costs, apparel and shoe factories in the late 1970s began to relocate to developing nations. Between 1975 and 1984 the number of clothing workers fell by a third; although the job totals stabilized by the end of the decade, they began declining again after 1996. On the other hand, more Arkansans in the 1990s punched the clock at food-processing factories than at lumber mills and electronics plants combined. If the razorback remained a cherished Arkansas icon, chickens were the centerpiece of an economy balanced between agriculture and manufacturing.

During the late 1950s the per-pound price for broiler chickens dropped by around 50 percent. Battered by the free fall, leading firms completed the vertical integration of the poultry industry, linking production, processing, and marketing. Within the state, the University of Arkansas was essentially the research and development arm of the industry and never flagged in pursuit of the better bird. In the 1950s a broiler required fifteen pounds of feed and fifteen weeks to grow to three pounds, but in the 1990s fewer than six weeks and eight pounds of feed were necessary to produce a four-pound chicken. Processors supplied chicks and feed to contract growers, who were responsible for maintaining houses and supplying labor. A unique set of farmers, the growers operated within a quasimarket system. While enjoying the security of a contracted price for the broilers they shipped, growers often went into debt to acquire equipment demanded by the processors and had little control over the numbers and conditions of chicks sent to them. Beginning in the 1960s the processors' insistence that growers expand their flocks forced the construction of three-hundred- to four-hundred-foot-long chicken houses and the installation of automatic feeders. By 1997 over 80 percent of growers sold at least one hundred thousand birds annually, and the average market value of capital investments (land, buildings, and machinery) was about $450,000, a figure over a third higher than the average for state livestock producers.

Dissatisfied northwest Arkansas growers in 1962 formed an association to negotiate uniform contracts with the processors. Major firms such as Tyson and Arkansas Valley Industries preferred to accept the inefficiency of dealing with many individual growers rather than diminish their control over production costs. The organization died in the face of such hostility. Nevertheless, the idea of grower bargaining rights gained force as industry consolidation left farmers without the leverage of negotiating with several companies. One Berryville grower noted, "The rule of thumb for Tyson's around here is, you do it our way or you don't do it at all." In 1991 Frank Conley of Nashville founded the Contract Poultry Growers Association (CPGA), which expanded throughout the decade to include members in about a dozen states. Poultry companies insisted that while numerous growers clamored for the opportunity to sign on with the firms, only a comparatively few enrolled in the association. In 1997 a state legislator and grower noted that conditions had improved since the early days when farmers were "treated like sharecroppers."

In that year the Arkansas chapter of the CPGA drew up a bill to prohibit intimidation, unilateral contract terminations by processors, and the coercion of growers to make capital investments. The organization was unable to secure a sponsor in the General Assembly. Opponents such as the National Broiler Council pointed to a pending congressional measure drafted by the national CPGA and proposed Department of Agriculture (USDA) rules as preferable alternatives to a jumble of state laws. The federal legislation was designed to extend bargaining rights to the growers' associations, while the regulations were to govern growers' compensation as well as the weighing of feed and live birds. In the end, the proposed bill never emerged from an agricultural subcommittee of the House of Representatives, and the USDA in 1999 issued a modest rule requiring the issuance of printed scale tickets to verify accurate weights. In contrast to its oversight of the beef and pork industries, the regulatory agency within the USDA did not have the authority to issue fines against or halt unfair practices by poultry companies.

During the 1997 public comment period on the necessity of regulating the relationship between growers and processors, slightly over half of the 226 letters sent to the USDA from Arkansas opposed any revision. A processing-company president condemned those demanding a new system: "I am quite confident you will be strongly opposed by those very independent, very successful growers that represent over 90% of the individuals in that part of the business. Less than 10% do believe in socialism because they are not interested in competing, performing the work they have agreed to perform, or accepting pay based on what they have earned versus a welfare type handout. . . ." The federal agency received hundreds of form letters from both the poultry firms and the growers association. Still, many letters were drafted personally. A number of growers who favored stronger federal intervention asked not to be identified to avoid retribution: "I will sign my name but would appreciate it if you don't use it. Fear is a terrible thing." Others echoed the plaintive despair of 1930s tenant farmers: "I have never written to anyone like you before. I didn't even know there was anyone who could help us." Each decade fewer growers raised more chickens.

Marketing was the final stage in the integrated poultry economy, and Don Tyson proved to be the industry's most gifted innovator. He understood that his company would continually be at the mercy of volatile commodity price swings as long it sold only whole chickens to grocery wholesalers. In 1966 Tyson Foods began offering frozen Rock Cornish hens as a specialty item at a fixed cost per bird rather than by the pound. Don Tyson pushed his strategy of value-added products even more aggressively when he became company head after his father, John Tyson, died in an auto accident. As married women entered the work force, the array of Tyson's convenience foods occupied larger sections of the grocery display cases: chilled chicken portions, precooked fried chicken, chicken patties, and processed sandwich meat. By 1990 only 20 percent of retail chicken sales were whole birds. With the 1984 acquisition of the firm that had the Kentucky Fried Chicken account, Tyson Foods became the supplier of ready-to-cook products for forty-two of the fifty largest fast-food chains. However, the company's venture into the seafood market during the 1990s proved a failed experiment.

The meat-packing industry in America, beginning with Gustavus Swift in the nineteenth century, had pioneered the techniques of vertical integration. Nevertheless, the beef and pork industry evolved into a virtual oligopoly largely through horizontal integration, or the absorption of competitors by giant companies. In the 1950s a series of magazine articles that warned consumers about diseased chickens instigated consolidation in the poultry industry. Industry trade associations pushed Congress to authorize uniform inspections by the USDA to restore public confidence and to supersede state oversight of plants. After Congress in 1959 approved mandatory inspections, marginal processors that had survived through the forbearance of tolerant local inspectors folded.

The next phase of industry concentration during the 1970s drove out the large national food corporations. Unwilling to cope with boom-and-bust price cycles, Ralston Purina, Swift, and Pillsbury unloaded their poultry divisions, opening new frontiers for the expansionist Tyson Foods. Tyson's acquisitions not only extended its domination of the market but also advanced the development of value-added products and saved the expense of constructing and equipping new processing plants. The 1986 purchase of Lane Poultry, a western Arkansas firm that had earlier acquired Arkansas Valley Industries, vaulted Tyson past Omaha-based ConAgra as the nation's largest poultry-processing firm. The Lane takeover also illustrated the interconnections characterizing the state's business community.

In 1982 cash-strapped Lane maneuvered to fend off a Tyson raid on its operations by taking out a nine-million-dollar bank loan. Tyson then turned to Stephens, Inc., the bond house founded by Witt Stephens and managed by his brother, Jackson. In credit-starved Arkansas the Stephens firm was an oasis, rising to become for a time the largest investment house outside of New York City. It had underwritten the initial corporate stock offerings for such Arkansas entrepreneurs as J. B. Hunt and Sam Walton. Through Stephens, Tyson purchased the Lane bank loan and then pushed its rival into bankruptcy by demanding repayment of the note. However, Tyson did not secure its prize until it bought the holdings of Texas investors who initially acquired Lane under the auspices of the federal bankruptcy court. In 1989 Stephens, Inc., was again the financial advisor for Tyson during the protracted, monumental struggle with ConAgra over the purchase of Holly Farms, the third-ranking poultry firm. The Holly Farms acquisition boosted Tyson's production capacity and aided its penetration of new global markets. Starting in 1989, Tyson began sending chickens raised in the United States to Mexico for processing before selling the meat in Japan.

In August 1997 the USDA issued its largest recall of tainted meat when *E. coli* bacteria was discovered in hamburgers produced at a Nebraska plant owned by Hudson Foods of Rogers. The plant had been a major supplier for Burger King, which terminated its contract with Hudson after the recall. Within a month, founder James T. Hudson dissolved his company by unloading the beef operations and agreeing to sell the poultry holdings to Tyson. The one-billion-dollar deal, brokered by Stephens, set a record for Tyson acquisitions and gave it 27 percent of the domestic market.

In 1969 James Hudson had encouraged J. B. Hunt to purchase several refrigerated trucks to haul frozen chickens for Ralston Purina. Transportation had been a sideline for Hunt's company, which was marketing discarded rice hulls from Stuttgart mills. Revenue from the rice-hull operations helped insulate Hunt's company when deregulation of truck routes set off fierce rate wars. Nevertheless, Hunt understood his company's growth rested with the poultry processors' demands for reliable shipping. He relocated his corporate headquarters from Stuttgart to the northwest Arkansas community of Lowell and in 1983 divested the rice operations. Just as the poultry processors' had launched vertical integration to control costs, Hunt standardized his operations by employing drivers to operate his company fleet vehicles rather than contracting with independent truck owner-operators. By the 1990s the ranking of J. B. Hunt Transport as the nation's top trucking company demonstrated that northwest Arkansas had evolved into a major carrier hub. Six of the one hundred largest trucking companies maintained headquarters in the region, a greater number than found in any other state.

The successful food processors set in motion the concentration of transportation firms in the northwest corner, but the proximity of good quail hunting lured the area's most famous corporate founder. In 1950, after his landlord refused to renew the lease on his successful Newport variety store, Sam Walton opened Walton 5 & 10 on the town square in Bentonville. By 1962 Walton owned sixteen variety stores affiliated with the Ben Franklin chain throughout Arkansas, Kansas, and Missouri. As fierce competition and eroding prices had inspired the innovations of Tyson and Hunt, Walton understood that the old-fashioned five-and-dime outlets were threatened in the 1960s by the onset of full-scale discount merchandisers such as the Texas chain Gibson Products. Arkansas had comparatively few discount operations in July 1962 when Walton welcomed the first customers to his Wal-Mart Discount City in Rogers.

Walton had a single-minded confidence that low retail prices would entice patrons willing to overlook the early Wal-Marts' cheap furnishings and inferior-grade merchandise. Strong profits underwrote regional expansion, but Walton's management by improvisation and refusal to develop a store-placement strategy suggested an uncertain future. In addition, national distributors and large trucking lines were unwilling to extend services to the geographically isolated Wal-Marts. If not a visionary, Walton understood the nuts and bolts of merchandising, and his answer to the distribution bottleneck was the turning point in his company's fortunes. In late 1969 the firm began supplying Wal-Mart stores from its own recently completed sixty-thousand-square-foot distribution center. Located south of Bentonville on 12.5 acres crossed by a railroad spur, the center was also adjacent to the corporate offices. Since the motto "we sell for less" would be an empty boast without strict management of costs, the company in 1971 added a division to construct new stores according to a uniform floor plan. By the mid-1970s the hometown Wal-Mart looked the same everywhere.

Whether measured by the relentless negotiations with vendors or the utilitarian look of the corporate headquarters, the Wal-Mart passion for cost reductions gave it an advantage over larger discount merchants during the inflationary 1970s. Strong economic growth in the region surrounding Bentonville also aided the company. Walton's frugality on occasion threatened his company's preparation for future technological changes. His suspicion of computers as unnecessary overhead was quelled through the perseverance of David Glass, his eventual successor. Varying from its customary practice of building its own outlets, Wal-Mart in 1981 purchased Kuhn's, a rival southern chain. With the additional stores, only Kmart could boast a greater number of outlets than the Arkansas firm. Walton recalled, "I think the Kuhn's deal gave us a new confidence that we could conquer anything." By early 1991 Wal-Mart had surged past both Kmart and Sears to become the nation's largest retailer.

In the beginning Wal-Mart avoided direct competition with the national retailers by confining its store openings to small towns. Walton staked his company's growth on his assumption that shoppers outside urban centers would choose the better bargain over loyalty to the hometown merchant. This strategy accelerated the restructuring of small-town retailing, which originated with the arrival of chain groceries before World War II. Downtown merchants offering items available at a new Wal-Mart on the edge of the community suffered from the chain's loss-leader inducements and volume pricing. On the other hand, restaurants, repair shops, and other service establishments rose and thrived by catering to out-of-town Wal-Mart patrons. However, charges that the company was administering last rites to small-town America resounded in nationally published columns and articles. Criticism echoed in the company's home state as well. In 1993 a Faulkner County chancery court ruled in favor of three local pharmacies that sued on the grounds that Wal-Mart sought to injure competitors by pricing goods below wholesale costs. The Arkansas Supreme Court overturned the ruling two years later, finding that aggressive pricing was not in itself proof of predatory practices.

Walton maintained in his autobiography that from his first five-and-dime in Bentonville to the erection of giant Wal-Mart Supercenters in the heartland, his operations kept small towns viable by offering residents an array of products once found only in metropolitan areas. Yet in each town the Wal-Mart remained a world apart. The standard format and goods offered few concessions to local taste. The single-minded devotion to sales figures during the company's expansionist phase discouraged its store managers from civic involvement or from making significant contributions to local charities. By contrast, Wal-Mart diligently strove to mold its workers into a self-contained community devoted to the well-being of the company. In Arkansas the Wal-Mart employee cheer, often led by Walton on his store visits, vied in volume and ubiquity with the cheer for the university's Razorback teams.

The designation of employees as "associates" would have been merely an artful management technique if the company profit-sharing plan had not reinforced the sense of partnership. By Walton's account, his wife Helen's admonishments about the generous salaries of company officers forced him to take into account those lower on the corporate ladder. He also acknowledged that union attempts to organize stores and the distribution center "helped hurry along our thinking in this direction." The extraordinary rise in Wal-Mart stock during its expansion allowed long-time hourly employees to plan early retirements and dream homes. The company confronted critics of its labor practices with testimonials such as that from Joyce McMurray, who worked at a Springdale store: "I live and breathe Wal-Mart. Sam always gives so much to the associates, I want to give as much as I can in return. . . . This year my profit sharing amounts to $475,000." Walton incessantly denounced unions throughout his life as inimical to the harmony of the Wal-Mart family. At times, appeals to filial loyalty were edged with threats. In 1984 the Teamsters lost an organizing election at the Searcy distribution center after Walton told the employees that he would restrict their participation in profit-sharing if they affiliated with the union. In 1988 Jay Bradford, a Pine Bluff state senator, charged that Wal-Mart's inadequate compensation of part-time workers left them eligible for public assistance, and in effect compelled taxpayers to subsidize the company. The firm countered that such personnel decisions prevailed in the discount industry. Certainly in Arkansas, the company's defenders well outnumbered its detractors.

In a state making the long transition from an agricultural to a diversified economy, entrepreneurs were important players whose stories and achievements personified the changes. Walton was the epitome of businessman as folk hero. His frequent visits to his stores and his casual, unaffected rapport with hourly-workers inspired genuine affection. Everyone in Arkansas knew that the nation's wealthiest man drove a pickup truck around Bentonville. While Walton lived in a spacious home designed by the noted architect E. Fay Jones, his distaste for "a big showy lifestyle" buttressed his company's no-nonsense image. Only after Walton's 1992 death did the new rich of the Wal-Mart corporate family in Bentonville construct grand houses with crown moldings, wine cellars, and chandeliers.

Unlike Walton and Tyson, other notable Arkansas capitalists only made their marks by moving beyond the state's borders. Opening his first store in Nashville, William Dillard in the 1960s anticipated urban resettlement patterns and anchored his upscale department stores in suburban malls. Charles Murphy Jr. completed the transition of his family's south Arkansas oil company into a global enterprise with a reputation for flexible integration of exploration, refining, and marketing of petroleum products. Frank Hickingbotham created the TCBY chain to satisfy the sweet tooth of consumers who exchanged ice cream cones for low-calorie frozen yogurt treats. Charles Morgan Jr. led Acxiom from pioneering the use of direct-mailing lists to compiling a massive information base on the habits and preferences of 195 million Americans. A 1998 *Washington Post* article on the business of "data mining" called attention to the Conway firm: "You've probably never heard of Acxiom. . . . But chances are that Acxiom knows quite a bit about you." The 1990 acquisition of Systematics revealed that Joe Ford had prepared Alltel (formerly Allied Telephone) to take advantage of the subsequent deregulation of the telecommunications industry.

In the 1990s many living in booming section of northwest Arkansas insisted that wealth had not undermined cultural integrity. "This part of Arkansas didn't come out of the Depression until the early 1960s—the chicken pluckers, truckers, and retailers here don't know they're rich," declared one local economic developer. Undeniably, the urban counties along the western border (Benton, Washington, and Sebastian) and rural counties to the east (Carroll and Boone) represented the "Arkansas Miracle" even as they became less representative of the Arkansas economy. Whether during the stagnant 1980s or in the rebounding 1990s, new residents streamed into the northwest locales. Between 1987 and 1997, Benton County, the center of the Wal-Mart empire, led the state's counties with a 43 percent population increase and registered the second highest per capita income.

Northwest Arkansas enjoyed other advantages besides a corps of determined capitalists. The region was unburdened by dependence on a single agricultural commodity, and its low-skilled workers were readily available for the new food plants. The area's proximity to major Midwestern markets and shipping terminals curtailed transportation costs and encouraged the development of trucking as an auxiliary business to the processing of local resources. Private investment was complemented by the infusion of public funds. While federally subsidized drainage districts helped keep the Delta counties agricultural, the ambitious lake projects in north Arkansas underwrote tourism and made the area appealing to retirees wanting both temperate weather and seasonal changes. The projects also averted the water shortages that came to plague other sections of the state. Isolation and deprivation persisted in several Ozark interior counties—Newton, Stone, and Searcy—in part because of a substandard and disjointed road system. Nevertheless, the primary transportation initiatives of the era included knitting together the western centers from Bentonville to Fort Smith through the five-hundred-million-dollar construction of Interstate 540 and the push to integrate U.S. Highway 71 into an international highway between Mexico and Kansas City. The Federal Aviation Administration provided nearly forty million dollars in construction funds and additional grants to complete the Northwest Arkansas Regional Airport. In late 1998, when Pres. Bill Clinton flew into the new airport near Highfill for the dedication ceremonies, he followed the example of his predecessors by lauding another monumental federal project as an economic asset for Arkansas.

The region's inability to keep up with the voracious appetite for entry-level workers was not a typical Arkansas problem. In a biracial state that had few ethnic communities and a chronic surplus of low-skilled laborers, the arrival of Hispanic migrants changed the northwest corner and brought it even closer to the American experience. Between 1990 and 1997, the 127 percent Latino increase in Arkansas was the highest in the nation. About half the immigrants settled in the flush Ozark areas. Most commonly, these workers emigrated first to California and Texas from Mexico and Central America before following relatives who had found work in processing plants hanging live chickens on conveyer-belt shackles or eviscerating the birds. They did not saturate the labor market. The proportion of Hispanic poultry workers in the area rose from 3 percent in 1991 to nearly 22 percent in 1995, while the northwest counties' unemployment rates fell from 4 percent to slightly under 3 percent during the period. The decision to move to Arkansas from other states was often sparked by the ambition to find employment more stable than seasonal harvest stints as well as by a belief that smaller towns were less plagued by crime.

Even though the Census Bureau's 1998 estimate of 49,473 Hispanics represented a substantial undercount, the new Arkansans remained a small portion of the 2.5 million residents of the state. Still, the consolidation of Latinos into certain sections of Arkansas and within identifiable neighborhoods hastened cultural changes. Whether by publishing a Spanish edition of the town newspaper or posting bilingual instructions on an automatic teller machine, businesses began to cater to an expanding consumer market. A distinctive economy emerged within the immigrant communities. While area Wal-Marts expanded their Mexican food sections, Hispanic entrepreneurs opened businesses to provide goods and services less readily available in chain stores and franchise outlets. Small cafes began serving the first authentic Mexican and Central American cuisine tasted in Ozark climes, and Mexican soccer leagues elevated the quality of competition in a sport embraced earlier by middle-class Anglo families. By the late 1990s, central Arkansas increasingly became the most common destination for Hispanics, many of whom found reasonable housing in a working-class section of southwest Little Rock. Reflecting the growing diversity, the neighborhood supermarket began to stock corn husks for tamales, mole sauce, and candles for religious observances, while down the street the Discoteca Mexico rented videos such as "El Padrecito" staring Cantinflas, and the Mercado San Jose supplied imported canned food, inexpensive jewelry, and *pan dulce.* One of the early migrants to Little Rock, Maria Rodriquez, by 1999 was feeling more at home in a changing society: "At first we felt alone. I still miss my family in Mexico, but now there are many Hispanic families."

The Latino migration into Little Rock demonstrated that in the 1990s the central urban districts did not fall behind the economic pace set by the thoroughbreds of the Ozarks. Metropolitan Pulaski County reached national per capita income levels, and continued higher levels of employment in business and government rather than in manufacturing underscored its differences from the rest of the state. Still, more individuals departed than entered the state's most populous county, while the surrounding commuter counties of Faulkner, Saline, and Lonoke boasted rates of in-migration comparable to those of the northwest magnets. Following the evolution of urban areas elsewhere, the suburban bedroom developments surrounding Little Rock were eclipsed by nearby older towns bursting at the seams. Local leaders in Conway, Benton, Bryant, and Cabot cited solid schools, low crime rates, and small-town amenities as lures for newcomers. Critics argued that whites were abandoning the Little Rock School District, which enrolled a majority of black students. During the 1980s the numbers and percentages of the African-American population declined in Saline and Lonoke Counties while the ratio of the black to white residents in Faulkner County remained unchanged. Between 1987 and 1997, these three expanding central Arkansas counties, along with Benton and Washington Counties in the northwest corner, accounted for 65 percent of the state's total population growth.

Economic recovery in the 1990s benefited those commonly left out of previous upturns. According to the Center for Budget and Policy Priorities, the poorest fifth of the state's families achieved a 19 percent gain in real income during the decade, which contrasted with the stagnate overall rate for the nation's poor. The improvements, however, did not unloosen the state from the bottom of the poverty rankings. Arkansas did reflect national trends in the failure of its middle-class citizens to close ground on those with the greatest incomes. Regional inequalities also deepened. In historic terms, the divide between the have and have-not regions in Arkansas introduced a more complex economic sectionalism than the customary agrarian resentment toward Little Rock domination. New urban centers thrived throughout the state while poverty burdened the static rural sections. The inability to replenish population loss and keep up with state income growth weighed upon the north-central mountain area, the old agricultural southwest region, and the tarnished jewel of the traditional economy, the Delta.

The chronic labor surplus and reliance upon row crops anchored the vast east Arkansas landscape to an atavistic past. During the postwar era, mechanization and consolidation continued to allay the demand for year-round hands in traditional row-crop counties. Modern operations dwarfed past empires. Between 1945 and 1992 the number of Delta farms declined over 88 percent, while the average size of the holdings increased by more than 700 percent. Seasonal labor was also critical to the operations of the pine plantations. In south Arkansas, a neo-bracero program permitted tree farmers to employ contingents of Mexican citizens who performed the skilled but exhausting task of planting pine seedlings. As in the 1940s, the new exchange program extended unique labor benefits, including pay schedules far exceeding the national minimum wage. In 1997 about two-thirds of the 47,354 Arkansas farm workers were employed 150 days or fewer.

In 1998 the executive director of the Agriculture Council of Arkansas estimated that at least twenty-five farming operations exceeded ten thousand acres. The dominant farm empires held firm throughout the postwar era. Prudential Insurance Company apparently remained the largest holder of Arkansas farmland, followed by Carter Jones in Bradley and Drew Counties, Lee Wilson and Bo Adams in Mississippi County, David Brooks Griffin in Phillips County, the Barnett family in Jefferson County, and the Ritter family in Poinsett County. Even a familiar commodity of Delta agriculture staged a modest comeback. By the late 1980s the rising demand for natural-fiber clothing stimulated a rise in cotton acreage, although only amounting to about a quarter of the land harvested for soybeans. Another persistent reality was the link between size and government favor. A 1999 Arkansas Public Policy Panel analysis of census statistics concluded that 7 percent of the largest Arkansas farms delivered 60 percent of agricultural sales and procured the greatest benefit from federal subsidy programs.

The enduring connivance between local agricultural department agents and county committees stacked with prominent landholders drove African Americans out of farming. During the troubled 1980s black farmers received a cold shoulder from the Farmers Home Administration, the major financing agency bailing out overextended operators. The 1983 abolishment of the civil rights office in the Department of Agriculture by the

Ronald Reagan administration exacerbated the unequal consideration of loan applications. In 1999 the department agreed to settle a lawsuit filed by the National Black Farmers Association by paying at least $300 million in claims arising from denial of aid. For many it was too late. Between 1982 and 1992 the number of African-American farmowners in Arkansas fell by nearly 40 percent. During the following five years, even a slight resurgence in numbers still left fewer black owners than in 1987, and dim prospects for younger operators kept the median age of African-American farmers above that of their white counterparts. Many of those still in business were saddled with debts and aging equipment. During the years when he could not secure a federal loan, James Stephenson of Chicot County had little choice but to farm "out-of-pocket," renting acreage for his rice crop and combing scrap-metal yards to keep his tractors in working order. He estimated that a decade of rejected applications for federal assistance cost him $4 million.

In 1997 an Associated Press reporter interviewed eighty-two-year-old Jeanie Branch, who continued to farm seventy-three acres of inherited land as well as sharecropping thirteen additional acres. Subsisting on Spam and crackers, he and his ill wife lived in a small Desha County house without indoor plumbing and lit only by a single sixty-watt bulb. Branch wearily observed: "This ain't no living. Poor people in the delta kiss the devil to survive." Deprivation in eastern Arkansas was not hidden. Journalists for decades ventured down worn dirt roads and gathered without much difficulty evidence of bitter, enervating poverty. Official recognition of the plight of the Delta was also generous. In 1988 the Congress passed a measure introduced by Dale Bumpers to form the Lower Mississippi Delta Development Commission to "identify and study the economic development, infrastructure, employment, transportation, resource development, education, health care, housing, and recreation needs" for the entire region covering several states. The commission issued its report in 1990. Eight years later the federal Agriculture Department announced the formation of a new compact of states to examine the earlier report. According to the press release, "recommendations expected as areas of action for the new agency compact include improvements in transportation, education, and health and safety of Delta residents."

The 1990 census revealed that the three counties with the lowest median household income and the highest percentage of impoverished individuals in Arkansas were the Delta counties of Lee, Chicot, and Phillips. Employment was disproportionately agricultural in these counties, where a shrunken middle class teetered between stark extremes of wealth and poverty. If the counties lagged behind in broader economic measures, local farmowners clustered at the top of the agricultural sector. Between 1992 and 1997 the growth in the net cash value on sales from farms in these counties dramatically outpaced the statewide average. Success in the marketplace did not removed the federal safety net as government payments to these farmers were on average a third higher than for their counterparts throughout Arkansas.

The most commonly touted antidote for Delta misery was industrialization. Certainly the mechanization of agriculture meant Delta boosters no longer confronted planters' opposition to any enterprise threatening to drain the labor pool. Still, the case of Mississippi County and the new steel mills suggested heavy industry alone would not transform the region. On the one hand, the county's increase in per capita personal income between 1987 and 1997 exceeded the growth rate for the state. On the other hand, its continued high unemployment rates, large numbers of impoverished families, and sobering infant mortality rates were common Delta maladies. Many of the well-paid steel employees were dispersed throughout neighboring counties and Tennessee. The comparative prosperity of Jonesboro in adjacent Craighead County indicated that urbanization was the key to Delta resurgence. State and local governments were able to improve only marginally the poor roads, tiny schools, and inadequate health services plaguing rural life.

The considerable attention to hardship in the Delta threatened to obscure in the popular mind the harsh poverty embedded in other sections of the state. The isolation and want associated with Appalachia overshadowed the Ozarks as well. Remote Newton County, home of Boxley and Lost Valleys along the Buffalo River, waited longer than any other county to secure a paved state highway. Still classified in 1990 by the Census Bureau as completely rural, Newton relied on tourism rather than lumber and sawmills to generate most of the jobs. No other county had more homes with little or no plumbing, and almost 10 percent of the households were without telephone service. The percentage of its adult population graduating from either high school or college did not match the state average. Yet, the Newton County poverty rates fell below those in the Delta in part because its poor tended to be elderly. Older recipients there enjoyed a 17 percent higher Social Security income than their Lee County counterparts. In the Delta the majority of children live in poverty, and aid to families with dependent children (AFDC), or welfare payments, were substantially below the average Social Security stipends.

The enactment during the 1970s of measures to index social security old-age payments to the rate of inflation and the Reagan program during the 1980s to purge the welfare rolls consolidated social welfare expenditures into programs for older Americans. In Arkansas the number of families receiving welfare began declining during the prosperous 1970s, but the trend quickened even as unemployment rose in the wake of credit tightening. Between 1980 and 1985 the average number of AFDC families fell by over 25 percent, a drop far steeper than the national rate of decline. During the same period the average monthly Social Security benefit sent to Arkansas retired workers rose by 42 percent. AFDC funds began flowing to more families after 1985, but the totals never equaled those on the rolls in 1980. The average AFDC monthly grant of $182 in 1996 had risen 26 percent since 1980, an annual growth rate of 1.6 percent. The drive to liquidate public income assistance culminated in the national "The Personal Responsibility and Work Opportunity Reconciliation Act of 1996," which enacted deadlines on how long individuals could collect benefits.

In 1997 the Arkansas legislature adopted the nation's briefest eligibility period for lifetime cash assistance. During the following two years, state human services officials passed along only a fraction of the federal block-grant money to counties for child care, transportation, and job training. Bureaucratic inertia was only one reason that Arkansas was among a majority of states that failed to use designated federal funds. A full-employment economy and prodding from local caseworkers sped the transition of recipients into the job market. Between 1997 and 1998 the state notched substantial budgetary savings as over 40 percent fewer people applied for assistance. This rate exceeded the decline nationally. What became of those who left the rolls was largely a mystery. Few disputed that the ones who found employment had done so largely on their own. Those remaining in the welfare system had few practical alternatives. By 1999, 41 percent of the welfare caseload in Arkansas consisted of children who lived in households with no adult recipients of public income assistance.

State leaders continued to treat business enticements and subsidies as effective weapons against poverty. Publicly financed promotions touting the state's advantages inexorably appeared in national publications. However, this approach became suspect after a 1985 full-page display advertisement appeared in the same issue of *The Wall Street Journal* as a newsstory map that placed the state in the vicinity of Colorado. The industrial bond programs originating in the 1950s were supplemented by mushrooming tax exemptions and direct capital subsidies for infrastructure and training. Faced with the reality that the era of industrial relocation from north to south was ending, Arkansas development leaders trumpeted their intentions to nurture the expansion of operations already within the state. In 1985, when International Paper threatened to shutdown its plants in Pine Bluff and Camden, Gov. Bill Clinton lobbied legislators to enact the Manufacturer's Investment Tax Credit, which waived sales and use taxes up to 7 percent of the cost of plant expansions. This generous new program was the source for two-thirds of the over $500 million in state subsidies that flowed to corporations during the 1990s. Although the director of the state economic development department insisted that Arkansas gained over three times in tax funds what it spent in business assistance, no independent researcher had collected or analyzed the data from all local and state incentive programs to verify this claim.

Just as earlier boosters had decried the state's over-reliance on agriculture, latter-day leaders worried about a similar dependency on manufacturing in a digital world. The Arkansas Industrial Development Commission changed its name to the Arkansas Economic Development Commission (AEDC) to mark a broader mission. Throughout the decade, AEDC surveys revealed that the state's employers ranked poorly trained workers as their chief headache. While the AEDC's Internet website continued to tout the state's antiunion legislation and low taxes, it also boasted of publicly funded custom training programs. In April 1998 Little

Rock–based Alltel, a digital communications company, fed anxieties about an ominous deficit of skilled employees when it located a new production center in Atlanta rather than in central Arkansas. Nevertheless, the argument that technical positions were going begging ignored the flight of educated residents venturing elsewhere for opportunity. Arkansas had the lowest percentage of college graduates within its population despite rising matriculation rates. Two-fifths of the engineering graduates from the University of Arkansas secured their first jobs out-of-state. The Arkansas economy at the close of the century did not reliably reward the most highly educated workers with suitable jobs.

A 1997 analysis by Charles E. Venus and Dana Venus Hoover compared the recent economic performance of Arkansas with that of other southern states that had also once put all their eggs into the low-wage manufacturing basket. Whereas after 1980 the other states had diversified their economies and approached national income levels, Arkansas adhered to the older strategies that had brought it to within three-quarters of the U.S. per capita income. Nearly a quarter of the state's workers labored for food-processing companies, a quarter were in wholesale and retail trade, and about a fifth were employed in various service establishments. The compensation of Arkansas manufacturing workers hovered around 80 percent of the American average, and wage increases during the 1990s were insufficient to close the gap.

Above all, elements of the traditional economy persisted to the end of the century. In Arkansas, agriculture's share of the gross state product was almost twice the average for the southeast and three times that for the nation. The link between the farm and factory remained stronger in Arkansas than elsewhere. The processing of agricultural products accounted for over 40 percent of the value of the state's manufacturing output. In the 1990s, lumber manufacturing once again led the durable goods employment index. The post–World War II industrialization drive had boosted the state into the national market without undermining established political and business structures of influence. Yet, it remained to be seen whether or not Arkansas leaders would risk provoking more fundamental changes by reconfiguring the state's economy to keep pace with global forces.

And what of Arkansas Power and Light, the parent of modern economic development? Jerry Maulden, who became president in 1979, followed the path of Couch and Moses, delivering around one hundred speeches a year, exhorting civic club gatherings to prepare their communities for an economic revival: "Arkansas has all this unrealized potential, and it's just around the corner." Yet a 1984 ruling by an administrative judge for the Federal Energy Regulatory Commission (FERC) to force Arkansas customers to pay for a Mississippi nuclear power plant turned the state's largest electrical utility into a pariah.

In 1974 Middle South Utilities (MSU), AP&L's parent holding company, began construction on the Grand Gulf nuclear power plant south of Vicksburg to generate energy for its other operating companies in Mississippi and Louisiana. By 1984 AP&L itself was awash with power, having built Nuclear One near Russellville as well as four coal-fired units. Cost overruns at Grand Gulf propelled the other Middle South companies to renege on an earlier agreement and demand that AP&L be assigned part of the construction bill even though it would not use the generated power. In 1985 the FERC agreed to assign AP&L a greater share of the expenses than it did the other MSU utilities. That same year the Arkansas Public Service Commission authorized a settlement obligating AP&L ratepayers to shoulder 80 percent of the utility's allotted Grand Gulf costs. Maulden's sustained and public denouncements of the FERC ruling did not appease an enraged public. One lawmaker introduced a bill in the General Assembly enabling the state to take over the company.

The company survived as a private entity and fell back on a familiar formula to regain at least the good will of local business organizations. In 1987 AP&L announced a new economic development program labeled "Teamwork Arkansas." The utility essentially repackaged Hamilton's Moses 1950s "Arkansas Plan." All of the elements of the earlier program were still in place: community assessment, leadership training, and deploying expeditions to lure industrial prospects. While AP&L may have shored up its traditional base among town chambers of commerce and local business leaders, its comparatively high electrical rates alienated the enterprises it had welcomed to the state over the decades. In addition, Entergy, the rechristened holding company, signaled its determination to more closely integrate its multistate operations by changing the name of the utility to

Entergy Arkansas and closing local service offices throughout the state.

By the mid-1990s, major industries within Arkansas eagerly anticipated the deregulation of electrical utilities, confident that they could lower their power costs by haggling with a variety of providers. Fearful that it could not recover its substantial capital investment in generating plants through a competitive market, Entergy initially fought to extend the transition phase. In 1997 large manufacturers, timber companies, and trucking firms in Arkansas became restive with the state chamber of commerce's continued deference to its long-time patron, forming a separate business interest group. To the surprise of many observers, Entergy Arkansas's chief lobbyist, Cecil Alexander, lassoed the dissident corporations into a formidable coalition supporting the utility's deregulation bill before the 1999 General Assembly. Voluminous and complex, the Entergy proposal would have restricted the oversight of the Public Service Commission by freezing numerous rules into statute. Opposition by the state's electrical cooperatives and the attorney general forced a compromise, which commanded huge legislative majorities.

Whereas Harvey Couch's vision of a modern Arkansas economy had once captured the popular imagination, his company's prospects had come to depend upon the shrewd and domineering Alexander, a backroom gamesman whose formidable skills had earned him the nickname "Slick." This transition, as well as the passing of the first generation of native entrepreneurs, brought down the curtain on an era in which Arkansas corporations were known by the individuals in charge.

Life in the New Arkansas

Arkansas moved to town, reluctantly. Urbanization surged between 1950 and 1970 but barely advanced the following two decades. Twenty years after crossing the urban threshold, the 1990 census reported only 53.5 percent of residents living in incorporated towns of twenty-five-hundred residents or more. While municipalities of over twenty-five-thousand people outpaced state population growth, they comprised only 12 of the 107 urban places in the state. With per capita incomes higher than those the rest of the state, the three largest statistical metropolitan areas within

Arkansas (Little Rock, Fort Smith, and Fayetteville-Springdale-Rogers) drew job seekers. However, taking work in the city did not necessarily mean moving to the city. Arkansans put more miles on their vehicles than other Americans, and the state's commuters (over three-fourths of whom drove solo) took nearly as long to reach the workplace as other Americans.

In contrast to earlier decades, nearly all rural homes were stocked with the same appliances and amenities as those in towns. Satellite dishes blossomed in front of country houses located beyond cable-television lines, and local Internet service providers, the mom-and-pop enterprises of the early digital era, cast a wide net throughout the state. Older media businesses expanded as well. Between 1984 and 1997 the number of Arkansas television stations grew from nineteen to thirty-three, while radio stations increased by 14 to a total of 229. Consistent with evolving national habits, fewer people subscribed to Arkansas newspapers. Unexpectedly, weekly papers retained their proportion of overall newspaper circulation. Nevertheless, these readership levels were an imperfect measure of the durability of small-town culture. Newspapers serving the planned retirement communities of Hot Springs Village, Bella Vista, and Cherokee Village, as well as the Little Rock–based *Arkansas Times,* were among the largest of the weekly publications.

National social trends modified but did not obliterate unique characteristics of the Arkansas family. An aging population and rising divorce numbers compressed the size of Arkansas households below the national average. Even as couples nationwide ended their marriages in record frequency, Arkansas continued to stand out as a divorce-friendly state. In the era before no-fault divorce, the liberalism of the Arkansas code on the matter rested on the recognition of "general indignities" as a justification for marital dissolution. Subsequently, the legislature reduced the waiting period after separation from three years to eighteen months. Undoubtedly, the fact that Arkansans married younger and more often stood as the primary reason for the proliferation of divorce suits. Beginning to escalate during the 1980s, the state's marriage rate almost doubled that of the nation by the mid-1990s.

As they had since the 1930s, Arkansas women continued to bear fewer children than American mothers overall. By the 1980s the increase in births to unmarried Arkansas women reflected national trends, although a larger proportion of teenage mothers in the state were married. A 1998 report by National Center for Children in Poverty determined that for the period 1991–95, 25.8 percent of children in the U.S. under eighteen years old lived in a household headed by a single mother as opposed to 21.9 percent in Arkansas; in addition, the national percentage of children living in a two-parent household was 69.9 compared to the 74.4 percent of Arkansas children. In that span of time, less than 1 percent of all mothers in the state with children at home were unmarried teenagers.

The experience of Arkansas women on the job came to resemble national realities while retaining the distinctive traits associated with the state's economic development. By 1998 the 58.4 percent rate of wage-earning women in Arkansas was nearly identical to the national figure, as was the gap yawning between their earnings and those of men. More women entered the workforce despite the shutdown of the female-dominated clothing factories as well as their continued absence on the production floor in better-paying manufacturing firms. The swelling health care industry enlarged the numbers of skilled positions in an area traditionally open to women. By 1990 three-fourths of the state's medical technicians and technologists were female. The most notable improvement between 1970 and 1990 was the doubling in the percentage of employed women who held professional and managerial positions other than public school teaching. In addition, the National Foundation for Women Business Owners reported that in 1997 Arkansas women owned 77,000 companies, a 1,000 percent increase over the number of such businesses operating twenty years earlier.

Yet, advances did not herald equality. The Institute for Women's Policy Research noted that in the 1990s Arkansas continued to rank near the bottom in the percentage of women holding managerial posts. Only 12 percent of Arkansas women completed four or more years of college, a figure lower than the overall percentage of the state's college-degree holders. In 1990 women in the state filled about 80 percent of administrative support or clerical positions.

The statistics only sketched the outlines of everyday experience. A 1998 *Arkansas Times* survey of central Arkansas women revealed that two-thirds of the respondents believed their job opportunities lagged behind those afforded men. The exhaustion endured by married women in the 1940s pulling double shifts at home and in the workplace echoed through the observations of women in the 1990s. "We have to carry more responsibility and take issues more seriously than men do," observed a Little Rock woman. Married women continued to take on cooking, laundry, and bill paying. Ambivalence over changing roles and a desire for balanced obligations apparently prodded all but 12 percent of the respondents to prefer either to care for their families full time or to work only part time at an outside job if family income would permit.

The lesions of historic racism were not healed in the course of Arkansas modernization. By 1990 African-American women, in comparison to white, employed females, were substantially underrepresented in the managerial, professional, and sales occupations while they were over-represented in service positions and as cashiers. Similar imbalances accounted for the suppressed wages of African-American men, who were more likely than white counterparts to work in the wood-products industry while holding proportionally fewer jobs in metal and machinery manufacturing. The difference between black and white incomes in Arkansas was even more profoundly unequal than the gap existing for the nation as a whole. In an astute and rigorous analysis of 1990 census data, Lawrence Santi concluded that only about half of the racial disparity in Arkansas incomes originated in divergent social and demographic characteristics. While black households, in general, were younger and less-educated and had fewer breadwinners available, these households also registered smaller income improvements as the members aged and completed additional schooling. In other words, economic inequality would endure even if African-American and white households resembled one another. The finding that experience and training did not render the same rewards for blacks as for whites suggested that the absence of African Americans from higher paying occupations originated in purposeful exclusion.

Despite formidable obstacles, the efforts of black Arkansans between 1959 and 1989 showed results as the rate of growth in their median family income surpassed that of whites. During the period, those African Americans employed as professionals and managers rose from 3 to 13.6

percent. As with whites, moving to town boosted African-American income even as inequities persisted. Composing about 16 percent of the state's population in 1990, black Arkansans were more likely than whites to live in the heart of larger cities while residing less often in suburbs and edge communities. Among black households in 1989, one-quarter of those in urban centers commanded incomes of $25,000 or more, whereas only one-fifth reached that level in rural areas. African-American businesses were also concentrated in cities. In 1992 nearly half of the state's 5,738 black-owned firms were located in Pulaski (Little Rock) and Jefferson (Pine Bluff) Counties. Yet the income gap between black and white households in metropolitan areas was about the same as that for the state as a whole.

For African Americans in Arkansas, middle-class identification was generally both more expansive and more fluid than that recognized in the white community. Fred Hokes, a social worker in Little Rock, pinpointed the threshold as the wherewithal to afford basic services: "I've had people tell me they were happy just to come home on a Friday night and find all the utilities still connected." Public relations consultant Stacy Williams suggested a more common outlook by listing education, family standing, and civic involvement as the hallmarks of middle-class status. By the 1990s the entrance of African Americans into a broader range of occupations extended the traditional circle of influence and leadership beyond the clergy. At the same time, certain urban families preserved their prominence, although now based almost exclusively on professional credentials. Cleon Flowers, the brother of civil rights pioneer W. Harold Flowers, was a Pine Bluff physician as were his son and daughter. Sterling Roaf, an obstetrician-gynecologist, and Clifton Roaf, a dentist, were the sons of a well-known Jefferson County minister; Clifton Roaf also was married to state appeals court judge Andree Layton Roaf. Henry Wilkins III of Pine Bluff was among the first African Americans to serve in the state General Assembly and was succeeded by his wife, Josetta Wilkins, who was elected to the seat following his 1991 death. Their children extended that legacy. Cassandra Wilkins Slater, married to U.S. transportation secretary Rodney Slater, became a senior adviser to the Social Security commissioner. In 1999 Henry Wilkins IV entered the General Assembly representing a Jefferson County house district.

To a greater degree than their white counterparts, prestigious black attorneys were likely to seek posts in state government or wield influence from the bench. Serving on the appeals court with Judge Roaf was Olly Neal, a VISTA activist from Lee County appointed in 1996 by Gov. Jim Guy Tucker. Wiley Branton Jr., the son of the former dean of Howard University Law School, was circuit-chancery judge in Little Rock. The best known heir to the legacy of Flowers and Branton was John Walker. Reared in Hope, Walker served two years on the staff of the Arkansas Council on Human Relations before earning his law degree from Yale. His first case upon returning to Arkansas in 1965 was defending black Forrest City high school students arrested for protesting discriminatory policies. Shortly afterward, Walker became involved in the Little Rock desegregation case and eventually represented the three metropolitan districts' African-American parents and children, a class known as the Joshua Intervenors.

In 1998 Gordon D. Morgan, a University of Arkansas sociologist, observed that the restoration of black political rights during the 1960s produced a statewide class of leaders. They in turn supplanted older, community-based power brokers whose influence depended on control of segregated institutions and respected personal qualities. The diversity of interests and backgrounds of the new elite more faithfully represented the growing socioeconomic complexity of the African-American community while also encouraging black Arkansans to look to national figures to articulate with passion and authority the multitude of their concerns.

The nationalization of Arkansas society revived the impulse to define an Arkansas culture. During the Depression the crisis of dislocation prompted an appreciation and distilling of Arkansas traditions into the vessel of rural mountain culture. Aided by federal revenues and policies, collectors of folk materials linked the retrieval of valued customs to the anticipated benefits of tourism. In subsequent decades sustained government investment and widening affluence stoked cultural preservation.

The revival of Ozark crafts in the 1960s originated with a series of federal rural-development pilot projects and the formation of the Ozark Foothills Handicraft Guild, modeled after the Southern Highland Handicraft Guild in Appalachia. Turning out largely nontraditional carvings to meet tourist expectations, woodcarvers became fixtures at festivals.

One person involved in neocraft promotion explained: "We are a business here. We are creating a market for these people to sell their work." Basket makers could also turn a profit thanks to promising venues such as amusement parks or convenient distribution through the Arkansas Craft Guild (the new name for the Ozark Foothills organization after 1991). In contrast, several nineteenth-century craft occupations such as blacksmithing and coopering declined because of their complexity and limited commercial potential.

A rare folk practice that endured independently of the tourism trade was the employment of herbal remedies for various illnesses. The scarcity of medical professionals in the Ozarks and Ouachita hill region kept viable the old knowledge about slippery elm, pokeweed, and sassafras. In the mid-1990s Justin Nolan interviewed "granny-women" and "yarb doctors" recognized for their familiarity with the curative properties of local flora. Although no longer midwives, the granny-women had expanded their treatments to respond to a range of complaints "from arthritis and dysentery to poison ivy and toothaches." Nolan discovered that for the healers, ancestral teachings rather than the particular availability of local plants determined which species were judged medicinal. Tradition in this case overrode practical observation and convenience.

For students and lay visitors, music had long represented the heart of the state's mountain culture. Folklorist W. K. McNeil concluded that while traditional Ozark music resembled that heard in Appalachia, it diverged in terms of singing style, origin of songs, and evidence of native material. As in the case of eastern highlands, the introduction of musical instruments influenced and altered Ozark music. After 1900 banjo players adopted the less-genteel finger-picking style, while black steamboat hands taught those in Ozark river towns to play the six-string guitar. Available through mail-order catalogues since the early twentieth century, the autoharp retained its popularity with hill musicians long after it was abandoned by Americans elsewhere. Often believed to be the quintessential Ozark folk instrument, the mountain dulcimer before the 1960s was less prominent at dances and programs than the more robust-sounding hammer dulcimer. Bluegrass songs also occupied a new segment in the repertoire at folk concerts. A post–World War II commercial adaptation of older string band styles, this musical form (associated with Kentuckian Bill Monroe) appealed to Ozarkers—as it did to many other Americans—as an acoustic rebuke to mass-culture.

Mountain View became a prominent outpost of the national folk revival during the 1960s through staging what promoters christened the "Arkansas Folk Festival." The popularity of the event, which came to attract tens of thousands of visitors each year, inspired the director of the state branch of the federal antipoverty agency to lobby for a congressional appropriation to construct a center to teach traditional crafts to regional inhabitants. The agency head believed that not only would individuals acquire a marketable skill, but the center also would enhance the chances of Mountain View to secure a desperately needed grant to construct a water system. Although the federal dollars arrived, the state tourism department took over the construction of the center after the original contractor filed for bankruptcy. Department officials wanted the center to be self-supporting and believed that attracting paying visitors to the site was a more creditable form of economic development than folk-art training. The school was restructured into a spacious outdoor museum with an expanded performance area and accompanying restaurant and lodge. Jimmy Driftwood, composer of the popular ballads "Battle of New Orleans" and "The Tennessee Stud" as well as founder of the traditionalist Rackensack Musical Society, became the center's first director.

Other enterprises based on mountain tourism were less salutary and attentive to local customs. In 1975 the first Governor's Conference on Tourism convened at an amusement park in Newton County modeled after the hill village in Al Capp's *Lil' Abner* comic strip. Seven years earlier the small town of Marble Falls had become Dogpatch, and former governor Orval Faubus was set up as general manager of the theme park by a group of Harrison investors. As the promoters predicted, the enterprise did generate employment, at first. Local residents conscientiously erected sturdy buildings in the park but then were instructed to redo the work. The park owners wanted replicas faithful to the comic strip's rickety, sway-roofed cabins. The park staggered on its unprofitable course until closing permanently in 1993. In 1997 the local population successfully petitioned the postal service to restore the name Marble Falls.

In the 1990s only Hot Springs attracted more tourists than the late-nineteenth-century Ozark resort town of Eureka Springs, which had historically traded upon genteel Victorian architecture rather than ersatz folk offerings. Thirty years earlier it appeared that quaint charm would not save the village from falling into the same obscurity of other forgotten spas. Then in 1964 Gerald L. K. Smith, an old-line right-wing demagogue and publisher of the anti-Semitic magazine *The Cross and the Flag,* retired to Eureka Springs and decided to make it the site for outsized commemorations to his career. The following year he commissioned the building of a seventy-foot statue of Jesus Christ. A rigid concrete rendering without grace or realism, the *Christ of the Ozarks* inspired Smith to continue his bid for immortality. By 1968 he built a vast amphitheater hollowed out of the side of a mountain to stage a production of the final days before the crucifixion of Christ. Each summer larger and larger crowds flocked to Eureka Springs, visiting the shops and gingerbread cottages along the sharply curving streets during the day and then attending the nightly performance of *The Passion Play.* The drama included a cast of 150 local actors as well as camels, horses, sheep, and donkeys moving across a four-hundred-foot-long stage representing a section in ancient Jerusalem.

Shortly before his death, Smith began to plan an amusement park duplicating the Middle Eastern shrines revered by Christians. He intended for his New Holy Land to spare devout tourists from having to visit Israel and finding themselves "paying cash to a Jew." The vision expired with its creator. Smith's crypt at the foot of the gigantic statue of Christ came to be largely ignored by those who traveled to see his handiwork.

The civil rights era broadened the cultural preservation program in the state to include African-American traditions. By the 1980s, Helena, the old capital of the delta blues empire, resurfaced as a destination for those cherishing the music pioneered by Sonny Boy Williamson and Robert Jr. Lockwood. Inaugurated in 1986, the King Biscuit Blues Festival each October attracted leading performers and sizable crowds to the Cherry Street Historic District. Without costly refurbishment of buildings, the old city blocks served as period backdrops for the performances. Visiting musicians assumed they were seeing the town as Robert Johnson knew it. Whereas Sonny Boy Williamson's visage had once help to sell cornmeal, it now adorned the caps and ice coolers hawked during the festival. Previously, Helena leaders had highlighted the antebellum and Civil War eras as the marketable past: "Helena. Long ago is not so far away." Yet, the blues revival proved more invigorating. In 1990 the state also made cultural renewal an agent in Helena's economic revitalization when it established the Delta Cultural Center.

In contrast to other sites in the state that offered culture as a tourism curio, the new center straightforwardly presented a comprehensive examination of the injustice and endurance embedded in Delta society. Those who argued that the molding of history for public consumption was necessary to keep it alive pointed to the success of the centers at Mountain View and Helena. However, the sifting through the past for remunerative nuggets risked distortion of the historical experience. In Helena, festival goers parked their vehicles on empty lots where juke joints once stood and in which musicians played a music so raw and powerful that none could have imagined it domesticated into a legacy.

The most gifted and influential musical talent to emerge from the Arkansas Delta in the years following the Great Migration and the demise of Sun Records was the incomparable Al Green of Forrest City. Green served his apprenticeship in a family gospel group before recording a series of early 1970s hits with Hi Records in Memphis: "Tired of Being Alone," "Let's Stay Together," and "I'm Still in Love with You." The songs were honeyed by the influences of Sam Cooke's and Jackie Wilson's soul ballads and toughened by the grit of next door's rhythm and blues. Recognized as the preeminent male soul artist of that decade, Green combined the blistering integrity of his rural roots with a graceful, worldly sophistication. He was a righteous man who understood the world's possibilities. Following a crisis of faith, he began to edge away from popular music, established a church in Memphis, and after 1980 released only gospel albums on a small specialty label. Following his 1995 installation in the Rock and Roll Hall of Fame, the Reverend Green once again began to include his popular songs in concerts.

Fortunately Green was not the only modern artist from the state who reinvigorated traditional elements through contemporary realism. Other major figures also navigated between naive romanticism and postmodern dissolution.

The actual Newton County gained a parallel fictional existence as the home of Stay More, a familiar locale to readers of novelist Donald Harington. The author began his task of building a new town in his native county while teaching art history in New England, later claiming a more convenient posting at the University of Arkansas. Beginning with *Lightning Bug* (1970) and continuing through *When Angels Rest* (1998), Harington wove the rich narrative of Stay More's history through recurring characters rather than the plumb line of chronology. He linked familiar modernist techniques of shifting perspective, multiple narrators, and the blurring of imagination and reality to the older oral folk conventions of direct address to the listener, unapologetic treatment of sexuality, and alteration of the facts on retelling. The fulcrum of Harington's universe is his widely acknowledged masterpiece, *The Architecture of the Arkansas Ozarks* (1975). In this lavish chronicle, Stay More's development was explicated through successive houses representing the cloistered dreams of the builders. Walking in and out of *Architecture* were characters who figure more prominently in both earlier and subsequent Harington novels. As with William Faulkner's Yoknapatawpha and Gabriel García Márquez's Macondo, Harington's village was more than the sum of the books, because its creator honestly revealed that any single description was only one of countless ways to recount the story. Harington invited his readers to complete his narrative and decide the fate of the characters.

The open and contingent character of Harington's Ozarks echoed the lessons in the career of the folklorist Vance Randolph. The works of both men demonstrated that folk practices originated from necessity and adaptation, never frozen in nostalgia. The standard unit of measurement in Stay More was a "hat," or approximately the distance that the town's founder commonly tossed his coonskin hat. While this ancestral tradition persisted, subsequent generations erected the houses of Stay More as they saw fit and not as rote manifestations of lifeless customs. In Harington's *Butterfly Weed* (1996), Randolph was the character narrating the saga of Doc Swain, whose reputation derived from his encyclopedic grasp of the medicinal properties of native plants, including those of the butterfly weed. In the vein of both local-color writing and folklore, Swain influenced events and people through his dreams. Were these simply tall tales? At one point in the narrative, Randolph issued a caveat: "I reckon I bring this up just to remind you that the story I've been telling you, no less than the Bible, can be taken either as the exact history of some people, of the love between a doctor and a young girl in a remote part of the Ozark Mountains, or it can be taken as a clever yarn."

Born in Union county on the opposite side of the state from Harington, Charles Portis poised his assault on regional literary conventions from a different direction. Although as firmly outside the mainstream as Ozark uplanders, the characters in Portis's novels did not stay put, always pursuing something last seen falling off the horizon. More than any other major twentieth-century novelist, Portis resembled Mark Twain in portraying drifters, con artists, and cranks as foils and reproaches to established opinion. While the genteel tradition excoriated by Twain had withered long before Portis's emergence, the Arkansas author continued to find the comic form the finest instrument to uncover modern society's secret obsessions, fears, and failed hopes. In 1964 Portis abruptly ended a promising career with the *New York Herald Tribune* to return to Arkansas and write his first novel. In both *Norwood* (1966) and *Dog of the South* (1979), the protagonists were uprooted innocents, partly through their ignorance of the surrounding conditions, but primarily because they did not comprehend the internal dissatisfactions driving them to hit the road. Norwood Pratt unknowingly set out in a stolen car for New York City, thinking to collect a small debt, but returned to his rural Texas home with both a fiancée and a chicken adept at sums. Ray Midge lights out for Central America to recover the Ford Torino stolen by his wife and her lover and returned to Little Rock with only his wife, who does not remain long.

In Mexico, Midge gives a lift to Dr. Reo Symes, who was unable to salvage his converted school bus, "The Dog of the South." Symes's eccentric cure for arthritis has deprived him of his medical license, but his dreams of easy money intermingled with his aspirations to locate the secret writings of John Selmer Dix. Dix scribbled his ideas while crisscrossing the American Southwest by bus, but his papers were never recovered after his death in a Tulsa hotel room. Symes was convinced that a profound revelation, a key to knowledge, would be contained in Dix's missing trunk. This fusion of the American dream for the one big jackpot and the conviction that one big idea explains it all was the foundation for Portis's

Masters of Atlantis (1985) and *Gringos* (1991). In the first book the Gnomon Society held out the promise of the wisdom of vanished Atlantis to attract the dissatisfied and the dispossessed, while in the other novel edgy dreamers and deep-enders plunged into the Yucatan jungle in search of the Lost City of Dawn.

The flow of Portis's literary reputation would be a fit subject for one of his novels. On the one hand, he was a cult novelist or as described in a 1998 appraisal in *Esquire,* "perhaps the most original, indescribable *sui generis* talent overlooked by literary culture in America." Yet, he also was able to subsist as a writer on the revenue from his tremendously popular *True Grit* (1968). A work of astounding craftsmanship, the novel was the purported first-person account of Mattie Ross from Dardanelle, Arkansas, who hired Marshal Rooster Cogburn to help her hunt down her father's killer after he fled into the Indian Territory. The fourteen-year-old Mattie was already imbued with bourgeoisie values of piety and thrift, but her demand for vengeance attracted her to the dubious Cogburn, whose taste for violence and contempt for rules made him little different from the outlaws he pursued. Her experiences on the bloody trek confirmed Mattie in her independence without deflating her commonplace convictions. The serious child grew to become a somber banker and rigorous Presbyterian. Yet her recollections unintentionally revealed that riding with Marshal Cogburn saved her from an altogether ordinary life. Even though most of Portis's characters end up back where they started, their travels become memories of a restless time when they stop doing the same thing for awhile. Ray Midge mused toward the end of *The Dog of the South:* "A lot of people leave Arkansas and most of them come back sooner or later. They can't quite achieve escape velocity."

As with many rural states without a metropolis, the literary center of Arkansas resided at the university in Fayetteville. Established by James Whitehead and William Harrison, the well-regarded Creative Writing Program drew as students young poets and novelists from throughout the nation. A number such as Ellen Gilchrist, Barry Hannah, Lee Abbott, and Lewis Nordan earned notable literary reputations. Teaching in the program, the poet Miller Williams shared the aesthetic of the other Arkansas writers by displaying a mastery of form without falling into sterile imitation. As the critic Lewis Turco noted, Williams has been "committed to both tradition and personal vision." Williams's poetry was deceptively straightforward in both its depiction of ordinary lives and its accessible language and imagery. Yet, he often displayed a dexterity of technique that few can match and a high democratic purpose by making his characters intellectually curious. In 1997 Williams, a native of Hoxie, delivered the presidential inaugural poem, a commission awarded to Maya Angelou four years earlier at the first inauguration of Bill Clinton.

Born in Fayetteville, Edward Durrell Stone began his architecture studies at Harvard and continued them in Europe before joining a New York City firm. His early work, such as the collaboration on the Metropolitan Museum of Art, were in the international style, but the forging of his signature blending of classical and modern characteristics was evident in his design of the Kennedy Center for the Performing Arts in Washington. His plans for the University of Arkansas Medical Sciences campus became his most extensive contribution to his native state.

Remaining in Arkansas throughout his career, E. Fay Jones designed structures no less distinctive than those of Stone, though sharply contrasting in style and materials. Born in Pine Bluff, Jones grew up in El Dorado, where his first building project was an elaborate tree house with a brick fireplace. Shortly before his high school graduation, he saw at the Rialto Theatre a short film on the newly erected Johnson Wax headquarters in Racine, Wisconsin. Designed by the modernist titan Frank Lloyd Wright, the curving, light-filled structure proved to Jones that one could be both artist and builder through architecture. In 1953, after gaining an architectural degree from Rice University, Jones was invited to work with Wright at his Taliesin workshop in Wisconsin. Wright was the prime exponent of the organic style, emphasizing both the internal cohesion of a building and its integration with the natural environment. The lessons Jones took from his mentor included open-floor layouts, use of fieldstone and unvarnished wood, and suffusion of light from hanging wall lanterns.

Nevertheless, Jones did not confuse organic architecture with the futile preservationist impulse to restore nature to its original state. He knew the end of his craft was artifice. An architect enabled individuals to live more completely within the environment by redeeming nature's promise through thought and art. "We have the power and responsibility to shape new forms in the landscape—physical and spatial forms that will nourish and express that all-important intangible of the human condition at its spiritual best. As architects, as transformers of the landscape, we *must.*"

Jones's appreciation for the sacred in everyday life led him to design only two types of structures: residences and places of worship. Following Jones's stint at Taliesin, John Williams recruited him for the newly established architectural program at the University of Arkansas. If Wright cared little for the expense of his projects, Jones early learned restraint by designing houses for professors whose desire for originality was checked by modest bank accounts. His reputation soon grew beyond the academic community, and in 1964 Orval Faubus turned to Jones to build a large retreat on a mountainside overlooking Huntsville. In 1978 James Reed asked Jones to design a small chapel in a wooded glade off a busy highway two miles from Eureka Springs. A self-described "frustrated cathedral builder," the architect braced the glass walls with an elaborate interior lattice that both framed the natural light and directed the vision up through ascending planes. Thorncrown Chapel brought international recognition to its creator. A series of impressive awards culminated in 1990, when Jones became one of only fifty individuals to earn the American Institute of Architects Gold Medal for lifetime achievement.

Like Harington, Portis, and Williams, Jones worked with materials at hand, eschewed ideology and fashion, and understood history without being in thrall to it. If there was an Arkansas aesthetic, its pragmatism and integrity were evident in what Jones called the "countenance of principles at work."

State Government, National Politics

For Orval Faubus, there was no life after politics. He had neither wealth nor profession. His segregationist reputation and Republican occupation of the White House made cushy appointments unlikely. Being governor had been his only vocation.

In the 1974 gubernatorial campaign, Witt Stephens and other former supporters jilted Faubus in his second comeback bid and threw their support to David Pryor, who had entered politics in the early 1960s as an anti-Faubus insurgent. The new governor in his first term adopted the more modest elements of the reformist programs of Winthrop Rockefeller and Dale Bumpers. He consolidated government agencies, including the establishment of the Department of Natural and Cultural Heritage; supported the calling of a constitutional convention; and appointed the first women and black representatives to several judicial and administrative department posts. Pryor decided that frugality rather than new programs would be his hallmark and slowed expenditure growth after two decades of exponential increases.

After his re-election Pryor proposed that the 1977 General Assembly reverse decades of consolidation to transfer a large share of state responsibilities to the county level. Under Pryor's proposal the state would reduce income taxes by a quarter while granting the counties the authority to raise revenue through any method of taxation rather than depending solely on the property levy. In a series of town meetings, Pryor explained to his listeners that they could apply their windfall from the income-tax cut to maintain local services or for "a new shotgun or coon dog." Since what came to be dubbed the "Coon Dog Plan" would also lead to the end of state turnback funds to local governments, county officials quickly realized they would be saddled with additional obligations while hostage to the willingness of their constituents to vote new taxes. County judges did not wish to regain independence at that price. The rough handling of his plan by the General Assembly relegated Pryor to the customary irrelevancy of second-term governors. In 1979 he followed his predecessor, Dale Bumpers, to the U.S. Senate.

Pryor's woes stemmed, in part, from a changing legislature less willing to submit to gubernatorial dominance. Election reform and newly redrawn urban districts reduced the sway of local power blocs over the General Assembly while strengthening the influence of larger business interest groups. In general, legislators began to develop a sense of institutional responsibility. The restructured committee system made lawmaking more open and less arbitrary. Legislators expected creditable information as well as favors from lobbyists. The incremental reforms also began to pare away the buffoonery and rowdiness. Diane Blair has aptly noted the changes in legislative culture: "Both lobbyists and liquor have been officially banished from the chamber floors, and the occasional hog calling or fiddle playing is a rare tension-reliever rather than a routine occurrence." The 1993 term-limits amendment expunged the last of the outlandish characters.

Throughout all the changes, white males continued to fill an overwhelmingly disproportionate share of the seats in the General Assembly. In 1964, when Dorathy Allen of Brinkley was elected as the first female state senator, three women were serving in the house of representatives. Over the course of the next thirty-five years, no more than one woman served during a senate session, and in 1999 the absence of any female members left the body as the only all-male legislative chamber in the nation. In that year, the house included twenty women, a decrease of two from the previous session. As part of evolving black political activism, in 1972 the century's first African-American legislators—one senator and three representatives—were elected from Little Rock and Pine Bluff. In 1989 Ben McGee ended the long political drought in eastern Arkansas. McGee won his house seat after filing a successful federal lawsuit that charged that Crittenden County's multimember district effectively ensured an all-white delegation. In 1998, fifteen African Americans were elected to the state legislature, the highest number since the 1891 disfranchisement laws.

Corresponding to southern patterns, women and African Americans discovered it much easier to secure mayoral posts than offices serving larger and more rural constituencies. By the end of the century, no woman had been elected attorney general, lieutenant governor, or governor, and no African American had filled one of the seven state constitutional offices. In 1992 Blanche Lambert Lincoln was the first woman elected from Arkansas to the U.S. House of Representatives; six years later became the first woman since Hattie Caraway to represent the state in the U.S. Senate. The dispersed residences of African-Americans in the state thwarted the formation of a black-majority or near-majority congressional district. In contrast, gubernatorial appointments of African Americans to state commissions and as agency directors widened black political influence and strengthened government accountability.

Changes in the corporate guard rippled through the capitol's hallways. In 1973 Witt Stephens relinquished control of Arkla Gas to his protégé Sheffield Nelson, only to discover that his heir intended to break off the utility's ties with other portions of the Stephens empire. The 1977 session revealed the decline of the old power broker's influence. Nelson mustered votes to defeat a bill that would have boosted natural gas prices by forcing Arkla to renegotiate a supply contract with Stephens Production Company. By 1985 legislators were sufficiently immune to Stephens's blandishments to approve Gov. Bill Clinton's establishment of the Arkansas Development Finance Authority. The new agency undermined the near-monopoly of Stephens, Inc., in the underwriting of public bond issues in the state, although the investment-banking firm continued to thrive through its far-flung holdings.

If Arkansas politics broke from its traditional local moorings, the long-standing characteristics of weak party structures and a part-time legislature magnified the dominance of corporate interest groups. Economic diversification only slightly enlarged the circle of the most influential groups. The utility operations, the original statewide firms, competed for lawmaker's attention with the Poultry Federation and the trucking industry. Much like traditional agricultural interests, the up and coming business associations skeptically regarded claims that Arkansas required additional government services to prosper. The new economic powers, taking up the old causes of low taxes and minimal regulations, neutralized the impact of the nonbusiness and public-service groups that emerged in the wake of urbanization. Certainly, the maturation of the state's economy provoked clashes among powerful interests with contrary goals. The General Assembly, for example, regularly found itself caught in the crossfire between the constitutionally autonomous Highway Commission and the formidable trucking lobbyists. The commission insisted that if the big rigs escaped the higher fees to offset the damage they inflicted on the roads, Arkansas prosperity would remain mired in the slow lane. For its part, the industry argued their taxes subsidized rural byways while the major arteries used by the long haulers fell into disrepair. However, business-group lobbyists generally sought consensus to smooth over their differences while legislators patiently waited to ratify the final settlement.

The fundamental legacy of the political reforms originating in the 1960s was that government in Arkansas came to function in the same manner as that in any other state. The cronyism and graft from the days when legislators were little more than agents of county bosses was no longer the rule. While corruption was less pervasive, its persistence suggested the incomplete transition to full government accountability. The most spectacular fall of a legislative kingpin occurred in 1999, when state senator Nick Wilson resigned following his conviction on federal tax evasion charges. In March 2000 Wilson pleaded guilty to defrauding publicly funded programs by receiving kickbacks from associates who overbilled for contracted services. During the previous two years, two other legislators, state representative Lloyd George and state senator Ben McGee, also gave up their seats after pleading guilty to federal charges arising from their abuse of public office. At the executive department level, Attorney General Steve Clark resigned in 1990 after his conviction for using state credit cards to entertain friends, and in 1996 former secretary of state Bill McCuen was sentenced to seventeen years in prison for accepting bribes and kickbacks while in office.

Even before these revelations, public sentiment had compelled new strictures. In 1988, after the legislature refused to enact a code of ethics drawn up by a citizen's commission, Governor Clinton secured its passage through a successful referendum drive. Ten years later the Center for Public Integrity ranked Arkansas eighteenth among states on the basis of its requirements for notification of conflicts of interest and for disclosure of financial records. Still, companies and industry associations continued to employ the part-time legislators and retain them as lobbyists. Other studies faulted the state's delivery of services and management of resources. And indeed a set of major scandals of the late 1990s revolved around the abuse of juvenile offenders in state custody and the failure to adequately inspect private care facilities for the elderly and mentally disabled. News accounts of these incidents emphasized bureaucratic neglect and incompetence.

As media exposure replaced local bosses in shaping election results, it was not surprising that the late-century politician who seemed best to fill the populist role of Jeff Davis and Orval Faubus hailed from Little Rock. In the early 1980s, Tommy Robinson, the Pulaski County sheriff, fastened himself into headlines and evening television news segments with flame-throwing rhetoric and erratic actions. He laced his verbal assaults on judges in racially provocative language, arrested county officials for not providing the funds he demanded, and left county prisoners chained to a fence at a state correctional facility. Robinson transformed an investigation into the murder of Alice MacArthur, wife of a noted Little Rock attorney, into a media event through strident charges of a cover-up by political insiders. If Robinson's appeal tapped into a tradition of rural insurgency, his early career was nurtured by a group of moderate Democratic businessmen, including utility executives Sheffield Nelson and Jerry Maulden. Around 1980, what had begun as an economic alliance among childhood friends and University of Arkansas alumni took on political overtones. The ambitious business coterie spied opportunities in the power vacuum in Little Rock that existed after the death of William Rector and the loosening of Witt Stephens's grasp over the legislature.

Although Robinson was elected to Congress in 1984, the group disintegrated soon afterward. The sharp downturn in the real estate market in mid-decade excited recriminations and suspicions among the businessmen as their shared investments in commercial property went sour. In addition, Bill Clinton's Faubus-like longevity as governor clogged the pipeline for political aspirants. In a 1990 gubernatorial primary election, Robinson lost to his former benefactor Nelson, marking the final chapter of what *The Wall Street Journal* likened to a "Russian novel." That the two men squared off for their high profile duel in the Republican, rather than the Democratic, primary heartened those who believed reform was a chimera in a one-party state.

While Arkansans voted along with fellow southerners for Republican Party presidential candidates, the state GOP was organizationally anemic and unable to recruit candidates for the full range of elected offices. Nevertheless, the migration of new people into Republican northwest Arkansas portended good news for the party when future census results compelled reapportionment. Republican leaders also anticipated that appeals to the conservatism of white Arkansas voters would expand membership beyond the Ozark confines. The poor showing of liberal Democratic presidential nominees confirmed the assessments of Republican activists that Sunbelt conservatism rather than Winthrop Rockefeller's moderation was the path to redemption. Victories by Republicans Ed Bethune (1978) and Jay Dickey (1992) for congressional seats outside the upland Third District bore out the benefits of a top-down electoral strategy. However, state Democrats were vulnerable on ideological grounds only if they were perceived as pressing for government action to redistribute resources and influence to those historically excluded from position and power.

Bill Clinton's political demise and recovery was an object lesson for moderate southern Democrats in the era of Ronald Reagan. In 1979 the first-term governor proposed an ambitious road, education, and environmental program, a seeming return to the days of Rockefeller and Bumpers. Yet, Clinton may have taken insufficient notice that his predecessor's fiscal conservatism played sufficiently well with voters to land Pryor in the U.S. Senate against strong candidates. Nevertheless, the legislature obliged the young chief executive by funding his highway construction program through higher automobile and truck registration fees. Clinton defended the assessment of higher taxes on the largest vehicles with the impeccable logic that they caused the greatest road damage. However, poorer Arkansans tended to drive older and heavier cars and were hit with the full increase when they renewed their annual vehicle registration. The numbers of aggrieved drivers grew each month as the renewal deadlines rolled around.

Misfortune magnified Clinton's political miscalculation. In May 1980 Pres. Jimmy Carter transferred to Fort Chaffee about eighteen thousand refugees who had fled Cuba after Fidel Castro threw open the gates at the port of Mariel. Carter disregarded Clinton's demands for additional military security. In June several hundred refugees left the fort and clashed with state police near the small town of Barling. When the Carter administration continued to relocate Cubans to Fort Chafee, Clinton did not publicly excoriate the president for fear that doing so would reawaken the nation's memories of Faubus's 1957 resistance. In that fall's general election campaign, Frank White, a former savings and loan executive and recent GOP convert, adeptly used footage of rioting Cubans in his advertisements to indict Clinton for endangering Arkansans to placate the Democratic president.

White had been director of the Arkansas Industrial Development Commission in the Pryor administration, but his pro-business outlook was not the only factor leading him to find a more congenial political home in the Republican Party. Strongly religious, White and his wife, Gay, were among the founders in the late 1970s of the Fellowship Bible Church, a nonsectarian fundamentalist congregation in Little Rock that grew rapidly in numbers and influence. At Ronald Reagan's inauguration festivities, White was a minor celebrity, a socially conservative, fiscally responsible businessman who had brought down one of the Democratic Party's rising stars.

For the 1981 session, the governor's program was little more than undoing a number of Clinton initiatives and curtailing agency budgets. He did endorse legislation allowing local governments through a referendum to levy sales taxes as a way to offset the anticipated demise of federal revenue sharing. Under this progeny of Pryor's Arkansas Plan, state lawmakers shifted the responsibility for tax increases to local officials, who retained the customary buffer of state turnback moneys. White did not propose the most prominent measure associated with the Religious Right agenda nor read the bill before signing it. Still, as the furor rose over the adoption of the creation science law, the governor firmly defended its purpose and constitutionality.

Approved by solid majorities with perfunctory debate, Act 590 effectively mandated that students in biology be informed that existing species had not evolved since the sudden creation of the universe. The American Civil Liberties Union filed suit on the grounds that the act violated the constitutional separation of church and state. The ensuing proceedings prompted unflattering comparisons to the 1925 Scopes Trial in Tennessee. After federal district judge William Overton struck down the law, Arkansas attorney general Steve Clark decided not to appeal the decision. In contrast to the reaction to unpopular court findings during the civil rights era, neither White nor legislative leaders set out to arouse popular outrage to pressure the attorney general to keep up the fight. The direst pronouncements erupted from national religious conservatives such as media evangelist Pat Robertson, who condemned Clark for offering only a tepid defense of the law.

Like Winthrop Rockefeller, White had not been hoisted into office by a permanent coalition, nor did his tenure foster Republican Party competitiveness. While the affable governor was generally well liked, his political ineptness was also reminiscent of Rockefeller's miscues. The outcome in the 1982 rematch of the 1980 gubernatorial contest was a personal triumph for Bill Clinton while also reconfirming Democratic supremacy. Clinton's coalition generally resembled that of other moderate candidates, but African Americans supported him more fully than they had other white politicians.

In his 1983 inaugural address, Clinton proclaimed, "Over the long run, education is the key to our economic revival and our perennial quest for prosperity." The argument was the heart of the enduring consensus in post-agricultural Arkansas that government activism was politically legitimate as long as it enhanced economic development. Education in particular enabled individuals to climb the ladder for themselves and in turn enrich Arkansas. In a 1987 speech to the national two-year college association, Clinton described the students enrolling in a Delta community college: "You see all those desperately poor kids coming in there, knowing that its their only shot to liberate themselves from the ravages of the world's economy." Throughout the modern era, viable political leaders tilted to the right or left edges of this consensus, differing only by degree on whether state support should be weighed toward business demands or toward school and infrastructure needs.

While Clinton's 1983 legislative program was modest in scope, a state supreme court ruling on school funding presented the governor an opportunity to restructure education more thoroughly than he had even dared hope during his ambitious first term. The *Alma v. Dupree* decision required that the state revamp its distribution of aid to narrow the gaping disparities in school-district income. With lawmakers resigned to the prospect of enlarging the education fund, Clinton proposed a one-cent increase in the sales tax, raising enough revenue not only to finance equalization but also to pay for a mandate that all schools offer a minimum set of courses and services. In a series of meetings throughout the state, an education standards committee chaired by Clinton's wife, Hillary, called attention to troubling statistics. At least half the school districts did not offer physics, advanced math, foreign languages, or music. The governor sidestepped the persistent controversy over consolidation, a political litmus test in rural communities, by endorsing the survival of small school districts if they met the basic standards. With the passage of the Clinton program, education became the state's core business.

While previous governors had made education a centerpiece of their administration, none had thrown themselves so completely into the enterprise as Clinton nor sought to extend its benefits beyond the schoolhouse doors and across generations. He pursued increased funding for adult training and literacy programs while touting early childhood development initiatives as critical to improving student academic performance. The Home Instruction Program for Preschool Youngsters (HIPPY), for example, trained lower-income mothers to teach the skills and concepts that would start their own children on the same footing as all their classmates. Clinton treated education as an instrument for social change. Those individuals and groups committed to a broader range of liberal principles became disenchanted with his insistence that educational improvements were more realistic avenues for progress than contentious measures to advance equity and workers' rights. In 1983 critical legislative support for the tax program depended upon the approval of a mandatory competency examination for all employed teachers. Clinton steadfastly defended the tests against sustained and passionate opposition from the Arkansas Education Association and in the face of evidence that those forced to leave the profession were disproportionately African American. During the same session, Clinton promised to back a tax rebate for low-income families if labor activists lobbied for his sales tax. He reneged, however, after state senate opposition to the rebate threatened to derail the entire measure.

Throughout the remainder of the decade, a shaky economy, along with the Reagan administration's cut in federal aid to states and localities, left Clinton largely fighting a holding action. General state government revenues increased by the smallest percentage in twenty years for 1985–86 and again in 1986–87. As part of a general belt-tightening, state officials ordered cuts in the school aid fund just as districts confronted the deadline imposed in 1983 for meeting the basic standards. Seeking to construct a legislative majority for another sales-tax rise, Clinton in 1989 included a provision to remove 260,000 poor residents from the income-tax rolls. The tax package failed by one vote in the senate. A bitter governor characterized the turn of events as "a disgraceful retreat."

In that year's session, a rancorous battle in the legislature over the desegregation of Little Rock schools exacerbated Clinton's despondency. After the court of appeals overturned Judge Henry Woods's order to merge the three metropolitan districts, the parties, including representatives of the district's black students, agreed to a settlement that required the state to provide $109 million to the districts as well as additional funds for magnet schools in Little Rock. Many lawmakers denounced the plan as plundering rural communities on behalf of big city kids, while urban representatives brandished figures documenting the disproportionate contribution of Little Rock taxpayers to the general education fund. Settlement supporters, however, played upon the opponents' dread of capricious federal judges to secure approval on the last day of the session. The settlement removed the state from the case. Officially, Arkansas closed the book on its part in the events of 1957.

As had Orval Faubus in his last run as an incumbent governor, Bill Clinton in 1990 won his final gubernatorial contest with a 57 percent victory margin over a formidable Republican candidate. Clinton's initial reluctance to stand for a fifth consecutive term lent weight to the claims of his opponents that ten years in office was long enough. Tom McRae, his challenger in the primary, was the past director of the Winthrop Rockefeller Foundation, which had issued reports during the Clinton years criticizing the state's regressive tax structure, lax environmental regulations, and inadequate health services. In the general election, Sheffield Nelson attacked his former ally as a big-government liberal whose policies discouraged business investment. These challenges from the Left and Right could not counter Clinton's entrenched network of local supporters and a nimble campaign operation that danced to the tune of its own polling results. While he had demonstrated the energy for another election battle, many wondered whether Clinton could avoid the atrophy that marked the twilight of the Faubus administration. The governor's prospects brightened with the outcomes of state legislative races. In senate contests, the victories by young, urban professionals sympathetic to the governor's goals accompanied the fall of east Arkansas intransigents.

The 1989 court decision forcing the state to redraw legislative district lines to represent equitably black residents did more than increase African-American numbers in the General Assembly. Jay Bradford, an incumbent white progressive, defeated perennial senate boss Knox Nelson after the two were thrown into the same Pine Bluff district. Nelson had been the mastermind behind the defeat of Clinton's 1989 tax measure. Although Clinton relished the consequences of redistricting, he had earlier joined with other members of the state board of apportionment to appeal the federal judge's decision on the issue. He assured his black supporters that he had done so primarily on technical grounds. Throughout his time in office, Clinton's commitment to power sharing had been exercised almost totally through the diversity of his appointments. He named the first African Americans to a wide number of boards and commissions as well as to be directors of the top-echelon Departments of Finance (Mahlon Martin), Human Services (Walter C. Patterson), and Health (Joycelyn Elders).

The new legislators joined like-minded moderates and liberals from earlier influxes of young Turks to enact Clinton proposals that had languished in previous sessions. Throughout the debates the advocates for the new programs described the higher expenditures as investments to stimulate creation of better-paying jobs and capital development. This tenet of modern Arkansas public policy became the foundation of the economic program of the first Arkansas president.

The General Assembly forced the governor to accept a .5 percent sales tax increase earmarked for education rather than his proposed 1 percent. The heads of large business enterprises swept aside the protests of their smaller brethren to accept a corporate income-tax hike to upgrade the state's poorly equipped vocational schools into technical colleges. The heavyweight leadership of the Arkansas Business Council—Tyson, Walton, and Murphy—shared the growing apprehension that a dearth of trained workers effectively saddled modernizing industries with a labor shortage. Clinton's broad conception of education was evident in the establishment of a state-supported residential math and science high school, grants for preschool enrichment programs for poor children, and college tuition scholarships for students from middle- and lower-income families. Higher gasoline taxes were put into place to jump-start road maintenance and new construction. In this session and again in 1997, the legislature enacted measures that exempted a large number of poor Arkansans from the state income tax. The reforms partially compensated for the regressive effect of escalating sales taxes. Still, a 1998 analysis concluded that Arkansas imposed the seventh heaviest income-tax burden upon families living at the federal poverty line.

Political observers ranked the 1991 session as the most constructive and activist since the 1971 legislature, which had enacted Bumpers's reforms. Without the new measures, Bill Clinton would have entered his first presidential campaign touting notably fewer accomplishments, dating primarily from the 1983 school equalization crisis. On 3 October 1991 Clinton announced his candidacy in front of the Old State House in Little Rock, declaring that he represented a new generation of leadership that would not be bound by the sterile liberal or conservative identifications. Outside the gates stood unnoticed a former governor who had raised taxes for education, formalized the state's industrial recruitment campaigns, and displayed an uncanny gift for connecting with ordinary Arkansans. Still incensed that Clinton had dismissed him in 1983 from a state patronage post, Orval Faubus was not among the cheering supporters.

As the crowds thinned that fine autumn day, Faubus crossed the street to the Stephens, Inc., offices, where the patriarch, Witt, held court at daily lunches attended by politicians, reporters, and business leaders. The closest approximation to an Arkansas salon, Witt Stephens took puckish delight in inviting guests with contrary opinions and then introducing a controversial topic to judge its effect. On this occasion Faubus found himself sitting at the same table with J. O. Powell, the former *Arkansas Gazette* editorialist who had written few kind words over the years about his luncheon companion. Whatever their observations on Clinton's prospects —conversations at Stephens's lunches were always off the record—these astute and knowledgeable men had helped shaped the era that had just culminated on the portico of the old capitol. Though suffering from failing health, Orval Faubus would live another three years. Making deals almost to the end, Witt Stephens died in December 1991. The *Arkansas Gazette* did not survive the month.

Reverence for the *Gazette* had deepened in the post-segregation era when many looked back proudly at its editorial criticisms of Faubus during the Little Rock Crisis. Its traditional layout and paucity of feature stories earned the *Gazette* the affectionate nickname of "the old gray lady." Although the uniformly liberal editorials and columns ran counter to grass-roots opinion, few questioned its primacy as the state's newspaper of record. By the mid-1970s the *Gazette* had almost a two to one advantage over the rival *Arkansas Democrat* in circulation and advertising revenue. With his paper on the edge of extinction in 1978, *Democrat* owner Walter E. Hussman Jr. defied expectations and began pouring money into the woebegone daily. His new managing editor, John Robert Starr, relished the underdog status and continually reminded readers in his daily column that he was making war on the *Gazette:* "I'm a street fighter and I know how to compete." A larger staff and expanded news coverage raised the *Democrat*'s creditability, and color graphics reinforced the contrast with its competitor. For its part, the *Gazette* strengthened its investigative reporting and devoted space to extended analyses of politics and education. In the end, however, improvement in the papers' overall quality was a sideshow to the war.

In 1986 *Gazette* publisher Hugh B. Patterson, whose father-in-law's family had owned the newspaper since 1902, withdrew from the fray. Drawing upon revenue from his profitable media operations in southwest Arkansas, Hussman had been able to discount *Democrat* advertising rates. While Hussman insisted that he only sought to reach parity with the *Gazette,* Patterson understood that Little Rock would not withstand the pressures toward a monopoly market any more successfully than other American cities. The sale of the *Gazette* to the Gannett Corporation seemed the most unlikely of pairings. The style of the expansionist chain was typified by their national daily, *USA Today,* which then offered casual readers vivid illustrations, abbreviated hard-news stories, and an abundance of human-interest features. The Gannett make-over of the *Gazette* represented one consumer trend that did not take hold in Arkansas. Those who had grown up with the *Gazette* resented the changes, and the new owners could not boost readership to compensate for their ample investments in production facilities. The *Democrat* also lost money during this phase of the war, but by 1991 it had virtually pulled even in circulation numbers. Impatient with losses exceeding $100 million over the course of five years, Gannett surrendered. On 19 October 1991, the day following the announcement that Hussman had paid $69.3 million to Gannett for the oldest newspaper west of the Mississippi River, *Gazette* and *Democrat* subscribers alike unfolded an edition of the *Arkansas Democrat-Gazette.*

Notwithstanding the rechristened banner or the *Democrat-Gazette's* official history, which traced its origins to William Woodruff's founding of the *Gazette* in 1819, the war ended with an acquisition and not a merger: the *Democrat* endured and the *Gazette* died. Contrary to expectations, Hussman did not attempt to recover from the years of red ink by slashing operating expenses; in fact, the paper became larger. The publisher was aware that his newspaper would continue to face heightened competition from television and digital news sources. In addition, the continued comprehensive coverage of state developments prepared the ground for the *Democrat-Gazette* to begin publishing in 1998 a special regional edition for the thriving northwest corner. Although *Gazette* loyalists gave Hussman grudging respect for the quality and breadth of his newspaper, they deplored the persistence of the *Democrat's* ideological bent. If the *Gazette* had suffered from liberal myopia, the *Democrat-Gazette's* conservative rigor was only slightly diluted with a careful rationing of moderate columnists. In contrast to the pragmatic originality of the state's artists, Arkansas political discourse continued to taper into echoing monologues and was ill equipped to counter the misconceptions about the state that flowered during the Clinton presidency.

Not unexpectedly, Pres. George Bush during the 1992 campaign both disparaged his challenger's record and questioned if leading "a small state" prepared one for the presidency. Normally, partisan depictions of Arkansas would have eventually faded as critics retrained their assaults on Clinton's presidential policies; indeed, in 1996 Sen. Robert Dole said little about the state during his unsuccessful run to unseat the incumbent. But the national media examinations accompanying the official Whitewater investigations customarily outlined an intricate scandal with its roots in "Arkansas political mores."

In December 1993 a *New York Times* article suggested that in the early

1980s Governor Clinton prevented the closing by state regulators of an insolvent savings and loan owned by James McDougal, his coinvestor in the Whitewater real estate development in Marion County. Crescendoing demands for a full accounting prompted U.S. attorney general Janet Reno in January 1994 to appoint Robert Fiske as special prosecutor to probe all matters relating to the financial ties between Clinton and McDougal. In August 1994 a panel of federal judges replaced Fiske with former Bush administration solicitor general Kenneth Starr. In the fall of 1998 Starr reported to the House of Representatives that while he made no recommendation concerning the Whitewater controversy, he did conclude that the president committed impeachable offenses while contesting a sexual harassment civil suit filed by Paula Jones, a former Arkansas state employee. On 12 February 1999 the U.S. Senate acquitted Pres. Bill Clinton on the two articles of impeachment that the House had approved on party-line votes the previous December. The stands in the Arkansas delegation mirrored the partisan split on the issue.

The prevailing thumbnail sketch of Arkansas changed little over the years of the Clinton presidency: members of an entrenched elite hold and exchange political offices to advance their common financial interests in a system devoid of the normal checks and balances. In the hands of Clinton's political opponents, the stock view was embellished with generous helpings of stereotypes. In late 1998 Republican presidential speechwriter Peggy Noonan characterized the president's efforts to counter the impeachment proceedings: "He acted as if he were still in Little Rock, still up against legislators in plaid suits who own the Chevy dealership. When Bill Clinton was governor and it was Yalie vs. the yokels, the yokels folded when you leaned on them. But Washington is not Little Rock." Outside Arkansas, neither southern editors nor southern historians condemned such moth-eaten derision, deepening the state's sense of itself under siege.

As it came to a close, the special prosecutor's exhaustive inquiry into Clinton's gubernatorial practices had rendered only one set of indictments touching upon public corruption. In August 1996 a jury refused to convict bankers Herby Branscum and Robert M. Hill on charges they illegally transferred bank funds to Clinton's 1990 campaign in exchange for patronage appointments. Whitewater's most long-lasting effect on Arkansas politics rose from indictments over the commission of fraudulent business practices in the mid-1980s by a future governor.

Elected lieutenant governor in 1990, Jim Guy Tucker became the chief executive following Clinton's presidential victory, and two years later he easily won a full term in his own right. Kenneth Starr's investigation into James McDougal's dealings produced the indictment of Tucker, who had been a McDougal business partner. When a federal grand jury returned a guilty verdict on 28 May 1996, the governor announced he would vacate the office on 15 July. (The state constitution prohibited those convicted of a felony from holding public office.) On that date, Tucker stunned those who gathered at the capitol to witness lieutenant governor Mike Huckabee's installation by declaring that he would not formally resign until the presiding judge ruled on whether a juror at his trial had been tainted. Late in the day, the state teetered on the edge of a constitutional crisis as both Huckabee, a Republican, and Tucker asserted their right to be governor. By evening, however, Tucker submitted his resignation after Democratic leaders urged him to step down.

Even though unelected, this third Republican governor of the century enlivened the hopes of his party that he would be more successful than his predecessors in breaking the Democratic monopoly over state offices. Five years earlier Huckabee had deftly reconciled fundamentalist and moderate factions during his tenure as president of the state's Southern Baptist Convention. As governor he was the nominal head of a growing party showing signs of developing an ideological wing within its northwest base of social and antitax conservatives. In 1996 Tim Hutchinson, the U.S. representative from the Third District, defeated the state attorney general to become the first Republican sent to the U.S. Senate since Reconstruction. His voting record in both the House and the Senate earned Hutchinson plaudits and high rankings from national conservative interest groups. While Huckabee had appeared to be allied with the religious right in his early political campaigns, the governor's positions blended with the prevailing economic development model.

The volatile 1997 legislative session, in which the General Assembly overrode an unprecedented number of gubernatorial vetoes, did Huckabee little political damage. In 1998 no Democratic officeholder took on the popular incumbent, who won easily over an earnest opponent. That election year was also the first decisively shaped by the 1993 term-limits amendment to the constitution. A large corps of veteran officeholders had exhausted the permitted three terms for representatives and two terms for senators. Even as new members made up over half of the one-hundred-seat house of representatives, Republicans modestly increased their number of delegates from fourteen to twenty-four. In 1999 the balm of prosperity and robust tax revenues smoothed the sharpest differences between Huckabee and the Democratic legislative majority as they agreed to underwrite the tourism industry, raise taxes to improve the highway system, and accept the deregulation compromise forged by the electric-utility interests. This bipartisan cooperation demonstrated the endurance of consensus politics even as the system became more democratic and inclusive.

On 25 September 1997 two natives of Hope, Arkansas, stood on the steps of Little Rock Central High to greet the nine men and women who had returned to the school they had desegregated forty years earlier. During the commemoration ceremonies, Ernest Green declared that much more had been at stake than the education of nine students: "What we needed was the same thing to which all people are entitled, a community that wants its children to blossom and not bleed, a society that encourages us to reach for our dreams and recognizes us as whole persons." When the speeches were finished, Pres. Bill Clinton and Gov. Mike Huckabee held open the tall wooden doors, and the nine walked into the building.

Selected Sources

No study of recent and contemporary history can rely only upon secondary works. This is particularly true of Arkansas, which attracted the attention of few scholars of southern history and did not support an academic press until 1980. Despite recent notable works, many topics lie fallow.

The Institute for Economic Development, located at the University of Arkansas at Little Rock, is a clearinghouse for demographic and economic data for counties and for the state as a whole. The information is readily accessible at www.aiea.ualr.edu. At Special Collections, University of Arkansas, Fayetteville, I consulted the manuscript collections of Daisy Bates, Robert Leflar, Virgil Blossom, and Hamilton Moses. In addition, I conducted interviews with Sen. Dale Bumpers, Marcus Halbrook, Brownie Ledbetter, Gov. Sydney S. McMath, Emon Mahony, Sheffield Nelson, Sen. David Pryor, and Judge Henry Woods.

Arkansas makes an appearance in several overviews of recent southern history: Numan V. Barley, *The New South, 1945–1980* (Baton Rouge: Louisiana State University Press, 1995); Jack Bass and Walter De Vries, *The Transformation of Southern Politics: Social Change and Political Consequence since 1945* (Athens: University of Georgia Press, 1976); Earl and Merle Black, *Politics and Society in the South* (Cambridge, Mass.: Harvard University Press, 1987); James C. Cobb, *The Selling of the South: The Southern Crusade for Southern Development* (Baton Rouge: Louisiana State University Press, 1982); Pete Daniel, *Breaking the Land: The Transformation of Cotton, Tobacco, and Rice Cultures since 1880* (Urbana: University of Illinois Press, 1985); Gilbert Fite, *Cotton Fields No More: Southern Agriculture, 1865–1980* (Lexington: University of Kentucky Press, 1984); Dewey W. Grantham, *The South in Modern America: A Region at Odds* (New York, HarperCollins, 1995); V. O. Key Jr., *Southern Politics in State and Nation* (New York: Knopf,

1949); Jack Temple Kirby, *Rural Worlds Lost: The American South, 1920–1960* (Baton Rouge: Louisiana State University Press, 1987); and George Tindall, *The Emergence of the New South, 1913–1945* (Baton Rouge: Louisiana State University Press, 1967).

The most thorough and useful general history of the state is Michael Dougan, *Arkansas Odyssey: The Saga of Arkansas from Prehistoric Times to Present* (Little Rock: Rose Publishing, 1994). More concise surveys are Harry S. Ashmore, *Arkansas: A History* (New York: Norton, 1978) and David M. Tucker, *Arkansas: A People and Their Reputation* (Memphis: Memphis State University Press, 1985). Indispensable guides to political developments are Diane D. Blair, *Arkansas Politics and Government: Do the People Rule?* (Lincoln: University of Nebraska Press, 1988) and Timothy P. Donovan, Willard B. Gatewood, and Jeannie M. Whayne, eds., *The Governors of Arkansas: Essays in Political Biography,* 2d ed. (Fayetteville: University of Arkansas Press, 1995). The evolution of governmental institutions and policy can be followed in Kay Collett Goss, *The Arkansas State Constitution: A Reference Guide* (Westport, Conn.: Greenwood Press, 1993). Those researching the state's history should begin with Michael B. Dougan, Tom W. Dillard, and Timothy G. Nutt, comps., *Arkansas History: An Annotated Bibliography* (Westport, Conn.: Greenwood Press, 1995).

Deserving special consideration for its exhaustive research and incisive analysis is John Kirk, *Race, Community, and Crisis: Little Rock, Arkansas, and the Civil Rights Struggle, 1940–1970* (Gainesville: University Press of Florida, 2000).

Chapter One. Depression Arkansas

Social and economic developments in the era before 1930 are insightfully covered in Carl H. Moneyhon, *Arkansas and the New South, 1874–1929* (Fayetteville: University of Arkansas Press, 1997). A good introduction to the most studied region in the state is Jeannie Whayne and Willard B. Gatewood, eds., *The Arkansas Delta: Land of Paradox* (Fayetteville: University of Arkansas Press, 1993), while those looking at the uplands will need Milton D. Rafferty, *The Ozarks: Land and Life* (Norman: University of Oklahoma Press, 1980). Early-twentieth-century exploitation of resources elsewhere is addressed in Kenneth Smith, *Sawmill: The*

Story of Cutting the Last Great Virgin Forest East of the Rockies (Fayetteville: University of Arkansas Press, 1986); Stephen Strausberg, *A Century of Research: Centennial History of the Arkansas Agricultural Experiment Station, 1888–1988* (Fayetteville: Arkansas Agricultural Experiment Station, 1989); and George W. Balogh, *Entrepreneurs in the Lumber Industry: Arkansas, 1881–1963* (New York: Garland Publishing, 1995). The consequences of the 1930 drought are described in Nan E. Woodruff, "The Failure of Relief during the Arkansas Drought of 1930–31," *Arkansas Historical Quarterly* 39 (winter 1980): 301–13; Roger Lambert, "Hoover and the Red Cross in the Arkansas Drought of 1930," *Arkansas Historical Quarterly* 29 (spring 1970): 3–19; and John I. Smith, "Reminiscences of Farming and Business in the Depression, 1929–1933," *Arkansas Historical Quarterly* 45 (winter 1986): 321–29.

A solid brief overview of the Great Depression is Donald Holley, "Arkansas and the Great Depression," in *Historical Report of the Secretary of State,* vol. 3 (Little Rock: Secretary of State, 1978), while a more comprehensive treatment is David Rison, "Arkansas during the Great Depression," (Ph.D. diss., University of California, Los Angeles, 1974). A number of works describe everyday life during the Depression, but readers can start with *The WPA Guide to 1930s Arkansas* (1941; reprint, with an introduction by Elliott West, Lawrence: University Press of Kansas, 1987); John G. Ragsdale, *As We Were in South Arkansas* (Little Rock: August House, 1995); and Rebecca DeArmond-Huskey, *Beyond Bartholomew: The Portland Area History* (Portland, Ark.: Portland History Project, 1996).

The Parnell highway scandal is put in legislative context by Lee Reaves, "Highway Bond Refunding," *Arkansas Historical Quarterly* 2 (December 1943): 316–30. Works on the major political figures of the decade include Cecil Edward Weller Jr., *Joe T. Robinson: Always a Loyal Democrat* (Fayetteville: University of Arkansas Press, 1998); Brooks Hays, *Politics Is My Parish* (Baton Rouge: Louisiana State University Press, 1981); Calvin R. Ledbetter, "Carl Bailey: A Pragmatic Reformer," *Arkansas Historical Quarterly* 57 (summer 1998): 134–62; and Donald Holley, "Carl E. Bailey, the Merit System, and Arkansas Politics, 1936–1939," *Arkansas Historical Quarterly* 45 (winter 1986), 291–320. The election of Hattie Caraway is described in David Malone, *Hattie and Huey: An*

Arkansas Tour (Fayetteville: University of Arkansas Press, 1989). The struggle of state and federal authorities over relief programs is told well in Floyd W. Hicks and C. Roger Lambert, "Food for the Hungry: Federal Food Programs in Arkansas, 1933–1942," *Arkansas Historical Quarterly* 38 (spring 1978): 23–43. The advent of black political reform is introduced in John Kirk, "Dr. J. M. Robinson, the Arkansas Negro Democratic Association, and Black Politics in Little Rock, Arkansas, 1928–1952," parts 1 and 2, *Pulaski County Historical Review* 41 (spring 1993): 2–16; 41 (summer 1993): 39–47.

David Moyers, "Trouble in a Company Town: The Crossett Strike of 1940," *Arkansas Historical Quarterly* 48 (spring 1989): 34–56, is one of the few accounts of an industrial strike. By contrast, much has been published on the rise and fall of the Southern Tenant Farmers' Union, including worthwhile examinations such as Donald H. Grubbs, *Cry from the Cotton: The Southern Tenant Farmers' Union and the New Deal* (Chapel Hill: University of North Carolina Press, 1971) and Jeannie Whayne, *A New Plantation South. Land, Labor, and Federal Favor in Twentieth-Century Arkansas* (Charlottesville: University Press of Virginia, 1996), as well as memoirs such as H. L. Mitchell, *Mean Things Happening in this Land: The Life and Times of H. L. Mitchell* (Montclair, N.J.: Allanheld, Osmum, 1979) and Howard Kester, *Revolt among the Sharecroppers* (New York: Covici, Friede, 1936). The definitive study of the resettlement communities is Donald Holley, *Uncle Sam's Farmers: The New Deal Communities in the Lower Mississippi Valley* (Urbana: University of Illinois Press, 1975). The saga of a radical college is traced by William H. Cobb in "From Utopian Isolation to Radical Activism: Commonwealth College, 1925–1933," *Arkansas Historical Quarterly* 32 (summer 1973): 132–47, and in "The State Legislature and the 'Reds': Arkansas's General Assembly v. Commonwealth College, 1935–1937," *Arkansas Historical Quarterly* 45 (spring 1986): 3–18.

Wendy Richter, "Celebrating Fifty Years of the Arkansas Historical Association," *Arkansas Historical Quarterly* 55 (summer 1996): 167–72, relates the founding of the organization. Examples of community life during the Depression are conveyed in Raymond L. Muncy, *Searcy, Arkansas: A Frontier Town Grows Up with America* (Searcy, Ark.: Harding Press, 1976); Nancy Apple and Suzy Keasler, *History of Lee County, Arkansas*

(Marianna, Ark.: Lee County Sesquicentennial Committee, 1987); and Stephen H. Dew "The New Deal and Fayetteville, Arkansas, 1933–1941" (M.A. thesis, University of Arkansas, 1987). The Depression-era search for cultural authenticity is noted in Pamela Webb, "By the Sweat of the Brow: The Back-to-the Land Movement in Depression Arkansas," *Arkansas Historical Quarterly* 42 (winter 1983): 332–43; Ben F. Johnson III, *Fierce Solitude: A Life of John Gould Fletcher* (Fayetteville: University of Arkansas Press, 1994); and Robert B. Cochran, "'All the Songs in the World': The Story of Emma Dusenbury," *Arkansas Historical Quarterly* 44 (spring 1985): 3–15. The discovery and celebration of Ozark folklore is cogently observed in Robert Cochran, *Vance Randolph: An Ozark Life* (Urbana: University of Illinois Press, 1985); Ethel Simpson, "Arkansas Lives: The Ozark Quest of Otto Ernest Rayburn," *Arkansas Libraries* 39 (March 1982): 12–19; and Ellen Shipley, "'But a Smile Looks Better in Print': The Literary Enterprises of Otto Ernest Rayburn," *Arkansas Libraries* 39 (March 1982): 20–23.

Interest in the state's image is not confined to civic boosters as indicated by the literature on the topic. A catalogue of Arkansas references in national publications is found in William Foy Lisenby, "A Survey of Arkansas's Image Problems," *Arkansas Historical Quarterly* 30 (spring 1971): 60–71, while Bob Lancaster, "Ill Fame," chap. 8 in *The Jungles of Arkansas: A Personal History of the Wonder State* (Fayetteville: University of Arkansas Press, 1989) is a shrewd commentary by the finest writer of Arkansas popular history. The influence of the federal jobs programs on cultural and tourism development is revealed in Joey McCarty, "Civilian Conservation Corps in Arkansas" (M.A. thesis, University of Arkansas, 1977); Fred H. Lang, "Two Decades of State Forestry in Arkansas," Arkansas *Historical Quarterly* 24 (winter 1965): 208–19; Lynda B. Langford, "The Works Projects Administration in Pulaski County District," *Pulaski County Historical Review* 35 (spring 1987): 2–15; Fon Louise Gordon, "Hattie Rutherford Watson and 'Mother-Wit': Exploring the Themes of Black Women's History" (Paper presented at the Arkansas Historical Association meeting, Pine Bluff, 17April 1999); and William B. Worthen, "Louise Loughborough and Her Campaign for 'Courage and Fineness,'" *Pulaski County Historical Review* 40 (summer 1992): 26–33.

The movement to preserve African-American history is brought to light in Bob Lancaster, "Early Hurt," chap. 7 in *The Jungles of Arkansas;* Thomas E. Jordan, "The Collection of Ex-Slave Narratives in Little Rock by the Federal Writers' Project," parts 1 and 2, *Pulaski County Historical Review* 40 (spring 1992): 2–14; (summer 1992): 42–47; and Fon Gordon, "Black Women in Arkansas," *Pulaski County Historical Review* 35 (summer 1987): 26–37. Students interested in two native African-American composers can consult Barbara Jackson, "Florence Price, Composer," *The Black Perspective in Music* 5 (spring 1977): 30–43, and John Michael Spencer, "An Introduction of William Grant Still," *Black Sacred Music: A Journal of Theomusicology* 6 (fall 1992): 1–60.

The conflicts surrounding the electrification of Arkansas are detailed in Stephen Wilson, *Harvey Couch: An Entrepreneur Brings Electricity to Arkansas* (Little Rock: August House, 1986); Clayton Brown, "Hen Eggs to Kilowatts: Arkansas Rural Electrification," *Red River Valley Historical Review* 3 (winter 1978): 119–26; E. F. Chesnutt, "Rural Electrification in Arkansas, 1935–1940: The Formative Years," *Arkansas Historical Quarterly* 46 (autumn 1987): 215–60; and Clyde Ellis, *A Giant Step* (New York: Random House, 1966). Background on the Flowers family of Stamps is offered in Bettye J. Williams, "Self-Representation in Maya Angelou's *I Know Why the Cage Bird Sings,*" (paper presented at the Arkansas Historical Association meeting, Pine Bluff, 17April 1999).

Chapter Two. Wartime Arkansas

Robert Palmer, *Deep Blues* (New York: Viking Press, 1981), is a wonderful history of Delta blues music. Both Palmer's later *Rock & Roll: An Unruly History* (New York: Harmony Books, 1995) and Robert Cochran, *Our Own Sweet Sounds: A Celebration of Popular Music in Arkansas* (Fayetteville: University of Arkansas Press, 1996) are necessary guides to the state's contributions to popular music.

The starting point for understanding 1940s Arkansas is C. Calvin Smith, War *and Wartime Changes: The Transformation of Arkansas, 1940–1945* (Fayetteville: University of Arkansas Press, 1986). A serviceable introduction to the period is Boyce Drummond, "Arkansas, 1940–1954," in *Historical Report of the Secretary of State,* vol. 3 (Little Rock: Secretary of State, 1978). A full history of an Arkansas military unit is Donald M.

Goldstein and Katherine V. Dillon, *The Williwaw War: The Arkansas National Guard in the Aleutians in World War II* (Fayetteville: University of Arkansas Press, 1992). Several strong essays examine the operations of government internment camps in the state: Cynthia Morris, "Arkansas' Reaction to the Men Who Said 'No' to World War II," *Arkansas Historical Quarterly* 43 (summer 1984): 153–77; Russell Bearden, "Life Inside Arkansas's Japanese-American Relocation Centers," *Arkansas Historical Quarterly* 48 (summer 1989): 169–96; C. Calvin Smith, "The Response of Arkansans to Prisoners of War and Japanese Americans in Arkansas, 1942–1945," *Arkansas Historical Quarterly* 53 (autumn 1994): 340–66; and Merrill Pritchett and William L. Shea, "The Afrika Korps in Arkansas, 1943–1946," *Arkansas Historical Quarterly* 37 (spring 1978): 3–22. The STFU's unequal fight with landowners is documented in Nan Elizabeth Woodruff, "Pick or Fight: The Emergency Farm Labor Program in the Arkansas and Mississippi Delta during World War II," *Agricultural History* 64 (spring 1990): 74–85.

In addition to the local histories cited above, the effect of World War II on town life is also covered in Odie B. Faulk and Billy Mac Jones, *Fort Smith: An Illustrated History* (Fort Smith, Ark.: The Old Fort Smith Museum, 1983); John Fergus Ryan, "An Argenta Memoir," *Arkansan* (August 1979): 12–21; B. C. Hall, "When Mississippi County Was the Land of the Pharaohs and Sunset Carson Was King," *Arkansas Times* (June 1983): 48–56; James W. Bell *Little Rock Handbook* (Little Rock: Publishers Bookshop, 1980); and Jim Lester and Judy Lester, *Greater Little Rock: A Pictorial History* (Norfolk, Va.: Donning, 1986). Histories of the largest church organizations in the state include E. Glenn Hinson, *A History of Baptists in Arkansas, 1818–1978* (Little Rock: Arkansas State Convention, 1979); Walter N. Vernon, *Methodism in Arkansas, 1816–1976* (Little Rock: Joint Committee for the History of Arkansas Methodism, 1976); and James M. Woods, *Mission and Memory: A History of the Catholic Church in Arkansas* (Little Rock: Diocese of Little Rock, 1993). Carolyn Gray LeMaster, *A Corner of the Tapestry: A History of the Jewish Experience in Arkansas, 1820s-1990s* (Fayetteville: University of Arkansas Press, 1994) is a comprehensive chronicle of a small but influential community.

Relatively few essays have been devoted to the experience of women in the post-1930 era. The general considerations include Janet Allured, "The Women of Arkansas: A Historical Overview," in *Behold Our Works Were Good,* ed. Elizabeth Jacoway (Little Rock: August House, 1988); Carol T. Gaddy, "Women of Arkansas," in *Historical Report of the Secretary of State,* vol. 3 (Little Rock: Secretary of State, 1978); Kitty Sloan, ed., *Horizons: 100 Arkansas Women of Achievement* (Little Rock: Rose Publishing, 1980); and Shirley Abbott, *Womenfolks: Growing Up Down South* (New York: Ticknor & Fields, 1983). Irene Hunter Jackson was interviewed by Susan Young for inclusion in "Good Times and Sorrow," Oral History Collection, Shiloh Museum, Springdale, Arkansas.

Federal investment in wartime Arkansas is surveyed in S. Charles Bolton, "Airfields, Camps, and Plants: Little Rock District U.S. Army Corps of Engineers Military Construction in World War II" (Little Rock: U.S. Army Corps of Engineers, forthcoming). An evolving twentieth-century industry is covered in Ray Poindexter, *Arkansas Airwaves* (North Little Rock, Ark.: n.p., 1974). The beginnings of industrial recruitment are disclosed in C. Hamilton Moses, "The Arkansas Plan," *Arkansas Economist* 3 (spring 1961): 1–7. A sympathetic, but not uncritical, examination of the poultry industry is Stephen Strausberg, *From Hills and Hollers: Rise of the Poultry Industry in Arkansas* (Fayetteville: Arkansas Agricultural Experiment Station, 1995). The impact of mechanization on cotton agriculture is explored in Donald Holley, *The Second Great Emancipation: The Mechanical Cotton Picker, Black Migration, and How They Shaped the Modern South* (Fayetteville: University of Arkansas Press, 2000). The antiunion campaign can be followed in F. Ray Marshall, *Labor in the South* (Cambridge, Mass.: Harvard University Press, 1967) and Edward Chess, "Agrarian and Labor Unions in Arkansas from 1870 to the Union Control Legislation of the 1940s" (M.A. thesis, University of Arkansas, Little Rock, 1996).

Guerdon D. Nichols, "Breaking the Color Barrier at the University of Arkansas," *Arkansas Historical Quarterly* 27 (spring 1968): 3–21, describes the state's initial public desegregation. C. Calvin Smith, "From 'Separate but Equal to Desegregation': The Changing Philosophy of L. C. Bates," *Arkansas Historical Quarterly* 42 (autumn 1983): 254–70, outlines the early career of the important civil rights leader.

Hot Springs is chronicled in Dee Brown, *The American Spa: Hot Springs, Arkansas* (Little Rock, Rose Publishing, 1982), while the rise and fall of a political boss is described in Nancy Russ, "The Life and Times of Leo P. McLaughlin," *The Record* 24 (1983): 65–71. A vanished era in the city's history is retold vividly by Shirley Abbott in *The Bookmaker's Daughter* (New York: Ticknor & Fields, 1991).

The effect of reforms on public institutions is evident in Jerry E. Hinshaw, *Call the Roll: The First One Hundred Years of the Arkansas Legislature* (Little Rock: Rose Publishing, 1986); Arkansas Game and Fish Commission, *Arkansas Wildlife: A History* (Fayetteville: University of Arkansas Press, 1998); Robert A. Leflar, *The First 100 Years: Centennial History of the University of Arkansas* (Fayetteville: University of Arkansas Foundation, 1972); T. M. Stinnett and Clara B. Kennan, *All This and Tomorrow Too: The Evolving and Continuing History of the Arkansas Education Association* (Little Rock: Arkansas Education Association, 1969); Xavier Zinzeindolph Wynn, "The Development of African-American Schools in Arkansas, 1863–1963: A Historical Comparison of Black and White Schools with Regards to Funding and the Quality of Education" (Ed.D. diss., University of Mississippi, 1995); and Linda Pine, "A Minimum Degree of Opportunity: A History of the Minimum Foundation Program Aid in Arkansas, 1951–1983" (M.A. thesis, University of Arkansas, Little Rock, 1986).

Electoral politics is deciphered in Boyce Drummond, "Arkansas Politics: A Study of a One-Party System" (Ph.D. diss., University of Chicago, 1957). An accomplished, underrated study is James E. Lester, *A Man for Arkansas: Sid McMath and the Southern Reform Tradition* (Little Rock: Rose Publishing, 1976). Randall Bennett Woods, *Fulbright: A Biography* (New York: Cambridge University Press, 1995) is a well-regarded portrait, although a dissenting perspective is found in Lee Riley Powell, *J. William Fulbright and His Time :A Political Biography* (Memphis: Guild Bindery Press, 1996). A notable contribution to recent political history is the exceptional Roy Reed, *Faubus: An American Prodigal* (Fayetteville: University of Arkansas Press, 1997). An important social welfare reform enacted during the Faubus years is described in Elizabeth F. Shores, "The

Arkansas Children's Colony at Conway: A Springboard for Federal Policy on Special Education," *Arkansas Historical Quarterly* 57 (winter 1998): 408–34.

The progress of industrial recruitment winds its way through Becky Thompson, "The Evolution of the Arkansas Industrial Development Commission from 1955 to the Present" (Report, Economic Development Institute, University of Oklahoma, 1996); James E. P. Griner, "The Growth of Manufactures in Arkansas, 1900–1950" (Ph.D. diss., George Peabody, 1957); and Kornelis Walraven, "Financing New Industry," *Arkansas Economist* 3 (winter 1961): 1–7. The career of Witt Stephens is detailed in an incisive series of articles by Ernest Dumas for the *Arkansas Gazette,* 27–29 June 1977.

A first-hand account of the revival of deer hunting is Herbert H. Lunday, "Memories of Buckeye Deer Camp," *Rivers & Roads & Points in Between* 13 (summer 1985): 2–8. The definitive history of the university football team is Orville Henry and Jim Bailey, *The Razorbacks: A Story of Arkansas Football,* rev. ed. (Fayetteville: University of Arkansas Press, 1996). A rockabilly pioneer tells his story in Jeannie Whayne, "Interview with Billy Lee Riley," *Arkansas Historical Quarterly* 55 (autumn 1996): 297–318.

The desegregation of the Fayetteville schools is scrupulously explained in Willard Gatewood's introduction to *Civil Obedience: An Oral History of School Desegregation in Fayetteville, Arkansas, 1954–1965,* ed. Julianne Lewis Adams and Thomas A DeBlack (Fayetteville: University of Arkansas Press, 1994), while another fine examination of early moderation is Jerry J. Vervak, "The Hoxie Imbroglio," *Arkansas Historical Quarterly* 48 (spring 1989): 17–33. The attempt to integrate southern minor league baseball is related in Jay Jennings, "The Black Bathers," *Arkansas Times* 17 (July 1991): 40–43, 52–57.

Chapter Four. Arkansas Divided

Shaped by the expansion of civil rights historiography and new research approaches, the narrative of the 1957 Little Rock Crisis has shifted from a focus on personalities to a greater recognition of community involvement, economic structure, and political culture. The range of perspectives is demonstrated in the essays appearing in Elizabeth Jacoway and

C. Fred Williams, eds., *Understanding the Little Rock Crisis: An Exercise in Remembrance and Reconciliation* (Fayetteville: University of Arkansas Press, 1999) and in *Arkansas Historical Quarterly* 56 (autumn 1997), a special thematic issue of the journal.

Memoirs of leading participants include Daisy Bates, *The Long Shadow of Little Rock.* (1962; reprint, Fayetteville: University of Arkansas Press, 1987); Harry Ashmore, *Hearts and Minds: The Anatomy of Racism from Roosevelt to Reagan* (New York: McGraw-Hill, 1982); Orval Faubus, *Down from the Hills* (Little Rock: Pioneer Press, 1980); Virgil T. Blossom, *It Has Happened Here* (New York: Harper, 1959); and Brooks Hays, *A Southern Moderate Speaks* (Chapel Hill: University of North Carolina, 1959). The shifting boundaries of white moderation are explored with considerable dexterity in Tony Badger, "Southerners Who Refused to Sign the Southern Manifesto," *Historical Journal* 42 (1999): 517–34; David L. Chappell, *Inside Agitators: White Southerners in the Civil Rights Movement* (Baltimore: John Hopkins, 1994); and Elizabeth Jacoway, "Taken by Surprise," in *Southern Businessmen and Desegregation,* ed. Elizabeth Jacoway and David Colburn (Baton Rouge: Louisiana State University Press, 1982).

Among the first attempts to consider the crisis within a broader context were Irving J. Spitzberg, *Racial Politics in Little Rock, 1954–1964* (New York: Garland Publishing, 1987) and Tony Freyer, *The Little Rock Crisis: A Constitutional Interpretation* (Westport, Conn.: Greenwood Press, 1984). Contrasting portraits of the 1957 school year inside Central High School are offered in Elizabeth Huckaby, *Crisis at Central High: Little Rock, 1957–1958* (Baton Rouge: Louisiana State University Press, 1980) and Melba Patillo Beals, *Warriors Don't Cry* (New York: Pocket Books, 1994). Neil R. McMillen, "The White Citizens' Council and the Resistance to School Desegregation in Arkansas," *Arkansas Historical Quarterly* 30 (summer 1971): 95–122, and Graeme Cope, "'A Thorn in the Side'? The Mothers' League of Central High School and the Little Rock Desegregation Crisis of 1957," *Arkansas Historical Quarterly* 57 (summer 1998): 160–90, study segregationist activism. The background and activities of the Women's Emergency Committee are related in the discerning Lorraine Gates, "Power from the Pedestal: The Women's Emergency Committee and the

Little Rock Crisis," *Arkansas Historical Quarterly* 55 (spring 1996): 25–57, as well the noteworthy Sara Alderman Murphy, *Breaking the Silence: Little Rock's Women's Emergency Committee to Open Our Schools, 1958–1963* (Fayetteville: University of Arkansas Press, 1997). Murphy's book also details the beginnings of the Panel of American Women.

Describing another urban reform group is Gary Delgado, *Organizing the Movement: The Roots and Growth of ACORN* (Philadelphia: Temple University Press, 1986). Urban development in Little Rock is sketched through Stuart Eurman, "Consolidating Cities: An Urban Fiction," *Pulaski County Historical Review* 42 (spring 1994): 19–22; Martha Walters, "Little Rock Urban Renewal," *Pulaski County Historical Review* 24 (March 1976): 12–16; Margaret Arnold, "Little Rock's Vanishing Black Communities," *Arkansas Times* (June 1978): 36–43; and Raymond Rebsamen, "Urban Renewal: Progress on a Timetable," *Arkansas Economist* 4 (fall 1961): 1–8. Henry Woods and Beth Deere, "Reflections on the Little Rock School Case," *Arkansas Law Review* 44 (1991): 972–1006, holds that federal appeals court decisions elevated the interests of the metropolitan school districts over those of black public school students.

Election reform is described fully in Calvin R. Ledbetter, "Arkansas Amendment for Voter Registration without Poll Tax Payment," *Arkansas Historical Quarterly* 54 (summer 1995): 134–62, while the fate of one of the casualties of the change is detailed in Robert Thompson, "Barefoot and Pregnant: The Education of Paul Van Dalsem," *Arkansas Historical Quarterly* 57 (winter 1998): 377–407. The first twentieth-century Republican governor is examined in Cathy K. Urwin, *Agenda for Reform: Winthrop Rockefeller as Governor of Arkansas, 1967–1971* (Fayetteville: University of Arkansas Press, 1991); John Ward, *The Arkansas Rockefeller* (Baton Rouge: Louisiana State University Press, 1978); and Billy B. Hathorn, "Friendly Rivalry: Winthrop Rockefeller Challenges Orval Faubus in 1964," *Arkansas Historical Quarterly* 53 (winter 1994): 446–73. Jim Ranchino, *Faubus to Bumpers: Arkansas Votes, 1960–1970* (Arkadelphia, Ark.: Action Research, 1972) reports the findings of the state's first professional political pollster.

Conditions in Lee County and the conflict over the health clinic are noted in Juanita D. Sandford, *Poverty in the Land of Opportunity* (Little Rock: Rose Publishing, 1978) and Marvin Schwartz, *In Service to America:*

A History of VISTA in Arkansas, 1965–1985 (Fayetteville: University of Arkansas Press, 1988). Largely forgotten now, the once-influential George Benson is examined in Edward Hicks, *"Sometimes in the Wrong, but Never in Doubt": George S. Benson and the Education of the New Religious Right* (Knoxville: University of Tennessee Press, 1994) and Lori Bogle, "Creating an American Will : Evangelical Democracy and National Security, 1913–1964," (Ph.D. diss., University of Arkansas, 1997).

River development is catalogued in S. Charles Bolton, *25 Years Later : A History Of The McClellan-Kerr Arkansas River Navigation System in Arkansas* (Little Rock: U.S. Army Corps of Engineers, Little Rock District, 1995); Mary Yeater Rathburn, *Castle on the Rock: The History of the Little Rock District U.S. Army Corps of Engineers, 1881–1985* (Little Rock: U.S. Army Corps of Engineers, Little Rock District, 1990); Gary B. Mills, *Of Men and Rivers: The Story of the Vicksburg District* (Vicksburg, Miss.: U.S. Army Corps of Engineers, Vicksburg District, 1978); and Sherrel Johnson, "Rolling on the River: Ouachita River Navigation in Arkansas" (paper presented at the Arkansas Historical Association meeting, Hope, 21 April 1989). A fine account by one of the state's pioneer environmentalists is Neil Compton, *The Battle for the Buffalo River: A Twentieth-Century Conservationist Crisis in the Ozarks* (Fayetteville: University of Arkansas Press, 1992). An informative overview of the effects of the environmental movement is Carol Griffee, *Environmental Quality Index* (Little Rock: Arkansas Wildlife Federation, 1994).

Chapter Five. An American State

Hope, Arkansas, is fondly described in Berton Roueché, *Special Places: In Search of Small Town America* (Boston: Little, Brown, 1982).

Essays that survey recent history include Dan Durning, "Arkansas, 1954 to Present," in *Historical Report of the Secretary of State,* vol. 3 (Little Rock: Secretary of State, 1978) and C. Fred Williams, "Modern Arkansas: World War II to the Present," in *Historical Report of the Secretary of State* (Little Rock: Secretary of State, 1998).

Most histories of Arkansas corporations are commissioned works, including Marvin Schwartz, *J. B. Hunt: The Long Haul to Success* (Fayetteville: University of Arkansas Press, 1992); Leon J. Rosenberg,

Dillard's: The First Fifty Years (Fayetteville: University of Arkansas Press, 1988); and Marvin Schwartz, *Tyson: From Farm to Market* (Fayetteville: University of Arkansas Press, 1992). A notable exception is the balanced Sandra S. Vance and Roy V. Scott, *Wal-Mart: A History of Sam Walton's Retail Phenomenon* (New York: Twayne, 1994), which can be read along with Walton's autobiography, *Made in America* (New York: Doubleday, 1992). The latest in a series of studies examining income and population trends is Jeffery T. Collins, "Arkansas Per Capita Income and Population: 1987–1997," *Arkansas Business and Economic Review* 32 (summer 1999): 1–7.

The barriers to African-American opportunities are revealed in Lawrence Santi, "Black-White Differences in Household Income in the State of Arkansas, 1989: Results of a Regression Analysis," *Arkansas Business and Economic Review* 31 (spring 1998): 1–13. Reasons for the slowdown in the growth of the state's per capita income are examined in Charles E. Venus and Dana Venus Hoover, "Comparative States Growth Study: The Arkansas Dilemma" (n.p., August 1997), while disagreements with certain of the Venus and Hoover findings are noted in Barbara I. Pardue, "Arkansas' Economic Development: Past, Present, Future," *Arkansas Business and Economic Review* 31 (fall/winter 1998): 9–19.

An indispensable overview of the evolution of mountain folklore practices and studies is W. K. McNeil, *Ozark Country* (Jackson: University Press of Mississippi, 1995). The persistence of folk medicine is documented in Justin M. Nolan, "An Investigation of Medicinal Plant Use and Classification in the Ozark and Ouachita Mountains" (M.A. thesis, University of Missouri, 1996). The folly that was Dogpatch is finely rendered in the "Marble City" chapter in Donald Harington's extraordinary *Let Us Build Us a City: Eleven Lost Towns* (New York: Harcourt, Brace, Jovanovich, 1986). A shaper of modern Eureka Springs is portrayed in Glen Jeansonne, *Gerald L. K. Smith: Minister of Hate* (New Haven, Conn.: Yale, 1988). A suggestive examination of the Helena Blues Festival is David S. Rotenstein, "The Helena Blues: Cultural Tourism and African-American Music," *Southern Folklore* 49 (1992): 133–46. Robert Adams Ivy Jr., *Fay Jones* (Washington, D.C.: The American Institute of Architects Press, 1992) is a generously illustrated consideration of a rich legacy. A unique examination of the evolution of a rural working-class African-American community is found in Charles E. Thomas, *Jelly Roll : A Black Neighborhood in a Southern Mill Town* (Little Rock: Rose Publishing,1986).

A number of essays devoted to post-Faubus political topics are reprinted in Richard P. Wang and Michael B. Dougan, eds., *Arkansas Politics: A Reader* (Fayetteville: M&M Press, 1997), but special attention should be paid to two articles in that volume by Diane Blair, "The Arkansas Plan: Coon Dogs or Community Services," 160–80, and "The Big Three of Late Twentieth Century Arkansas Politics: Dale Bumpers, Bill Clinton, and David Pryor," 371–400.

The production of works on Bill Clinton continues to gather steam, although few systematically examine his public career in Arkansas. Among the initial considerations of the gubernatorial phase are Phyllis Finton Johnston, *Bill Clinton's Public Policy for Arkansas: 1979–1980* (Little Rock: August House, 1983) and Charles F. Allen and Jonathan Portis, *The Comeback Kid: The Life and Career of Bill Clinton* (New York: Carol Pub. Group, 1992). Although devoted to the first year of the Clinton presidency, John Brummett, *Highwire : From the Backwoods to the Beltway—The Education of Bill Clinton* (New York: Hyperion, 1994) also recounts the Arkansas background from the perspective of a veteran state reporter. The most comprehensive personal portrait of the years leading up to the presidency is David Maraniss, *First in His Class: A Biography of Bill Clinton* (New York: Simon and Schuster, 1995).

Arguing that the Whitewater charges against Hillary and Bill Clinton had merit, James B. Stewart, *Blood Sport: The President and His Adversaries* (New York: Simon & Schuster, 1996) has been countered by Gene Lyons, *Fools for Scandal: How the Media Invented Whitewater* (New York: Franklin Square Press, 1996) and Joe Conason and Gene Lyons, *The Hunting of the President: The Ten Year Campaign to Destroy Bill and Hillary Clinton* (New York: St. Martins, 2000). Contrasting views of the impeachment and trial of the president are provided by Richard A. Posner, *An Affair of State: The Investigation, Impeachment, and Trial of President Clinton* (Cambridge, Mass.: Harvard University Press, 1999) and Jeffrey Toobin, *A Vast Conspiracy :The Real Story of the Sex Scandal that Nearly Brought Down a President* (New York: Random House, 2000).

Index

So they served as home missionaries, and Mother remained a worrywart but survived. When Dad entered the pastorate, each of his churches got not only a fine pastor but also an ideal minister's wife, who could teach at any level, excelled in girls' work, worked with young people, joined the women's society, invited groups to her home, visited in hospital or home with Dad... In a junior high class she discovered that one boy couldn't read. She tutored him every school day until he could. He became teacher of the men's Sunday School class. One year the head of the Baptist girls' organization in New York State was Adah Brokaw, my humble little mother.

Neither couple put pressure on their children to become missionaries, but we came by it naturally. Norm dedicated his life to Christian service at a summer camp during his high school years. I had been impressed with the missionaries who visited our little church, and well before I was ten I had determined to be one too.

We met in college. Norm began his studies aiming for a career in electronics, but various factors changed his mind. His freshman year he took calculus and radio. Radio wasn't a freshman course, and calculus seemed to have nothing to do with math as he had known it. He found both of them difficult. Then religion prof Al Pitcher advised, "If you have skills in technical fields and also in fields that help people, choose helping people. Our society is way ahead in technology and way behind in people relations." Norm remembered that he had taken aptitude tests showing he had abilities needed by a surgeon. Then he got interested in a certain young woman who was determined to be an overseas missionary.

We had met early in our freshman year. Jo, a freshman woman older than the rest of us, was engaged to a man back home, but she encouraged other freshmen to get together. She arranged a double date for her and me. Norm was her date. Now this was wartime. The only men on campus were 17-year-olds, like Norm, and 4-Fs, who had flunked the physical exam for the military. So our president had invited the armed forces to send V-12s, Navy and Marines who attended classes with us. They occupied the freshman women's dorms. And we freshmen women lived in the fraternity houses! Jo brought the men over to my house and introduced them. I looked at Norm and then looked higher and higher and finally reached the top. He measured 6'3". The other fellow, my date, was short with platinum blond hair. Both looked like engineering types, with slide rules dangling from their belts. We took a picnic to the local wayside park, where we sang "Smoke Gets in Your Eyes" and talked about the stars and theology.

After that Norm and I saw each other Sunday evenings at Fireside Fellowship, which happily crowded the pastor's house, but Norm was dating a professor's daughter. About Christmas time they broke up, and in the new semester Norm asked another freshman for a date. She was busy; he tried me. I was not busy, but that first date flopped. For some reason we went to a movie midweek. Norm was working in one of the dining halls, so the film had started before we got there. In those days, freshman women had to be in the dorm by a certain hour; we had to leave before the movie was over. The only time to talk was while hurrying down to the theater or hurrying back to campus.

Fortunately, there was a second date—the first time either of us had ever attended a movie on Sunday. This time we relaxed and talked over a soda, and many dates were to follow.

Summer came; we went to our respective homes in New York State and wrote to each other. Norm's mother invited me to come for a visit, and I did. On the way back to school Norm stopped to visit me. One evening we drove out on Lover's Lane, where Norm asked me to marry him.

"If it's God's will," I replied. It didn't take us long to decide that it was.

Then we had three years to wait. He gave me his fraternity pin at the end of our sophomore year. Instead of singing "Sister Jean has seen the light," my dorm mates exclaimed, "Well, it's about time."

Jean and Norm in the early years

Another year passed before my sweetheart serenade, at the end of which Norm was allowed to come up to my room (!) and put a ring on my finger. We graduated the following May, and in August my dad married us. Norm was accepted at the University of Rochester Medical School and found a room we could rent with breakfast privileges.

I trained as a teacher, specializing in English, French, and also biology because I was planning to marry a doctor. I never taught biology; that was just as well. I never would have cleaned up the lab in time for the next class. English as a second language was not offered in those days; it would have been more useful than Shakespeare, but I loved Shakespeare.

Our first year in Rochester I taught junior high English and discovered that I wasn't a junior high teacher. The second year I worked in an office. I taught Sunday School that year and discovered how delightful second graders are. The last two years I was privileged to teach second grade in a fine city school.

Our friends and classmates were graduated from seminary and ready for their careers. Norm had a fourth year of med school, then three more years of internship and residency after med school, in order to become a general practitioner with some experience in surgery. At that time most of our mission hospitals were one-doctor institutions; the physician needed to turn his hand to whatever needed to be done. Specialization was not appropriate.

Now was the time to start a family. Bobby was born ten years after Pearl Harbor.

During residency in Detroit we finally completed the application process and were commissioned as missionaries of the American Baptist Foreign Mission Society (ABFMS). We met the board in New York City on Jan. 20, 1953, the day President Eisenhower was inaugurated. I was pregnant with Grace and wore a peplum dress that I hoped would hide my condition. I was mistaken.

We were excited about our assignment to the Chin Hills of Burma. The ABFMS had two mission stations in the Chin Hills, Falam in the north and Tiddim in the south, but no medical work. Our job—Norm's job—would be to establish a hospital at Haka, centrally located between Falam and Tiddim.

We took advantage of being in New York to see some of the sights. One day we journeyed to the United Nations buildings. Because we hadn't allowed enough time for the subway trips, we missed an appointment with Dr. Freas, a Congo missionary in the States at that time. Had we talked with him, we probably would have saved a year out of our lives.

Norm completed his residency by the end of 1953. That Christmas saw our little row house in Detroit very full, with my parents, Norm's

parents, his brother and sister and brother's girlfriend all come to celebrate together. Most stayed to help with the move. The mothers took charge of the kitchen while Norm's sister, also named Grace, worked with us in the basement, recording each thing we put in a box to go overseas. Some friends, having read Gordon Seagrave's *Wastebasket Surgery,* donated used medical instruments. Grace inadvertently left out an "l" from "scalpel," so that her list of contents included "1 box scalpes."

Dr. Spock's book *Baby and Child Care,* the bible for new mothers, had warned me that moving was not good for a child right around two. Bobby had turned two in December. Having the house full of relatives no doubt caused enough stress already, but worse was to come. A couple in our church generously offered to take Bobby and eight-month-old Grace for a day so we would be freer. We gladly accepted, not considering that the children really didn't know the couple at all. They seemed to have a good time, and the host couple brought them to the farewell party at church that night. So far, so good. In the middle of the night Bobby started crying, and we weren't able to wake him up completely so we could comfort him. Furthermore, there was no place to take him so he wouldn't disturb others. Every bedroom was full, and to go anywhere else we'd have to take him through the living room, where parents were sleeping, or trying to. I thought, "If he's this upset now, what will it be like when we actually move?"

Moving day did come. Our pastor stored the boxes ready for Burma in the parsonage basement. I don't remember what happened to the furniture, but everything else went in or on our little Ford, named Henry, of course. We packed the back seat full from the floor up to the backs of the front seats. In the middle, dividing the space in two, stood a vertical, folded card table, reaching almost to the ceiling. When we were ready to depart, we slipped a snow-suited child lying down on each side of the card table, we got into the front, and off we went. Imagine what would happen if we tried that now! But the little ones didn't seem to mind at all. As soon as we were in the car, just the four of us, Bobby settled down and enjoyed the actual move.

I'm sure our long-suffering parents stayed behind and cleaned up after us. What would we have done without them!

We were traveling to Berkeley, California, for one semester at Berkeley Baptist Divinity School. The trip didn't go very fast; dear old Henry required a present each day. Albuquerque is the place where we bought the new water pump. Going across the desert we purchased a desert water bag, but unfortunately we hung it in front of the radiator, making the coolant boil faster.

Finally we arrived in Berkeley, in time to start the spring semester. Grace celebrated her second Easter before her first birthday, as

Easter came earlier the next year. The kids enjoyed playing with other small ones in the apartment building for married students. Norm took a full load of classes, including homiletics, while I remember a fascinating course in apologetics and an evening class in missions. I recall the prof asking us, "What will you do when you run out of love for the people you're working with?"

Usually willing to raise my hand, I answered, "I guess we ask God for a new supply."

We also took a course in linguistics at the University of Berkeley, with an exciting woman prof who talked about her friendship with the prince of Thailand. He knew many languages. Once she asked him, "Your highness, what language do you think in?"

"Mademoiselle," he replied. "I don't think!" Too many languages running around in his head.

Somewhere along the way I learned my first Burmese words, *"Bey go thwameley?"* It means, "Where are you going?" and I learned it as a greeting. Amazingly, people who know Burmese still recognize it when I say it! Of course I never learned anything to say after that.

Now why was that? When we had left Detroit for California, we'd thought we'd be sailing from the west coast. No, they sent us back east, speaking in churches along the way, to attend New Missionaries Conference in Meadville, Pennsylvania. That year the World Council of Churches met in Evanston, and we were blessed to hear some great world figures, including the literacy pioneer Frank Laubach and Canon Max Warren, head of the Church Missionary Society (CMS) in England, who taught our Bible study. What a privilege! For those of us who would be traveling through London—we had passage on the *Queen Mary* to Southampton and then on a P&O boat to Rangoon (Rangoon!)—he asked what we'd most like to do in London. One wife longed to see the queen, and Canon Warren promised to try to arrange that. We wanted to attend a Gilbert and Sullivan production; that would probably be easier to manage than seeing the queen. We didn't get to London that year, but Canon Warren wrote a special letter each Christmas to those green American missionaries he had taught, and many years later, when he had retired from the CMS and become a Canon of Westminster Abbey, we stayed overnight with him and his delightful wife at the Abbey. Our younger daughter's classmates didn't believe her when she said she'd slept at Westminster Abbey.

We never did see the *Queen Mary*, much less a P & O Boat. Burma did not grant us visas. While we waited, we lived alternately with Norm's folks in Jamestown, New York, and mine, near Utica, New York. When Christmas came and no visa, we decided we'd better start brushing up on the French we'd taken in college, because the next choice for us was the Belgian Congo. Now if we had talked with Dr. Freas that day two years before, he would have persuaded us to forget Burma and go to Congo. He was a great persuader.

Neither Jamestown nor Utica is a large city, but in each place our parents found a French tutor and someone else with whom we could practice French conversation. Our helpful mothers took care of the children so we could both have a lesson every day and study for the next day. Then the mission board sent us to Yale for a crash French course in the summer. We lived in half of a Quonset hut in a village built for students who were veterans. In the summer they were allowed to sublet. It was hot; the students would play hoses over the metal roofs of their homes, while the children splashed in little round pools. Every child's toys were marked with his name because everyone played with everyone else. We took the kids to a babysitter in the morning, then went to class. I did housework in the afternoon and studied in the evening. I haven't been so well organized since.

Back in Detroit I had entitled a deputation talk "We Don't Know Where We're Going, But We're on Our Way." How true that turned out to be! Finally on that September day in 1955, we were definitely, literally, geographically on our way—not directly to Congo but to Belgium for a year of study to prepare us to work in their colony. The four parents had waved good-by to us from the pier, with mixed feelings. They wanted us to go; we were fulfilling their dream as well as ours. But how they would miss us, especially my folks, because they had no other children to visit them! I found out much later that my mother had cried until Norm's mother finally told her, "That's enough, Adah."

CHAPTER TWO

Belgium

The ocean voyage passed smoothly. Experienced passengers described the Atlantic as a mill pond. One day the staff gave a party for the children, with balloons and professional photographs to keep the memory. We were surprised to have the steward announce, "Your bath is drawn, madam." One bathed first in sea water, and then rinsed off with a pail of fresh water provided for the purpose.

In the lounge one evening we were delighted to overhear a young Englishwoman say to an American friend, "You know, you really don't seem like an American." We knew she was paying her a compliment.

When the ship docked at Cherbourg, France, we were sent to a lounge to wait until called to go ashore in the lighter. People went out, and people went out, and finally we were almost alone. Fortunately we took the initiative just in time to avoid being left behind and going to Southampton by mistake.

Next lap: the boat train (the train that meets ships at the port) to Paris. With us were Joe and Ethel, another new American Baptist couple—in all we totaled seven couples and four single women

The party for the children on the *Queen Elizabeth*—how Bobby enjoyed it!

Yes, the *Queen Elizabeth!* Enjoying the deck—now Grace is having a good time too!

studying in Belgium that year—and a single woman who had already had a term in Congo. She described the French course we would take in Brussels. There were two sections, the *forte* or advanced class under the redoubtable professor Gilsoul, and the beginning, or *faible,* class, with a much easier prof. The French words mean literally "strong" and "weak." People dreaded M. Gilsoul but knew that they would learn a lot more if they studied under him.

We had supper at a nice little restaurant in the *Gare du Nord* before taking a night train to Brussels. The trip posed a problem for both our little children. There was no drinking water on board. One could buy pop or fizzy mineral water. Little Grace was thirsty but couldn't stand the fizzy stuff. She'd make a face and give up; then after a while thirst would make her take another drink, just as unsatisfactory. For Bobby the trouble came in the rest room. The toilet emptied directly onto the ground between the tracks. With the land rushing by at the bottom of that hole, he just couldn't do anything.

Arriving in Brussels, we must have been met by Mr. Coxill, whose job it was to take care of the many Protestant missionaries passing through Belgium on their way to the colony. Interesting for a tiny country to possess a colony many times larger than itself. Perhaps this would be a good place to speak up for the Belgians, who have been blamed for everything that ever went wrong in the Congo. Beginning in 1885, King Leopold I owned the Congo as his own personal possession, called, interestingly enough, the Congo Free State. It was free in the sense that other European countries didn't have to pay any customs duties. Leopold leased rights to companies that exploited the resources and the people. Vachel Lindsay's poem immortalized the custom of cutting off the hands of thieves. Surely the Belgian companies did not invent that method of punishment; it must have been practiced by chiefs before the Belgians ever came. No doubt people were much more willing to steal from the company than from an individual. At least, when we were there we found that people who would never steal from each other saw nothing wrong with taking from an institution, a school or a hospital. Its resources must have seemed limitless.

In 1908 the Belgian parliament took over the colony, which then became the Belgian Congo. They really did a lot of things right. They just about stamped out sleeping sickness with their public health program and kept down malaria in the agglomerations by spraying. Christian missions started schools long before the government did, but the government subsidized the Catholic schools, Belgium being a 99% Catholic country. When a free-thinking government came into power, they didn't stop subsidizing the Catholic schools; they subsidized the Protestant ones as well. Seeing what happened in India, where the British gave higher education to a few and no education to many, the Belgians decided to bring everyone up together, emphasizing primary education for the masses and delaying higher education. One result was that the literacy rate in the Belgian Congo compared favorably with that in almost all other African countries at that time. Officials at different levels of government varied, of course, in their attitudes and actions, but in general the colony was well administered. Of course, it was a paternalistic system, doing many things for the Congolese but not with them.

Obviously we didn't know all that on our first morning in the very European city of Brussels, with its medieval town hall, cathedral, and green market. Mr. Coxill took us to a hotel, explaining, "You'll stay here until you find a place to live."

Studying the menu for our first noon meal, we ordered, *"Filet américain* with *sauce anglaise, s'il vous plaît."*

Fortunately the kind waitress informed us, *"Filet américain* is ground beef served raw." Why they would call it American we never did find out.

We found an apartment on the third floor of a typical Belgian building touching its neighbors with no space between. There was a

What a fun place for Bobby and Grace to play!

tiny balcony in front, over the sidewalk. Since the September weather was definitely cool and the apartment boasted no refrigerator, I used to keep my milk bottle on the balcony until the neighbor on the second floor informed me, "The neighbors don't appreciate your displaying a milk bottle on the balcony. There's a *cave* (basement) where things will stay cool." It seemed a long way to go for a bottle of milk.

Right across the street a kindergarten was located, taking children from three to five. How ideal for Bobby! That was my first experience of the very formal, regimented style of Belgian education. In class the children did interesting things like making applesauce, but I was not allowed to visit. When it was time to go home, the children lined up and met their parents in order.

Most of our fellow missionaries were in Brussels to take the colonial course, required for teachers who wanted to be certified by the government so their schools could receive government subsidies. Doctors and nurses, however, studied tropical medicine in Antwerp.

Norm commuted, taking the tram to the train station, a train to Antwerp, then another tram to the School of Tropical Medicine.

His studies started with a crash French course for foreigners, which had already begun when we arrived. The colonial course had not yet started, and I, along with our colleagues, took the placement exam, a *dictée de sélection.* Belgian and French people, perhaps Europeans in general, love dictation. I think dictating whole sentences is a much better way to test spelling than giving individual words, but they use a dictation to test language capability in general, judging that if you can write down what the professor said you probably understand it. It's very hard to get a good grade because every wrong letter or punctuation mark counts against you, a grammatical error counting a whole point out of ten. To my surprise, the *dictée* was much easier than the one we had been given at Yale. It came from an early lesson in the French text we had used in the States! It began: *La petite Hélène est malade.* "Little Helen is sick." Not surprisingly, I was placed in the coveted and dreaded *forte* class, but I never did meet the famous Prof. Gilsoul.

Norm came home one day and announced, "If I have to commute I'm not going to pass the course." So we moved to Antwerp. Bobby dropped out of kindergarten and I did not take the colonial course. We American doctors' wives in Antwerp tried a session with a tutor and a night school course for Flemish speakers, then settled down to just living in Antwerp.

I'll never forget our last night in Brussels. I thought I'd better wash the blankets by hand, in the bathroom, and hang them in the bathroom to dry. I have no idea what we slept under that night. The landlady lived in Paris but happened to be in the house at the time. Our bathroom was on the landing between two floors, and her bedroom stood under it on the landing below. In the night she woke up feeling what she first thought was a small animal on her bed. It turned out to be drops of water coming through the ceiling from my dripping blankets. Oh dear!

Our apartment in Antwerp occupied the ground floor. The landlady lived next door, but her daughter and family were in the basement below us. When we took a bath we went down there. A toilet hid in a tiny closet across the marble-floored hall from our apartment. To wash your hands you used the kitchen sink. There was, however, a *bidet* in the bedroom. We ignorant Americans made fun of the *bidet,* but it came in very handy. We euphemistically called it a foot-bath; it was intended for washing the bottom. I think it was big enough for bathing the tots.

Here the kitchen was located at the back of the house, facing a walled courtyard where I hung clothes and the children played in safety. The kitchen window included a window box both inside and outside. Not having a green thumb, I used the box as a refrigerator outside at first, and inside when the outside temperature got down to freezing.

Passing from the kitchen, where we ate, through the bedroom, where all of us must have slept, one came to the living room, which looked out on the Avenue of the Americas, a beautiful boulevard with trams going right by our door. Once Bobby had been in the kitchen watching snow come down in the back courtyard. Then he walked into the living room for some reason, looked out the front windows and remarked in surprise, "It's snowing out there too!"

Bobby had a little sister, but he really wanted a baby brother too. I pointed out that Bobby was still wetting the bed. "How would I have time to take care of you and Grace and a baby brother too?"

That afternoon Bobby woke up dry from his nap. I was congratulating him when the doorbell rang. The three-year-old asked hopefully, "Is that the baby brother?" Talk about instant gratification!

The neighbors had two boys, Jean-Paul, seven, and Jean-Jacques, five. Bobby turned four in December. He used to play with Jean-Jacques, but of course he knew very little French. Jean-Jacques would tell him to do something, and Bobby would reply, *"Oui, oui,"* but not understanding, he wouldn't do whatever it was. This got very frustrating for the five-year-old.

Grocery shopping went on every day—to the bakery to buy *pain gris,* literally "gray bread" but very tasty; to the butcher's to buy meat—they left the door open on the coldest winter days so customers would come in, and the personnel all got frostbite; to the grocery store for packaged items; to the outdoor market for vegetables. There were so many kinds of cabbage, and they were always the cheapest vegetables. Now the Belgians made a wonderful soup with all sorts of vegetables and followed it with meat and potatoes for their main meal. I had the meat and potatoes and vegetables at noon and made soup with the leftovers for supper. So-called red cabbage is actually purple, isn't it? And when you save the cooking water to use in soup, it's blue. Bobby got tired of cabbage; I started calling it by its French name, *chou.* One day he proclaimed, "I don't want any more cabbage or *chou.*"

You didn't have to make your own soup if you didn't want to. In Brussels I could take my pan to the corner store and buy a liter of soup. In Antwerp the soup cart came to the door, holding vats with two kinds of delicious soup to fill my pan. On a nearby corner we could watch people making French fries in a glass-walled kiosk on wheels, and buy some wrapped in a paper cone. My neighbor Mme Neal found it easier to make her own!

Norm's French professor was delightful. His wife would invite students and their wives to their lovely home for an evening. She showed us their fireplace, lined with white tiles, each one hand-painted and different from every other—even those that were all blackened with soot.

At Thanksgiving time the prof talked with these American doctors about that American holiday: *les pères pèlerins,* "Pilgrim fathers," and *la dinde,* "the turkey." Then he asked, "Does anyone know how to say 'stuffed turkey'?" Well, during our tutoring days we had learned that you don't translate "I'm full" literally in French. If you're a man it means, "I'm drunk"; for a woman, "I'm pregnant." Our tutor had taught us the refined way to express the idea of having eaten plenty: *rassasié.* Norm had asked, "How do you say 'stuffed'"? Well, it depends on what you're talking about. A cushion is *rembourré,* but a turkey may be *farcie.* Norm wowed the prof by properly describing a stuffed turkey.

The tropical medicine course included different professors for different subjects. Norm took me along for one lesson on languages of Congo. Final exams were difficult because the Belgians believed in oral exams. That meant the prof asked you one or a few questions, and if you weren't up on the subject he chose for you, too bad. We heard about one luckless missionary who had missed a class in one subject and neglected to borrow a classmate's notes for that day. The prof selected that material on that student's final, and the student had to repeat tropical medicine. Norm passed, and was certified on a higher level than some of his colleagues because he had studied Latin in high school!

While our friends in Brussels had two full semesters of class, Norm finished about the end of January but had to wait several weeks to hear the results. We used the time to do a little touring. The organist of my dad's church in New Hartford, New York, was Welsh and had invited us to visit his estate in Wales. We took the ferry to the white cliffs of Dover and rented a little Austin to travel around England and Wales. Now we saw London for the first time. We drove down through Sussex and Surrey, then west to Stratford-on-Avon, but we didn't see a Shakespeare play. It was cold in England in February. We found out that it doesn't do a bit of good to let your sixpenny heater work while you're out; it doesn't heat the room but works only by radiation. It warms you only if you're standing in front of it. In Stratford we were given bricks to keep our feet warm in bed. The bathroom was again on the landing, with a sign on the door in case a line formed: "There is another WC at the bottom of the garden." We Americans had visions of digging down through the snow to the bottom of the garden.

Eventually we arrived in Wales, with its beautiful, unpronounceable place names. The address of the organist's estate comprised no numbers, only a series of names. We drove through North Conway and eventually found it. I had envisioned something on a cliff, perhaps a little more modest than Daphne du Maurier's Manderley. The estate turned out to be half a house on a quiet residential street. We received a warm welcome. The next day we were taken to visit the castle and other sights, including what was billed as the smallest house in the world. There were two floors. We were told that the fisherman who had occupied the house was tall, so his legs stuck out the upstairs window. The neighboring women used to take advantage of him by hanging their laundry on the projecting lower extremities. The house actually existed; the story about it was something else again. Across the bay we visited Llandudno, with a statue of Alice in Wonderland.

With another couple we spent one day touring the Netherlands. I was surprised to find the country at least half Catholic. In the States you find rest rooms at gas stations; it was not so in the Netherlands. We had to stop at a restaurant or tea shop to attend to those needs. A missionary already in the Congo had asked us to buy her a light woolen blanket, so we looked for the proper store in the narrow streets of Amsterdam. It was easy to find the word "pure"—*zuiver*—but how to say "light"?

By the way, did you wonder why we learned French, not Belgian? There is no Belgian language. Belgium is made up of Walloons in the southeast, who speak French, and Flemings in the northwest, who speak Flemish. The Dutch say Flemish is a dialect of Dutch, but the Flemings are sure it's a separate language, and our friend and colleague Don told us it's the language closest to English. We did not try to learn it, although it's the language of Antwerp, and people there did not like to use French. (Our neighbors the Neals were an exception.) I tried very hard at the train station to ask for a round-trip ticket to Brussels in French good enough so I wouldn't be answered in English. One day Bobby remarked, "God knows all languages, even Flemish."

Back in the Netherlands, we finished the day driving through fishing villages in the northwestern provinces. It felt cozy to be able to look in through undraped windows that went down almost to the floor and see families at their evening meal.

For our last trip we rented a Renault and drove first to Paris. It was so cold! We'd drive until our feet felt freezing, then walk a while till our hands got too cold. Bobby lost his cap in the Seine. We visited Notre Dame but couldn't climb way up on account of glare ice on the stairs. Versailles was amazing; it went on and on. Louis XIV slept in a very short bed. People weren't as tall in those days, but also I understand they sort of sat up in bed. Then the gardens went on and on too, with lots of statuary. Finally we got to the Grand Trianon and the Petit Trianon, where Marie Antoinette put on plays. Too bad Bobby was too young to remember. When he was in high school I tried to tell him about Versailles for a test he had to take the next day, but he was so sleepy his eyes glazed over and nothing penetrated.

CHAPTER THREE

To the Congo by Freighter

Our American Baptist colleagues came from Brussels to the pier to see us off on the *Armand Grisard.* Since Norm was a doctor, we were allowed to travel by freighter. We never found out who Armand had been, but the ship carried a cargo of ferry boats and salt fish. With us went John, another American doctor, with his wife and little girl. John had grown up in the Congo, so his experience and knowledge of the Kikongo language were invaluable. Becky was a little younger than our Grace. Grace wore her hair long and her dresses short; Mennonite Becky did just the opposite.

As soon as we had unpacked in our staterooms, Jeanne suggested, "Let's ask where we can find an ironing board and iron our clothes."

"That's a good idea," I assented. I never would have thought of it myself! The room they showed us was small and hot, and I felt a little seasick, but it didn't last.

There were two other passengers, an American single woman missionary and a Belgian woman. It must have been lonely for the Belgian: I don't remember our reaching out to her at all. How selfish of us! The American woman loved children and was happy to watch ours. And I was happy to let her. During that trip of two weeks or so I wrote 75 letters, put our tiny grayscale photos from Europe in an album, and gave myself a Tip-Toni. Photos taken since that time never made their way into albums, our correspondence is woefully neglected, and I have never again given myself a perm. The children had a ball exploring the ship and did not fall overboard. Once Bobby was allowed to hold the wheel that steers the ship. We were given a photo to prove it.

Life on a freighter was quite luxurious for the passengers. The meals always included several courses, with a selection of cheeses just before dessert, and coffee last of all in solitary splendor. A small meal was served mid-morning. The last evening they brought out Baked Alaska flambé. I was so disappointed! The brandy they had poured over it and ignited spoiled the flavor.

Actually the food was too rich. Grace and I both developed diarrhea two or three days before we landed in the Congo. I wondered if we couldn't just keep on enjoying the food and worry about the diarrhea later, but the good doctor limited us to white foods—potatoes and rice, primarily. We didn't really recover till we were eating wholesome Swedish food at the mission guest house in Matadi.

In the meantime we had stopped in the Canaries—not on Ténérife, as most ships did, but at Las Palmas on Palm Sunday! We saw the Palm Sunday procession, with a number of barefoot men carrying a representation of Jesus on the donkey. We were impressed with the wealth of the Catholic Church—lots of gold in the church buildings—and the poverty of the people, some of whom lived in caves. And we took pictures of goats. We had taken pictures of goats in Switzerland, which we visited after Paris, and we would take more pictures of goats in the Congo. Goats seem to be quite ubiquitous.

We made port again at Pointe Noire in what was then French Equatorial Africa. There are now two countries called Congo, the former French Congo (Republic of Congo) and the former Belgian

Congo (DRC or Democratic Republic of the Congo), across the river—very confusing. This was our first sight of Africa and Africans, our first hearing of Kikongo.

We were still on the ship on Easter Sunday. John held a service for the African crew. They all took off their shoes before worship.

Grace had her third Easter on shipboard, before her third birthday.

April 2, 1956, we made our way some 100 km up the Congo River to the port of Matadi. That's as far as the first Portuguese explorers got. Upstream from Matadi there are rocks and rapids; the river doesn't become navigable again till Kinshasa, which was called Leopoldville in those days, after the Belgian king who owned the country for 23 years. *Matadi* means rocks. The men unloading our freighter sang or chanted, *"Rrrhaa!";* maybe it corresponded to "Yo ho, heave ho!"

Matadi ascends from the river. The post office and government buildings and hotels occupy a level well above the docks, and then the streets climb up and up before you arrive at the Swedish mission—simple, clean, welcoming—our first taste of life in the Congo. It was good to see our first indoor lizard in the guest house living room with other people about, who assured us a lizard was good to have around, as it ate insects. This one was the small white kind, almost transparent. Years later Bobby's little brother would watch them crawling on the outside of the window screen and try to mark one's white belly through the screen so he would know it was his.

At the post office I encountered my first example of discrimination. There were two lines, a short one for whites and a long one for Congolese. I knew I should not accept the privilege, but I justified taking advantage of it because my time was limited. Did I think their time didn't count?

"We'd better buy enough bread and a few other things here to carry us through our first week in the bush," John told us. So we did. What did we know? On the day of our departure the Swedish missionary in charge of the guest house made us lunch to take on the train, including green bananas. They were ripe and overripe by afternoon.

The train was scheduled to arrive at Sona Bata, 50 miles before the capital city of Leopoldville, at 2:30, but it was rainy season and there had been a washout. We waited four hours. Then we were going again. Bobby looked eagerly for villages along the way. At first they were all well removed from the railroad right of way, but when he finally spotted one he wanted to get off the train and tell the villagers they needed to wear shoes. We had impressed upon him the necessity of wearing shoes in that country where hygiene may be minimal and walking barefoot presents various hazards. He wanted to share his protective knowledge. A couple of years later, at Sona Bata, he would rush into the house exclaiming, "There's a boy here who's not Congolese!"

"Not Congolese? He isn't black?"

"Oh, he's black all right, but he's a shoe boy! He wears shoes like us!"

CHAPTER FOUR

Sona Bata

The train arrived at Sona Bata at 6:30. By that time it was dark. I turned to the Belgian in our compartment, who had befriended these newcomers to the country, and asked, "Is this really Sona Bata?"

He assured me it was. The station had no electricity, only a lantern. We disembarked with our luggage; Norm asked for the stationmaster. *"C'est moi,"* replied the man. "It's me," or "I'm it."

Norm replied, "I'm the new doctor."

"Tiens, tiens!" replied the *chef de gare*. That translates, "Well, well," or in this case I think, "Well, whaddaya know about that!"

The Sona Bata missionaries knew we were coming but didn't know what day to expect us. The stationmaster sent word up the hill to the mission station by means of a boy, I imagine, and in due time our senior missionary, Roland, arrived in a Combi (Comb-bee)—Volkswagen bus—to pick us up. He had been working on the electricity in our house; Sona Bata possessed a generator that was operated from 6:00 p.m. till 9:00. Roland had inadvertently cut off the current for the whole station.

It's possible that no other missionary was ever greeted exactly the way we were that evening. Ordinarily, when new missionaries arrived, the school boys and girls were brought out to sing to them. We had come during Easter vacation—no school kids around. But Norm was the long-awaited new doctor. Sona Bata had seen our first American Baptist hospital in the Congo, with Dr. King in charge, before we were born, and our first Protestant nurses' training school. Dr. Tuttle and his British colleague had moved that school to Kimpese, where there was more room to expand. The school at Sona Bata now gave two years of training, turning out something between practical nurses and nurses' aides. After the departure of the four-year school, Sona Bata had continued with one doctor, and for the past six months a missionary nurse had been in charge.

When the Combi reached the top of the hill, we were told we were outside our house, the doctor's house, separated from the hospital by a tennis court. Of course we couldn't see anything, but from the darkness came singing. The hospital staff, patients' relatives, and patients were standing on our lawn singing to welcome us.

In the morning a wizened little woman came over, took Norm's hands, and knelt in front of him. Of course we couldn't understand her words, but we gathered the sense of them: "Thank God you've come."

The early years of mission work in the Congo—the late 1800s—were terribly difficult. Few missionaries lived to return to their home country after one term. They died of malaria, sleeping sickness, or some tropical infection they had never developed resistance to. Language had to be learned with no manual and no informant who knew the language you were coming from. Living conditions were starkly primitive, and missionary efforts were met with suspicion.

In recent years missionaries have again met with suspicion and mistrust, to say nothing of riots and civil wars. Runaway inflation, political instability, and collapsed infrastructure have made it very hard to carry on the work.

We arrived in the Congo in the halcyon days. Missionaries were welcomed and appreciated. Boys and, increasingly, girls were eagerly sent to school. Life went along on a pretty even keel. There were problems, of course, but in comparison with those who went before and those who came after, we had it easy.

Back to April 4, 1956. Eventually the songs came to an end and the Combi moved on, straight up to the steps of a duplex shared by Eva and Esther. Esther was the nurse who had carried the whole responsibility of the 100-bed hospital since the doctor had left and who would continue to carry a good deal of it as Norm studied Kikongo and learned the ropes. Eva, an experienced missionary, directed both the primary school and the teachers' training school. During the brief time that we waited down at the station, Roland or someone, probably Esther, had alerted the hospital to our arrival and Eva had fixed supper for us. We enjoyed a royal welcome.

After supper we were introduced to our house by the light of a kerosene lamp or two. In our large bedroom stood a 3/4 bed and a single hospital bed. There was a small bedroom for the two children, but the place seemed so new and strange we decided to share the 3/4 bed and put the children in the single bed, one at the head and the other at the foot. We had done that trick while visiting England. Of course the weather here was hot; we probably put only a sheet over them, and it wasn't tucked in well enough; the bed was pretty high, and the floor was made of concrete. Grace fell out and met people the next day with a swollen lip.

Morning came about 6:30. Daylight allowed us to explore our new home. Early missionary bungalows were spacious and airy. Our square house was divided into four parts: living room, dining room, bedroom, and the other quarter divided into a long bathroom and a walk-through closet. A screened veranda went all the way around the house. Behind the veranda in back stood a four-room cookhouse: sink kitchen on the left, with the storeroom behind; stove kitchen on the right, with a laundry room behind. That was the original house. In the early days Congo missionaries sent their babies back to the States for health reasons, but after one brave missionary wife pioneered keeping children on the field with their parents, another bedroom was needed. In this case, a corner of the veranda next to the bathroom was closed in for the children's room. Another corner had been walled in for the doctor's home office. Every room opened onto the veranda. I counted 11 outside doors. That first term we never locked any of them unless we were going to be away overnight. It was a good place to live. The living room included a fireplace, but we almost never used it. I had supposed that dry season would be hot, but the mornings could be surprisingly chilly. However, who has time to sit around the fireplace in the morning?

Our senior missionaries had made up a meal schedule so we didn't have to cook for ourselves the first week. We didn't need all that bread we'd bought in Matadi! The next year a new couple came, and we were one of the host families. As Orville and Virginia left after the first meal, they thanked us.

"You'll be back here on Thursday," I assured them.

"Oh, I hope not!" Orville burst out. We laughed, realizing he meant, "We don't want to be a burden."

During that first week we got acquainted with the beautiful station of Sona Bata, built on seven hills, like Rome. Two of them, near the hospital, held the dormitories for male and female nursing students and hospital staff. Our senior nurse had been trained when students were required to be married. Each man needed a wife to grow food and cook for him. He had had five years of primary school and then five years of nurses' training at Sona Bata, after which he performed like a doctor, diagnosing and treating patients and performing minor surgery. Now the four-year students at Kimpese completed nine grades before entering nurses' training; ours had had six, and they were young and unmarried.

Missionaries called the two main hills Prayer Hill and Pill Hill. We, of course, lived on Pill Hill. The other hill housed the church, Eva's two schools and a homemaking school for girls, and the homes of those who worked there plus students' dormitories. I preferred to call it Pulpit Hill, contending that just as much prayer went up from the medical side. In the valley between those hills stood the precious generator, which supplied electricity from 6:00 to 9:00 p.m.

Roland and Lillian occupied the big, light, airy house nearest the road that went by both our mission station and the village of Sona Bata. Another large house on that side was called the Coop. It had been made for two single missionaries. Only Madelyn was occupying it now. She had charge of the homemaking school and did me the great favor of transferring her cook to our employ. He had previously been a painter at the hospital; she had trained him to cook. Before I started being on my own for meals, with Kikongo lessons beginning the same day, I took her three small pieces of paper on which I had written words and phrases I'd need to know those first few days. She filled in the Kikongo equivalents.

Right away I ran into a snag with Tata Nzeza. Dear Eva came over to help me get started. The first thing I said to the new cook was: "Go get drinking water." We had running water in our houses, but the spring water was considered better for drinking.

The ex-painter informed Eva (since I wouldn't understand), "I don't fetch water, I'm a cook. She needs a boy (helper) to get water."

Tactfully Eva suggested, "Since she doesn't have a boy yet, perhaps you could go for water this one time."

He agreed, I breathed a sigh of relief, and Eva went back to her work.

When Tata returned from the spring I consulted my little sheets and told him in the Kikongo on my little paper, "Mop the floor."

He replied, *"Ka mambu ko; si ya sukula."* What did he mean? I knew *sukula;* it was the word I'd used for "mop" (wash). But what did the rest of the words signify? Was he refusing again? I hotfooted it as fast as I could go to Eva's house, repeating all the way, *"Ka mambu ko; si ya sukula."*

Eva and Esther got a good laugh when I burst breathlessly into their living room saying, "He says, *'Ka mambu ko; si ya sukula.'* What does that mean?"

"It means, 'All right. I'll mop.'" Madelyn had given me *"Ka diambu ko"* for "all right," literally "no problem," but how was I to know that *mambu* was the plural of *diambu* and was used the same way?

After that Tata Nzeza and I got along all right. He didn't read, so if I wanted him to make something Madelyn hadn't taught him I had to show him how. The first time I wanted pancakes I said the word in English—no comprehension. I tried the French word, *crêpes*—no.

Then I started making them in front of him, and the light dawned: "Oh, *panakukasi."* Kikongo seldom puts two consonants together and ends every word with a vowel, so "pan-cake-s" had to have three more syllables.

I think of two incidents connected with Tata Nzeza. Once I threw away a doll of Grace's that had lost a leg or an arm.

He picked it out of the wastebasket and asked, "Could I take this home to my little girl?"

"Yes, indeed, Tata," I replied.

Later I told Grace, "Tata Nzeza's little girl doesn't have any dolls."

She responded immediately, "I'll give her some."

Much later, on a more primitive station, Grace was attending second grade in the local school. The teacher remarked one day, "You girls should really have three dresses: one for school, one for work and play, and one for church."

Grace came home troubled: "I have lots more than three."

Once Tata Nzeza came to work upset. Someone had put a hex on his house, he informed me. He had found a bunch of grass in front of the house that he was sure was a fetish intended to harm his family. He wanted to move from his concrete block house to a grass hut. I couldn't change his mind. I hadn't realized he was not a Christian. After that I talked to him about Jesus, but I'm sadly sure his life was not changed as a result of that conversation.

After a week to get settled at Sona Bata, Norm left for a month's *stage* at the Evangelical Medical Institute in Kimpese, called by the French initials IME. This was the medical complex founded by the two doctors who had been at Sona Bata and looked for more room to expand. From the train we had seen some of the buildings; now Norm was to have his Congo internship there, learning how to practice medicine in tropical Africa. Toward the end of the time the children and I joined him. That night I woke up crying out, having dreamed that a snake was coming in through the ventilation opening high up near the ceiling.

That same weekend a patient named Rémy was brought in. Rémy was such a fine, gifted Christian teacher that senior missionary Mary had found a way to send him to Belgium for normal school, a teacher training institute on a junior college level. He was the first of our mission to go that far in education. He had returned from Belgium shortly after we arrived there. The missionaries were thrilled to have a well-trained Congolese teacher taking over some of the courses.

But now he was desperately ill. IME was the best hospital around, but in spite of all efforts he died. I remember praying for a resurrection!

Autopsy showed that a parasite had localized in the brain tissue—very unusual. That was the scientific explanation. Many local people believed that sorcery had been used against him because he had got too far ahead of his fellows. Americans admire heroes who stand head and shoulders above the crowd. In Congo you don't want to stand out.

Years later I was looking for a student who could take charge of the PE class that day, since the teacher was sick. I stuck my head inside the classroom door and called out, "Who's the best soccer player?"

The answer came back, "We're all identical."

After his time in Kimpese Norm had another week or two of internship in Leopoldville, the capital, also the headquarters of the American Baptist Foreign Mission Society in the Congo. We joined him there too and got acquainted with the missionaries in the city. I went up to someone's house one day and knocked on the door. The missionary called out, *"Nani?"*

I replied, "It's not Nani, it's me." That was how I learned that *nani* means "who."

Back at Sona Bata Norm got into the routine of hospital work, saving half the day for Kikongo study as long as Esther was there. Rémy's death made a difference at our station. Educational missionaries Jim and June were transferred from Sona Bata to Nsona Mpangu to take Rémy's place. I don't know what they did about other courses, but I was asked to teach sixth grade French. At that time the Belgian colonial government was trying something new: They separated out the best students finishing fifth grade and made an elite sixth grade of those preparing to go on to secondary education, which then consisted of two three-year sections. We had no secondary school at our station. Nsona Mpangu had the first section. In our area only Kimpese offered a complete high school education. It was a union station, where several missions worked together in educational and agricultural work as well as medical.

Grace had celebrated her third birthday shortly after arriving at Sona Bata. Before Jim and June left she enjoyed playing with their Betty Sue and admiring her new baby sister. One day she reported, "Betty Sue's baby is all made of little stuff."

My class came early in the morning. One day I came home to find the children at the breakfast table joyfully throwing the dishes at each other. I had asked Tata Nzeza to watch them, but unfortunately I used the wrong verb, one that means to look at rather than to supervise. So he obediently watched them throw the dishes around.

We spent over three years at Sona Bata. Norm was very busy, the only doctor for the 100-bed hospital, also in charge of the nursing school and several rural dispensaries which required regular visits. Kimpiatu, the head Congolese nurse, was an invaluable help with learning the language, learning the customs, understanding what was going on and just listening when Norm needed to share problems. Once every three months Norm made a surgical visit to Boko, a mission station a long, difficult day's journey away. Boko had a hospital run by a missionary nurse but no doctor. I remember complaining to that nurse, "I'm so slow."

She responded, "I am too, so I have to work long hours." All right, Jean, that's what you do about it.

Norm was a slow, painstaking surgeon and a good, patient teacher. When our second-year nursing class was to graduate we had equal numbers of girls and boys. The girls excelled! Norm had no time to

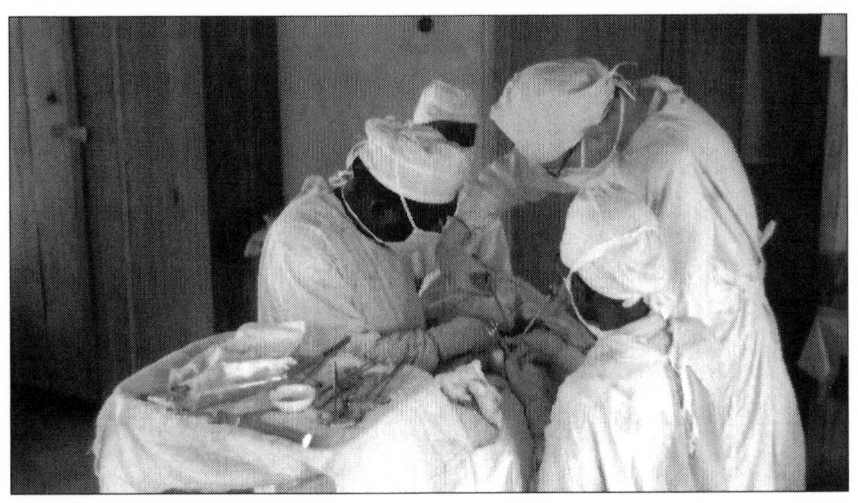

Norm and his team of nurses in surgery

prepare his speech. He asked the Holy Spirit for help, and the Spirit gave him a fine message.

Missionaries would come from Leopoldville to have their babies. Norm delivered seven missionary babies our first term, all girls. The most exciting was Tonda.

Norm congratulating the second-year nursing class

Mwesi, our nursing graduate on her wedding day

Don and Betsy came to the Congo two years after we did. They were assigned to Nsona Mpangu, a station downriver from us. It was the successor to Mbanza Manteke, the very first American Baptist mission station in the Congo. The Nsona Mpangu hospital did not have a doctor. Betsy was almost seven months pregnant and had a history of losing babies either just before they were born or just after. It was thought that Don and Betsy, with three children already, should stay at a station with a doctor, i.e., Sona Bata.

Yes, of course. But where would they stay? The Coop seemed a good idea, since it had more rooms than one single missionary would need. Well, no. Sharing a house with another single woman was one thing. Sharing it with a couple and three children was another. Sorry, but no.

Well, how about George's house? George was a single missionary in his early 20's, an exception to the usual practice of sending people 25 and over. He had been sent out to care for all the mission trucks and radios. We had eight stations at that time. Each possessed at least one or two trucks. Five had radios. It meant a lot of road travel and a lot of responsibility. It also involved problems that didn't normally occur in the States—communication problems. English, French, Kikongo? Does he really understand? Do I understand what he's saying? Availability—or unavailability—of parts. A worldview that does not include the idea of routine maintenance when nothing is broken yet. And the fearfully and wonderfully made roads of the Congo. George was very good at his job, but once he dreamed all the trucks on the eight stations were broken down at once.

George was living in a large house that later became the station pastor's. And he was away a lot. Wouldn't that be a good place for Don and Betsy? Well, no. It contained lots of radio equipment. George was not about to welcome children aged eight, four, and eighteen months into that house.

In the end Maurice and Judy invited Don and Betsy to share their duplex. It was the house where Eva and Esther had been when we came to Sona Bata. It had a common living room, dining room, and kitchen. On each side was an apartment for a single woman: office, bedroom, and bath. Maurice and Judy, with two boys and two girls, were occupying it. But the boys went to school in Leopoldville. The rest of the family would use one side of the house and give Don and Betsy, whose son would also be going to school in Leopoldville, the other side.

Somehow it worked. Tonda was indeed born two months early, but she survived and thrived. About the same time Judy had a miscarriage, so it was we who temporarily moved into George's house while ours held Norm's three missionary patients. I don't remember how we kept George's precious electronic stuff safe from our five- and four-year olds, but nothing untoward happened to it.

After that first French class on Pulpit Hill, I taught French and math to our nursing students. I remember telling one girl, "Denise, you'll never make a nurse if you don't learn the multiplication table." I doubt she ever learned it, but she turned into a very good scrub nurse.

Bobby started kindergarten at home with the Calvert course, which I found excellent. In first grade he went to the local school (in Kikongo) in the morning and worked with me in the afternoon. I thought he was quite poetic. One morning he woke up earlier than usual, when it was just light. He looked out the window and exclaimed, "Isn't it beautiful! Nobody has woke up yet. There the road is, waiting for the people."

That makes me think of Christmas at Sona Bata. It started earlier than that, while it was still dark. Someone would come out of his house and start singing a Christmas carol. As other people and families heard, they would come out and join the singer. Gradually the group got larger and larger. Other groups would come from the other hills, and the whole population would arrive at the church for a sunrise Christmas service. Jesus is born!

One day Bobby was to dictate a story to me. He showed no signs of ever stopping, so finally I told him, "That's the end of the page, Bobby—no more room." I considered his story very good for a kindergartener and sent copies to both sets of grandparents.

One grandmother wrote back, "That's a wonderful story! I'm sure Bobby will grow up to be a writer or a preacher—somebody who uses words well."

The other grandmother responded, "I'm sure he'll improve as he grows older."

It was a slow 50 miles from Sona Bata on the dirt road to Leopoldville. During the dry season the road would fill up with sand, and eventually workers would shovel it out, off to the side. Over time this made part of the route a sunken road between dirt banks lined with trees. Now a Belgian company started paving the road. They made a contract with the Sona Bata hospital to treat all their workers. It made a good, dependable source of income for the hospital. We came to know a French couple working with the construction company. Their headquarters were nearby, and we exchanged visits. I made the mistake of serving them steak and French fries. Never try to serve someone their specialty when you can't do it very well. We enjoyed the couple, and they were very patient with our French. They invited us to their home, and I meant to say, "That would be great!" I thought of using the French word, *épatant,* for which we'd been given the translation "swell." Remember that word? But unfortunately, instead of *épatant* I said *épouvantable,* which translates "dreadful, horrible, appalling"! Madame graciously never turned a hair.

She wasn't so gracious with everyone, though. They showed us a little home movie her husband had made. They were walking along a path behind some Congolese women. The Frenchman carefully filmed his wife managing to give a little kick to the woman walking in front of her. Now why would she do that? I once saw a boy show his kid brother how to give a little kick to their sister as she went up the stairs ahead of them. Why would the Frenchwoman want to act like a pesky brother? Was she bored with no French neighbors, only Belgians, perhaps Flemings who scorned speaking French?

Then she and her husband showed off her clever trick to these Americans. They must have been proud of it! It was a good joke. We wanted to get acquainted with our Congolese neighbors. The company building the road treated their Congolese employees fairly, meeting their needs. This couple apparently wanted to make fun of them. We didn't say anything.

Norm took the children and me on one of his dispensary trips. The nearest dispensary was at a palm oil factory, very interesting. They used the debris from the palm nuts to stoke their boilers—sustainable energy! Norm checked the nurse's supply of medicines, saw patients, and talked with the nurse about his work. In order to help with one mental patient's diagnosis, Norm asked him to count to three. The man obediently recited, *"Mosi, zole, tatu."* Apparently he thought that was something the doctor really wanted to hear, because for the rest of the afternoon he would keep turning up saying, *"Mosi, zole, tatu."*

To get to the next dispensary Norm took a shortcut he had heard about. It turned out to be a long cut and very bumpy. At one point we came to two cemeteries. On the left was a traditional cemetery, with a plate, a lantern, or another useful item on each grave. They were for the spirit's life in the afterworld. Each object had a hole punched in it so it wouldn't be stolen for life in this world. On the other side stood a Christian cemetery with gravestones, some quite large and ornate and painted different colors. Five-year-old Bobby took one disgusted look and announced, "It isn't right to break up a road and then decorate it!"

Bobby had a small truck with a crane, which we had given him in Belgium. Another boy was playing with a hoop—the rim of a discarded bicycle wheel. They happily exchanged toys, to the satisfaction of both.

Our ocean freight included 40 barrels and boxes, and they arrived six months after we did, held up in customs at Matadi because they included a still for making distilled water for the hospital. Customs wanted all sorts of documents, including a photograph of the still. How do you take a picture of an apparatus housed in a box that you aren't permitted to have until you've submitted the photo? They also

Bobby admired the other boy's hoop

wanted to know what we were going to use it for. Our mission treasurer suggested, "Why, to make that good ole moonshine down in the holler."

Among the things we had packed were sundresses for Grace. The little square bodices didn't always cover everything, and sometimes she felt a bit embarrassed, but on the other hand, as she pointed out, "It makes it easier to nurse my dolls." She knew how because she saw the Congolese women nursing their babies.

Trucks and people had to cross the river by ferry

Our Congolese guide and helper, Grace, Bobby, and Norm crossing on the ferry

One day Norm started suffering severe back pain, which he eventually diagnosed as a herniated disc. He took to his bed. But the next night a bad accident occurred on our newly paved road. As a Belgian had predicted once in our living room, "People will drive on it as if it were an *autobahn,* but it isn't." Two trucks loaded with men,

Unloading our much-anticipated ocean freight onto our house veranda

women and children ran into each other head-on. Thirty people were brought in to the hospital. Norm got on his bicycle, rode it to the hospital, and leaned on it as he examined the patients.

The following day we drove—I drove with poor Norm flat on his back in the truck that we euphemistically termed our ambulance—southwest on the main road, away from the capital, to the big union hospital at Kimpese, which boasted a missionary orthopedist. The short, stocky doctor hoisted tall Norm on his back and jounced him in an effort to put the disc back in place. It didn't work. Then Norm had to endure the trip back to Sona Bata. The road was paved from Sona Bata to the capital but only a short distance in the other direction. From there on it was full of ruts and holes and bumps. How I wished I could drive as smoothly as Norm!

Eventually he ordered a back brace from the States and wore it until we went on furlough. In the States the orthopedist commanded, "Take that thing off and throw it away. I've gotten hod carriers back to work!"

As the months went by we understood more and more of what we heard in church. Sometimes the pastor would preach; another time it might be a teacher, a nurse, or a mason. Anyone could be called on to pray; no one declined. The preacher kept the congregation involved by starting a sentence and letting the people finish it. If he thought they might not be able to, he'd say the whole sentence and then repeat the first part. Once one of our nurses remarked, "I just wished he'd call on me to pray so I could fill out what was lacking in his sermon."

One very sharp teacher was a man named Lulendo. His son was about the same age as our Bobby and they played together. Most of Bobby's friends were a little older and made allowances for this little white kid. It was good for him to have one peer who gave as good as he took. Lulendo preached one time on the subject *"Kulumuka."* The word means "come down." Jesus said it to Zaccheus when he was up in the tree. Tata Lulendo told his compatriots, "We love to climb a tree and see what's going on. Anybody who starts a new sect gets lots of followers. We need to come down from the tree and commit ourselves."

One day I heard that one of the women had lost a child. I asked a nursing student to take me to the woman's home. She was there, and I tried in my limited Kikongo to comfort her. Later Tata Kimpiatu, who sometimes served as our language informant, heard about it and asked the student, "What did Mama Abell do there?"

"She exhorted her."

"I didn't know she knew that much Kikongo."

I wonder what I said. I wonder what the woman made of it. At least I paid her some attention.

In those days the Congo was still a Belgian colony. In 1958 Brussels hosted Expo 58, the first world's fair after World War II. There was a Congo pavilion, and the Belgian government brought some Congolese each month to act as docents. Kimpiatu was one of those chosen. Before he left he confided, "I'm afraid I'll be hungry with no manioc in Belgium."

When he returned he looked well fed. I told him so, and he admitted, "There were lots of other good things to eat."

Besides Kikongo and one or two other Bantu languages, he knew French and English, but there were visitors to the Expo who knew none of those. Kimpiatu described how they would ask through gestures, "Did the sun burn you that color?"

And nurse Kimpiatu would reply through gestures, "No, I came out of my mother's womb this way."

"On the way home," he told us, "I prayed the plane along till we'd crossed the Mediterranean. Then I figured the pilot could manage from there on, so I went to sleep."

When Norm went to Leopoldville he would visit the dispensary next to the Baptist Church in Kintambo, one of the sections of the city. This dispensary was in the capable hands of Mama Mattie, one of the first two female Congolese nurses, trained at Sona Bata under Dr. King when the first nursing school was very new. While Norm checked out what she was doing, the church women were having their meeting in the sanctuary. I was along on one trip, so I went in and sat in the back in time to hear one of the women praying for the doctor. "Give him wisdom and patience and love," she asked.

I thought, "What a good prayer!" We often found ourselves praying, "Lord, help us get through all this work that needs to be done," but

Mama Mattie and her children

she was praying for what was really important: wisdom and patience and love.

Much later I found out that the baby layettes American Baptist women sent over in White Cross to that dispensary were given only to those mothers who belonged to the church. I didn't think that was right. Mama Mattie explained, "We were afraid there wouldn't be enough for us if we gave them to everyone." It still wasn't right, but didn't I do the same thing? If I bought bananas at the market and on the way home someone asked me for one, I wouldn't give it because by the time I got home they would all be gone. But I could afford to get more, and maybe the people who asked couldn't.

We had known an Africa where only two countries were independent; all the rest were colonies of the UK or France or Spain or Portugal or Germany or Italy or Belgium. Now things were changing. In 1959 France gave autonomy to its African colonies. Germany and Italy had lost their colonies in WWII. The Belgians had had no plans to change the status of their colony, but with the new ferment for freedom they began to draw up a plan for independence in 30 years. That was too slow. All right, four years. The first elections were held for burgomasters (mayors) for the various sections of Leopoldville. And then it became clear that the Congolese were not willing to wait four years. Belgium was weary of war and did not want conflict with the colony it thought it had treated so well. Independence Day was set for June 30, 1960. Remember, the only elected officials were those burgomasters in the capital city. Who would replace all the Belgians in government posts? Who had the training? Who had any experience? I remember asking Lulendo, "Do you think the country's ready for independence?"

"Wouldn't you want to be free?" was his reply.

The church was already well on the way to independence. In 1956, just a few months after our arrival, we attended the last missionary conference, at which everyone looked eagerly at the blackboard that showed who would be going to what station for the coming year. There were always changes because some missionaries went on furlough each year and needed to be replaced. Distribution of the money sent out for the work was also handled there. Of course, needs always exceeded the supply, so competition was hot. Which station, which work needed the money more than another? Whatever anyone else said, one missionary would always counter, "Have you seen the boys' dorms at Sona Bata?" The following year and from then on, these matters would be discussed at *Mbundani,* the gathering of Congolese leaders. A few missionaries were included.

Two topics came up at that missionary conference that were of special significance to us. The Salk vaccine for polio had just come out in the States. Should we have some sent to the Congo so our children could be vaccinated? New missionary Jean Abell raised her little hand and suggested, "Since two of our doctors (Freas and Osterholm) have contracted polio, shouldn't we vaccinate adults as well as children?"

The idea was accepted, and the Abells became responsible for receiving the vaccine and seeing that it stayed cold on its journey to the other stations. A little later it would have been easy to send the vaccine by MAF (Mission Aviation Fellowship), but MAF didn't come to the Congo till after independence. Of course Norm vaccinated the Sona Bata missionary community first. One day I unthinkingly asked him at the table, "Are you going to shoot the missionaries today?"

Later a troubled little boy asked me, "Is Daddy really going to kill the missionaries?" Thank goodness he asked!

We took Boko's vaccine by truck, packed in a thermos bottle with ice cubes. Unfortunately the road was so bumpy that the bouncing ice cubes broke the delicate glass of the thermos. Fortunately, and somewhat to our surprise, we were able to stop at a town that had a store with both thermos bottles and ice. Now we knew we had to crush the ice before putting it in the bottle.

The other one-time question concerned the education of our children. The Presbyterians had a school for missionary children (or kids, also known as MKs) at Lubondai, near the middle of the country. American Baptists partnered with them in the high school; our children were paying guests in the elementary school. Now the baby boom or perhaps the influx of missionaries—our class of American Baptists was the largest ever to go to the Congo—had caught up with them, and they informed us that there might not be room for our children when their parents were ready to send them. What should we do? Should we start our own school for American Baptist MKs? It seemed very parochial. The MKs whose parents lived in Leopoldville had been going to the local Belgian school and getting along all right. Should we establish a hostel where children from the bush could live in the city and go to that school? It was a difficult decision, with lots to be said on both sides. Eventually we decided on the second alternative. Reidar and Sigrid, new missionaries just coming out, would be the first hostel parents, with, I think, seven boys and two girls. It's better to start working in a second language as young as possible. The Leopoldville parents recommended that we teach our children first grade at home so they'd get a start reading and writing English and then send them to first grade in the French language Belgian school. Since European education tended to be at least a year ahead of ours in academics, they would be able to skip a grade when they went back to the States.

Bobby was homeschooled; he could take as long as he needed on his work. That was a mistake. To this day he has trouble with deadlines because he's very painstaking.

I had vowed I would not send a child of mine away to school unless he wanted to go. Bobby wanted to go to Leopoldville to school. Visiting the city was fun; why not go to school there? I tried to teach him some French, but he wasn't interested. He'd learn it when the time came.

The time came. We were given a long list of books and notebooks he had to have, along with a schoolbag. Each book and notebook must be covered with blue paper which you bought along with the books. Bobby proudly carried his new bookbag into the first grade class in the Belgian school and hung it on the hook on the side of his desk as the other children did. Imagine his consternation when the teacher came along and took out most of the books! She would keep them for him until the time came to use a particular book, but how was this little American to know that?

Bobby has not one single good memory of that school. The other boys in our hostel all went into second grade; there was no one to interpret for him or speak up for him to his teacher. We were not allowed to visit or to have a conference with the teacher. We lived only 50 miles from the city, but Bobby was not encouraged to visit home on weekends; re-entry became more difficult. When we visited the city, Bobby's schoolbag would be full of papers he had never handed in because he hadn't finished them. Some he did finish later but lacked the courage to give the teacher.

Bobby did come home for his birthday. That first year we brought all the boys down to Sona Bata to celebrate. The cake I made for the occasion barely rose.

One of the boys exclaimed, "That's a birthday pancake!"

Somehow Bobby survived the year. He did have happy times at the hostel. Sigrid reported that once he said to her, "Aunt Sig, I'm sick."

"Where do you hurt, Bobby?"

"What's that kind of sick? HOMEsick."

The school year ended. What about second grade? Now he knew French. The second year should be much easier. We sent him back. Don and Bunny were hostel parents. I think the whole hostel went swimming to celebrate the week Bobby didn't cry once.

Years later I asked Bunny, "What would you have done with this boy who's having real problems at school and in the hostel?"

She replied, "I'd give him a roommate like Tim." Tim was Bobby's roommate—smart but easygoing, cheerful, a lifelong friend.

Grace had a very scary adventure our first year in the Congo. We took daraprim to prevent malaria. It was a very small pill, easy to swallow, not bitter like most antimalarials. We kept it in a little red pill box. We were supposed to take it once a week, but we would forget, so one day I decided to keep the box on the dining room table to remind us. I should have been warned when three-year-old Grace called it "MY daraprim." One night she vomited off and on all night long. Norm was away. In the morning I discovered the pill box was empty. I asked Tata Kimpiatu, the wonderful head nurse at the hospital, what I should do. Since Grace had vomited thoroughly and seemed all right, there didn't seem to be anything to do, except thank God with a full heart. Friends of ours, missionaries in Thailand, lost a child that way. Why the difference?

We were supposed to take four Kikongo exams during our first two years, or certainly during our first term. We arrived in April of 1956, so it must have been dry season (summer in the States) of 1957 when Madelyn went on furlough. We had had a little over a year to learn the language. Madelyn was directing the homemaking school. This level of homemaking school took girls who had started school late and had now completed second grade but would be nearing marriageable age in another three years. Their three years of homemaking school emphasized cooking, sewing and other needlecraft, cleaning, laundry (most Congolese men ironed their own shirts), and agriculture. They also included rudiments of French, arithmetic, and other general subjects. Madelyn was very good at it. When Madelyn went on furlough,

Eva added that school to the two she was already directing, the regular elementary school and a course for teachers. By Christmas time Eva realized it was too much; someone else had to take the homemaking school. On paper I had the best qualifications; homemaking skills were not among them, but when the second semester started, there I was in Madelyn's office, trying to make sense of my new job.

I enjoyed the course I taught the girls. It was called Conversations. It turned out the subject matter was geography. Instead of starting with their school and town, it began with the universe and worked down. I consulted my encyclopedia since there was no textbook. I told the girls, "There's a star called Betelguese that's so big, if its center were at the center of our sun, the earth would be swallowed up in it."

One girl got the point and asked, "If one star is that big, how big are the heavens?"

A moment for worship.

But now I needed to find out what was going on in all the courses. And what were those little black pellets rolling around in Madelyn's drawer? Oh, papaya seeds. That must have been an extra good papaya and she'd saved the seeds to plant.

I don't remember how much I learned in her office that day, but I'll always remember the second day. The agricultural inspector came. We lived in dread of a surprise visit from a Belgian school inspector. On his report depended the subsidies our schools received, that paid the Congolese teachers' salaries. The inspectors left us free to teach religion as we saw fit, but they did expect us to keep high academic standards. Now here was an inspector. He wanted to see the girls' gardens. I didn't know where the gardens were! Fortunately there was one woman whose job was to supervise the girls' work in their gardens. She showed the inspector around.

The other crisis appeared when one of the three homeroom teachers got sick. Norm diagnosed tuberculosis and decreed that she had to quit teaching until she got better. Also, she was not to carry heavy loads up and down hills. When she was rebuked for toting a five-gallon demijohn of water up from the spring on her head, she protested, "Only one!" Ordinarily women would carry three in a large round dishpan on their head.

The other woman teacher in the homemaking school had seven children. When a new one came along, she brought her to class, where the baby slept in a washtub at the back of the room. When she woke up hungry, Mrs. Tsiebele would nurse her, going on teaching. A real demonstration of practical, indigenous homemaking! But now someone had to take the other teacher's classes until I could find a substitute. Norm eventually lent me his best nursing student! In the meantime I tried to teach all the regular courses—not cooking or sewing; we had special teachers for those. The hardest were agriculture and Kikongo grammar. The homeroom teacher taught agriculture from a book; the Congolese woman, who had never read the book, supervised it in the fields. I never found out whether there was any relationship between the two. Only the teacher had the book.

So I developed the following didactic method: I would read a paragraph from the book and ask the class, "Do you understand?"

"Yes, Mama," they would assure me.

"Then who will explain it to the class?"

Someone would always volunteer, and by the time she finished I would understand what I had read. The subject matter was fruit trees, and I learned that you don't plant orange trees; you graft them on to lemon trees. Now I wonder why we were teaching this to the girls; women grow manioc and corn and peanuts, but it's men who plant trees. Maybe a more experienced teacher would have skipped that chapter.

I was studying Kikongo grammar, but I was studying it in English. The textbook we were using was written by French-speaking Catholics, and they used a slightly different spelling. I was lost. The first day I asked the girls, "What page are you on?"

They told me.

"And what were you doing on this page?"

They told me.

"OK, keep on doing it."

Finally they came to a word I recognized, and it all became clear. They were taking a verb—in this case *sonika,* "to write," and making it into a noun, the doer of the action. I knew *nsoniki,* "writer," as it's the word used for "scribe" in the Bible, and our Kikongo text was strong on Bible passages. (Norm learned medical Kikongo, I learned kitchen Kikongo, and we both learned Bible Kikongo.) Then they added the object and put it in the plural, so we had *nsoniki a minkanda,* "a writer of books." But what could be more absurd than a first-term English-speaking missionary trying to teach Congolese village girls their own language?

The Sona Bata mission station had been founded in 1908, so 1958 marked Sona Bata's fiftieth anniversary, its golden jubilee. Great plans were made for a celebration. "Eva, will you create a play to show the history of Sona Bata?" asked Roland.

"Yes, I will. I'll invite the oldest chiefs over for tea and listen to their memories of the early days." She found three elderly chiefs and laid in a supply of cookies. When the old men were ensconced in her living room with their tea, she emptied a boxful of cookies onto a platter and offered it to the oldest chief. He graciously accepted the whole platter. Fortunately she had two more boxes and two more platters, so each chief could be treated the same. When the conversation was over and it was time to go home, Eva returned each chief's uneaten cookies to their box and sent each one home satisfied and provided with a supply of cookies for the future. She now had lots of ideas for the play, scenes to cover the fifty years. Of course there would be speeches too, and singing.

Station people were not the only ones making plans. During the 50 years, many boys and young men had graduated from the Sona Bata schools, beginning with the most rudimentary education. In recent years girls had graduated too, including the first female Congolese nurses, and of course now there were multiple schools. Most of these grads now lived in Leopoldville, and many of them planned to come to the celebration at Sona Bata. The train made it convenient. They also ordered a steer from the ranch down the line, which they would cook at Sona Bata.

The big day came. Actors were ready in costume for the great history play. Speechmakers, local and old grads, were looking forward to their turns. Of course there were no beds for the horde of old grads, but people were not worrying about that. Then the steer arrived several hours late. It takes time to cook a steer. By the time everyone had eaten, the program began about the time it was scheduled to end. You remember, the generator, in its little house between the two major hills, could run from 6:00 to 9:00 p.m. It was now 9:00. The play began. It had multiple scenes. Roland watched the generator and wondered how long he could stretch its performance without burning it out. Finally, at 11:00, he turned it off. Consternation! Anger! Resentment. Those speeches were never made. Finally people gave up in disgust and in the dark and found some place to sleep. The great day ended with a thud.

In the morning the sun rose on a sorry sight. People had slept in the church and outdoors. All the trash and garbage of the night before littered the space that had been filled with celebrating people. When our good doctor saw the situation, he started cleaning up. After a while another man joined him, one of those from the city. I hope there were several others who helped in the work. Some time later, one of the local men asked Norm, "Do you know that man who was helping you?"

"No," Norm admitted. "Who is he?"

"That's Kasavubu."

Mr. Kasavubu was the head of ABAKO, the political party of the Bakongo, the large tribe that inhabited our part of the Congo. Educated in Catholic schools, he had become Protestant. He had held various jobs, including work for the colonial government. He had begun striving for independence while still holding the government job. At first he had gone along with the Belgians' 30-year-plan, but as the party grew stronger he insisted on an earlier date. He was not a Sona Bata graduate, but of course it was important for him to be part of this large gathering of Bakongo at the 50-year-old station of Sona Bata. He made no speech; he just quietly joined in the grungy cleanup work.

January 4, 1959, Kasavubu was to speak at the enormous stadium in Leopoldville. Passion for independence had grown. The crowd pushing its way into the stadium was immense. Police tried to regulate the flow. The temper of the people was such, and there were so many of them, that they were not about to tolerate any constraint. There was also conflict between political parties. Because it represented the large area from Leopoldville to the coast, and because it had been the most active in the struggle for independence, ABAKO was the dominant party, but of course people from all over the country came to the capital, and every large tribe had its own party. A riot broke out; some people were killed. The Congolese named January 4 the Day of the Martyrs, calling those who were killed martyrs for the cause of independence. Kasavubu did not get to speak, but he was imprisoned as having caused the riot. Two months later he was restored to freedom.

CHAPTER FIVE

Moanza

Flash back to the pioneer days of missions in the Congo. Mpambu was a dedicated young pastor from the other side of the Congo River. He started out on foot with two American missionaries to establish a mission station many miles away on the Inzia River, leaving behind his new bride. He became separated from the other men and ended up walking without them the last eight days to Moanza to share the gospel with people who had never heard it. He was a Mukongo. His dominant tribe populated the large area that extended from the seacoast to Leopoldville, the capital city, also south into Angola, where San Salvador was the capital of the old Kongo kingdom, and north into what was then French Equatorial Africa. Of course this was the first tribe to have contact with Europeans and to receive missionaries, evangelization, literacy.

Trekking east and north, Mpambu was leaving family, clan, tribe, friends, language, and culture. The Basuku, who included Moanza in their territory, were still untouched by any Christian influence. Like other tribes, they believed in *Nzambi-Mpungu,* "God Almighty," but they thought he had created the world and then gone fishing, leaving humans at the mercy of spirits, mostly evil, who had to be propitiated. Illness, accidents, and death were always caused by other people, usually family members. Life was ruled by fear. These beliefs were not strange to Mpambu. He knew what he and others of his tribe had been delivered from. He wanted the Basuku to be delivered too.

The Basuku spoke a different language from the Bakongo, but it was close enough so Mpambu could understand some things, and they could understand some of what he said. In fact, as he approached one village the first man who spotted him spoke loudly enough so Mpambu heard, "Here comes our meat. Let's eat him." Mpambu prayed and by God's grace, the villagers did not act on that idea. In fact, the village chief sent some men with him till he arrived at Moanza, where the other missionaries must have rejoiced to see him.

The Americans stayed three months, working with the local people to construct the first buildings of the mission station. A few people followed their teachings and were baptized. Then the two men left and Mpambu was on his own. His wife joined him and was baptized at Moanza. The couple worked hard, earning money by farming to start a school, teaching young people to read and to follow Jesus. As soon as the boys could read a little they were sent back to their villages to teach others. Four years after his arrival at Moanza, Mpambu reaped the first fruits of his labor, baptizing four men and one woman, and the church at Moanza was born. Seven years later a missionary named Hill joined him. Moanza people used to talk about *Nzambi a Tata Hilu*—Mr. Hill's God.

After his wife's death Mpambu married a Musuku. Few frontier missionaries go that far! By the time we got there Mpambu had died, and his widow had married a Mumbala. What? Another tribe? Yes, some Basuku must have reached into the tribe to the north, and they were now represented at Moanza too. I thought of this strong Christian woman as a bridge between tribes. It's hard being a bridge; you get walked on.

Now, in 1959, the senior missionaries at Moanza were Marguerite (Miggs) and a couple we called Ted and Pete. Pete's real name was Matilda; she was very feminine. Cliff and Joy, who'd been in Belgium with us, rounded out the missionary staff. Norm already knew Miggs. While we were at Sona Bata he had been asked to diagnose her by radio. She had an acute attack of something that the Moanza missionary nurse described and Norm diagnosed as a pulmonary thrombosis. Later on the doctor from Vanga saw her and thought it had been a coronary. She was ordered to return to the States. Norm flew in the helicopter that went to pick her up and brought her to Leopoldville. One of the Moanza missionaries contributed a cake pan at the last minute when it was realized that there was no bedpan. Then Norm flew on to the States with Miggs by Pan Am. There his diagnosis was confirmed. In the few days before he returned to the Congo, Norm visited his alma mater, the University of Rochester Medical School, to meet Dan, an American Baptist missionary candidate. Dan had previously taken seminary work. Now, a full-time med student, he was also pastoring a small church! Getting acquainted with Dan filled Norm with hope and excitement for the day when Dan would arrive in Congo. Those hopes were more than realized.

The Moanza station included a beautiful little church, made of the local pinkish stone, a fine elementary school, and a 40-bed hospital, run by a missionary nurse with local staff. Now Moanza was to have a doctor!

All our goods and chattels in the Sona Bata truck, with a Congolese driver along to bring the truck back, we made the arduous trip from Sona Bata to Moanza. Of course that courageous pastor had done it on foot, with no friends from his tribe to welcome him when he got there. We had three missionary homes welcoming us, and somewhat discombobulated because we arrived a day later than expected. We knew not to expect many gas stations along the way, so we had brought

Moanza's beautiful church—building and people!

two extra barrels. When we ran out of gas the men simply went to the back of the trunk to open a barrel. Oh-oh! *"Tala, Tata. Mpamba."*

"What did he say, honey?"

"The barrel sprang a leak. It's empty."

"What do we do now?"

"There's another barrel."

Graduation at the elementary school

"Oh, good."

"Oh-oh! It's our water supply."

Norm turned to the driver, "Tata Diyenga."

"Eyu." (Here I am)

Then Norm told Diyenga in Kikongo, "Take the bicycle to the nearest Catholic mission station. Buy 20 liters of gasoline; don't settle for less."

It was a long wait. Night came on; the children and I curled up in the cab; the men slept under or beside the truck. Finally Diyenga returned, pushing the bicycle with its load of fuel. The first mission station had had only 10 liters of gasoline, so he had obeyed instructions and gone on to the next, almost to Moanza. There he had bought 20 liters and strapped it to the luggage carrier. It proved to be too heavy and broke the carrier. So Diyenga fastened the fuel on in some way and pushed the bike back. We had sometimes criticized him for doing his own thing instead of what he had been told. This time we wished he had used his own good sense!

I've always thought Moanza was our most beautiful church center. The Inzia flows far below the little plateau where the mission station was built. In the mornings fog fills the valley, like a wide white river. Across the river rise range after range of hills. In the other direction a road goes on up to a village at the top of the hill. Near the river the hills are covered with trees, rising very tall from the riverbank to find the sun. In other places they're all grass, looking velvety green from a distance. If you walk through them you find they're not at all velvety.

The mission station was built around the church, with paths leading to it from the hospital at the upper end, the missionary homes overlooking the valley, the school and houses on both sides. Ted and Pete greeted us warmly, assuring us, "Anything you need and don't have, just tell us, and we'll tell you how to get along without it." Actually they met all our needs. There was no market; there was no store. We ate what people came to the door to sell us, plus what we had brought with us. We had imported a lot of canned goods, including large tins of powdered milk, boxes of raisins and other goodies stored in a small metal barrel or box, oatmeal in cans. It was compressed so that when you opened a two-cup can you got seven cups of raw oatmeal out of it. In the past some missionaries had given each other onions for Christmas—bunches of locally grown shallots, which weren't always available. I tried to have a garden, but I'm no gardener, and it turned out our outdoor man wasn't either. In Congo people plant in *plate-bandes,* "square beds" instead of rows. When the plants came up, the ones near the path did pretty well, but those on the other side of the bed looked very sorry. It had been too much work to throw the water that far. My watermelons did not make it. One year when we went to the coast on vacation, we found watermelons on sale at Matadi. They were such a treat I bought one to take with us and even made watermelon rind pickles at the beach house rather than waste any of that precious fruit.

Moanza folk spoke Kisuku, which had a good deal of resemblance to Kikongo. Also, the older people had learned Kikongo, as the missionaries had decided around 1930 that all our stations should use the same language. People were very happy to have a resident doctor. A doctor from Vanga had been coming four times a year to do surgery, as Norm had done from Sona Bata to Boko.

The hospital had 40 beds. There was no X-ray; there hadn't been at Sona Bata either. Old Tata Kitsangi was the senior nurse—no ball of fire, but a man of integrity. He suffered from asthma, and once while we were there he had such a crisis his wife thought he was a goner and started wailing. He protested, "Louise, please!" He lived another 20 years. A younger nurse had graduated from the four-year course at Kimpese and brought more knowledge. The hospital also had a couple of young men who had been trained at Sona Bata. The rest of the staff had pretty much learned by doing. Norm was a good teacher.

Tata Kitsangi consulting with an expectant mother

One day the local government requested (ordered?) Norm to perform an autopsy in a village we did not know. The body had not been buried very deep or very long, so Norm was able to dissect it and find the poison that had killed the man. He sent a sample to the government lab. He also asked one of the men who had been helping him, "If you were going to poison somebody, what plant would you use?" The man readily showed him a plant, and Norm sent samples of that to the lab too. Yes, it matched the poison found in the body. Norm was not required to identify the poisoner.

Sometimes when a patient died at the hospital, Norm wanted to perform an autopsy to make sure of the cause of death. The family had to be convinced to give permission, and convincing them was rarely possible. We were surprised to find that here in the States the family may try to have an autopsy done and find it difficult and very expensive.

Down in Leopoldville, Chet had become the mission secretary. His wife, Margaret, saw that teachers needed help with their religion lessons. All they had was a curriculum that gave them a topic and a Scripture reference for each lesson. So Margaret went over the excellent American Baptist Sunday School materials used in the States, picking out lessons that could be adapted for use in the Congo. For each of the six grades she asked one teacher, "Will you adapt each lesson to your children's needs, teach it, and then write it in Kikongo?"

"Yes, Margaret," I replied. "I'll tackle sixth grade. Sounds interesting."

What a lot of mistakes I made! I started out the first lesson jumping into the story, as it was written in English. "Timoteo didn't even hear his mother calling him that morning." You don't do that in the Congo. You give the title and carefully set the scene before you go into the action.

If I didn't know a word and couldn't find it in our Kikongo dictionary I would look for it in the Bible. This is dangerous, especially in the Old Testament, where scholars don't agree on how to translate some verses. It seems to me there was one word that might mean "orgies" or perhaps "little hills".

There was one girl in my class who was persecuted by the other kids because she was from a different tribe. For one lesson I used the book of Philemon, putting her name in place of Onesimus. I don't know whether it helped or not.

I remember asking the students, "What is the hardest thing you do? Chopping wood, digging gardens, what?" I submitted that forgiving was the hardest. Another time I asked them, "What is the work of a pastor?" and was disappointed to get the answer, "Raising money and building church buildings."

One unit started with Acts and went through the history of the early church. When we got to Revelation, I explained that some scholars thought it had been written by the John who wrote the gospel and the epistles, and others thought it must have been some other John. Someone suggested that it might have been John the Baptist.

I reminded them, "Remember? He had his head chopped off by Herod. Could he have written Revelation after that?"

"We don't know," they replied. "Could he?" It makes a difference when you believe in the living dead!

The missionaries got together for a special meal on Thanksgiving, Christmas, New Year's, and Easter. Since we were four households, we each had a turn at hosting the others. When my turn came, we were to have a goat leg. I thought one leg might not be enough, so I was given two. When it came time to eat, the precious goat legs were not done. *Kiadi!* (sorrow). Also *nsoni!* (shame).

Another time we were having company and had hired an extra boy to help in the kitchen. I went out and found him washing the ice cubes in hot soapy water.

At Moanza we met driver ants, also called army ants. They bivouac and then invade houses in armies, eating everything animal. They don't cross kerosene, so once I supposed I could keep them from going into the dining room by pouring kerosene on the threshold. They simply crawled up the wall and went in higher up. You can dip a little palm frond broom in kerosene, set fire to it, and go along their ranks, burning them up as you go, or you can vacate your house for a day and come back to find it thoroughly rid of cockroaches and all other small pests. The ants travel in columns, with larger ants at intervals along the sides, apparently keeping them in order. Once George and I noticed a small detachment composed of only the larger ants. "An ROTC unit!" he exclaimed.

Bobby had started second grade in the Belgian school in Leopoldville. We brought him home for his birthday in December. Because the country, especially the capital city, was in something of a ferment leading to independence, many Belgians had already left. We did not send Bobby back. What a relief for him! He jumped right into Calvert School in English with his friend Tim. You remember he had done first grade at home and then first grade in French the following year. Now he was plunged into the middle of third grade in English. At first he literally couldn't spell "the," but he was a good sport and caught up fast. One day he was relaxing in the bathtub and informed me, "Mom, I'm a dreamer. You know what a dreamer is?"

"What's a dreamer, Bobby?"

"A dreamer is somebody who's supposed to be doing his work, and he gets to looking at something and thinking all about it, how it's made and everything, and all of a sudden the teacher shouts, 'Abell! *Tu dors?'* [Are you asleep?]"

Grace went to the local school. She told us one day that she knew seven languages. She was right about English. She felt she knew French because in school she had learned to close the door in four tenses. She had learned Kikongo at Sona Bata, playing with other children. Here boys played with boys and girls with girls, and spoke Kisuku, so she was learning that. The other tribe represented at Moanza was the Bambala, who spoke Kimbala. *Mbala* happens to be the word for "sweet potato," so when Grace first heard about Kimbala she exclaimed in delight, "The language of sweet potatoes!" The other two languages? Someone had taught her a phrase in Chinese, which she thought was Japanese, so she counted that as one of her languages. And the seventh was pig latin.

At Moanza, girls played with girls

I was assigned the job of preparing the annual Christmas pageant. I hoped the people from the village up on the hill would come down for it, so I wanted it to be in Kisuku. "All right," my committee agreed, "but when government people (Roman officials in the play) speak they have to use Kikongo *de l'État* (government Kikongo, the trade language also known as Kituba)."

Instead of trying to change scenes on the platform in church, we had the audience move from one scene to another along the road. The first little temporary house built for the performance showed a Christian family on Christmas Day, visited by a little girl from a non-Christian family. That gave the father an opportunity to open the Bible and start telling the Christmas story. The audience moved to the next *fokola* (temporary shelter), where the angel visited Mary and from which she started off to see Elizabeth. In the third *fokola* Joseph and Mary were gazing in awe at their newborn baby. Behind the church and the road we were following was an open space that served as a soccer field.

This day it was a field where shepherds were keeping watch over their sheep—real sheep, one per shepherd. After they visited Bethlehem and saw Jesus, we ended up at the church, where Simeon welcomed the Messiah, blessed and warned his parents. At Moanza several old men had lost their sight from river blindness. We chose one of those men for Simeon. He was reduced to making balls of string for a living, but his faith was still strong.

In 1960 *Mbundani,* the annual Convention of Baptist Churches of Western Congo, was to meet at Moanza, and we missionary women, under the capable direction of Pete, had the responsibility of preparing meals for 54 people. I remember finding out how an avocado from the tree near our house dressed up a green salad very nicely. Now I wonder how many of the Congolese appreciated raw vegetables. I was responsible for the squash for one meal. I discovered that 54 people do

Visiting Bethlehem, they saw Jesus! I loved directing the Christmas pageant

not eat nine times as much squash as six people. That might be because Congolese are used to eating the seeds, not the flesh.

Pete was concerned about Joy working too hard because she was pregnant. Unfortunately I let it slip that we were expecting a third child also. In due course Norm delivered Linda, a breech baby but just fine. Linda and Marjorie were to become great friends.

Independence was coming! Out here in the boondocks few people had any idea what it meant. It was something wonderful, but what? Con artists sold boxes of dirt, which they assured people would turn to gold when independence came. Tim's friends teased him: "We're going to get our independence, and you're not going to get any."

One loyal pal assured him, "When I get my independence, I'll give you some."

Sometime during that Moanza year we made a trip to Leopoldville. The Bontragers found us one evening where we were staying at the Mission Guest House. They were Leopoldville missionaries, in charge of the Protestant printing press. They asked Norm if he would go with them to visit a patient. Of course he agreed. Where they took him in the city I don't know, but the patient turned out to be Mr. Kasavubu. Norm examined him and told him, "You need medical attention. You should be in a hospital."

"Not in the city," decreed the politician. "The Belgians would find me right away."

"Then go to IME," Norm suggested.

"No, I need to be close enough to keep my finger on things. I'll go to Sona Bata."

The hospital at Sona Bata was now the responsibility of a recently married woman doctor. Norm wanted to spare her the responsibility of treating, and housing, the head of ABAKO, but he was not able to influence Kasavubu to change his decision. The hospital had no private rooms, and no one was about to put Mr. Kasavubu in a ward. The doctor was, naturally, occupying the doctor's house, where we had lived for the previous three years. Kasavubu was given the children's veranda bedroom. So yes, Grace, Kasavubu did stay in your room—but not while it was yours. It must have been difficult to keep his whereabouts a secret, since an armed guard was always on duty outside his room—supplied by Kasavubu or ABAKO, not by the hospital!

We were scheduled for furlough. Frank, a physician, and his wife, Joan, were to replace us. In fact, they came a month before we left, giving time for an orderly transfer of the work. We moved out of our house so they could move in. I provided three boxes for Bobby and Grace to sort their stuff into:

The hospital staff during the transition of supervision from Norm to Frank

Take to the States. Store here. Give away. When I checked on their progress, almost everything was in the first box and nothing in the third.

There was a small guest house just down the hill from our house; we occupied that. It was so hot in that bunk bed at afternoon siesta time, and Marjorie was getting bigger and heavier. When the time came to leave, we had a sale, displaying things in the living room of the little guest house and inviting people in to buy at rock bottom prices. Foolishly I had included gift wrapping paper, and when everyone had left we discovered some had secreted things in the paper and had got even more for their money than we had planned. We had got rid of not only everything we had for sale but also the cushions from the guest house chairs.

Our departure was set for June 24. We would miss Congo's Independence Day by less than a week. Kasavubu was elected the first president of the newly independent country. He would serve five years, during a succession of prime ministers. When Kasavubu was no longer in office, he retired to his natal region, a good deal downriver from our area. There he died. A rumor circulated that he had been poisoned. It's not impossible, but that kind of rumor was very common, and Dr. Abell knew that Mr. Kasavubu had suffered for years from enough medical problems to take his life without any human assistance.

CHAPTER SIX

Watermelon

We had sailed from New York to Europe and again from Belgium to the Congo, but by 1960 it had become more economical to fly. My parents were in New York City to meet the Pan Am plane and were duly impressed by my rounded appearance. Mother called it my watermelon. Not realizing how very well one was fed on transatlantic flights, they took us to an expensive restaurant in the terminal. I remember being served 7-Up in an elegant glass surrounded by crushed ice.

On June 30 the Congo became an independent country. We scanned the New York Times for news. There wasn't any. Never has it been so apparent to us that no news is good news. Finally on July 7 the news broke, and it was not good.

Way back in the bush people had no idea what independence meant. In the capital and the area between it and the coast where our down-country stations (those between Leopoldville and the mouth of the river) were located, expectations rose high. Not only would all the government officials be Congolese; of course all the Belgian army officers would be replaced by Congolese; and furthermore, Congolese would get the Belgians' houses and wives.

Congolese did take over all the government posts. In many cases the man who had been a clerk in the territorial administrator's office succeeded to the main desk. No one else knew as much about the job. Many Belgians did leave, and of course some houses must have changed hands. Wives did not. And the Belgian army officers were not immediately replaced, nor did the soldiers become richer. Having guns, some decided to take matters into their own hands. This happened at one army camp near our Nsona Mpangu station; our missionaries were attacked, beaten and mistreated. There was a general evacuation of white people, whether Belgian, American, or Portuguese, as many storekeepers were. Frank, the doctor, never did go back to Moanza. The New York Times gave fragmentary accounts. One small item reported that a helicopter landed at Kimpese to pick up missionaries but didn't find any. There was never any follow-up in the paper, and we wanted to know. It turned out that a different helicopter had arrived there first and evacuated the folk in question.

At Sona Bata, nurse Kimpiatu, who had assisted Norm in surgery, took over the leadership of the hospital, doing minor surgery and emergencies (Caesarean sections and hernias), and reported later that he had not lost a single surgery patient.

In the States, we were planning to spend our furlough in one of the two houses in the Boston area that our mission board kept for that purpose. We were to live in Judson House in Malden, a large house built in 1742 where Adoniram Judson, the first American Baptist foreign missionary, was born.

However, we stayed with my parents, the Brokaws, in New Hartford, New York, until mid-August. The baby was due in September. When the time came to travel, for once we were all ready the night before, with suitcases packed and in or on the Brokaws' car. Norm had been in New York City and came back that night after I'd gone to bed. He felt my abdomen and informed me that I was in labor. So the next morning, instead of heading for Massachusetts, we unstrapped my suitcase from the top of the car and went to see a doctor.

After examining me, he pronounced, "Well, you may have been in labor, but you're not in labor now."

"Should we go to Boston today?"

"I can't tell you that."

We decided to go ahead and arrived safely in Malden. Judson House was divided into two apartments. At the moment the widow of a Baptist minister was living downstairs, taking care of the house until missionaries came. She welcomed us but, not surprisingly, could not recommend an obstetrician in Malden. She handed us a phone book and we went to the yellow pages. August is a good month for vacations. We went down the list alphabetically and finally contacted Dr. Wilder. Since my watermelon was quiet, we made an appointment for the next morning.

"You're not in labor now, but it could happen any time."

Mother stayed. After a week or so Dad went back to his church.

We moved into the upstairs apartment and waited for the baby. Bobby and Grace started school. Every night I had false labor. Every night it went on for a while and then stopped. I became impossible to live with. Mother finally went home.

Early one September morning it was the real thing. Norm woke the kids up and took them to the hospital with us, where they stayed in the waiting room. The doctor came. The nurses prepped me, and everybody waited for the moment to take me to the delivery room. Finally Norm had to take Bobby and Grace to school; the doctor popped home for breakfast. That was when Marjorie decided to make her appearance.

Because of a diarrhea scare in the nursery, they were taking a throat swab on all mothers. They found staph aureus in my throat, although I had no symptoms, so I was not allowed to have Marjorie with me.

Since I wanted to nurse her, and Mother had returned to help, they let me take her home at two days.

So a very young Marjorie went to live in the house where Adoniram Judson had preceded her by some 150 years. In her room there was a crib that surely did not date back to Adoniram's birth but wasn't very up-to-date either. The side did not go up and down but stayed at a perennial mid-height. When Marjorie grew able to pull herself up, she could easily fall out, and did. At first all I could think of to do was put a folded blanket on the floor to cushion her fall.

Soon a couple from Burma came to the downstairs apartment. Ed was very ill; they had been unable to treat him in Burma and expected him to die. He and his wife wanted to try the Lahey Clinic in Boston. Lo and behold, the obstruction in his stomach was caused by a knot of whipworms. Once they were removed he was able to eat again and quickly gained strength. Judson House was full of praise to God!

One day Bobby came home with a friend from school. The other boy asked, "Do you have any sisters?"

Bobby replied, "Yes, this is one of them," indicating Grace. It was a new thought to me that now he had two sisters.

Norm sharpened his skills by observing in the Surgery Department of Massachusetts General Hospital. He attended grand rounds and operations, refreshed his memory on things a bush doctor might forget, and acquired new knowledge that hadn't been available when he went to med school and did his residency.

We attended First Baptist Church in Malden and had opportunities to speak in the black Baptist church as well. On the way we would pass a Catholic store that had figurines of Mary and others in the window.

Grace, seven, called it the *biteki* store. *Biteki* is the Kikongo word for idols, also dolls. I used to attend the women's meetings. One month the subject of the meeting was dollhouses. When I spoke to the group the following month, my talk was entitled "Trivia." Do we really want to devote our precious time together as Christian women to talk about dollhouses and such?

In January Don and Betsy with their four children came to live in the downstairs apartment. They had been at Nsona Mpangu when it was attacked. When they were new in Congo Norm had delivered Tonda, who was now two years old.

In July of 1960 there were no Congolese doctors who had been trained in the Congo. The first class graduated from the medical school later that year. There were some 750 expatriate doctors for a country of 22,000,000 people. After the massive evacuation 250 were left. Norm was impatient to get back. The mission board now planned to send him and Don back together. Betsy and I would hold the fort at Judson House until the school year ended, when we'd be allowed to rejoin our husbands on the field.

At the last minute the board changed their minds. They decided Betsy had suffered enough that she should not be deprived of her husband. They must have been divinely guided. Norm went off in January 1961 without Don. He lived with Wes at Moanza, in Ted and Pete's house. It was an emotional moment when Norm walked into their dining room and saw Pete's sweater over the back of the chair where she always put it. Later he found the Moanza people had also kept the drinking water she had had boiled before they were evacuated.

CHAPTER SEVEN

Five Months Is Too Long

Norm had plenty to do to keep him busy. Frank was sent to the 100-bed hospital at Vanga to replace the experienced doctor, who had already retired once or twice and come back because he was needed. He would not return again after evacuation. He was a competent, rapid surgeon. Besides supervising all the medical work, he took care of administration and finances. Now these fell into the laps of the Congolese staff, nurses and less trained people. With the heady ferment of independence, they were glad to have the responsibility for what only the white man had done before. When Frank arrived, they saw no reason to share administration and finances with him. He could do surgery. They were very surprised to find that the new doctor was not willing to stay under those circumstances. He was sent to IME, the big union hospital at Kimpese, where he eventually became director.

Now Vanga lacked a doctor and was added to the hospitals Norm needed to visit. He was in charge of the small hospital at Moanza, where he lived, but he couldn't spend much time there because he needed to visit other institutions, both mission and government, that had lost their doctors.

As the months went by, the Vanga staff learned that administration and finances could become quite difficult; also, a doctor sent to take charge of a hospital will expect to have some say in administration and finances. This prepared the ground so that when Norm visited Vanga he was able to have serious talks with the staff and prepare the way for the new missionary, Dr. Dan, who would expand the Vanga hospital's ministry and reputation beyond anyone's dreams, except perhaps his.

At Moanza Norm had a portable reel-to-reel tape recorder, which he sometimes used to send me messages. Early one morning he was out walking around with the recorder hanging from his shoulder, recording for me. He told me, "Yesterday was payday at the hospital, but there wasn't enough money in the box to pay everybody." Since he was moving as he spoke, his voice came out quavery.

George was taking graduate work at Harvard and came to see us from time to time. He predicted, "If you play that tape in the churches, people will immediately reach into their pockets and shell out so the box will have enough money next month." Alas, I didn't take the tape to churches. It wouldn't have been a good solution to the problem—it was an example of what Norm called "aid dropped by parachute" in contrast to a long-term solution such as more patients, better bill collection, perhaps moving a staff person to a different position, such as a rural dispensary. But it would have been fun to see if folk would respond to that quavery voice telling the sad news.

One thing Norm talked about was Wes' adventures. Wes was an outstanding missionary who cared greatly for his Congolese brothers and didn't shrink from taking chances. Once he was driving people somewhere in a truck when a group of soldiers flagged them down peremptorily. Oh-oh, what now? It turned out they needed him to take a woman in labor to the hospital.

Another time Wes had a group of students in the truck when they were stopped at a checkpoint. Some of the students didn't have all the identification papers they needed, so they were hauled off to jail. "If they're going, I'm going too," Wes informed the soldiers. Accordingly he spent the night in jail with the students—and the bedbugs, no doubt.

Recounting this, Norm complained, "Nothing ever happens to me!"

Well, one Sunday something did happen. Mission Aviation Fellowship had not worked in the Belgian Congo. Norm had to make all those trips to other hospitals by truck. But after independence MAF did start flying there. Norm was commissioned to find a good site for an airstrip at Moanza—not an easy assignment, if you remember that the terrain there is hills and more hills. He had been scouting around and found a possible site, and men had started clearing it. Officials at the nearest government post got wind of this, and one Sunday during church a truckload of them drove into the station demanding of the Moanza people, "Turn your doctor over to us!" They were afraid the airstrip would be used for landing paratroopers!

Worshiping in church, Norm knew nothing of this until the service was over and he came out, to find the government truck surrounded by men with machetes, not about to surrender their doctor! He was able to reassure the officials, "No paratroopers will land here. The strip will be long enough for only very small planes."

After several months Norm developed tendonitis, an inflammation of the rotator cuff which gave him shoulder pain. He had no doubt used his arm unwisely. Also, he'd been separated from his wife and children too long. What do families do when one is in the military?

At Judson House, Don was off on deputation. Their little Becky had been unwell for some time, and Betsy took her to the doctor. The diagnosis: leukemia. Don came home as fast as he could. Good thing he wasn't in the Congo. There followed many medical visits and lots of talk about the Jimmy Fund, set up to combat leukemia and pay for its costs. Becky was a charming three-year-old; they said, "Her picture will make lots of money for the Jimmy Fund," but when a camera appeared Becky's smiles went into hiding.

In those days there wasn't enough that could be done for leukemia. As her parents put it, "It took two years watching her suffer before we were willing to let her go."

June came; the kids were out of school. They had been given the opportunity to set up little savings accounts. With her savings Grace went to the store and proudly bought her own Cinderella watch.

We were to fly to Congo July 4. I busily bought our refit, items we would need for the next term, the term Norm had already started. There were shoes for the children in several sizes for the next few years. I replaced some of the tableware we had taken out the first time. When we first left the States aluminum tumblers in different colors were in style, but when we offered one to a senior missionary at Moanza she stated, "I don't drink out of a tin cup." I searched for a glass tumbler and tried again. She added, "Or a jelly glass." So now I bought proper glass glasses. We never left anything in the store packing; we always took it out and protected it between cloth items we were taking anyway, to save space. I think I lost one of those pretty little jelly glasses that way on the first experience. That was the only breakage. But for a later term we lined a metal barrel with a 2-inch foam mattress and then filled the interior with miscellaneous household items, including a bottle of vanilla, which managed to break, adding unusual color and temporary fragrance to several other things.

My parents came again to help me with the packing. It would have been good to send the things off a month or so before we left, but we were never that foresighted. The transport people must have come for them July 3rd, and the Fourth of July we were on our way for our second term.

CHAPTER EIGHT

A Multicolored Cloth

Our plane duly arrived in Leopoldville and we were met by a very happy husband and daddy. We stayed in the capital city a little while. During that time we took a trip to Nsona Mpangu, the station where Don and Betsy had been. Their house had been left exactly the way it was when they evacuated. On the way we stopped at our first station, Sona Bata, glad to see old friends. One was a young male nurse who had married his sweet Catholic bride during our time there. When their first baby came, she had to be delivered by Caesarean section. The father was so grateful for the good outcome for mother and child that they named the baby Abelline. That was flattering, but less so when we discovered the child's other name: *Mpesi.* That means "cockroach." We asked, "Why would you name a child Cockroach?"

We were told, "A cockroach eats everything. We want to be sure this child will always have enough to eat." But if we'd asked someone else we might have got a different answer. On this visit we posed for a photo, Abelline's mother holding Marjorie and I holding Abelline. Many years later we found Abelline working as an auxiliary nurse at IME.

Jean with Abelline, her mother with Marjorie

Bobby and Grace had stayed with friends in the city. The children were taken to a swimming pool, where Grace took off her prized watch at the last minute and laid it carefully on the bench in the changing room. When she came back after swimming, the watch was gone. *Kiadi!* (sorrow). Grace learned early to weather disappointments.

It was August by the time we actually made it back to Moanza. And our beloved colleagues Cliff and Joy didn't get there till September. The mission board decreed Norm should not leave Moanza before the other missionary family came. He was happy with the decision, as he needed time to work at his own hospital, but what was the board thinking, he shouldn't leave his family "alone"? Didn't they count our Congolese "family," who surely would have protected us if any protecting was needed?

When both families were back, the pastor held a special welcoming service for us in church. This is the way he put it: "You know, in our country the women wear cloths of different, bright colors, but we men wear plain khaki shirts. For a while we were like a khaki shirt, all the same color, but now that our white friends are back we're like a multicolored cloth."

It was good to be back. We lived in the house on the other end of missionary row this time, the one Miggs had occupied. Neither she nor Ted and Pete would be coming back; they were about ready for retirement anyway. Cliff and Joy had the big house that had been Ted and Pete's, where Wes and Norm had led their bachelor existence for five months.

At the beginning of our furlough we had talked about speaking French one meal a day and Kikongo one meal. That lasted about one day. Now Bobby went out and played with his friends and soon got his language proficiency back. Grace's friends didn't come so often; girls had to help their mothers and were free only on Sundays. And when they did appear she hid behind a curtain because she'd forgotten how to talk with them!

Grace had promised, "I'll take all the care of the baby!" She had turned eight in the States and was indeed a great help. We celebrated Marjorie's first birthday in September. She sat happily in a playpen, enjoying the gift wrap more than the presents.

Remember the stuff we had shipped just before we left the States July 4? It arrived in the port of Matadi, made it through customs all right, must have been put on a train to Leopoldville, then a boat up the Congo River, branching off into the Kwa, then the Kasai. At Mbandaka, where the Kwilu runs into the Kasai, it was transshipped to a smaller boat to ascend the Kwilu and eventually the beautiful little Inzia River on which or above which Moanza was built. The trouble was that by this time it was October and rainy season had begun. Our barrels and cases came safely off the boat into the little warehouse on the bank, but the road from there to the church center stayed so muddy the truck couldn't make the trip down to get our freight. The barrels and cases stayed in the warehouse.

One day toward the end of October 1961, a boy was brought in to the hospital who had fallen from a tree and been impaled on a broken branch on the way down. His intestine was pierced; Norm had to perform a colostomy to let the intestine heal.

A previous surgical challenge had involved a man whose gun had accidentally gone off while standing vertical between his knees and shot off his jaw. Norm needed a nasogastric tube so the man could be fed, but there wasn't any available. He tried another kind of tube. It was too small; it just curled up and never made it down to the stomach. That man had to be flown to Vanga. Thank God for MAF!

But now, operating on the boy, Norm wasn't feeling too well himself. He stayed in bed the next day, saying, "I guess I've got malaria"—a pretty likely diagnosis in the tropics.

"It seems more like flu to me," I judged, and so did a doctor who happened to visit Moanza in the ensuing days. Whatever it was, it wasn't getting better.

The time came to undo the boy's colostomy. Norm didn't have the strength to go up to the hospital, so they brought the boy to our house and laid him on sterile sheets on our living room floor. Norm knelt beside him and did the necessary surgery. When his strength ran out he would lie on his side and rest until he could get back to work. Grace remembers coming into the adjoining dining room and seeing the strange sight of her dad on his side and other members of the surgical team kneeling around someone lying in the middle of the living room floor. I hadn't thought to inform the kids of what was going on! Grace says, "I decided I wasn't supposed to be there."

It may have been the next day that Norm noticed weakness in his left hand and arm. Neither malaria nor flu would explain that. We got on the radio and asked a doctor in Leopoldville, "Could you come up on the next plane?"

He suggested, "Why don't you fly down to Leopoldville instead?" MAF pilot John and his wife had planned a little visit to Moanza. I had made a mango cake in preparation for their coming. Now we had to ask them instead of visiting us to take us to the city.

Joy offered to keep Bobby and Grace while we were away. The children had been together in school, one mother teaching Tim and our Bobby in the same grade and the other one taking our Grace and Rick, a year apart. Now Joy would have all the teaching to do, plus mothering. Little Marjorie, 13 months old, and I got on the plane with Norm, who lay on a mattress on the floor. "Can you walk?" the pilot had asked him.

"No," Norm admitted. Then he amended, "Well, I could walk a few steps." John didn't ask him to.

Some time later I saw the diary Grace was keeping at that time. The day after our departure she wrote, "They did not come back." The next day: "They stil [sic] did not come." The following day: "They stil did not come" and so on, day after day. It made very poignant reading until Grace confessed that it had been one of those times when you don't write in your diary every day and fill in whatever you can remember when you finally try to catch up. You can see what she remembered.

CHAPTER NINE

Unexpected Furlough

We didn't know it at the time, but boarding that little MAF plane to leave Moanza in late 1961 was to signal the end of our truncated second term in Congo, and a new kind of life for Norm. We had been rejoicing that our two missionary families were back at Moanza, resuming our work or starting new work. Now everything was changed again.

What did Norm have? Nobody thought it could be polio. We had all received a full course of Salk vaccine back in 1956. But for whatever reason, Norm's left hand was paralyzed, and he was steadily getting weaker. Someone suggested Guillain-Barré syndrome. It causes paralysis somewhat similar to polio. But it wasn't that.

In Leopoldville Norm was taken to the white hospital. It wasn't necessarily painted white; it was intended for white people, in contrast to the humongous hospital available to Africans—crowded, noisy, dirty, not brimming with hope. This time I did not complain that my husband got better treatment than the Congolese. We wouldn't have thought of taking him to the city hospital even for a relatively minor illness or accident; now he was undiagnosed with something major, mysterious and scary.

The white hospital had lovely big rooms, each with access to the veranda. We learned to our surprise that, just as in the hospitals we served, each patient needed a family member to stay with him—but I did not have to prepare his meals. Little Marjorie was just learning to walk; the stone tile floors, slanted toward the veranda to make mopping easier, didn't help any. Besides, she wasn't welcome. There was even a bed for me (I didn't have to unroll a mat under my husband's bed as a Congolese wife would do!), but no provision for a toddler. Margaret, whose husband, Chet, was mission secretary, graciously offered to care for her most of the time along with all her regular responsibilities. Once during that stay the young people staffing UMH, the interdenominational mission guest house, kept her for me for an afternoon. They introduced her to Coca-Cola!

Norm's paralysis proved to be more extensive than appreciated at first. Only his left arm and hand were completely paralyzed; his legs, back and shoulders had several partially paralyzed muscles and his nerves in general were jumpy. It was hard for him to sleep. Sometimes I took him for wheelchair rides; it seems to me we found out later that wasn't a good idea. The doctor gave him a small ball to squeeze in his paralyzed hand. Norm told me, "That's the index of his incompetence to treat this."

The doctor threatened, "If you're not better by next week, I'm going to send the physical therapist to see you." The therapist came and massaged his limbs. I tried to learn how. The doctor said to me, "Oh, you want to *voler le métier* (steal his profession)"!

Eventually Chet and others decided Norm should go to the States to recover—return to Strong Memorial Hospital in Rochester, NY, where he had trained.

So finally, Grace, Mom did come home, although Daddy didn't. I was ready to go with him, but Chet had a much more practical solution in mind: Jerry, mission treasurer, would go with Norm; I would return to Moanza to pack up our belongings and follow in some three weeks' time. Norm and Jerry left on Thanksgiving Day. Norm's brother David met them at Kennedy airport in New York. He remembers seeing Norm being carried down the stairway in a wheelchair. "I was shocked to find that he couldn't move any one of his four limbs." David accompanied him on the plane to Rochester and on to Strong Memorial Hospital, at his alma mater.

At Moanza I had plenty to do. Of course there was less to pack because those barrels were still in the warehouse down by the river. On the other hand, we needed some of their contents for the trip home. We had a list of the contents of each barrel, but were the shoes we needed the ones in #1 or #4? The road was still muddy; men carried the barrels we needed on poles on their shoulders the old way, not dependent on technology. It behooved me to figure out exactly which barrels I really had to have. When I did come to the shoes Grace had grown into, that I had ordered from a catalog, lo and behold, they were light blue velvet with rhinestones or sequins. Tim remarked in his admiring nine-year-old way, "Those are real diamonds, aren't they!"

Once during those days it occurred to me that Norm might die. Somehow I had never thought that before. I was crying a little as I walked through the house, and our cook decided I was pretty weak.

Many friends came to say good-by and wish us well. They usually included something like this: "I'm sure you'll come back, but in case you don't, could I buy your bed?"

At the hospital in Leopoldville, Norm had received visits from friends, usually from Sona Bata. Their wishes went, "We're praying with all our hearts that you'll get well and come back to help us."

Marc was different. Marc had graduated from the Sona Bata nursing school about the same time as Kimpiatu. He made an excellent nurse, but he decided to go back to school, hoping to become a doctor. He took the first cycle of secondary school at Nsona Mpangu, downriver from Kimpese, and then moved to Kimpese for the second three years. He had four children when he began this endeavor. He would come to

Marc and family

Sona Bata to work at the hospital during vacations. One year he asked me to tutor him in history; I was glad to do it. The next year it was physics. I had never taken physics myself, didn't think I was capable of understanding it, but I took his book and started working on it. I found out I had been right; willing as I was, I could not help Marc with physics. Now Marc came to see Norm in the hospital and simply said, "We're praying with all our hearts that you'll get well." Over the years he became Norm's best friend.

The children and I were to fly from Leopoldville December 15. MAF would come for us December 13, giving us two nights in the city.

We really needed that day: Bobby had only short pants, which would not be at all suitable for arriving in New York State in December.

A problem arose. Before my return from Leopoldville a flu bug had attacked Cliff and Joy's children. Now it was Grace's turn. Then Marjorie came down with it too. While I was tending to one on the small plane, the other tossed her cookies just as we were landing. Marjorie was never very sick, but Grace was.

We were very glad to get settled in a large room at UMH. It even had its own bath. Not all the rooms did in those days. Grace made one trip to the bathroom after another. Then she got so weak I had to carry her to the bathroom, and finally I put a waterproof sheet on the bed and just kept changing her. There was a doctor staying at UMH. He gave me Kaopectate with Neomycin. I don't know what we would have done or how we could ever have gone on that plane without it. As it was, Grace gradually improved, and that evening she was hungry. She wanted an egg. This seems hard to believe now, but the kitchen was next door to our room and I was able to go in and soft-cook an egg for her. Then she wanted another. I prepared it and she ate it. The third egg turned out to be one too many, but she was on the mend.

The next day we did make that flight! On the plane was another doctor, a woman missionary on her way back to the States. She had paregoric. Grace was now strong enough to walk, and walk she did. It seemed as if she spent most of the flight in the tiny room at the tail of the plane, even when the RETURN TO YOUR SEAT sign came on. After every trip, another dose of bitter but blessed paregoric. In the morning breakfast was served. I was busy helping Grace when a very small hand came up to my tray table and helped itself to some of my scrambled eggs. Happily, Marjorie was not feeling sick. How grateful I was to God that he provided people to help us and the healing Grace needed!

When we left Leopoldville the temperature measured 80 degrees. In Syracuse, New York, it was 15. My mother had provided coats and caps and scarves and mittens, but they were with her in the terminal building. Now with jet ways, no problem, but getting down off the plane and walking across that windy tarmac—Bobby, Grace, and I with Marjorie—remains in my memory. I always said I never got warm that whole winter.

We took the girls to the doctor as soon as possible. He was more concerned about Marjorie because she was so young, but she got along fine. Grace was recovering too.

Finally we arrived in Rochester, where Norm was. He did have polio. Although the Salk vaccine did wonders, there were a very few people whom it did not protect completely. Perhaps Norm would have been more ill, even died, if he had not been vaccinated. When he was at Strong, there were only two other polio patients in that large hospital, 17-year-old twins who had not been vaccinated. The March of Dimes paid his hospital expenses, once we realized we needed to contact them. Our American Baptist Foreign Mission Society was taking care of them at first.

I had hoped to be able to stay in the missionary apartment at Colgate-Rochester Divinity School, but this was the middle of the school year and the apartment was occupied. Bill had been our pastor during our four years in Rochester. Now he was on the faculty at Colgate-Rochester. He and his wife took us into their home until a more permanent place could be found. How helpful people were to us, at Moanza, in Leopoldville, in Rochester! I'm sure we never expressed our appreciation, just accepted their help and sacrifice of their own convenience. We spent Christmas with Bill and his wife. Then we were allowed to move into a dorm intended for married students.

Strong Memorial Hospital was a far cry from the white hospital in Leopoldville. There were lots of nurses and therapists, and they all knew what they were doing. Norm received whirlpool baths, massage, and all the other treatments that helped polio patients regain as much use of their muscles as possible. I asked his doctor, "How soon will he be able to come home?"

The doctor replied, "In a couple of weeks." After a couple of weeks, the time had become a couple more weeks. This went on until April. It would be so much better to expect a longer wait and then be pleasantly surprised.

A couple we had never met did us a great favor. They were a mature couple, empty nesters, on their way to mission work in Hong Kong. They were buying a new car to take with them. Instead of trading in their old one, they gave it to us. When I visited Norm at the hospital he made me out a maintenance schedule.

Before we ever went overseas we had attended a Camp Farthest Out with Norm's parents and sister and heard of Agnes Sanford, now called "the Grandmother of the Third Wave." That's the third wave of the Holy Spirit. Back in 1954 we first heard of her remarkable success in healing through prayer. Now Mother Abell sent one of Agnes' books to each of us. Norm received her first teaching book, *The Healing Light.* But Mother knew me well and sent me Agnes' first novel, *Oh, Watchman.* All her novels were teaching books too. I opened the book at 10:30 one night when I went to bed in my lonely little room in Eaton Hall. I closed it at 2:30 a.m. when I'd read the last page. It told the most exciting news I could imagine. The Holy Spirit was doing what I'd always thought he should be doing but I didn't know he was —healing people in body and mind, working miracles! Norm took a little longer to read *The Healing Light,* and later when I read it, it took me quite a while because I felt I should put one chapter into practice before I went on to the next. The first chapter explains that God wants us well; if we pray for healing and it doesn't occur, it doesn't mean God doesn't exist, or that he's not able or willing to heal. It just means we need to learn more about how to pray.

As Norm gained strength and some muscles came back, he was able to move around the hospital some. His grandmother was admitted to the same hospital, and he could visit her. She was concerned that perhaps no one would come when she pushed her button. Norm reassured her, "There's always one nurse who comes."

The next time a nurse came into her room, Grandma addressed her, "My grandson tells me there's always one nurse who comes when you call. Are you that nurse?"

Norm also visited the hospital administrator's office. On our return to the Congo in 1961, we had found Kimpiatu, the head nurse who had been so helpful to us at Sona Bata, had carried on the hospital work magnificently after the missionaries were evacuated, performing emergency surgery. Now Norm was able to arrange for him to come to Strong Memorial Hospital and act like a surgical intern, getting valuable experience in surgery and hospital administration. His very first day in the operating room he got to see Siamese twins separated! He was paid as an orderly. Colgate-Rochester allowed him to room

Kimpiatu in the States

in one of their dormitories. An African-American student befriended him, showed him how to use the laundry, also took him to a Black Muslim meeting. Kimpiatu's verdict: "It's political, not religious." One time we were praying at our house (we had moved into an apartment by then) and at the end Kimpiatu said, "Maybe one day things will be much better in Congo, and we'll remember that we prayed."

He was at our apartment when he saw his first snow. He looked out the window and exclaimed, "It's beautiful!" Then he went outside and picked some up. "It's cold!"

At last came the final week of Norm's hospitalization. His roommate was discharged and left a newspaper behind. Norm picked it up and looked through it. There was no reason for him to read the church notices, but this time he did. Lo and behold, Agnes Sanford was coming to Buffalo for a week-long mission, teaching about healing. Norm felt sure the Holy Spirit had supplied that newspaper and directed him to that page.

Norm was discharged from the hospital, and the next week we drove 70 miles to Buffalo every night to hear Agnes Sanford. At one point she invited each of us to choose a subject to pray about in faith. She cautioned us to begin with a little thing, and I tried, but no little thing came to mind, so I prayed for Norm's healing. It didn't happen, but I didn't stop praying. We also were able to talk with Agnes personally after at least one of the sessions. She invited us to come to her School of Pastoral Care in Whitinsville, MA, where we could learn more about prayer for healing.

Norm's first act when he was released from the hospital was to get a book on how to do things with one hand. I helped him continue the exercises he

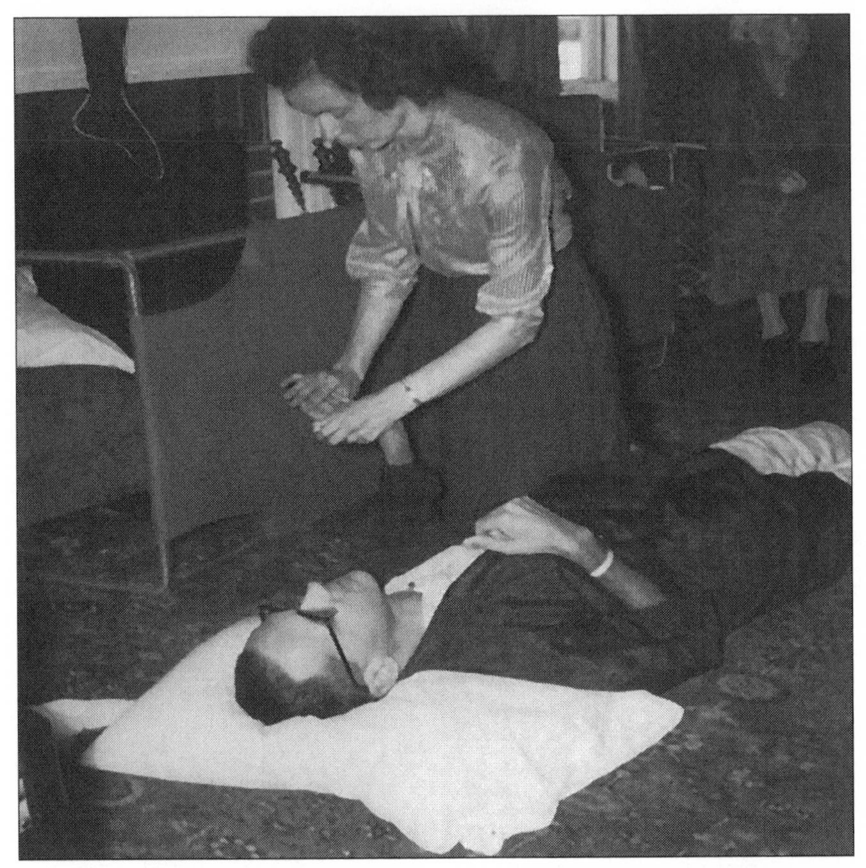

Jean works with Norm's hand

had done in the hospital, and we rejoiced together over any flicker of life in a previously dead muscle. After a while there wasn't any more improvement, but Norm never complained. He just found ways to compensate for the loss of activity in his left arm and hand. I would find just buttoning buttons with one hand terribly frustrating, but he did it for 50 years. Once in a while the top shirt button defied him; he found me a little tool made for overcoming recalcitrant buttons and allowed me to help that much.

In order to get insurance for the car, Norm had to give up his driver's license. It was in driving around Rochester with Norm in the passenger's seat that I really learned city driving.

There was a School of Pastoral Care in May. Norm would have liked me to go, but I didn't see how I could with Bobby and Grace in school, so Norm went. "Was it wonderful, honey?"

"I was blessed, but I felt as if I was on the outside looking in." When I went to the next session in August I determined that wasn't going to happen to me. I told Agnes Sanford about it, and she invited me to a small group that met in an upstairs room during a free time in the morning. I went, and she herself prayed for me to receive the baptism of the Holy Spirit. I was very conscious of the love in the room but didn't feel anything happened at the time of the prayer. I was encouraged to stay alone afterward and be open to speaking in a prayer language. I did for a while, but it didn't occur to me to skip lunch for that purpose! In the years since, I have sometimes used a prayer language but never been sure it was the real thing. But something happened. My roommates at the School saw a change. And when I got home, guess what Norm noticed. I was quieter! I remember taking Bobby to camp and driving home praying away. Good thing there wasn't much traffic.

We were able to attend another School of Pastoral Care together some years later, and since then I've read almost all of Agnes' books. It took a couple of years for *The Healing Light* to find a publisher. Nobody had faith that people would believe it. MacAlaster Park finally took the plunge, and *The Healing Light* met an overwhelming welcome. One day years later, Agnes wasn't feeling well. She told us during her school, "I don't remember what the problem was—sawdust leaking out somewhere." This was very unusual; Agnes could spill hot oil on her arm and just remind it she was protected. But now she was at a low ebb in general. She shared her discouragement with a neighbor on a train, who offered, "I know a book that could help you; it's called *The Healing Light.*" Agnes decided that wouldn't meet her need this time. She and two spiritual friends who were in a similar state "made a retreat" at a house in the western desert. First they prayed for healing, but no healing came. Agnes taught us, "When you've prayed for something for several days and nothing happens, ask God how you should pray." She gave us several examples of this. One time she felt that something bad was going to happen in the Pacific Northwest. She asked God if she could pray for it not to happen. He said no.

"Can I pray for it to be less?"

"Yes."

Agnes, in her delightful humility, often said, "My guidance is the most fallible thing there is." If her guidance was fallible, whose in the world is less so?

Another example: Her mother was stricken with Alzheimer's. Agnes asked, "Can I pray for it to be healed?"

"No, she's suffered too much. You can pray for her to remember only the good things."

Agnes did, and her mother quietly lived with only the good memories.

Back to the retreat house in the desert. The three women asked God how they should pray. Each of them separately received the word, "Ask for the Holy Spirit."

Agnes told us, "I thought I had the Holy Spirit." But they prayed two for one, two for one, two for one. Agnes told us, "If a fourth person had been there, he wouldn't have known anything happened. But each of us was conscious, first, that we had been healed of whatever was wrong with us, and second, that we had received power."

After that experience Agnes believed that when one receives water baptism he receives the Holy Spirit, but it's latent. Unless one is expecting to receive the Spirit in his power at that time, it takes another step.

During the summer of 1962 we moved to a half house on Field Street. People were very generous in lending us furniture. Marjorie celebrated her second birthday. One day Grace was washing clothes in the wringer washer in the basement. Marjorie caught the clothes as they came through the wringer. At one point one piece got twisted and

Grace made the wringer go backward briefly. Consternation! Here came Marjorie's fingers through the wringer! Grace did everything right. She hit the right place to loosen the wringer and brought Marjorie upstairs to me. Only then did she start to feel faint.

With the New Year we had passage to return to the Congo by freighter. At one time we were to travel on the *African Lightning.* That didn't seem a very good omen. Our travel was delayed; we finally sailed on the *African Glade.*

During the delay we stayed with my parents. They had a young woman living with them as she continued her education. They had become very fond of her; to some extent she filled the empty spot in their home, with their only child and all her family so far away. Now we met her and were living in the same house. Sadly, I found she rubbed me the wrong way. Was I jealous? I didn't think so, but the enemy got in his licks and robbed me of what the Holy Spirit had given. I was pregnant and not telling anyone but Norm, because you weren't supposed to travel during the first three months. That made me more ornery than I would have been otherwise. It's a period of which I feel very much ashamed. I caused my wonderful mother a lot of suffering.

Eventually we moved to Beacon on the Hudson, where Norm's folks were. One day I took the train to New York City to get a yellow fever shot. On the way back I amused myself by reading the fine print on our tickets. The freighter captain could do anything he wanted to: change the schedule without notice, change the port of call, go backward, even lie on the bottom!

That day I also noticed a small swelling over one hipbone, about the size of a bean. It itched. Norm was as mystified as I was.

On Valentine's Day of 1963 we finally set sail. There were more passengers than on the *Armand Grisard.* Our waiter was very friendly and helpful. "Eddie," I said, "I feel a bit seasick. I'll just have a little fruit, please."

Eddie, experienced with seasick passengers, explained, "Fruit isn't the best idea. Let me bring you some crackers."

He did, and of course he was right. The nausea went away, and we enjoyed the voyage, keeping a monopoly game going in the lounge.

CHAPTER TEN

A New Station

This time we were being sent to Vanga. Norm was supposed to work only half time, so we were going to a station where Dr. Dan was in charge of the medical work. Norm's assignment was the nursing school Dan had already started. Norm enjoyed teaching the students. Of course he wasn't the only teacher. Gini, for instance, taught obstetrics and midwifery. One unit Norm taught was on asepsis and antisepsis. Emphasizing the importance of the skin as a barrier to infection, he quoted an earlier doctor: *"Une piqure d'épingle est une porte ouverte à la mort."* (A pinprick is an open door to death!) Of course he also taught about Louis Pasteur and pasteurization. On the exam one student informed him, *"Le pasteur* (the pastor, rather than Pasteur) *a découvert la méthode de l' épingle pour tuer les microbes."* (discovered the pin method for killing microbes). Norm had visions of a pastor with a large open safety pin, stabbing each microbe as it came along.

We arrived in April; the baby was due in August. Miriam guessed my secret right away, despite my bouffant petticoat. We had left Bobby in the city to stay at the hostel and attend the new American school. Unfortunately the other boys at the hostel were suffering from some malady that had not yet been diagnosed. We were up at Vanga when we heard that it was hepatitis. By the time Bobby came down with it their spring vacation was coming. What to do? We didn't want to bring Bobby to Vanga and expose people there to hepatitis, and the hostel parents didn't really want to spend their vacation at the hostel while all the other children were at home, just to take care of Bobby. So little Marjorie and I went down to the city to take care of Bobby. We got gamma globulin shots and were very careful, washing our hands at every opportunity. By the time spring break was over, Bobby had recovered. The first evening everyone was back, the day before school resumed, we all sat on the floor while Uncle Don showed a move. (That's what the children called him—MKs referred to our missionary colleagues as Uncle or Aunt.) Marjorie felt she had to get up three times during the movie to go wash her hands.

Our first home at Vanga had been a guest house and had apparently grown like Topsy. Going from one room to another, one usually ascended or descended a step. The kitchen was a narrow room along the back of the house, lower than the dining room, and the door from the kitchen to the outside left space between it and the floor. One evening I was at the far end of the long, narrow bathroom and saw something on the floor between me and the door. When the something moved, I realized it was a thin snake. I called Norm; he came and pinned the snake down at the neck with a narrow board. Then he asked me, "Come hold this while I get a machete."

"I'm afraid I won't do it right and he'll get away!"

"Then go get help."

I never would have made a pioneer wife. My admiration for Norma surpasses all bounds. She lived across the (dirt) street in a large house with a basement. Once when she was going downstairs a snake plopped down right in front of her, and she was as scared of snakes as I was. This was her first term. Eventually a nest of snakes was discovered in that basement. I don't think I would have stuck it out. Another snake made its way under the kitchen door before we moved from that house.

At Vanga they spoke Kituba (the trade language based on Kikongo, different from the village Kikongo we had spoken at Sona Bata and Moanza). Kikongo is the name of the language and also the name of the church station where we would eventually live. We proceeded to study Kituba, which is much like Kikongo but with a simplified grammar and influence from Lingala. My recipe file for the cook (this one could read) shows my faltering progress from Kikongo to Kituba. One day I wanted the cook to make angel food cake, so I translated the recipe and called it *Gateau ya Zimbasi* (cake of angels). The next day I wanted a devil's food cake. I called it Chocolate Cake. The most interesting faux pas I'm aware of came when I attempted to translate "Serves eight." I tried to say, "This food will feed eight people." *Dia* means "to eat" in both languages. *Dikila* means "to feed" in Kikongo, so that's what I wrote. Unfortunately I had written in Kituba, "This food will poison eight people."

In July Dr. Dan gave me a prenatal exam. He announced that the baby was still quite small and would surely not be born before the due date in August. It was probably at that time that we showed him the interesting bean sitting over my right pelvic bone. He felt we should have it out posthaste in case it should be malignant. I had not heard of a cancer that itched so did not feel worried. Dan excised the little tumor and then said to Norm, "Well, shall we cut it open?"

Norm mildly replied, "Well, yes." I had supposed that was the whole idea, but Dan was always making deadpan jokes. So they cut it in two and it turned out to be full of a coiled-up little worm—*onchocerca volvulus.* I was lucky, or blessed; if it had been two worms they would have produced lots of eggs and given trouble all over my body. The amazing thing was that this tropical infestation had appeared at least 13 months after we had left the tropics.

Jimmy was born in July. I had intended to go to the hospital for this, my only delivery in the Congo, but there wasn't time. I'd been having false labor every night and had decided that this night I was not going to wake Norm—but I sure wouldn't mind if he woke up himself. And Norm did wake up in time. He examined me and was going to go for Dr. Dan, but I didn't want him to leave me alone, so he went to wake Bobby instead. Bobby, 11, was a sound sleeper, but this time he woke up promptly and did his errand with dispatch. While he was gone, all Dr. Norm could think of to do was boil water! Dr. Dan came, examined me, and directed, "Bobby, go back for nurse Miriam." It is convenient when the doctor's wife is a nurse. In the morning our cook was quite surprised to find a sixth inhabitant in the house.

Jimmy had problems nursing at first, as Bobby had done, but Miriam encouraged me and he succeeded. When he was a month old I wanted to get a picture of him naked; I changed my mind. His poor little bottom looked scalded. I had told the wash jack (laundry man), "Wash the diapers in spring water (carried in pails) because the river water is so polluted." I had also directed him, "Rinse them four times." Now I said, "Wash them in the river." The diaper rash disappeared right away. Congolese, used to washing clothes in a flowing stream, rub each piece thoroughly with bar soap. Of course, in a tub the soap accumulates in the water. Whether or not those diapers had been rinsed four times, a lot of soap had been staying in them. Whatever pollution

Welcoming brand new Jimmy

was in the river, the flowing water washed away the soap. Soon we got a charming picture of a clothed Jimmy in my arms with Norm and the rest of the family admiring him. Grace wrote an excellent story about him for Calvert School, and three-year-old Marjorie considered him her special responsibility. He was the only one of our children to learn colors before the age of three; I figured it was because Marjorie taught him from his stack of nesting rings.

Going back to his earliest infancy, one day I realized that Jimmy didn't startle when someone else came into the room and I spoke to that other person. If my voice was loud enough to carry to the door, it should have been too loud for the baby at my breast. Thunder didn't bother him. I tried clapping my hands over his head; no reaction. I told Doris, "I think my baby's deaf."

"I'll pray for him," she promised. And of course she did. I'll never know whether Jimmy was deaf at first or not, but as he developed he heard just fine. Thank you, Father.

That dry season Scotty and Dolores went on furlough and we moved into their house, all on one level and much roomier. It was the easiest move ever, as the houses were next door to each other and we just moved one room at a time. Our cook made breakfast for us in the old house, moved the kitchen and cooked the noon meal in the new house. He was really fast.

The wash jack was a young fellow. He and Bobby became good friends and even owned a canoe together. When we had lived in the new house for some time, the wash jack came to us and told us, "The cook is stealing things from your kitchen (like dishtowels) and giving them to his mistress." I was more upset about the mistress than the stealing.

We called both men in and talked with them together. After they left Norm told me, "I'm sure from their body language that the wash jack is telling the truth and the cook is guilty as charged." We let him go. I wonder if we could have acted redemptively instead of just dismissing him.

We found Vanga a difficult station. Congolese leaders and missionaries met together for station council. One time several missionaries had gathered in the missionary home where we were meeting; only two Congolese had arrived. One said to the other, "We're the only ones here."

On the other hand, one day one of the missionary women exclaimed, "I can't find Doris anywhere! I've been to every house." Of course she meant every missionary house.

A problem arose that has persisted and grown worse since then. The local people were eager for the school to take in as many students as possible so their children could get diplomas. The missionaries were concerned for the quality of education and pointed out that we didn't have enough teachers to teach all the hours required for the extra sections. We finally asked people to come up from the central office in Leopoldville to mediate. And we prayed that God's will would be done.

The missionaries were outvoted. I suggested that perhaps, even though it didn't seem right to us, the decision was God's will. I did not convince any other missionary. I was to teach French, mornings only. I had to choose whether to teach literature or grammar. I chose literature, hoping to get in some grammar along the way. We had a little library, enriched by a number of paperback books translated from English, not very appropriate for our students. At one time I asked each student in a class to take out a library book, read it, and report on it. I found out that they would read about three pages and then write their report. Some of those students went on to college in the States! How did they do it?

Norm's medical work was more stressful. One senior nurse's aide was especially prickly. At a staff meeting he became quite angry with Norm and, pointing a finger at him (very impolite in the Congo), enunciated with considerable heat, *"Vous êtes capable!"* His intention was clear, but instead of saying, "You are guilty *(coupable),*" he had declared, "You are capable!"

Another time a girl student had written, *"J'ai ceinté par Makalala."* That's execrable French by which she accused a senior nurse of making her pregnant. Talking with the nurse, for some reason Norm unthinkingly handed him the accusation to read, so of course he no longer had any evidence. The girl's reputation didn't lead to unbounded confidence in her anyway. It was at Vanga that Norm developed asthma.

There were some funny experiences. At one time there were two mentally ill people circulating at the church center—a man who would harangue people at the flagpole where the hospital staff gathered every morning, and a woman with a two-year-old boy. One of the missionaries gave her a pair of shorts for the little boy; she somehow managed to get them on herself. The house where we were living had a large veranda; some beds under construction for the nursing students were temporarily housed there. The woman (we started calling her "our lady") decided to take up residence on that veranda. Eventually Norm decided that wasn't a very good idea and moved her to one of the little rooms in the outbuilding behind the house. We found some of the local men were jokingly calling her his concubine!

Once we invited a few of the station leaders to come to our home to pray with us. It was very good. Why didn't we do it regularly?

Norm's dad was a sanitary engineer, and Norm had engineering interests and abilities too. Vanga needed a better water source; Norm decided to prospect for one. He found a good site with a spring down in a valley next to the nursing school. He supervised the construction of a concrete cylinder about six feet in diameter. Wooden forms, inner and outer, were built. Concrete was poured to a depth of three feet, with reinforcing iron. When the concrete was set and ready, the soil was dug out from within and beneath the concrete wall to lower the

Norm's successful engineering project

cylinder to the depth needed to get a good flow of water. A second section of concrete was poured on top of the first, making a six-foot tall cylinder of concrete about three inches thick. Such a heavy structure was not really appropriate for that job, but Norm was not an experienced builder! Anyhow, the work progressed, and sand and clay were removed from under the concrete, letting the cylinder settle. What was not foreseen was the difference in soil on the upstream side (clay) and the downstream side (sand). When the water started coming in faster, it began washing away the sand on the downstream side and it was hard to remove the clay on the other side. The cylinder tipped, impeding any further lowering of the structure. But that did not prevent the good flow of water, and the water source was a success, although Norm was not proud of his Leaning Tower of Vanga. A visiting builder from the States took on the job of piping the water to a reservoir uphill from the hospital.

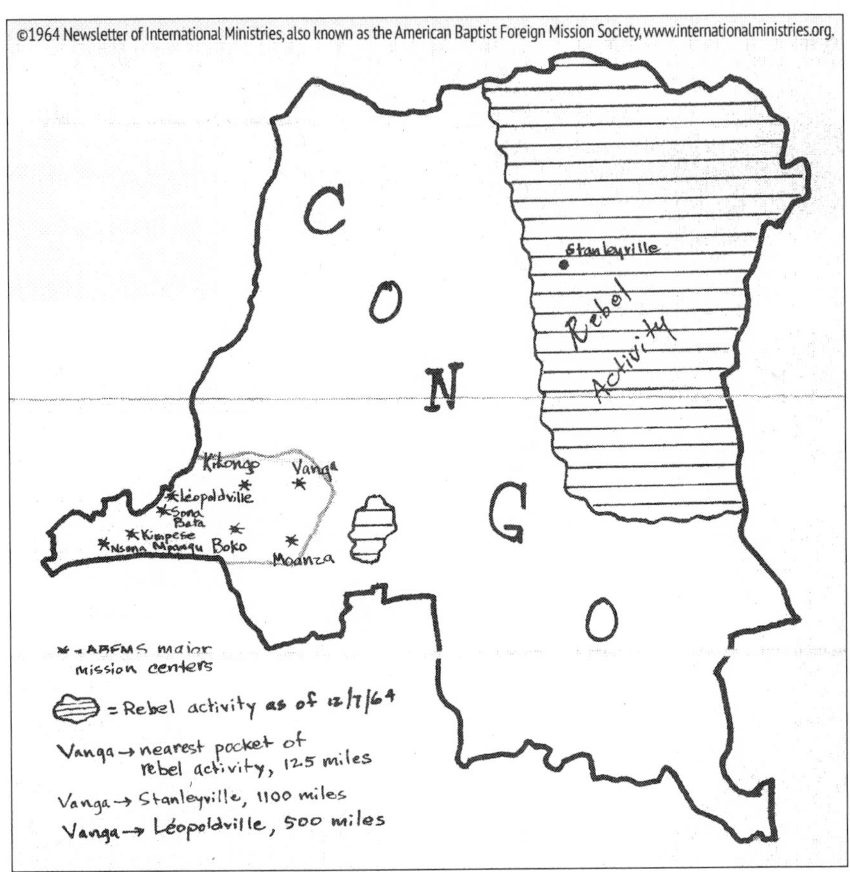

American Baptist mission work and rebel activity in the Congo, 1964

In 1964 Mulele started a rebellion in Bandundu Province, where Vanga was located, but east of us, on the other side of the Kwilu River. This was the precursor of the Simba Rebellion in the northeast part of the country. The rebels felt that the educated people were oppressing them, so they were out to get anyone with an education. A few missionaries and many Congolese were killed; much property was destroyed. We learned that even a concrete building will burn if soaked in gasoline. Missionaries from across the river began to flee, and we discussed whether we should evacuate.

Now I'm quite sure it was before this happened that a little revival had begun among the missionaries. One missionary couple, Norm and Von, made a room behind their house available as a prayer chamber, and we had a kind of prayer vigil there, with different people scheduled for different times.

It was after missionary prayer meeting at Norm and Von's that we had this conversation about whether to evacuate. I didn't want to. After the meeting it happened to be my turn to use the prayer room. While I was praying I began to hear a lot of noise down by the river. No, I wasn't afraid. I wasn't? My heart started beating faster, and that perspiration couldn't be blamed entirely on the muggy atmosphere. And what turned out to be the cause of the commotion? The riverboat had docked, and the usual crowd had gathered.

In February it was decided that women and children should leave the station. The high school principal (Congolese) said to me, "We'd like to be able to leave too."

"Yes, of course you would. I hope you won't need to." All the missionaries could be flown out and even repatriated if necessary. If MAF started flying Congolese to the city, where would they stop?

We arrived in Leopoldville to find many other evacuees from other missions there. Americans who lived in the city had contributed clothes so that those who had fled with nothing would have something to wear. We were not in that situation; nothing of ours had been destroyed, and we'd each been able to bring out a small suitcase. There were a lot of us. It may have been Margaret who asked me, "Would you be willing to go to Sona Bata with Marjorie and Jimmy? Grace can stay at the hostel. Bob's already there."

"Yes, that would be good. I know the station and the language. I'll feel more comfortable there than crowding a family in Leopoldville." I didn't realize for many years how hard it was for Grace to be unceremoniously assigned to the hostel with her parents in two other places. She was especially afraid for her dad left at Vanga.

At Sona Bata the Coop was empty. It was a big rambling house where two single missionaries ordinarily lived. For some reason, not even one was there at that time. Missionaries provided the furniture the children and I needed, and there we were. And thoughtful Jeannette gave me something to do—teach psychology to the nursing students. I had taken one psychology course in college. She gave me a book. I'm not sure what the girls learned. I was also provided with a man to cook and clean and wash. He also watched the children while I taught my one class.

Jimmy was eight months old. He wasn't nursing very much, so I weaned him at Sona Bata. I used to say I weaned him to the thumb because he drank so little from a cup at that time. But he survived and grew to be 6' 2½" and valedictorian of his high school class, so I guess he didn't suffer from malnutrition. Another thing he did at Sona Bata was crawl to the back door, push open the screen door and fall off the steps. That didn't slow him down either.

Even with my psychology class I found life pretty limited with no one over three to talk with at home. God provided for that need too. Two other missionary wives came to Sona Bata to have babies and stayed with me at the Coop while they recovered. First came Gloria with her baby; she left and Trissie brought new little John. So there were three babies at the Coop during that evacuation period. The men left at Vanga decided they should pare their number down so those left could fit in one MAF plane if they needed to evacuate. They had to eliminate only one man, and Norm was chosen. After all, he was the second doctor, and of course he was also crippled with polio. So he left Vanga by plane and enjoyed visiting Boko and other places as the plane picked up other evacuees. Then he finally arrived at Sona Bata, and I was no longer lonely.

After two months away from our stations we all went to missionary retreat in the city. People planning the gathering had decided to have three speakers on successive days and name a reactor to react to each speech. Norm was chosen to speak one day, with Janie as his reactor. Janie had great gifts and great energy. Later, working with student wives at the seminary in the city, she produced the most powerful Easter play I've ever seen. She asked her cast, "Have you ever seen a play in Congo that wasn't a success?" No. "Have you ever seen one that accomplished its aim?" Another story. It's so much fun to make people laugh, and so easy to make them laugh, for instance, at the soldiers trembling and falling down when the angel comes to open the tomb. Janie got the people to keep their minds on what they wanted the play to accomplish. It was shown in the city and televised, and we saw it on TV the following Easter in Kimpese. Janie also prepared Sunday School lessons for Congo, lessons on the same theme for all the different ages. This filled a great need.

Back in 1964, Norm introduced his talk by saying, "Each of us speakers has a reactor, but I'm the only one with an atomic reactor." That brought the desired reaction. But it was April Fool's Day, and Norm thought of a good April Fool. We were all expecting to return to our stations after the retreat, so everyone was surprised when Norm announced seriously, "We've received word from Valley Forge (our mission headquarters) that we are all to return to the States immediately, turning over our work to the Canadian Baptists."

Surprise. Consternation. Wonder. Why would the Canadians be able to stay if we had to leave?

In the back of the church where we were meeting, I had just heard news that made me think, "Oh, dear, he shouldn't be making an April Fool joke at a time like this." Congolese were passing around the word that Pastor Lubikulu had just died. His name means "forgiveness." He's the only Congolese I've ever heard of with that name. He was an old, highly respected, beloved pastor. Jeannette was crying. Then we found out that Tata Lubikulu's death was also an April Fool. Perhaps he had been dying every April Fool's day for a while. Pastor Lubikulu lived a while longer, and we did go back to our homes and our work.

God brought at least one good thing out of the rebellion. In some cases Catholic and Protestant missionaries found themselves refugees together for the duration. Up until that time each group had distrusted the other, feeling pretty sure that those who didn't believe like them were lost. Now Protestants and Catholics found out to their surprise and joy that the others were Christians too.

CHAPTER ELEVEN

One-Hand Surgery

After two years at Vanga we went back to Moanza. The nurse who performed surgery there, Kitswaka, had gone to the States for training, as Kimpiatu had done before. Now Norm was to resume responsibility for the hospital there, doing surgery with his one good hand and the aid of a capable nurse named Mukengele.

The Moanza people who had said, "We're sure you'll be coming back" were very surprised when we actually did return. People had spread the rumor: "That young fellow who was cooking for them paid to have some witchcraft done. The penalty for not following all the rules was this curse on his employer." Come back to the same place where you'd been cursed? Never! Norm surprised them.

The year before, Leon had begun a junior high school at Moanza. Now it became my responsibility to head it up, one section each of seventh and eighth grades.

But between Vanga and Moanza we took a month's vacation at the coast. In those days it was cheap to stay at the hotel at Moanda. That month is memorable for two things. First, most of the family got sick.

The night we slept in Leopoldville on our way down toward the coast Norm complained, "My chest feels as if an elephant was sitting on it." He had an X-ray done at the general hospital. Nothing specific was found, and by the next day he felt better, so we resumed our journey. For the following year he felt unwell off and on; we didn't find out why until we went back to the States on home assignment and he had a stool examination! Working in water for the construction of the Leaning Tower in the valley at Vanga, he had picked up a parasite called *strongyloides* (threadworm). That night in the capital city the larvae were migrating through his lungs. Later on the symptoms were different. Once it was diagnosed, he took the proper treatment and was cured. The *strongyloides* did put an end to his asthma for a number of years!

Down at the coast, it was the turn of the two younger children, Marjorie and Jimmy. They both contracted measles, one after the other. Measles in Congo seems to be more severe than it is in the States. Usually this is thought to be because most Congolese children are not as well-nourished as American kids, but now our own children were having it hard. However, they both got over it, and because we were at the coast for a whole month, there was time for everyone to have some fun. I don't remember my getting sick, or Bob either. Grace waited till the day we left and had an upset stomach on the way.

The other memorable event was much more pleasant. Norm took the two older kids deep-sea fishing, with a guide, of course. Neither of the males caught anything, but slim, 12-year-old Grace snagged a 4-pound barracuda and a 37-pound ocean perch. The guide grabbed her pole and pulled them in for her. The hotel kitchen staff prepared the barracuda for our family's lunch and in the evening brought in a huge platter of perch, which served many of the diners. (We still had to pay for each meal.)

Grace's surprising catch

Back to work at Moanza. Our tiny junior high consisted of a number of boys in the two classes and five or six girls in the first year. The boys lived in dormitories; the girls were placed in homes, with the idea that they would be more protected that way. One was the pastor's daughter and lived at home; the others had relatives on the station. One of them became pregnant that year anyway.

In those days the US was giving away surplus food to needy countries. Church World Service paid for the ocean transport; all we had to do was get it from the port to our centers. That way we were able to provide those growing boys with nourishing bulgur wheat every day. Unfortunately, they didn't appreciate bulgur wheat. One day as I passed by their open dining area they complained, "This food is terrible; taste it!"

"Does anybody have a clean spoon?" No one did, so I went home and got one. When I returned five minutes later I was unable to taste the unpalatable food because it had all been eaten.

We were three teachers—Joy and I and a new high school graduate named Reuben. The rule was that any student who completed secondary studies in our union school at Kimpese owed a year of teaching to the church community before he went on to university or another job. Many young men fulfilled this obligation grudgingly; Reuben was different. He willingly took on whatever we gave him, and did more. He taught science and of course the boys' PE, maybe second year math. He was gifted in music, but music was not required and drawing was, so I assigned him drawing. That was not an intelligent decision. He did his best. Fortunately he organized a choir outside of class and got wonderful music out of the students. Joy taught French and religion. I should have insisted she take drawing too; she would have taught it well. I had history, first year math, and girls' PE. Anyone who knew me would have laughed his or her head off at the idea of my teaching PE. The girls did enjoy having a tailor make shorts for them. I was doing exercises for my back and had the girls do them too. Later we branched out into something a little more exciting. I thought I was a fairly good runner; in the States I had paced Bob as he prepared for a race. The slowest girl was miles ahead of me. The fastest girl looked like an Olympic runner to me, but her brother in second year left her far behind.

How they grew in junior high school! We followed the European system: students rose to speak in class. One day a seventh-grade boy in the last seat was saying something, and I told him, "Stand up, Ndombe."

"Madame, I am standing up," he replied.

The eighth graders looked like giants in comparison. They loved soccer and looked forward to playing against other schools. I learned to hope—maybe pray—that the match would end in a tie. Otherwise the supporters of the losing team were likely to surge onto the field and start a fight. There was also the danger that the home team would bury a fetish under the goal posts. The boys felt sure the priest blessed the ball before they played a Catholic school. Once they asked me to catch the ball and return it to them before they left for a Catholic station. If I could do it again I would pray over it, "Father God, bless both teams, help them to do their best and love each other and make our guys magnanimous in victory (How would I say 'magnanimous' in Kikongo?) or mature and friendly in defeat."

One part of the seventh-grade math curriculum was the concept of negative numbers. I related it to the years BC in history. One day the pastor in charge of Marriage and Family Life for the whole field visited Moanza. He was a wonderful Christian man; you could just feel the love pour out of him as he came in and ascended the platform. Men and women sat separately in church; he encouraged them to sit together and to sing (in their language), "The more we get together the happier we'll be. For your children are my children, and my children are your children; your money is my money, and my money is your money, and the more we get together, the happier we'll be." Good concepts for a Congolese couple. But at one point he wanted to say that something had happened BC. He explained it this way: "Before Christ, people told time backwards. If this year (1965) were BC, it would be 5691." I observed my students murmuring to each other. They may not have

Investing in the next generation

understood negative numbers and time Before Christ very well, but they were quite sure that the pastor did not have it right.

In eighth-grade history we took a look at various civilizations and were encouraged to make value judgments about them. On the final exam I mentioned several of these civilizations of various periods and asked the students to say one thing that was good and one thing that was bad about each of them. Just for fun I included the contemporary US. Their response: "Good: They share their things with others." (They knew where the food in their refectory came from.) "Bad: They think they're the greatest!"

I thought about that response quite a bit. Years later, back at Sona Bata, I told it to a group of Swedes and Germans gathered around our table, and asked, "Don't the people of every country think theirs is the greatest?"

One of the Germans replied, "We don't—not since World War II." Were they ashamed of what Hitler had done or of being defeated in the war?

At Moanza that year Marjorie started school. How proudly she went off to kindergarten with her little bottle of water and a rag! The school at that time provided each child with a slate and a slate pencil; all they had to furnish was the wherewithal to clean the slate. About 10:00 a.m. the first day the teacher let the children out for recess; Marjorie thought school was over and came home. She cheerfully went back when she realized her error. That day she came home reciting, *"Deux plus deux égale gatre"* (2 + 2 = 4, with a slight error in pronunciation). The last day of kindergarten she came home reciting, *"Deux plus deux égale gatre."* Obviously her academic progress in that school year was not spectacular, but I'm glad she had the experience.

Back to Reuben. In high school at Kimpese, between Leopoldville and the coast, where education and Christian training had had time to exercise more influence, he had adopted the scientific method. He no longer believed in the power of witchcraft. But on his way home, he had got no farther than Leopoldville before family and friends from Moanza counseled him, "You'd better get yourself a fetish for protection before you go back to Moanza."

Reuben reported to us later, "I saw that no one had just one fetish, so I realized they didn't trust fully in any of them." Reuben came back without a fetish.

Then one day he got sick. In fact, he went off his rocker. He had malaria; that can make one susceptible to all sorts of things. When he went to the outhouse, he felt there was an evil spirit waiting for him inside. We heard about this on Sunday and prayed for Reuben in our missionary prayer meeting that evening, and he got better. But after a few days he relapsed. By this time Norm was away on a trip. I called together several people, missionaries and Congolese, who I thought were powerful in prayer, and we prayed intensively for Reuben. This time he got well and stayed well. The next week we had to meet again, with Reuben, to thank God for healing him. And thus was born the most exciting prayer group I can remember. We had come together because of a need, and none of us ever wanted to miss a meeting. Our group gradually grew until we numbered about a dozen. We took a long time praying because someone would introduce a subject of prayer and everyone would pray about that before we went to another topic.

After several months one of the members reported a problem. Someone—maybe several people—had heard about our group and were jealous because they had not been included. The member immediately invited them, "Come join us!"

But they said, "No, you didn't include us in the beginning." This member suggested that instead of continuing our original group, each one of us form a new prayer group. Moanza had tried cottage prayer meetings before. We agreed to do that.

Well, some groups succeeded and some didn't. Reuben's did; mine didn't. Our group was supposed to meet in a different home each week. One evening as I approached the house where we were to gather, I heard someone say, "Oh, here comes Mama Abell. We have to pray."

After that I wrote a note to each member of our group, saying, "I see that this way of praying does not appeal to you, and I don't want to force you. However, if any of you want to pray with me, you're welcome to come to my house, or I'll come anywhere you say."

One man responded in high dudgeon that I had intimated he didn't want to pray. But while I was still reading his note, all the women in the group appeared at my door! So our women's prayer group started, and grew. We would meet once a week in one of our homes, and we would also go to the hospital and pray for patients there. In one of our weekly meetings one of the women prayed honestly, "Thank you, God, for healing Mama Mpasi. We didn't think you would, but you did it anyway."

One day Norm came home from the hospital in the middle of the morning to ask me to pray with him. A woman had come from a village quite far away, bearing on her back her sixteen-year-old daughter, Nkeni, who looked about ten. Something was wrong with her leg; the mother hoped the doctor would put some salve on it. What was wrong was a sarcoma, which had almost certainly metastasized. Norm wanted guidance as to whether he should amputate the leg, since it seemed virtually certain that the cancer would kill the girl anyway. We prayed together, and Norm went back and took off the leg.

The next day or so a group of pastors, including my dad, who was visiting us, went to the hospital and prayed for Nkeni with laying on of hands. We women came later to pray. I didn't understand the girl's language, but she told one of us, "Something happened to me when the pastors prayed." She recovered quickly and well from the operation and went home with her mother.

Many months later Norm was traveling when a man flagged down his pickup to say, "I want to pay my bill." It was Nkeni's father.

"Could I see your daughter?" Norm asked eagerly.

"Oh, I'll send for her. She's in the field with her mother." Before long she came swinging along on her crutches, smiling and in good health. Norm took a picture. It's too bad he hadn't taken a "before" photo, because people in the States who saw the "after" one were impressed by how thin she was. But that's the normal thinness of people who work hard and eat one meal a day, based on what the women grow in their gardens. Once in a while a man brings home a little game from the forest or fish from the river. Nkeni was well. We were not able to claim a five-year cure because the next year she died in a flu epidemic. But something had happened when people prayed, in her body and in her spirit.

That year my parents came by ship to visit us. They arrived in October. Mother cooked our Thanksgiving turkey. (The station mason also raised sheep and turkeys.) At one point Mother told us, "I think the oven has got a little too hot." Our stove was wood-burning.

So I asked the cook, "Tata, open the oven door a bit for a little while." When we got home from church the door was still open! But the turkey eventually got done, and we had a fine feast.

In our junior high curriculum English was optional. We two missionaries didn't feel we had time to add it to our other responsibilities, but while Mother was there the students had English every day. Mother and Dad had studied French in night school before coming, and Mother had learned quite a bit, at age 70, but of course her spoken French was limited. Our students were very surprised when she wrote something on the blackboard in beautifully correct French.

Our family of six and Jean's parents, in their 70's

Unfortunately Dad had picked up hepatitis on the ship, and at Moanza it made itself known. He wasn't very sick, but when he expressed a craving for steak I got suspicious. I had learned that people with hepatitis feel a need for meat. Norm was away; I radioed him my concern, and he told me to try the ketchup bottle test. I put Dad's urine in one ketchup bottle and mine in another, capped them and shook them both up. Sure enough, the foam on mine was white, but Dad's was yellow. It's wonderful how you can make diagnoses without a lab.

Mother and Dad were staying in another house, although eating with us, and of course Mother took care of Dad. By Christmas time Dad was well, and he and Mother flew to Kikongo to visit that station. (Kikongo is the name of the language the Bakongo speak and also the name of a mission station.) There Mother arrived with both malaria and hepatitis. She was much sicker than Dad. They stayed in the Congo five months instead of three, but when they got back to the States their doctor pronounced them in better health than he had seen them before they left.

By the way, Reuben told us later that about the same time we had been praying for him, his family had given a goat to the uncle who claimed to have caused his illness. How would one prove which was responsible for his healing?

Once at school something was missing and we couldn't find out which boy had taken it. Reuben suggested, "Let's have each boy touch a doll, telling them the doll will tell us who was the thief."

I protested, "We don't believe in witchcraft."

Reuben countered, "But the boys do." Foolishly I accepted the ploy. It didn't work. We never did find the culprit.

April Fool's Day came. Congolese loved *poisson d'avril* ("April fish" it's called in French). Norm was away. Besides having charge of the hospital, he visited outlying dispensaries, as at Sona Bata. And occasionally he went to the city or to another church center for some reason. One of our schoolboys knocked on my door at 6:00 a.m., before I had my thinking cap on. He brought the following note (I translate): "Madame Abell, I have the honor to report to you that Mr. Solo has hit Pika. What are you going to do about it?" This was really incredible, because gentle little Mr. Solo, the man in charge of the boys' dorms, would never hit anyone—but if any of the boys could stimulate such a reaction it would be Pika.

While I was still absorbing that news, someone else came to tell me my office at school was in complete disarray; someone had got into it during the night. So I took my little self up to the school. I had never been there that early in the morning and was surprised to see a steady stream of boys going from their dorm area to the dispensary. It turned out to be sick call. I had no idea so many of them asked for medicine on a given day. The other people about were women sweeping the ground in front of the church building. As I drew nearer I heard the boys shouting joyously, *"Bien avalé!"* but I didn't understand it until

I looked at my office. It was indeed a mess, but it was the same mess I'd left it in the night before. *Bien avalé* means "well swallowed." This April fish had swallowed the bait—hook, line, and sinker.

At some time Reuben confided in me, "I can't talk to a girl without people thinking there's something between us. I'm used to the way they do things at Kimpese, where boys and girls talk freely together. I think that's a lot healthier. It helps make the sexes more equal, too." But it wasn't accepted at Moanza. So before the year was out, for self-protection, he said, he and Malia announced their engagement. She was the prettiest of the girl students and the daughter of a chief who lived in the village up on the hill. Her mother was a very nice woman, having to deal with another wife in the same compound.

The end of the school year came. Now in Congo the teachers gave final exams, then the pupils came back to school for a few more days while the teachers figured out their grades. It's a complicated process because some classes are taught more than five times a week and some less, so the grades are weighted accordingly. You don't just base everything on 100 and then average them out. But I thought it was silly to make kids come back after exams with no motivation and make teachers teach while struggling with their grades. I thought we three teachers could get our grades together in one evening. Well, Joy and I did all right, but poor Reuben got so sleepy he made several mistakes. By the time I discovered them the kids had already received their grades and it was too late to do anything about it.

Wherever we lived in Congo, we had people helping us in the house. We didn't call them servants; of course they were. We called them helpers or workers. They were that too. In the early days of mission work it was considered an honor and a boon to work in a missionary's house. A promising student could earn his school fees and learn a lot from working in a missionary home. Such a job was no longer prestigious in our day, but it certainly was useful. I'm a slow worker at best. If I had had to make all our meals, using a wood stove, and do the laundry by hand, ironing with a charcoal iron, I would have had no time left to teach or do anything else. So I appreciated our cook and wash jack. At Vanga and Moanza we also had a baby sitter for Jimmy when I was at school. It would have been good if we had always spoken Kikongo, or whatever the local language was, with each other when any of our help was within earshot. It would have been respectful, and they wouldn't have thought they needed to learn English to find out the secrets we were hiding from them. People at Moanza were sure they knew about our secret worship. During our first term the missionaries enjoyed an occasional hot dog roast on a small level area a little bit down toward the river from our house, in the opposite direction from the rest of the station. We would take the trouble to keep the grass mown and, before the picnic, use insect spray, then make the fire and toast our (canned) frankfurters and eat the picnic there outdoors, with a wonderful view of the ranges of hills across the river. Well, why in the world would people who had kitchens and dining rooms eat outdoors when they didn't have to? And they eat those things that look like people's fingers and probably are. This must be where they get their secret power by which they get so rich.

Well, let's get back to house helpers. Unfortunately it was all too easy to speak our native language among ourselves, so we missed that opportunity for a Christian witness.

Our cook at Moanza that year was a young man named Sammy. He was always cheerful and a good worker. When I dashed off to school before he came to work, without leaving him instructions for the day, he would present himself at my classroom door to ask what he should prepare. We got along very well.

Sammy's brother had been a village catechist. Such a man is responsible for the church and primary school (two grades) in a village that does not have a pastor. He works hard and is paid very little. It's a labor of love for the people and for the Lord. This catechist married Suzanne and they had three children. Then he died of tuberculosis, which is common where people are malnourished. Kongo tradition is like that of the Old Testament Hebrews: when a man dies, his brother is to take the widow as his wife. Where people have accepted monogamy, this is seldom possible as the brothers are usually already married, but in this case Sammy was single and took sweet Suzanne as his wife. Suzanne had already come to Moanza and been hired as a hospital worker. She had no training; she learned on the job. Her wedding gown was made of White Cross gauze. When our senior missionary heard that, she wished she had known so she could have provided Suzanne with something nicer.

Now Sammy was also a village catechist, but Suzanne was making more money than he, so it made sense for him to apply for a job at Moanza. That's how he ended up cooking for us.

Of course they had the three children sired by Sammy's brother, but naturally Sammy wanted children of his own. They didn't come right away. When little Noel was born at Christmas time, we all rejoiced with that family. Sadly, at about six months he fell ill with what turned out to be meningitis. Meningitis is hard to diagnose, and when it was identified it wasn't possible to save little Noel. The whole station mourned with them.

One day some women came to tell me, "We need to carry water for Mama Suzanne." Traditionally a woman who lost a child was to mourn that child for a whole year, staying in her house. That meant she couldn't work her gardens or go to the stream to do dishes or get water. Her "sisters" did that for her. By the time I found out about this custom, the year had been sensibly reduced to about a month. I willingly carried my pail of water on my head (having to hang on, as no one else did), but by the time we got to Mama Suzanne's house it was no more than half full. A good thing she didn't have to depend on missionary sisters!

Some time later, the women came back and told me, "It's time to bring Mama Suzanne out of mourning."

She welcomed us into her home but insisted, "I'm not ready to come out of mourning yet." She sat on the floor with her legs straight out in front of her and said, "I've been reading the Book of Job." Then she shared what she'd been learning. About a week later she was ready to come out of mourning.

After we had left Moanza, we came back for a visit and went to Sammy and Suzanne's house to talk and pray with them. We were all kneeling on the floor, holding hands and praying, when a cockroach crawled under my skirt. I did not scream, but my prayer was seriously interrupted. My legendary Aunt Fanny Tenney, in New York State some generations earlier, would have been grievously disappointed in me. When a mouse crawled up under her long, heavy skirt in church, she may have stopped worshiping, but no one else would have known it as she grasped that mouse in her hand through the skirt and squeezed until it died, presumably without a single squeak.

CHAPTER TWELVE

Tour of the Congo

If you put your thumb down on the middle of a map of Africa, it will also be in the middle of the Democratic Republic of the Congo, a country as large as the US east of the Mississippi, inhabited by tribes speaking more than 200 different languages. The Congo is shaped like a question mark on its side, the stem pointing west as the Congo River makes its abundant way to the Atlantic Ocean. The river begins as the Lualaba in the mountains of the southeast corner of the country. Flowing north and then west, the mighty river approaches the northern border of the country. The equator crosses it here; this is the dense equatorial rain forest. As the river makes its way south, dry season appears. Here the rainy season is interrupted and the vegetation becomes grassy savannah with forests in the river valleys.

In 1878 the first missionaries entered the Congo. Over the years one denomination after another, one country after another, sent its own missionaries, and gradually more and more parts of the country began to light up with the Good News. The Belgian Congo required the Protestant missions to form one umbrella organization to deal with the government. Thus the Congo Protestant Council (CPC) was born. The various missions divided up responsibility for the many areas of the country so that missions were not competing with each other. Most missions started churches, schools, and some sort of medical work.

In 1966 a missionary doctor named David was trying to cover the Medical Office of the CPC in addition to his other responsibilities. Hearing that it was no longer appropriate for Dr. Abell to be in charge of a hospital, including surgery, he suggested to the Congolese Director of CPC, "Why don't we try to get Dr. Abell as the first full-time Director of the Medical Office?"

"That's a good idea," Dr. Shaumba agreed. "I'll get in touch with Chet and see if his board will second him to us."

It was arranged, and Norm was adjusting to the prospect of an administrative job in the capital in 1967. Before that, on furlough, he planned to take a public health course at Harvard. In the meantime an exciting development was added to the mix.

The National Council of Churches in New York City was planning a month-long survey of medical institutions in the Congo. Dr. Nute

Dr. Abell, Dr. Nute, and the MAF pilot

was chosen to conduct the survey, but he needed someone familiar with medical work in the country to guide him. Who more appropriate than Dr. Abell?

The children and I returned to the States in August, while Norm and Dr. Nute prepared for their tour of the Congo in September. They visited some 30 institutions—Protestant, Catholic, and government—hospitals and training centers ranging from two-year nurses' courses to the medical school in the southeast corner of the country. Dr. Nute wrote up his notes on the plane between destinations. Norm waited until the tour was over, then had a big job writing up his report and getting it submitted.

After the tour came a meeting with 23 missionary doctors in Leopoldville, then contact with the General Secretary of the National Health Ministry. Mr. Ngandu was eager to cooperate with the Protestant Medical Office, which would be Norm's responsibility. So September and October rolled by. But Norm still had tasks to accomplish at Moanza, turning the medical responsibility over to nurse Kitswaka, setting up the new autoclave, straightening accounts, installing a new generator, working on wiring. This was complicated by transportation difficulties. The truck didn't arrive; the driver was sick. The MAF plane that was to take Norm to Moanza was needed for a family. George, who would have worked with Norm on the generator and wiring, left the same day Norm arrived. That meant that Norm had to do all the work by himself. He didn't leave things undone, he just stayed until they were done. As it turned out, he started his furlough in mid-November.

CHAPTER THIRTEEN

Meanwhile, Back in the States

Having stayed in Judson House in Malden during our first furlough, this time we were in Newell House in Newton Center, another residence our board kept for missionaries on furlough. Malden is a northern suburb of Boston. Newton Center lies southwest of the city. Its school system is such that Harvard professors like to live there so their children can start preparing for Harvard in first grade. Fortunately, neither our children nor I understood this right away. Later on I attended a parent-teacher meeting in which one father asked if he should learn "new math" while his child was being exposed to it. The thoughtful reply came back, "Only if you would learn Russian while your child was studying it."

Our new abode was a two-story, yellow clapboard house with two-car garage. We lived on the first floor this time. Upstairs was a family fresh from a term in Japan, deeply committed Christians, delightful neighbors. Andover-Newton Theological School is located in Newton Center. This couple knew a young Japanese woman studying there. She found her studies difficult, and they kept a very close watch on her, since in Japanese culture suicide is an approved method of reacting to failure. Once when we'd been talking about higher criticism (of the Bible) and the doubts it aroused in some pastoral students, our neighbor said about her husband, "They could prove the whole Bible was false from cover to cover, and it wouldn't affect his faith one bit. He knows his God."

The couple had five children, two older boys and three younger girls. Betsy, the oldest girl, had a crisis early in our stay. The doctor who gave her the school exam in Newton Center took her off the medication she'd been taking, and one day she was in trouble. Her dad was not at home, and her mother asked me if I would drive them to Children's Hospital in Boston. I agreed, of course, but was very relieved when another friend offered to make the trip instead.

The second daughter, Mary, was Marjorie's age, and they became good friends. Suzie, the youngest, was four, and our Jimmy had turned three in July. Suzie thought the sun rose and set in Jimmy Abell. In Sunday School, if her class was going outdoors she wouldn't go unless Jimmy's class was going too.

Bob started his sophomore year in high school. Junior high went through ninth grade, so all the sophomores were new to that impressively large school. One of his classmates asked Bob, "Where are you from?" meaning one of the two junior highs that fed the high school.

"Congo."

"Huh?"

"Congo, Africa."

"You mean with all those wild animals?" But it turned out the Newton Center kids weren't really interested in Africa. Another MK (missionary kid), Ted, lived in the area and would sometimes attend the church youth group with Bob. They occasionally talked to each other in Kituba or Lingala. That did not endear them to the girls they were cultivating friendships with.

Bob asserted one day, "That is not a youth group." What he meant was that it wasn't like the one he had known in Kinshasa. Kinshasa? Yes. Now, in 1966, the President changed the names of the largest cities from European to African; Leopoldville became Kinshasa. That made sense. Why should the independent Congo still call its capital city by the name of the Belgian king who exploited it as his personal possession until 1908?

Massachusetts was a lot more worldly than the Kinshasa our children knew. But the Baptist youth group in Newton Center did some good things. Once the youth group was in charge of the morning service. Bob was chosen to give the message, on Jonah. He left the congregation with the challenge: "Where is your Nineveh?" The only problem was that he almost passed out. It has something to do with being long and lanky, standing still for quite a while—and probably, adolescence and nervousness.

Getting back to the beginning of school, the guidance counselor expressed admiration for Bob's grades from The American School of Kinshasa (TASOK). Bob replied, "You should see my sister."

The counselor was so supportive. She told him, "We find that boys often bloom later than girls." And sure enough, Grace was the valedictorian of her high school class, but it was Bob who graduated from college summa cum laude.

At open house we parents were invited to follow an abridged version of our child's daily schedule, visiting each classroom and meeting each teacher. Thanks to Bob, we escaped getting lost. The biology teacher told us, "Teaching biology has changed a lot since you went to school.

You probably studied each of the phyla. Now we talk about what the DNA and the RNA are doing."

I wanted to ask, "What are they doing?"

One time Bob told that teacher, "I'm pleased that you don't talk about the conflict between faith and science."

The teacher responded, "I don't think there is any." Good for you!

Grace was in eighth grade. The school had wonderful opportunities. There were elective mini-courses one could take. One was on math games, another on Shakespeare. Grace studied "Richard III." In home economics, we studied sewing in my day; Grace's course was called Clothing. She made a pleated skirt. She had carefully marked the material following the pattern, when the teacher told her, "Since it's plaid material, you follow the lines of the plaid"; Grace did it all over. Of course, if you follow the lines of the plaid, the skirt doesn't get any wider as it goes down and you can't put it on. She did it a third time. At the end of the course the teacher evaluated each student and also asked them to evaluate the course, telling what they had learned. Grace wrote that she had learned patience.

One day the English teacher asked the students to write their impression of the objective case. Grace told what the objective case was, how it was used. No, the teacher wanted her impression of the objective case. Grace didn't have a clue, and I couldn't think how to elicit an impression from her, so I suggested, in a tearful voice, "I'm the objective case. I never get to do anything. People just do things to me." I suppose I wasn't the only parent to supply a child with an answer.

Marjorie started first grade, but that year got interrupted. After six years since her birth and an early consultation with a pediatrician, the general practitioner we went to for our furlough physicals diagnosed a congenital condition that required surgery. She spent two weeks in the hospital. She was in a ward with several other children. The charge nurse came in and told the children, "My name is Kitty, and when you want me you just call, 'Here, kitty, kitty!'" There was a playroom full of lovely toys. Marjorie loved the hospital; she didn't want to come home!

In PE Bob was playing a game in which two basketballs were in the air at once. Bob had caught one when another came at him. Trying to handle that, he broke his thumb. The school called me. I think we did not yet have a car; it seems to me I had to get a taxi to go to the school and take Bob to an orthopedist. He X-rayed the thumb, set it, and X-rayed it again. The thumb was nicely put back in its proper position. Unfortunately, there is no way to keep a thumb in its proper position, so Bob still has a slightly misshapen thumb.

Norm hoped we could all meet him on his arrival in New York City Armistice Day, 1966, but it didn't work out. For one thing, I don't think we got a car until he came. Now he was permitted to drive if he had automatic shift or a steering knob. Our car that year was a pale blue, used Volkswagen Bug. Since it was a bug and pretty colorless, we named it *Mbembele,* which means "mosquito." Bob taught himself to drive by turning Mbembele around in the garage. At Christmas time we visited Norm's brother and family in Philadelphia. The kids enjoyed getting acquainted with their Philadelphia cousins. In addition to the six of us, we took suitcases, of course, our contribution of food, Christmas presents, and Bob's guitar. We must have had a roof rack, and Marjorie and Jimmy traveled in the well behind the back seat. When it came time to set out, I couldn't find the grapes I was to take.

After we returned, they came to light in a low cupboard. I think Jimmy had changed their abode. Sadly, they had to be thrown out.

That was really an eventful year for Bob. He found he could rent a guitar to buy, so he did, and taught himself to play it. That guitar stayed with him through college until he needed to buy an engagement ring for his intended. Then the guitar was sacrificed for the greater need—but Anna's wedding present to him was a new guitar.

A less happy event for Bob was orthodontia. It was high time he had it. We contacted an orthodontist as soon as possible, but it was nip and tuck as to whether he could complete the work before we needed to leave. He offered a reduction in the price if Bob would be willing to have the work done faster (and more painfully). It was rough, but Bob and the orthodontist did it.

Of course it was too late for Norm to work on his Master of Public Health in the fall semester. He took the opportunity to have some corrective surgery done. Since polio his left arm had been pretty useless. Now a surgeon proposed to transplant a tendon so that he would be able to carry something, such as a briefcase, with that arm. That seemed pretty useful, so Norm underwent the operation, which involved opening the arm to the elbow. He recovered from that in time to enter the second semester at Harvard, but it really didn't help much without the first semester.

And what did I do? Well, take care of my husband and four children. One day Jimmy and Susie were playing in our bedroom. I heard Susie

exclaim happily, "Your mommy's going to like this snowstorm!" They had opened at least one of the pillows and were enjoying letting the feathers fly around the room. It was winter; they were wearing fuzzy clothes.

No, Susie, Jimmy's mommy does not particularly enjoy this snowstorm.

As usual, Marjorie's birthday came so early in the school year she hadn't had time to make friends yet. For Bob's December birthday we invited his MK (missionary kid) friends and also a classmate Bob had been befriending. Grace warned us that that boy would spoil the party, and in a way he did. He asked who had catered the meal. I suppose that was a compliment. We all went to see *The Sound of Music,* which he pronounced "pure schmaltz."

One Sunday I attended the old ladies' class in the First Baptist Church. The teacher encouraged us to expect God to do something special in our lives the next day. Well, the next day a woman telephoned me and asked if she could come over, would I be her friend. I had spoken in the church where she was Director of Christian Education. She did come, and we did become friends. I wasn't good about sensing people's needs and reaching out to them, so God put her in my lap. She had had a very traumatic life. Her husband was dead; she had one daughter who suffered from a congenital condition that made her bones break very easily. When Grace's birthday came along, she invited that girl and two classmates, one of whom was Jewish. First we drove to a nearby town to attend an outdoor event. It was a cold, rainy day, not very pleasant. Then we went home and made pizza. Grace's other friend had thought the Jewish one was not kosher, and we were putting sausage in the pizza. She said the smell made her sick, and she went home! Not a successful birthday party.

I didn't do a lot of deputation that furlough, but one time I was to speak at a church in Lynn, on the northeastern edge of the Greater Boston area. Mbembele did not possess a fuel gauge. Instead she had a spare gas tank which was supposed to hold about a gallon. On the trip around the circumferential, Rte. 128, the gas ran out and we (the car and I) switched to the auxiliary tank. Soon a sign for a service area came up and I prepared to turn off. But there was also an exit nearby, and I managed to take the exit instead of the service area road. By the time I got back on the highway the service area was past. Before another one appeared the engine starved to death. I pulled over to the shoulder and was happy to see a gas station on the road we were going over. I climbed down the embankment and trudged up again with a red can of gasoline. But when it was in the tank, the car still refused to start. I had to make my way back down the embankment and ask for help. Finally I was on my way again, and eventually I reached my destination and parked across the street from the church. Hurrying out of the car, I dropped my box of slides, which popped open, disgorging slides in random order on the pavement. I stuffed them back in the box and hurried into the church, where people were no doubt relieved that they would have a missionary speaker after all. They had reached the dessert course, so I re-sorted slides as I ate my pie and was somewhat bemused when the man who was to run the slide projector asked me, "How shall I show them, one after the other?"

One more memory of that year involves a Lay School of Theology given by Andover-Newton, every evening for a week or maybe two. I took a course given by Nels Ferré, and another in Old Testament. The two profs were both delightful and very different. The OT professor started at the top left-hand corner of the blackboard and taught very systematically. I remember asking him after class if the stories in the Book of Daniel actually happened. He answered that that wasn't the point. One time he told the class about opening the notebook of a female student and finding she had written on the first page, "He reminds me of a rabbit."

Nels Ferré, on the other hand, said things like, "Karl Barth believes in the Trinity, but not like three billiard balls (here he whirled to the blackboard and drew three contiguous circles), and not like a heavenly committee meeting in which two say to one, 'You go.'"

Someone in another class had asked Ferré, "And what do you believe? Where are you in all this?"

To which Ferré replied, "Square in the middle of God's truth."

Once after class I told Ferré how Bobby, aged four or five, informed his little sister, "God is everywhere. He's right in this sugar bowl."

Grace retorted, "No, he isn't, because if he was I'd eat him up."

The theologian then recounted how his son at age three had hit his head against the wall and announced, "In one sense God is in this wall, and in another sense he isn't."

CHAPTER FOURTEEN

City Dwellers

The school year came to an end. It was 1967, and back to the Congo we went, but this time to an administrative position in the capital city. We were not city dwellers. True, we lived in cities for the first years of our married life, but I had grown up in small towns and Norm had spent some of his happiest years on a farm. Denison University, where we met, is located in a very small town.

Now we were to live in Kinshasa. At independence time it had numbered some 350,000 people, about the same as our beloved Rochester. In the past seven years it had been growing by leaps and bounds.

We must have given our colleagues a hard time. On our arrival the Mission Secretary told us, "There isn't any place for you in the CBCO compound, but we've found a house in Parc Hembise, where the Belgians live." CBCO stood for the Baptist Churches of Western Congo, the denomination started by American Baptists. Our missionaries in Kinshasa lived in that compound.

Instead of expressing our gratitude, I burst out, "Oh, can't we live in the *cité?* We want to have Congolese neighbors, like we did at Sona Bata."

And our good friend the long-suffering Mission Secretary, who knew these crazy Abells, replied, “We'll see what we can do.”

Accordingly, we started our Kinshasa chapter in a large house built by Belgians. I deplored the waste space. The man across the street kept several dogs. Now this was a tense time in the Congo. Mercenaries from other countries who had helped the Congo government defeat the Simbas in 1964 were still around, and the government was not paying them. They now rebelled, and white people in general could be suspected of being mercenaries. We were told that the radio encouraged people to: “Take your machetes and drive them out!” The trouble was compounded by the similarity of the words “missionary” and “mercenary,” in French as in English. Long-haired teenage sons were especially suspect. Some missionaries had not been allowed to return at this time, and some had been stopped en route. This was the time we visited Rome on the way to Congo. What would we have done if we'd had to cool our heels in Italy?

Some Belgians had sent their wives home from Congo temporarily. In general nerves were on edge, and when the dogs barked at night I woke up and wondered what was happening. After a while we got used to it and slept through.

I did have a somewhat painful introduction to the house. When we first entered, I went around blessing the doors and windows. Then I tackled the old electric stove. Its dials no longer showed when a burner was on, so I tried to turn them on, hoping I'd be able to mark the dials. When I came back I put my hand on one (flat plate over the coils) and found that it was indeed on. We didn't have a refrigerator working yet, and it was one of those times when the water pressure didn't suffice to pump water out of the faucet. I finally found a spigot low down in the garage and an old chamber pot I could fill with water to soak my burned hand.

We lived in that house until Thanksgiving, when our mission secretary found a half house for us in the *cité,* the part of the city where the Congolese lived. This was an old section, and our particular part, called Camp Babylone, had had rather nice but inexpensive houses built by Belgians for Congolese before independence. This one was owned by a school director at Sona Bata, our first station (not the director we had known). He and his family lived in one half, we in the other. It was a two-story house, with living room, dining room, and kitchen on the first floor, four tiny bedrooms and a bath on the second. On the narrow, concrete-floored back porch we put a washer and ironing board, with a foot locker under the ironing board to hold clothes awaiting ironing. There was a fruitful papaya tree in the back yard, but we never got any papayas from it, because we would wait till they were ripe, and in the meantime neighborhood boys would harvest them. One day there were so many boys in the tree that a branch broke under one of them. It wasn't far to the ground; he didn't break any bones.

Remember my blessing the doors and windows of the first house? I prayed that only good would come in through them. That was so as long as we lived there, but while we were moving, thieves came in. For some reason we had stored wrapped Christmas presents on a shelf; no doubt we'd brought them that way from family in the States. The thieves liked those. When they came back for another load, we surprised the thieves, and they left without our seeing them. Unfortunately we didn't think to warn our neighbors, and after leaving us the thieves visited the MAF family living behind us.

The new home had two glaring deficiencies by our American standards. There were no closets, no shelves, no hooks, not a nail in the wall. We put a few shelves under the staircase and made or had made wall bookcases in the living room. Then we wanted an electric stove, but that street had only 220 volts, not the 380 a stove required. They put a line in for us eventually—amazing, come to think of it—but until the new year we did all our cooking on a one-burner hot plate. In the meantime Bob came home from The American School of Kinshasa (TASOK) one day and announced, "I promised to provide the manioc chips for our international feast."

"You did? How much do you need?"

"I dunno. Lots. We don't want to run out." So the cook, Bob, and I spelled each other all day long frying thin slices of manioc in deep fat.

So many memories from that house! The owner's family next door had a daughter about Grace's age, and we rejoiced that Grace would have a Congolese friend—but alas! The other girl's French was so much better than Grace's that Grace was too shy to talk to her. They played together but in silence.

There were plenty of neighbor kids for Marjorie and Jimmy to play with. Marjorie knew we hoped they would learn Lingala, the African language spoken in the city. Even the children of Kikongo-speaking parents spoke Lingala with their peers, to the extent of not understanding when the grownups spoke Kikongo. One day Marjorie came in all excited. "Jimmy's learning Lingala! He said, *"Ici!" Ici* means "here"—in French. Jim now informs me that he did learn some words in Lingala—bad ones!

Jimmy started school. When he came home from his first day in kindergarten, I asked him "Jimmy, what did you like best in kindergarten?"

"Rest hour!" At home he didn't get to lie on a towel on the floor while the teacher read to them. Jimmy loved his kindergarten teacher. She was tall and young and very good with the children. The summer following that year she was visiting Israel—Jericho, to be exact—when a stray bullet from across the river struck and killed her.

In kindergarten each child was to make a picture book about his family. Jimmy did fine on the cover, a picture of his house—well, a house, anyhow. Each succeeding page was to have a picture of a family member. Jim's pages were blank. He explained that he couldn't draw people. He could draw bicycles and guns (!), but not people. That got remedied later. In high school he painted both seascapes and action pictures with people in them.

One day the teacher's report stated, "Jimmy never does anything fast—even going out to play." Another time: "Jimmy is very good at making things out of useless materials." That was a skill encouraged in the schools for Congolese children. *Matériaux de fortune* meant whatever they could pick up—twigs, bottle caps—green grapefruit slices made good wheels for toy cars; they didn't need to learn that in school. In fact, kids made amazingly accurate vehicles out of light wood or wire: not just a car, a Volkswagen; not just an airplane, a Cessna 182. When Jim was in high school, his counselor encouraged him with the idea that if he couldn't have his first choice of profession he could become a fabricator—not a liar but someone who makes what he needs with what he has on hand. If he didn't have the tool he needed for a particular job, Jim, like his dad, would make one.

Camp Babylone was in the section of the city called Kintambo, where the American Baptist work had started. The Kintambo church was within walking distance. I trained Sunday School teachers there on a week night, and we took our children there on Sunday mornings. When that service was over we drove downtown to the English-speaking church. After a while I realized it was too much for the kids. Sunday morning was more hassle than worship. So we excused them from going to Kintambo. They enjoyed the English language Sunday School.

My Sunday School responsibilities eventually enlarged. Our colleague Eva, whom we had first known at Sona Bata, was now living in the city and meeting with Sunday School teachers in various parishes around town. American Baptist work had started with the one church in Kintambo; now there were CBCO (Baptist Churches of Western Congo) churches in an ever-increasing number of communes, as the sections of the city were called. Eva turned over another of these Sunday Schools to me, along with some of the responsibility for vacation Bible schools. What fun! Most of the teachers were high school students. At Bandalungwa, my second parish, one student had founded the Sunday School and the youth group and started a ministry to children at the nearby prison. Children in prison? Yes. Some with their mothers, some arrested for vagrancy. The young people brought song and worship to them, also soap and other necessities. Not surprisingly, that young man married a fine Christian young woman and became a leader in the church. There was one girl who didn't join the Sunday School teachers but did teach in Vacation Bible School. She was a fine, intelligent young person. One time we were discussing how we spent our money and she remarked, *"Il faut être belle"* (you have to be beautiful), meaning it's necessary to spend money on cosmetics and hairdressing. That young woman went into Christian work. She visited us years later. She had a ministry to young girls, encouraging them to wait for marriage. She said, "When I talk to 13- and 14-year-olds and see the sad looks on their faces, I realize it's too late to tell them to remain virgins. I need to talk to 10- and 12-year-olds."

At that time the Bandalungwa church did not have a church building. The church met in the courtyard of a relatively well-to-do family. The husband worked at the American embassy. Our Sunday School teachers' class convened on the porch of that home. One evening Norm was busy elsewhere and I had no one to leave the younger children with, so I took them with me. The host family had a litter of puppies; Marjorie carried one around all evening. When I got ready to go, the woman of the house smiled and said to me in her best English, "I give the dog for the children."

Gulp. Nobody had asked me if I was ready for a dog. "Thank you. Is it male or female?"

"It's female."

Gulp. So Spotty came home with us. Later people wondered why she was called Spotty. Her puppy spots had spread out to a general mottled effect. Poor dog! When she went into heat, every dog in the neighborhood treated her like a woman of the streets. Then when she came home, the next-door dog felt sure she was his wife. No peace anywhere. Eventually her first litter announced their arrival. Unfortunately it was at night. Now we had a driveway beside that house but no garage. Bob had got some chicks from fellow missionary Murray and built a small concrete block henhouse at the end of the driveway. While he was building the house the chicks stayed in their box under his bed. Building took longer than he had planned; the chicks grew fast. Everyone drew a sigh of relief when they could finally emigrate to their own dwelling. And for a while Bob had eggs to sell. Then one night thieves came and stole all his roosters. Hens don't lay well when there are no roosters, we found. But to prevent further theft we took to parking our Volkswagen smack in front of the henhouse door. What we didn't realize was that Spotty had carefully dug a hole in the sandy soil of the henhouse floor as a bassinet for her babies. And just when she needed it, she couldn't get in! Our bedroom window looked out on the driveway, but we had an air conditioner in it—the only time we had air conditioning in Congo—so it took a long time for Spotty's frenzied moans to get through the white sound and wake me up. I went down to see what the trouble was and then had to go upstairs again for the car key so I could move the car. Finally the poor mother was able to get to her birthing room. She had already delivered one pup and covered it with sand as best she could. That one was already cold. I think another one died, but there were at least four little roly-poly canines soon moving around. Before they grew very big, tragedy struck again. One by one they died in great pain. The mother grieved for each one, then ate it. In those days the government sent men around to spray the outsides of houses with DDT to keep down mosquitoes. I suspected that Spotty had ingested enough DDT to kill her pups through her milk. People told me that couldn't happen. If not, I can't imagine what killed Spotty's pups. Another time Spotty scared us. After receiving a rabies shot, she gradually became paralyzed. First she was dragging her hind legs behind her; then she couldn't walk at all. We had to bring food and water to her. But gradually she recovered.

Working with Sunday School teachers was rewarding. Traditionally the teacher told the children, *"Kanga maboko"* (fold your arms) and then did all the talking. The children's only participation came in singing, as loudly as possible. When the next-door class wanted to pray, that didn't work too well. I encouraged the teachers to ask the children questions, get them talking, find activities to relate to the story. In our Stateside Sunday Schools, children at least have paper and crayons, often things to cut out. And teachers' books suggest all kinds of activities. These teachers had to dream up their own. We used drama quite a bit, playing the story. And we used what came to hand. Once for the Easter story we made a little garden in the sand, with twigs for trees. Buildings and walls were made of concrete blocks, some with decorative holes in them. A discarded part of a block made the empty tomb.

There was always a pageant or play at Christmas. How people loved to make fun of the census takers, supplying them with adding machines! I saw one Herod lolling on his throne with one or two wives beside him. What troubled me was seeing Mary dragging her way into Bethlehem, her pregnancy almost to the ground, already in labor. I asked them, "Would you make fun of your mother like that?"

The high school students took up new ideas quite well. One older man in the group had a harder time changing. "But the children don't have anything to say."

"No, Tata, you have to get them used to the idea that they can think."

You never know what consequences your teaching may have. In vacation Bible school the rooms were packed with children, especially the youngest ones. I thought one activity pre-schoolers could do would be leaf rubbing, giving each child one crayon and a piece of paper to put over the leaf, but I found even that was hard for them. In another class a pastoral student was supposed to be teaching, but I found him cutting out the letters he should have made the night before. They were to create a hanging with leaves and flowers and a verse praising God for creation. Here was the teacher in a back seat, leaving the children with nothing to do. It was second grade, so I told the teacher, "Give them directions on the blackboard."

"Oh, they can't read," responded the teacher.

So I went to the blackboard and wrote, in their language, "Go outdoors. Get leaves and flowers." To my delight, the children looked at the words, then looked questioningly at me, and started out. I hope that pastoral student learned two things that day.

Then there was the young teacher who came to me with joy, reporting on how he had put my teaching into practice. "I was teaching about Pentecost, so when we came to the tongues of fire I gave each child a match and had them light them and hold them over their heads!"

I was also teaching English in the Kintambo Baptist high school, located next to the church. One time one of my young Sunday School teachers asked if I could get him into my school. I asked the principal if he would give the boy an entrance exam. Instead he just accepted him on my recommendation. I sure wish he hadn't. Come exam time, we teachers monitored each other's exams, and of course we were supposed to prevent cheating. I had learned to be suspicious of long sleeves rolled up. Later I think I had all the boys unroll their sleeves before entering the room. But this time, as soon as everyone had started the French exam, I strode to the back of the room (rather than begin at the front, where all the kids could see what I was doing), and felt in the rolled-up sleeve of the first student I came to, who happened to be my Sunday School teacher. Sure enough, there was a long slip of paper with a list of authors on it. I marched the boy to the front, took his paper, and sent him on his way. It took him a long time to forgive me. I wonder if he thought some magic power had cued me in.

What was Norm doing all this time? He was administering the Medical Department of the CPC. His trip with Dr. Nute had given him an excellent overall picture of the Protestant medical work throughout the country, problems and needs. Perhaps the most important accomplishment of his tenure was the formation of CEPAM, a pharmacy created to supply medicines to Protestant hospitals around the country. Before that, hospitals received some medicines through Interchurch Medical Assistance. Others they had to look for in the commercial pharmacies in the capital. Often the doctor had to make the long journey there and then go the rounds of various pharmacies for several days to try to find what he was lacking. After CEPAM got going, its pharmacist, Warren, had access to European pharmaceutical firms and was able to furnish a more consistent supply.

Another task that Norm enjoyed was orienting new missionary doctors. During their first days in the capital they would come to his office, ask questions, and get briefed for what lay ahead of them. Norm had the right combination of experience on the local level and the overview of hospitals and nursing schools, Protestant, Catholic, and government, to be very helpful to the newbies. Also, he cared about each of them, as well as the Congolese they would work with and those they would minister to.

One day I decided to invite the neighbors on our block to come to our house to pray. After my experience at Moanza, I shouldn't have been surprised that it was the women who came. I asked them, "What would you like to pray about?"

They answered, "Our homes and our families. It's different for us than it is for you. Your husband listens to you."

I remember hearing about a woman whose husband had left her for a younger woman. That happened distressingly often. There came a time when the first wife needed the father of her children. She went to where he was living and called to him. Now in Congo, at least in that part, a person was sometimes addressed as the mother of a child. I might be called Mama Abell, or *Mama Dokuta* (Mrs. Doctor) or Mama Jeanne, but I also could be called *Mam'a Babi* (the mother of Bobby). This woman stood outside her husband's home and called, "Tat'a Catherine! Tat'a Albert! Tat'a Josephine! Tat'a Marc! Tat'a Joseph!" naming each of their children in an effort to get him to respond. He never did.

Our children went to the American school, but we did have Congolese friends. The house on our right was occupied by the wife of a member of Parliament. People were pleased that this Christian man had risen to a significant position in the government, but with worldly advancement had come worldly lifestyle; he was one of those living with a younger, more sophisticated woman. His first wife said he visited her just often enough to keep her pregnant. One thing I remember about her was that she had a hedge of manioc around her house. There was no room in the city for a garden, but she made sure she had some manioc. Otherwise one had to buy everything at the local market, just a few blocks away.

The house on the other side was occupied by an interesting family. The mother was a very sweet lady who became president of the women's society in the Kintambo church. Her first daughter had never developed properly. She was a teenager when we knew them and had grown physically according to her age, but she just lay in a bed, could do no more for herself than a small baby. That mother fed and cared for her all those years. A younger daughter, Bernadette, was normal. Then there was a boy named Daudet (after the French author!). He became a friend to Jimmy, although he was several years older. He would take Jimmy to the market, where Jimmy wanted to buy a palm grub—not to eat, as the Congolese did, but to have for a pet. Failing that, he once adopted a rice worm, making a little Lego house for it. Then he wondered what to feed it!

We knew two African-American couples. That is, the husband was Congolese, the wife African-American. John taught at the seminary. He was one of three Congolese who had been sent to the States to study theology. Baptist women of California had paid for their wives to join them in the States, but his wife's family had not allowed her to come, and before long she died in the village. While in the States John met Anne and married her. She tried very hard to be a good Congolese wife. Probably the hardest part was adjusting to the idea that the whole extended family is welcome in your home for as long as they want to stay. One of their daughters was Jimmy's age, in first grade, but she was attending a local school. They came to our house one evening, and at my request she recited one of the fables of La Fontaine, her eyes glazing over in proper Congolese fashion as she quoted.

The other couple we knew less well. He was working in child evangelism. I think he was the one who told me about his baptism. He was in catechism class with other boys of his age, preparing to be baptized, when someone decided he was too young or for some reason should not be baptized at that time. He was devastated. His mother took him aside and asked, "Do you love Jesus? Is he your Savior?"

"Yes!" the boy protested.

"Then that's what counts. He's your Savior. You have him in your heart."

"When my friends were baptized," the man recounted, "I sat in the congregation and watched them, and it was all right. I knew I had Jesus in my heart."

The first year we lived in the Camp Babylone house, the rent was amazingly low—what a Congolese family would have been able to pay. The second year our landlord doubled the rent, but it was still very reasonable. The owners of the house moved back to Sona Bata and rented their side to a Belgian couple, then a Swiss one. When I invited the Swiss for a meal, I remembered that Europeans do not eat sweet with savory, so I refrained from glazing the ham—but it didn't occur to me that pineapple salad is sweet too!

In between tenants the other side of the house was empty. This worked out very well for us. Our friend Reuben had had a very sad college career. He was enrolled in science in the first year—he wanted to become a psychologist—when the President decided teachers were needed so badly in the far east of the country that they drafted university students to go out there and teach, whether they were trained or interested in education or not. They would then automatically be in the next year when they returned to college. Reuben was one of those who went. It was a very broadening experience, of course. He saw Stanleyville, which had been hit so hard by the rebellion, and people who had lived in the forest for many months. Then he was sent much farther east, where the people were not Bantu but Nilotic, and darker than Bantu. Reuben discovered he had prejudice against people who were darker than he!

Back in college, Reuben found that all those drafted teachers were now education majors, but that was not what he wanted. We suggested he apply to the rather new Protestant university in Stanleyville, which was looking for students. He did, and was accepted, but on getting there he discovered that they had too many enrolled in the sciences and he could only audit classes, not get credit for them. Reuben developed hepatitis, couldn't attend class anyway, returned. Now an uncle in the bush commissioned Reuben, back in Kinshasa, to buy a house and lot for him. After doing this Reuben realized that the same seller had sold the same lot to a couple of other people and he did not have clear title. The uncle was furious. Reuben's fiancée was unhappy because he wasn't writing her often enough, and Reuben's answer to that was to punish her by writing less often. We knew Reuben needed rest so he could recover, so we rented the other half of our house and invited him to stay there. He had meals with us. We learned a lot that year about the local culture and a little about witchcraft that we never would have known otherwise. Reuben wanted to know more about witchcraft but realized he couldn't find out all he wanted to know without getting involved himself. He read the New Testament through while he was with us. He told us, "I wish God hadn't given us free will."

Also during that time, Norm's folks came to visit. There was room for them, along with Reuben, in that other half house. They came by ship and brought a piano with them! At one time we played a duet, Mother on the piano and I on the harp. Later, after Norm's parents and Reuben had left and the Swiss couple lived in that side of the house, they finally told us, "It sounds as if the piano were right in the room with us." We moved it to the outside wall.

We had other pets in that house besides Spotty and her short-lived puppies. There was a darling white kitten the children named Snowsoft. One day we came home to find that boys from the next

Norm's parents joined the crowd rejoicing at the arrival of the piano

block had stoned her to death, just for the fun of it. We also had two parrots, one named Blue Eyes, the other, Puffin. One of them was in the house while we were playing Clue and bit the head off Professor Plum.

The third year the rent jumped from 16 zaïres a month to 100. We refused. At this time the Congo Protestant Council, for which Norm worked, was building new offices and associated two-family homes. He was invited to take one half house and accepted. The rent we had to pay was actually higher than the 100 zaïres we would have paid to stay in the Kintambo house. I prayed hard that we wouldn't have to move, but we did. A dedication date was set for the new buildings, and people rushed to finish them before that date. Most permanent houses in the Congo had concrete floors; they were often painted red or green. Ours were painted red. Unfortunately they were painted before the concrete had completely dried out. The result was that the paint never did dry. Norm ended up paying men to unpaint the floor, that, is, to scrape off the ill-fated paint. That done, we did move in. Electricity was not connected yet. Our first supper in the new house was eaten by the light of a flashlight stood upright in the middle of the table. Surprising how much light it gave!

One of Norm's roommates during his internship days (and nights) was now a successful allergist in Detroit. Allergies were a big problem in the Congo, and Norm invited Rudy to come for a visit and suggest ways to help. Rudy accepted. "As soon as I stepped off the plane," he reported to us, "I smelled mold." Rudy was particularly interested in training someone who could specialize in allergy prevention and treatment after he left. Norm did find a young nurse (male), who enjoyed learning about allergies. Then Norm took Rudy and nurse

Constantin to the Evangelical Medical Institute at Kimpese to speak to the students there. Later the three of them flew to a similar school at Tshikaji, in the south central part of the country, for the same purpose. They had various adventures. The government took their passports when they entered Tshikaji and didn't give them back till they were on their way to the airport to depart. In fact, they were so late that when they arrived at the terminal building there were only two boarding passes left for the three men. Rudy, being a man of action, extended his long legs over the counter and possessed himself of a third boarding pass. They boarded the plane with no difficulty.

The problem announced itself when they landed at an intermediate city. Passengers got off; others got on. Departure time came, but they couldn't depart because there was one more passenger than the number of seats! Our three men kept very quiet during the long delay. How the problem was solved they don't know, but they eventually arrived safely back in the capital.

Before Rudy left he told me, "You're spreading yourself too thin. You need to take care of your husband and children." He was right, of course. I rather abruptly turned my Sunday School teachers' classes back to Eva. She must have felt somewhat overwhelmed.

After the extensive surgery on his arm Norm had been prescribed sedatives. They got to be a habit. It's very easy for a doctor, especially in the Congo, to keep himself supplied with a prescription drug. Now we realized that Norm had become habituated to that sedative. It was no longer so effective, and he started taking it earlier and earlier so it would take effect by bedtime. Then he might half wake up in the night and act almost drunk with sleepiness. He didn't get free of that until our next furlough.

A pediatrician came from Sweden to help out in this needy country. She brought a brand-new Volvo. After a few months she became discouraged and decided to go home. She gave the Volvo to Norm and the Medical Department for his work. We then had two vehicles. Norm had hired a chauffeur who could drive around the city doing errands for him. Now they could go different places at the same time. One day Norm had our Volkswagen bug, so I took the Volvo to pick up our kids at the American School. It was my first time to drive a Volvo, and I felt very cautious. The road to the American School goes up a hill. It has one lane going each way with a middle lane for passing. The American School had begun on our American Baptist mission compound. Recently it had built new, larger quarters on the main route going south out of town. The entrance, on the left as you go up the hill, was not clearly visible from the highway. If you didn't know it was there, you might not realize there was a road going in.

So here I was, driving cautiously up the hill, looking in my rear-view mirror, signaling, moving cautiously into the passing lane. Once there, I stopped looking behind me, needing to watch for anything coming around the curve ahead. There was nothing, so I slowly turned to enter that inconspicuous road that led to the American School. When I had just about reached it, I realized there was an enormous government truck coming up on my left! Every lug in his front wheel made a little hole in my door. The driver, who had already lost his license, had assumed that I was moving over to pass a slower vehicle ahead of me, but I was too slow for him, so he planned to pass me in the far left lane.

I don't know how our kids got home from school that day. Someone in the government drove by and saw our two vehicles and realized what had happened, so we had a credible witness that it was the government driver's fault. The government would have paid for the repair to the Volvo, but it might have taken years. Our chauffeur knew someone in the bowels of the city who could repair our door cheaply, so we let Martin take the Volvo to him. When it came back, the door was repaired, but there was a new problem. Someone must have driven the Volvo in some pretty rugged terrain, because the front axle was bent, and there were telltale pieces of bark on it. Now the Volvo needed more repair. So much for not waiting for the government to act.

In 1969 Bob graduated from the American School of Kinshasa. Grace was two years behind him. She must have been about 15 when she received her first proposal of marriage. One of Bob's Congolese friends came to our home in Camp Babylone sometimes. One day he presented Grace with a poem he had written, in English: "Son of Africa, girl of America, can you be one?"

Grace responded mildly, "I'm too young to think about marriage." Come to think of it, she was a year older, and several years further along in school, than Reuben's Malia had been when they became engaged. No wonder the young man thought the time was ripe.

Both Bob and Grace participated in the excellent musicals the American School put on. The Class of '69, including a number of American Baptist boys, really shone. They produced *Oklahoma*—a very sad play, to my way of thinking, with great songs. Bob's good friend Glen played Curly, while Grace's friend's older sister, Anne, had the female lead. One of our American Baptist girls made a great Ido Annie, and John played the ill-fated Jud to perfection. Bob and Grace enjoyed being part of the chorus.

Let me not forget *Harvey*. Remember the friendly six-foot rabbit? Tim was offered the part of Elmer, Harvey's alcoholic but lovable friend. Tim didn't want it, and our Bob was the next choice. He did a fine job, and that activity gave just the boost he needed to his self-confidence. Many years have flowed under the bridge since then, but at a recent Congo reunion Bob entered the room holding the door for an invisible someone about his height and saying, "Come on in, Harvey. Do you remember these people?"

During Bob's senior year he dated an English girl named Juliet. I had read in Mencken's *The American Language* that there is more difference in speech from one English county to another than between standard British and American English. Hearing Juliet, I could believe it. Sometimes she could say a whole sentence without my understanding a single word.

It was probably during spring break that we went to the coast on vacation—our family of six, Cliff and Joy's family of six, and Juliet. Fortunately the vacation house was pretty well furnished at that time and included several bedrooms. Cliff and Joy had a bedroom, shared with their youngest child; so did we. A third bedroom housed the girls—Juliet, Grace, Linda, and Marjorie. That left the laundry room for Tim and Rick and Bob. It was not too comfortable. One day Juliet was going to make Banbury buns for us. I had brought food supplies from home, of course, and oh dear! I had put some soda in a baking powder tin. Juliet used it instead of baking powder, and though the Banbury buns tasted fine to us, she was understandably quite disappointed with her creation.

Graduation came, and Bob went back to the States to enroll at Kalamazoo College. He and Juliet had decided to go their separate ways; it would be difficult to carry on their relationship so far separated from each other, geographically and culturally as well. Our mission board gave each of our children in college one trip back to the field during his/her college years. Bob chose to take it the summer after his freshman year. A very responsible young man, he felt he could not come unless he could earn some money while in Congo, so I scouted around for him and found a job with an American construction company called Kalicak. Like many freshman students, Bob put on some weight during that year and arrived in Congo looking filled out and healthy. Then he went to work, doing the outdoor physical labor and also serving as an interpreter at times. Kalicak got a good deal when he hired Bob. He invited Bob to his home one time and gave him a shot of whisky—Bob's only taste of hard liquor ever, as far as I know. We were grateful that he got home safely. Those welcome pounds Bob had put on at college melted right away as he toughened his muscles and have never come back.

Bob had arranged to quit his job in time to have a couple of weeks for himself before going back to the States. He spent both weekends camping out at the rapids in the Congo River with his friend Ted, providing food for hungry mosquitoes. None of us thought about the fact that since we took our antimalarials on Sunday, Bob missed them both weeks.

Jimmy's birthday came in July, and his friends tended to be away. We had a tradition of inviting as many guests as the birthday child's years. We couldn't find seven boys that summer of 1970, so we had to invite girls. It turned out that, counting Jim, there were four boys and four girls. Thinking about it before the party, I remarked, "Isn't it interesting! All the boys are white, and all the girls are black."

Jimmy retorted with some indignation, "Blondine is not black. She's exactly the same color as Riaz."

He was right. Blondine was the daughter of the very black Congolese and the very fair African-American we told you about earlier. Riaz was Pakistani. (Why did I consider him white?) When they came to the party, sure enough, they were exactly the same color.

There were a lot of Pakistani businessmen in Kinshasa, and elsewhere in the country, and a number sent their children to the American School. A couple of Pakistani boys were in Marjorie's fourth grade. One day we were driving into the CBCO compound when Marjorie spotted two boys coming out and exclaimed, "I know them! They're Pakistaniels. Oh, no, that's some kind of dog, isn't it?"

CHAPTER FIFTEEN

Back to Sona Bata

Sona Bata needed a doctor. Norm was eager to get back to hospital work. But first he had to find a replacement as Medical Director of the Congo Protestant Council. He thought it should be a Congolese, and he thought of Marc, who had trained as a nurse at Sona Bata and worked there, then gone back to school for six years and graduated from high school and had the preparatory year for university. After that he went into education and worked as a school principal. He had training and experience in the medical field and in administration, and he was a committed Christian, honest and dependable, who worked well with others. Would he come?

Yes, he would! And he turned out to be very good in the job. He knew how to compromise and get along with others without sacrificing his principles. He was one of the finest persons we've ever known, and Norm's best friend in Congo. But it was a while before he could take over the work.

In 1970 we moved to Sona Bata, where Norm was the only doctor as before, with responsibility for hospital, nursing school, and outlying dispensaries, but now he had had polio and left the surgery to Tata Kimpiatu. Norm was there to give advice if needed. However, he didn't stay at Sona Bata all the time. He spent part of every week at the CPC office in Kinshasa, sleeping on a board he put across the bathtub. The building had been a private house before. After Marc came—affectionately called ya-Marc—Norm still made trips to the city to help him get broken in to the new job.

Bob had returned to the States. He visited my parents in Glens Falls, NY, and then Norm's. He felt unwell before he left them, but he went on to Eastern Baptist College to see his classmates Glen and Tim. While there he became really ill and was hospitalized at Bryn Mawr Hospital. Bob and his friends were sure he had malaria; then he remembered those mosquitoes at the rapids. But Stateside doctors do not believe in malaria until they see a positive smear, and people who have been taking antimalarials don't always show positive smears. Bob was in the hospital a week, unable to keep anything down, before treatment started. The second week he started to get well. Of course we didn't know any of this until it was all over. But something good, something very good, came out of it. The other students in Glen and Tim's prayer group found out about Bob, and some visited him in the hospital. One of the young women heard about this dreamy guy and decided she was not going to follow the crowd and visit him. Anna didn't meet him till he was out of the hospital and praying with the group before he headed back to Kalamazoo, now late to start his school year. But that prayer meeting started a relationship that culminated in their wedding two years later. Or should culmination include their children and grandchildren and ministry together?

As soon as the school year started, Grace went to the hostel. Marjorie and Jimmy were thrown into the local school with the Congolese children. "Jimmy," I had told him, "at Sona Bata you'll be going to school in French!"

At first he rather liked the idea. Later he changed his mind, telling his sister, "I won't go to the French school. Well (remembering the facts of life), I'll go if Mom makes me, but I won't learn anything!" I remembered that with delight when in third grade he came home and cut equilateral, right, and scalene triangles out of cardboard just because he wanted to. But first he had to get through second grade. It was the first of the grades to be taught in French. In the Sona Bata school they had used the local language, Kikongo, in the first grade. So French was new to all the second graders. Jimmy had an advantage in the fact that Mary was in his class. Mary's father was one of those three men who had been sent to California for further study, so she spoke English fluently and could give Jimmy a helping hand. At the end of the first semester the teacher reported that Jimmy, the missionary doctor's son, had passed everything except health and religion! He mastered those too by the end of the year.

It was during the following year that I asked him, "Jimmy, do you speak French with Mary? Do you speak Kikongo with her?"

Jimmy responded, "Mom, I speak all kinds of languages. I don't know what I speak!"

Another time we were in our bedroom when we heard Jimmy on the veranda with some friends. They had spotted an outdoor thermometer on the outside wall and asked Jimmy what it was. He didn't know the word for thermometer, so he explained in French, "It's something to tell the temperature." Yay, Jimmy!

Discipline was harsher than in the American School. Children sat at double desks. Once the teacher set out to slap Jimmy's seatmate's hand with a ruler, but the boy drew back his hand quickly and it was Jimmy who felt the ruler. Our children participated sometimes in punishment administered to the whole class. Each child had to bring a palm frond broom to school. Palm frond brooms are very effective. You strip off the frond until you have a thin, flexible fiber. When you have enough of these, you hold them together with an empty 2-oz. tomato paste can near one end. The fibers are springy enough to do a good job. It took a lot of palm fronds and a lot of work to produce enough fibers to really fill out the tomato paste can collar. Our children's brooms were always very skinny, and the collar had to be squeezed to hold the fibers in place.

One day the President was to pass by on the road outside Sona Bata, that went from the capital city to the seaport. The children learned rhythmic slogans and then marched out in their blue and white uniforms to stand by the road until the great man passed. Unfortunately he was delayed and they stood for hours in the hot sun.

Marjorie had a problem in school that Jimmy would never encounter. Her long blonde hair posed a great temptation to the boy seated behind her. He didn't try to dip it in the inkwell, but he did want to feel it. It was so different from his or his sister's. Marjorie got tired of having her hair handled, so she found a solution. She braided it and wound it around on top of her head. Yay, Marjorie!

Marjorie's friends included the children of the Dutch missionaries in a nearby house and Nzuzi, the daughter of the hospital chaplain who lived in the tiny house in between. One day Marjorie reported that the teacher had scolded her and Nzuzi for whispering. I rejoiced. Marjorie had become a normal student in a class where she was a minority of one. Years later, when Marjorie was in college, she visited Kimpese and saw Nzuzi again. Marjorie was way ahead in education but she was impressed with Nzuzi's experience in life.

At the end of the year Marjorie finished fourth grade with flying colors. She asked if she could skip fifth grade, since she had lost a year by repeating fourth because of the language barrier. Her wish was granted. She had no trouble with sixth grade. With this move she caught up with Florence, Mary's older sister. They became great friends. Florence eventually moved to the States and came to Marjorie's wedding.

One day in fourth grade she had come home stating, "The teacher says we have to have a new notebook, bought by our clean daddy." What's that? Oh, yes, the French adjective *propre* ordinarily means "clean," but not when it's put before the noun. The teacher had said, "Your own daddy must buy this notebook." I wonder who had bought the other notebooks.

I also gave the children some lessons in English at home. Another Dutch family lived at the other end of the station. They had spent some time in the States, and the mother wanted the boys to continue in English. She asked if I would teach them, and I accepted. In English school Marjorie was in fifth grade that year, Jimmy in second. The Dutch boys fit in between, in third and fourth. The principal of the American School in the city had offered to help us get materials from the States. The only trouble was that they were late in coming. What to do? Since I had taught Bob and Grace, there were books left from them. I found a reader at the right level for each child, and I must have found math books. For science, I had read somewhere that we should follow the children's interests. So I found some sort of reference book for each child. Jimmy's was The Little Golden Encyclopedia. When they suggested a topic, each one looked in his/her book to see if it said anything about that subject. Once we were in the middle of studying volcanos when one of the boys brought in a turtle. We dropped volcanos and studied turtles. However, since their teacher was much more interested in language than zoology, we mostly learned how to say "turtle" in four languages—English, French, Dutch, and Kikongo. We had a ball—until the proper books came. Then it was a scramble to try to catch up. One of the Dutch boys did not enjoy reading, and I wasn't flexible enough to make it easier for him. I finally threatened, "If you don't try harder I'm going to send you back to your mother." He called my bluff. I felt bad about that.

The local people very much wanted to expand the nursing school. Since there were only so many patients to work with and only so many nurses to teach the students, Norm didn't feel the school could grow very much without sacrificing quality. Other people didn't see it that way. It was important to educate as many young people as possible.

Every year we gave entrance exams to the applicants. I loved making up French and math exams, with questions designed to see if they could follow directions and think. Once I told them, "Draw a patient under the bed and a box on the bed"—partly to see if they understood the difference between under and over, and partly to see if they would follow directions that went contrary to what they would expect. In math I asked, "Which is greater, 132/144 of an orange or one orange?" But one time I did a very foolish thing. I had been working on entrance exams at my desk in our bedroom, and I had made an answer key. The next day we were taking a little trip, and I went away and left everything on my desk. Our house worker was very grateful that I had been so generous, enabling him to share the information with the applicants he knew—or maybe just one, who passed it on to others. We found out when correcting the exam papers because I had made one mistake in the answer key, and of course all those who had received the free help made the same mistake. We had a hard time explaining to the government official why we had to give a second entrance exam. We didn't punish our house worker. I suppose he and I should both have been locked up and fed bread and water.

One day a woman whom Norm had seen in prenatal clinic came to the hospital to have her baby. He had determined she would need a Caesarian section, but Tata Kimpiatu was away that day. Norm commissioned me to drive her some 36 kilometers down the road to the Catholic hospital. I felt uncomfortable about the situation and asked for someone who knew midwifery to accompany me. Fortunately one of our recent graduates was going that way and would be willing to be taken all the way to the hospital and then delivered to her destination on the way back. It would have made a good comedy scene: the woman in labor crying out with each contraction, her relative telling her, "Trust in God!", the nurse-midwife in front with me trying to calm them, and me driving and saying, "Breathe!", demonstrating panting there in the driver's seat. We arrived safely at the Catholic hospital, where the woman delivered naturally, without surgery.

In 1971 came the great name change. The President wanted "authenticity." The Belgian names of cities had already been replaced by African names. Leopoldville had become Kinshasa. The currency was already zaïres instead of francs. Now the President christened the country Zaïre. Our Dutch friends laughingly asked, "How would it be if the USA were called the Republic of the Dollar?" The President announced a competition to write the new national anthem.

In due time the winning song was chosen and published in the paper, complete with music. I sat at the piano and played it, and the children and I sang. And we laughed. Here we were, American and Dutch, lustily belting out, "We are Zaïrois!"

Grace graduated from what was now The American School of Kinshasa (TASOK), valedictorian of her class. She made her graduation dress. The night before graduation I was in her hostel room trying to help her. I wasn't too much help on the dress, which she was working on while memorizing her speech.

She chose Earlham College, although not because her Aunt Grace had gone there. She had two scary adventures that first year in college. Our sweet, pretty Rosebud had been a late bloomer socially. Her high school yearbook revealed that some boys had noticed her, but they had waited to write about it in the yearbook. In college that situation was rectified. She had all the dates she could handle. Once she naïvely told a young man, "I have the most beautiful view from my window! Come see." She was talking about the view from her dorm window. He interpreted the invitation differently.

The other adventure lasted longer. Grace got sick and figured she had malaria. She knew where to find the antimalarial we had given her for such a situation, but she didn't remember the directions for taking it. This powerful medicine was to be taken one pill a day for three days. She took all three at once. She wrote, "That weekend is just gone out of my life." Once again, by the time we heard about it the emergency was over. How good of God to take care of our children when we were far away!

As part of his college course, Bob worked one term of that sophomore year at St. David's, a camp for retarded children in the Philadelphia area, not far from the place where he had spent two weeks in the hospital with malaria. It never occurred to me at the time that he had chosen that opportunity to be near Anna. I was explaining to Marjorie and Jimmy, "Bob's at a camp for retarded children."

Jimmy asked innocently, "You mean big children like Bob?" I had to explain that Bob was working there, not one of the children. Now I understand that Anna was able to visit him there, both help and admire him as he played his guitar and led the kids in worship, and decide he would make a great daddy for her children.

I also had a scary adventure during that term. Remember our first term at Sona Bata? The 11 outside doors that we never locked unless we were to be away overnight? Times had changed. Now we locked all of them every night, but some weren't very secure.

One night we were in bed, but I wasn't asleep or at least not soundly, because I heard a man fumbling around on Norm's desk, beyond his side of the bed. I whispered to Norm. Of course the man heard me and left abruptly. He hadn't found the money he was looking for.

How did he get in? The dining room had French doors opening onto the veranda. I guess we didn't, or couldn't, lock the doors opening onto the veranda from the outside. The thief had entered the veranda and then pried out a pane from a French door so he could reach the latch from inside. Then he'd made his way through the dining room and living room to our bedroom, brave guy. He must have found Norm's little medical bag and carried it off with great glee, but when he saw it did not contain money he threw it down in disgust and we eventually retrieved it. Norm's reaction was to create a booby-trap of tin cans on top of our bedroom door. When one opened the door it would make a great racket and hopefully scare off the thief.

Some time later Norm was away on one of his many trips. A doctor who had occupied the house while we were elsewhere had converted half of the four-room cookhouse into an apartment for his mother-in-law. That made better accommodations for Marjorie and Jimmy than the veranda bedroom that had briefly been Kasavubu's. Between it and our bedroom were the breezeway and bathroom. I was reading in bed, by the light of a kerosene lamp, of course. For some reason I remembered that I had left laundry on the clothesline. So out I went in the dark in my nightgown and brought in the clothes. Perhaps it was the dog barking that had made me stop reading. Now I went back to bed. After a while the dog must have barked again. There was a window right beside the head of the bed. Outside, a man had pried up the window with a paring knife he had found in my kitchen. Through the opening were coming his hands and a gun. I jumped out of bed on the other side and dashed through the bathroom to the breezeway, picked up a pail and held it in front of my head, whatever good that would do, went outdoors and yelled at the top of my lungs in Kikongo, "Thief! Help me!" Later Jimmy, who had been back in the cookhouse apartment, told me, "I thought you were the girl thief yelling to the man thief to help her." Obviously he recognized my voice as female but not as his mother's.

No one shot me, and pretty soon men did come to help. The man who had come in through the window dashed out through the door to the living room, activating the booby-trap, of course. He also had the window drapery wrapped around him, unintentionally, I'm sure. The first helper was the very dark hospital chaplain, whose house was the closest. *"Tala! Mwifi!"* I yelled, mistaking my rescuer for the thief! Obviously I wasn't thinking very well. Sietzo, the Dutch missionary in the next house, set me straight. He found out that this was a group of men who had previously visited the Catholic station across the railroad tracks. One of the teachers (priests?) at their school had at some time flunked out one of the bandits, who this night had shot him. Then they had apparently decided to kill two birds with one stone and see what profits they could find at the Protestant center. We eventually heard that they were captured way down the road when their vehicle broke down. In the meantime Sietzo had arranged for one of the female nursing students to stay with me the rest of the night so this poor scared missionary would be able to sleep.

In the morning our cook heard the story and thought I was a pretty weak woman. He was right, of course. He explained, "I would have jammed the window down on his fingers. I wouldn't have screamed like a banshee."

Yes, Tata, you're a strong, capable man, and I'm a weak, bumbling woman. I would never have thought that I could succeed in imprisoning, or injuring, the man's fingers before he shot me. And there was a justification for the scream. I remembered the thieves who had visited our house in Kinshasa and then moved to the neighbors'. So I thought there was good reason to let other people know thieves were around.

You know the expression "afraid of your own shadow"? In the days—no, nights—following that adventure I found out what it means. After dark I'd hear the dog barking, look out the window and see someone moving on the veranda. It always turned out to be my shadow.

We had lived in the city three years. That meant there was only one year of our four-year term left for Sona Bata, but as that year drew near to a close there was no doctor on the horizon to replace Norm. There were plans to bring a Christian Indian doctor named Dhamaraj to another church center, if both governments and everything else cooperated. If he succeeded in coming, there might be another Indian doctor for Sona Bata. While we were thinking about this, Emmet and Eloys from California visited our station. They were an outstanding couple. We had been impressed by Emmet's prayer at an American Baptist Biennial a few years before. Now we asked him, "Will you pray that Dr. Dhamaraj will actually be able to come?" Emmet was happy to pray, and Dhamaraj did come—but no second Indian doctor for Sona Bata. Why hadn't I asked Emmet to pray for our own need? We lengthened our term by a fifth year.

Before we finally did leave on home assignment, the church center as usual had a good-by feast for us. There were the normal speeches, including somebody's words, probably in Kikongo, "We are very happy to say good-by to you." We interpreted that to mean that they were happy to give us this sendoff, not that they wanted to get rid of us. But maybe this time we were mistaken. That difference of opinion about expanding the nursing school loomed large in their thinking.

CHAPTER SIXTEEN

Highlights of a Furlough Year

Norm's work on a Master of Public Health degree at Harvard had not really accomplished anything, since he hadn't been able to take the first semester. Now, in 1972, he was going to do it right, at Johns Hopkins School of Public Health in Baltimore.

Where would we live? Just north of the city there was an institution called Koinonia Foundation (no relationship with Koinonia Farm in Georgia). It had been founded by Frank Laubach, Glenn Clark, and others to train people who were going abroad in any capacity—government, business, whatever—to share the gospel and to teach people to read. I had visited there for one weekend conference. They had been able to buy a 40-acre estate with lots of woods, a house big enough for conferences and several other useful buildings. People who came there for training had been blessed, but unfortunately not many actually went overseas after being trained. Koinonia had also started a literacy project in Sierra Leone. After some time they were in financial difficulty keeping up their extensive property in Baltimore and also the project in Sierra Leone. They decided to change the nature of Koinonia and make it a place where primarily college students came for an alternative semester. A young Episcopal priest became the director. He had a lovely wife and a toddler. A few of the "old Koinonians" stayed on. Dick, an older man, and Helen, whose youngest daughter was there too, reveled in organic gardening. Another woman was in charge of the housekeeping, a big responsibility with the various dwellings, meals for everybody, all the details. An African-American couple ran the large kitchen, but Dick made the oatmeal from steel-cut oats, which cooked quietly all night on the back of the large range. He also made whole wheat bread, in which he might put whole peanuts, pieces of carrot, a host of delightful surprises. Unfortunately our son Jimmy did not share my appreciation of that healthful bread from which I made his sandwiches every day. Eventually he confessed, "I lick off the peanut butter and throw away the bread."

"All right, Jimmy," I sighed, "from now on I'll make your sandwiches from 'cotton batting' bread."

Before coming to the States I had written to ask whether we could live at Koinonia for that year of study. Norm wouldn't be able to do a lot in the life of Koinonia, but I would. Their reply told me about the change in Koinonia but said we would be welcome to come, so we did. It was indeed a change. Things were very informal and free. Anyone who had anything to share was welcome to share it. I taught a little conversational French class for a few interested people. Once a man came who made and played hammered dulcimers. A woman from a church brought an art technique that initially stimulated a good deal of interest. The second week she came the enthusiasm had somehow leaked out. She commented, "Yes, it's very fluid here. It flows, and it ebbs." The students must have enjoyed their alternative semester, typified by the multicolor candlesticks they created by letting candles of different colors melt down the holders. The next semester they presumably went back to college. I wonder what effect Koinonia had on them. Any spiritual input would have been very low-key and due to the Christian personality and lifestyle of committed individuals.

I helped can the enormous tomatoes that came from Dick's garden. We even harvested green tomatoes toward the end of the season, and I shared my mother's idea of green tomato mincemeat. In the spring I worked in the garden a little, weeding strawberries. Strawberries are difficult to weed, because another plant looks very much like a strawberry plant before the blossoms come out. I mistakenly dug up more than one strawberry plant—but there were still a lot to freeze when harvest time came.

We had an apartment in a two-story building. Just above us lived a young public health doctor and his wife, a charming couple. They taught a class based on the book *I'm OK, You're OK.* The doctor was also helping some people to quit smoking. One young fellow was coming along well until McGovern (remember presidential candidate George McGovern?) was so soundly defeated. Then he turned back to his comfort habit.

We discovered an Episcopal church that knew about the gifts of the Holy Spirit and had healing services. One of our friends at Koinonia, one of the few older people like us, came to a service with us. She was amazed to see the church parking lot full on a weekday evening. "This is an Episcopal church?" she exclaimed. It was good to go there. I'll never sing "Walking and Leaping and Praising God" without remembering that powerful little church.

Our own church was in Towson, across the north side of Baltimore from Pikesville, the address of Koinonia. Down in the city there were some black and white churches, which we would have enjoyed, but they were down in the city, too far to drive. The Baptist Church in Towson was dually aligned American and Southern Baptist. Marjorie got to be a queen in Acteens. (Every girl became a queen if she fulfilled the requirements.) While we were there they started putting people together in home groups. We really shared from the heart and grew spiritually and bonded with the others in the group. We learned about the Church of the Savior in Washington, DC, where each member of the church was involved in some ministry. Here in Towson a group of women studied a book *The Eighth Day of Creation,* written by a member of that church. She encouraged us to look for gifts God had given us, try something new.

With that impetus, when the school was looking for den mothers for Cub Scouts, I decided to see whether that was one of my gifts. (It wasn't.)

The town of Pikesville was a golden ghetto, inhabited largely by well-to-do Jewish people. At the meeting, none of the Jewish mothers volunteered to mother a den, only another Gentile mother and I. Neither of us had any experience in the field. She lived in the country and had horses the boys could get acquainted with. I went to all the meetings for den mothers and tried to do what we were supposed to do. KISMIF was the slogan: Keep It Simple; Make It Fun. I tried but did not succeed. These boys were so sophisticated, and Jimmy and I were so clueless. I came to the conclusion that what the boys really wanted was not a Cub den but a basketball team. I think they all had basketball hoops attached to their garages. Poor Jimmy did not play basketball. Once I brought them out to Koinonia, where Jimmy was in his element, because he knew how to climb trees. It was the style that year for boys to wear their hair long. Our neighbor the public health doctor caught sight of my Cubs and commented afterward, "I never expected to see so many little Jesuses." But unfortunately I kept the boys too long that day. It was Friday, and they needed to be home before the Sabbath began. I should have been aware of that. As it was, one mother phoned me and explained the problem. I was very apologetic.

Another unforgettable adventure with the Cub Scouts: We were doing something connected with music, and these fourth-graders were way beyond a rhythm band. One boy brought his violin. The Koinonia director's wife offered, "You can take my Volkswagen to pick up the boys and take them home." For the trip home I opened the hood, in front of course on a Volkswagen, to put the violin in. On the freeway the hood popped open; I hadn't fastened it properly. No, the violin didn't fall out, but the hood stood in front of the windshield and I couldn't see where we were going. I was able to pull off and stop, no damage done, just a scare. My friend did not offer to lend me her car again—nor did I ask.

This was Jimmy's first year in the States since he was three, Marjorie's since first grade. They adapted pretty well. Jimmy got demoted to a lower math group (!) after the first marking period. The next section was on the metric system, and Jimmy had used that exclusively in Congo, so his grades went up considerably. Marjorie sang in the junior high chorus. We attended their Christmas program. The director, an African-American man dressed in striking red and black, had chosen a number of real, Christian Christmas songs, which those Jewish children sang and their Jewish parents listened to with pleasure. I visited Marjorie's school one day. She loved her English teacher. The social studies teacher managed her class superbly but with a good deal of sarcasm. She kept the boys in the back of the room busy but never called on our daughter on the rare occasions when her hand went up. I'm afraid I was mean. At the end of class I said to the teacher, "You know that blonde girl on the front row? Her name is Marjorie."

After those years in the tropics, the children were really looking forward to winter and snow. Someone lent them a saucer for sliding downhill. One late fall afternoon while we were raking leaves, it started to snow, and before nightfall the ground was covered. In the morning the snow was still there, and the kids looked forward to saucering after school. Alas! The sun came out and melted all the snow during the day. And all that winter it never snowed where we were. It snowed north of us; it snowed south of us; it snowed west of us; it snowed east of us, over the ocean, but not on Baltimore. At Christmas we went north to my parents' in New York State, and the kids enjoyed snow at least a foot deep, but no chance to use their saucer on the exciting hills at Koinonia. Spring came, and one afternoon snow covered the ground. The kids were wise by now and got up early the next morning to take advantage of the snow before school. They slid down the slope that was pretty bare of trees a number of times, then decided to try the side with more trees. Pretty soon Marjorie came to the door crying. "I don't know what day it is!" Her head had run into a tree; she must have suffered a slight concussion. Whatever day it was, a social studies test was scheduled. We figured if she didn't know what day it was she probably wouldn't remember the exports of Brazil; we kept her home that day. Some well-meaning soul lent her a fiendish jigsaw puzzle—round, with all sorts of candies jostling each other. What a choice for someone with a concussion!

Norm loved his Public Health course at Johns Hopkins. The profs were great. One of them, about Norm's age, invited the class to his home, where they got to know each other socially. Some of his fellow students came from countries where they might go back to be the Minister of Health. Norm made plans for a Health Zone centered at Sona Bata. The hospital would be the nucleus, overseeing the dispensaries Norm had supervised, which would be converted to Health Centers, with emphasis on wellness and preventive medicine—nutrition, immunizations, checkups—not just dispensing the proper medicines to treat diseases. The third layer—really the first one—envisioned a Mama Bongisa in each village. *Bongisa* means "improve, make better." A Mama Bongisa is a mature, respected woman who strives to make her village a better, healthier place to live. She encourages parents to see that their children get nutritious food every day, especially the little ones who have just been weaned. Traditionally the father gets the best food, the mother second best, and if there's any left the children can eat too. Mama Bongisa keeps track of pregnant women and sees that they get prenatal exams. If there are indications that the delivery may be complicated, she makes sure the expectant mother plans to arrive at the hospital before labor starts. She's aware of illness and accidents in the village, encourages immunization and sends people to the Health Center when they need to go.

Is Mama Bongisa remunerated? Yes, in the village way. She's already looked up to; now she becomes everybody's grandmother. She has her own gardens, with manioc and corn and peanuts, but if they didn't flourish, the other women would help supply what was lacking. A man might give her an especially delicious papaya from his tree or a stalk of bananas. If the village is near a stream, a big fish would find its way to Mama Bongisa's from time to time, and anyone who was able to kill a monkey or an antelope would make sure Mama Bongisa got a choice portion.

CHAPTER SEVENTEEN

Our Longest Home

At Johns Hopkins Norm had planned a Health Zone centered at Sona Bata. Now it was 1973, time to return to Congo and put that plan into action—but Sona Bata did not want Dr. Abell back. It wanted to triple the size of its nursing school, and Dr. Abell wouldn't cooperate.

Well, who did want him? IME, *l'Institut Médical Évangélique de Kimpese* (the Protestant Medical Institute of Kimpese)—the medical center Dr. Freas had tried to direct us to all those years ago. Norm would be their first full-time Public Health doctor.

Accordingly we moved to Kimpese, to the rambling house we would occupy for ten years, longer than either of us had ever lived in one house before. Actually, we would have two five-year terms there, with a year of home assignment in between.

IME was laid out in separate pavilions, all one-story—a medical pavilion, a surgical pavilion, obstetrics, pediatrics, and orthopedics, because one of the founding doctors had been an orthopedist. They even made artificial limbs there, excellent ones. A mile or so away stood Kivuvu (Place of Hope), a leprosarium. Few patients lived there any longer, because contemporary treatment allowed leprosy patients to go home and live in their villages. Those who did remain had suffered a good deal of damage before the new medicines became available, but they were able to do some useful things. For instance, they grew vegetables and sold them. People had finally accepted the fact that they would not catch leprosy by eating vegetables that leprosy patients had cultivated.

We found many Angolans living and working in the area. In fact, the man who came to be our cook was Angolan. Also some British and Canadian missionaries who served at IME had previously worked in Angola. How come?

The country of Angola borders the Congo on the south. Angola was for centuries a colony of Portugal. In 1961, when almost all the other countries of Africa had achieved independence, restless groups in Angola began guerrilla warfare against the Portuguese government. That war continued until 1975, when Angola finally became independent. During those years many Angolans had come north, fleeing the Portuguese, and had more or less integrated into society in the Congo, although Congolese tended to discriminate against them. Now when Angola was newly independent, some went back. The church at IME had a fine Angolan pastor, and another Angolan pastor lived at CECO, the mission station that trained teachers and pastors, on the other side of town. These men were among those who returned, and they asked Norm if he would help them plan the church's medical work in the newly independent country. So Norm made five trips to Angola to work with them. Marjorie and Jimmy and I accompanied him on two of the trips. On one our cook went with us. We would be driving by an area where all we could see was grass, and he would say, "There used to be a village here."

"How can you tell?" we wondered. If you'd lived in a village like that, I suppose you'd know.

We saw that the roads were all dirt, but well-kept, rolled dirt roads. The Portuguese government had done well on that. Dirt roads in Congo were not that good; the Belgians had relied on villagers with hoes to keep the roads in condition.

Once we all slept on bamboo mats on the concrete floor of a classroom. I think that's the only time we ever did that. It was hard, but we slept. How touched we were to see two old people reunited after being separated by years of war! Of course we tried to learn a little Portuguese. One of those pastors explained, "The Portuguese use their nostrils a lot." Angolan Kikongo—think of the Queen's English in comparison to American speech—differed from the kind we used in Congo, and also, where our Kikongo was liberally larded with French words, Angolan Kikongo naturally incorporated Portuguese vocabulary.

We visited the ancient cemetery where the Kongo kings were buried—vertically, in cylindrical tombs rising up above the ground! These are the ones we'd read about in African history. One of the kings became a Christian and sent his son to Portugal to be educated. He came back a bishop.

In 1975 the Portuguese transferred the government to a coalition of the three Angolan political parties that had been fighting for independence. Unfortunately, the coalition did not last. Just when the church in Angola was getting organized for medical work, and other things, of course, war broke out again, with three armies fighting each other. Instead of Norm's going over to help the Angolans, the Angolans came to us.

The village of Songololo, with a striking church and a thriving dispensary, numbered some 5,000 people. In one day its population tripled with the arrival of refugees from Angola. The first agency on the scene was Doctors Without Borders. They organized relief efforts, food, emergency medical care. Norm worked with them, of course.

And some of his first Village Health Zones were established in the refugee camps that soon got organized.

Norm supplies Angolan nurses with medicines

Refugees kept coming. Some arrived at the hospital at IME. Life in the villages in Angola had become very difficult. One army would descend on the village and demand their help, their food, etc. Naturally, with guns threatening them, the villagers gave it. When that army had passed through, the army that was fighting them would come and burn the village because they had aided the first army. So people fled to the forest and lived on palm nuts. Some who arrived at IME were wearing cloth made from bark. It worked, but it didn't last very long. And some died of starvation, with only grass in their stomachs. An Angolan family of five came in desperate condition. One missionary took the seven-year-old boy into her home to try to nourish him back to health. Another took the baby. The boy didn't make it, but the baby recovered, was adopted by a Congolese pastor and wife, and grew to be a fine young man.

A Congolese woman went with Norm to the refugee camps and talked to the women about the Christian family. "The wife is the driver," she explained, "and the husband is the mechanic." She discussed nutrition and encouraged them to grow manioc (the staple food) and become self-sufficient.

One of the Angolan women stood up and said, "We want to, but how can we?" holding up a manioc root attacked by blight. Another problem. We came to feel that the biggest medical problem was not malaria, not any other tropical disease, but malnutrition.

In addition to the hospital, IME included a school for nurses. These were called A2. A1 nurses corresponded to RNs in the States. A2s had a high school education, plus one year. They came to us after ninth grade and received four more years of instruction, mostly nursing subjects but some French, math, science, and history, with English optional. There was also a section for laboratory technicians. Helen had come to the field to train lab techs, but through the years she'd had to work as a nurse instead. Now at last there was a lab school where she could use her special knowledge. She was a very special person, too. Whenever she encountered someone, she would ask herself, "What does God see in this person?" or "What does God want me to do for this person?" One student was found to be drinking. She could have just put him out of the school. Instead she said to him, "If you have a drinking problem, we can help you."

During the years, I taught various subjects at that school, in both the nursing and lab sections. French was my responsibility in the lab school that first year, until we got a Frenchwoman who had taught in Canada before coming to the Congo. That first lab class was quite small, about twelve students, and only two girls. Several of the students had completed high school but had been unable to go on to the university, so they came here as a career option. One young man traveled all the way from the province of Kasai, where, he reported, all you had to do to pay your school fees was dig up a diamond. Another had completed the philosophy section and knew a lot but could not condense what he had to say. The girls suffered in comparison with those who had completed several more years of school. One day we were reading a selection entitled *"Les Vers du Roi."* I asked if they had any questions, and one girl raised her hand. "What don't you understand?" I queried.

Honestly she responded, "What it's all about!"

Now it happened to be about verses, poetry. It seems Louis XIV enjoyed writing poetry. The word *vers,* however, can also mean "worms," so I asked these lab students, "Is it about intestinal worms?"

"No." They knew better than that.

The word *verre* means "glass;" "Is that it?"

"No." That wasn't where the trouble lay. Actually, why should Congolese lab techs be reading about the machinations of a 17th century French king? I tried to find something more appropriate and less flowery for them and discovered a book by a French journalist that had to do with medical or paramedical problems. One chapter dealt with defoliants used in the Vietnam War. Remember Agent Orange? The writer said that it had been used *à grande échelle.* That means on a large scale, *échelle* being the word used on maps in "a scale of 1:500," for example. But the more common meaning of *échelle* is "ladder," so the other girl quite naturally envisioned our soldiers in Vietnam climbing a very tall ladder to apply Agent Orange to each tree. Isn't language confusing!

One part of the curriculum required the students to study Shakespeare (!)—in French. Shakespeare in French? Well, a Frenchman named Anouilh had translated four of Shakespeare's plays into excellent French, and our nursing school had the book in its library! Anouilh reported that it had been very hard work, much harder than writing a play himself, but what a good job he had done! I considered it as fine as Shakespeare himself. I chose "Twelfth Night" for my little class. After reading it, we picked out a few scenes that we could perform with a cast of twelve, including only two women. The countess and her mischievous maid were portrayed by females, but the heroine was played by a young man who resembled—in size and shape and color, anyway—the one who played her twin brother. Since the heroine (played by a male in our version, and in Shakespeare's theater, for that matter) disguises herself as a young man in all the scenes we showed, it was confusing for the audience, but they loved it, especially the sword fighting between two people neither of whom wanted to fight. Our philosophy major drove me up the wall by not memorizing his lines until the last minute, but he had them down pat at the performance.

I also taught history to the nursing students. I used to give them a five-minute quiz at the beginning of each period, based on the previous lesson or the reading assignment. Then I realized that they were forgetting earlier work and I needed to review. So one day, without warning them, I asked them questions like "Name a country of eastern Europe," because we were going back to eastern Europe, although we had just finished a lesson or two about the exploration of the Pacific. Students in the Congo, and I'm sure they're not alone in this, tend to keep their noses in their notebooks until the very last minute before a test. One girl reluctantly closed her notebook as she came into the classroom, took out her pen and wrote. Her country of Eastern Europe was the Bering Strait. I was reminded of geography class one of those very first years at Sona Bata, where we had studied a map of Africa and the then Belgian Congo, after which I rolled up the map and asked my students to draw Africa and the Congo. At least one girl had a rather large glob for Africa and a smaller glob out in the ocean for the Congo.

In the second semester, the final class in history took up general problems, the first being world hunger. I presented the first problem; teams of students presented the others. One bright boy, captain of his team, took the floor wearing a pair of glasses he had made, using them to read his notes and taking them off to look at the class, just as his teacher did with her glasses. That class came at 2:00 p.m., right after our precious siesta. At least once I went off without my glasses, and my dear husband, who was at that time director of the school, presented himself, and the glasses, at my classroom door.

Part of our study was African history, including those kings whose tombs I eventually visited, as well as other kingdoms that became part of the Belgian Congo. The first year I taught that, I discovered that the kids knew their original ancestors had been hunters, fishermen, and gatherers, and they knew the current president was Mobutu Sese Seko. Everything between was a blank. So the next year I took pains to teach about Diego Cão, the Portuguese explorer who discovered The River (Congo, later Zaïre) 10 years before Columbus arrived at Hispaniola. Then I told them about Livingstone and Stanley, who in searching for Livingstone got bitten by the exploration bug and ended up traveling the length of the Congo River, which he thought at first might be the Nile. On the final exam I reaped this delightful response: "In 1482 Diego Cão discovered The River. Four hundred years later Stanley went looking for him, and he found him!" Now to be fair, I'm not sure that's what the student meant. The same pronoun in French means "him" or "it." It may be she was saying that Stanley went looking for the river. That's considerably closer to the truth.

I taught an elective English course to nursing students, without much success. They tended to think that because the course was elective, attendance and homework were also elective. One day I had come across a little song used in Sunday School with the English-speaking children: "If anyone asks you who I am, tell them I'm a child of God." I thought, "My English students should be able to understand that." I tried it on a couple of them one day. They didn't get it. Finally I translated it for them.

"Oh, shield!" one of them exclaimed. That's how you might pronounce c-h-i-l-d if it were a French word.

"But that's not English," I explained.

"It's our English," she countered.

She had failed to turn in some important homework in history class and didn't do very well on the final exam, so she flunked. The director of the school, one of our other missionary doctors that year, asked me if I could regrade her exam so she passed, as history was the only subject she had failed. I found that I could look at her paper from another angle and pass her. The next year she failed anyway, not just history.

My most successful English class was the one I taught lab students. That's because it had a very narrow objective—to enable them to understand the English on things they used, such as labels and instructions for reagents. This was a brand-new school; Helen was making up the curriculum and courses. She asked me to create the one for English. I took the basic lessons she was teaching in French and put them into simplified English, limiting the new vocabulary introduced in each lesson. Most medical words are cognates, so it's pretty easy. I took a hint from my high school English teacher and had the kids write each new word in their notebook with a definition and a sentence. The first lesson was on the microscope and its parts. They had no trouble until they came to the microscope stage. How do you define it without talking about microscope slides? I hadn't introduced that word. The French word for a microscope slide is *lame*. It usually means "blade," so most of them talked about putting a blade on the microscope stage, but one smart fellow had a feeling that wasn't right, so he looked around for another translation of *lame*. Aha! It also means an ocean wave, so he put waves on his microscope stage. Well, they learned lab English pretty well. They couldn't say a correct sentence in English; one boy presented himself at the office saying, "I am come for to take the chalk." The assistant director figured out his English teacher needed chalk. But one of our graduates came back and told me that the doctor he worked under depended on him to read English.

I also taught religion. It was called Bible, but I thought it included more than that. The Old Testament in modern French was in process of translation. A partial edition of the Old Testament had come out that just touched the high points. I thought that would be ideal for the brief overview I had time to give them. They knew about creation, but after that they were very vague, so we started with Abraham. I tried to apply the Scriptures to their own lives. "Think of something very precious in your own life, something God gave you. Would you be willing to give it up if God asked you to (as Abraham was willing to give up his precious son)?"

One day I happened to tell another class about Frank Laubach's "game with minutes," how he tried to relate to God every minute of the day. I have tried at times to do that but never come anywhere near. One boy in that class was named Madituka. He was not an outstanding student, sort of average, a little bit of a clown. That young man became the leader of the local Scripture Union, probably the most vibrant and growing Christian organization in the country at that time. He was chosen with one other to attend the Hospital Christian Fellowship, an organization for nurses that then existed in Africa only in English-speaking countries. The meeting was held in Malawi. Madituka and his companion enjoyed meeting black and white nurses from South Africa who got along with each other. They were invited to visit Soweto on their way back to the Congo and miraculously were able to get visas and go there. Madituka came back and started organizing Hospital Christian Fellowship at Kimpese and then in the whole Congo. Now he's the national co-coordinator and the trainer for all of Francophone Africa. He married one of his classmates, and that couple bears an amazing Christian witness, tried in the fire of personal tragedy. One day long ago, when Madituka had become leader of the Scripture Union in the region, some of us were asking, "How did you get this way?"

He replied, "One day Mme Abell told us about the 'game with minutes.'" That boy I hadn't paid much attention to had put it into practice. Later I realized his parents must have been deeply committed Christians; he had a solid foundation.

Madituka and Fwauna, with God's guidance and the power of the Holy Spirit, produced four fine sons. They were especially proud of, and grateful for, the first-born, Patrice, who became a doctor. By this time the family was living in Kinshasa, so it was easy for Patrice to attend classes at the University. For his internship he went to IME, Kimpese, his parents' alma mater. At church in the city, his mother missed seeing and hearing her son play the piano as he always did, but God whispered to her, "He's where he belongs."

Later she found out the deeper meaning of that message. That Sunday afternoon, enjoying the freedom of the weekend, Patrice and some friends went to a small waterfall on the hill behind Kimpese, where we all enjoyed swimming. The young men would dive from a rock at the top of the waterfall and then swim in the pool below. They were about to go home when Patrice called out, "One more dive." He dove. He did not come up. Others dived in to find him. There was no trace of him. Eventually, horrorstruck, they returned to IME to tell the appalling news. By then it was dark. The next day a professional diver searched for Patrice. Still nothing.

If there was ever ground for believing in witchcraft, surely this was the case. How else could a full-grown, healthy man dive into a pool where people dived all the time and just completely disappear? His parents did not succumb to the temptation. They did pray, "Lord, give us back our Patou!"

Madituka went to Kimpese. Finally the body did float to the surface. Somehow it must have been caught under a layer of rock. They had planned to take the body to Kinshasa for burial, but it was in no condition to be taken, so it was buried at IME. Fwauna came from the city with her other sons. Now when someone dies in the Congo, people wail. If they have come some distance to the funeral, or to the wake, they don't wail all the time during the journey, but when they arrive and meet the other mourners they start wailing again. Fwauna stepped out of that car singing a hymn. God had repeated to her, "He's where he belongs."

The bereaved couple eventually wrote a book about Patrice, his life and death and life. They called it *La Rose Remise à sa Place* (The Rose Put Back Where It Belongs). We would probably not compare a man to a flower, but in African thinking that's all right. I've never known anyone whose faith and trust surpassed theirs.

Another opportunity came when Helen offered me a class called *séminaire.* It was far from a college seminar, but it was a discussion group, and I could choose what we would discuss. Wow! I realized that I wanted them to take notes, and the first thing I needed to do was teach them how to study. I remembered that when I started college we were given a little booklet telling us how to study, which I found very useful. The traditional way to study in the Congo is to copy in one's notebook whatever the teacher writes on the blackboard and try to memorize it. I wanted them to listen and understand and write down what they thought was important, whether it was on the board or not. I gave them math problems with extraneous information included, to try to get them to sort out what was necessary. I wanted them to think, and they found that difficult.

After that I started basing our discussion on books by Walter Trobisch, a German missionary to the Cameroun. Starting out in education, he came to specialize in marriage and family. His most famous book is called in English *I Loved a Girl.* The translation doesn't quite render what the French says. In French the tense makes a difference. The perfect tense, used in this title, indicates a one-time action, e.g., "I made love to a girl." Loving her over a period of time would be expressed by the imperfect tense. It's the thought-provoking story of a young man who is fired from his teaching position by the church because of adultery. He writes to his mentor, Trobisch, and

Trobisch replies. In a series of letters, the young man brings up one argument after another to justify himself, and Trobisch teaches him, letter by letter. Finally Trobisch sends his young friend a ticket to come see him, and the young man opens up and confesses deeply, is forgiven and starts home a new person. On the bus going home he meets a girl whom he sees with different eyes. They fall in love, and the sequel talks about their problems, as the girl's uncle wants her to marry someone else. After that book we went on to another and another of Trobisch's, and the students identified with his characters. This led to useful discussions. One of the girls said, "I'm a serious girl (not free and easy)," and I'm sure she was sincere.

The boys answered her, "Then pay attention to what you wear." I don't think she had ever thought about the relationship of the length of her skirt to how boys thought about her.

On another subject, the students told me about the bribery and corruption rampant in the country. "Little people," they explained, "are used to being gouged. They've finally realized they can gouge others too. They're seeing clearly now."

"It's possible," I tried to convince them, "to see even more clearly, to understand what happens in the long run when everybody gouges everybody else." It's hard to think of the long run when your children are hungry. We did hear about a group of Christians who had vowed neither to offer bribes nor to accept them. That takes a great deal of courage and faith. Missionaries don't always follow their own principles.

In our later years at Kimpese, Norm gave me responsibility for the cold chain. All the village health zones and dispensaries gave vaccinations. We had a supply of cold boxes in which we packed the vaccines with ice to send out to the villages. Vaccines that got warm could not be depended on.

We didn't see much cholera, but at one time we heard of some cases in the area. The hospital made preparations for any cases that might come to us—cholera beds in a special room and extra precautions to prevent its spreading to other patients. Then one day Norm came home saying, "Well, we have our first case of cholera."

"Oh, my. So they're using the cholera room." The patient was a habitual drunkard who was employed by the Catholic sisters of another mission in town. Unfortunately the staff on duty was so excited by the event that they forgot to put him in the room prepared for such patients. The hospital was crowded, and a woman waiting to deliver was ensconced on the floor in the corridor where the cholera patient waited. She contracted the disease. The man recovered; she did not. I learned that cholera can be successfully treated simply by giving rehydration fluids (water with a little bit of sugar and a tiny bit of salt) persistently, every few minutes. But it's much faster if you have the right antibiotic. We saw no more cases of cholera.

Great excitement at IME! Then Vice-President George H. W. Bush was visiting Kinshasa, the capital (called Leopoldville before the great name switch), and Barbara Bush was going to come down-country by plane and visit IME. Such preparations! In the Public Health Department, the posters about nutrition and hygiene and disease prevention were all translated into English. The English versions would not be useful after Mrs. Bush's visit, of course, but there they were. People from the Bushes' entourage came to prepare our staff. They practiced what they would do, down to the minute. Someone was to present the lady with flowers; they had to be inspected first. Everyone lined up on the sidewalk between pavilions as they would to greet Mrs. Bush. Well, almost everyone. A surgical operation was in progress. The petite missionary doctor and her patient remained in the operating room, but the nurses and the anesthetist obeyed the higher priority of getting ready for the big event.

On the anticipated day the weather did not cooperate, the flight did not take place, and Mrs. Bush never saw Kimpese.

That was a very minor incident compared with what occurred at the time of the famous Mohammed Ali versus George Foreman prize fight that was held in Kinshasa in 1974. The Department of Tourism, if there was such a thing, felt sure that many Americans would travel to Zaïre for the great occasion, and plans were made for tourists to come to Kimpese. Behind the town and the mission stations the Bangu raised its lofty head. It's not a mountain, just a deeply eroded plateau. It took us white adults about an hour to climb it; the local boys scrambled up in fifteen minutes. A stream called the Vampa tumbled down in two waterfalls; below each one a pool invited swimmers. Yes, that's where, years later, Patrice would drown. To get there we had to drive through town to the other Protestant center and through it to a manioc field where we found a swaying wooden bridge across the stream. On the other side of that we hiked through a mango grove and other foliage to reach the lower pool. But in preparation for the droves of tourists expected to come for the boxing match, a parking lot large enough for several buses had been carved out of the manioc field and a solid bridge built, held up by enormous tree trunks and wide enough for a car to drive across. Of course there was no road on the other side. In the mango grove slim tree trunks made benches in case folk wanted to stop and have a picnic. Then a little wooden bridge had been built so one could cross over to the other side of the Vampa without wading. To our knowledge nary a tourist used the parking lot, the bridge, or the benches. Eventually the small bridge was taken by somebody for firewood.

There were enough missionary kids at IME to justify a small school. The year we came there, Florny taught first through fifth grade. A young British missionary taught kindergarten. Florny was an experienced teacher in the States and had previously volunteered as an extra houseparent at our hostel in the city. She organized those children so that each one did his own work at his desk. When he needed her he would put up a little flag, and she would come to him as soon as she could. (Of course some were girls, but he/she is so cumbersome.) There were educational games in the back of the room to be used when regular work was done. The younger children came early in the morning, the older ones maybe an hour and a half later. Then the older ones stayed later. This gave Florny a chance to work with the two groups separately. Visiting her classroom, I exclaimed, "Florny, this is amazing! Every child is working at his own pace; no one's goofing off or disturbing the others. How do you do it?"

She said, "It took me six weeks to get everything working smoothly," but once she did, it was amazing.

In addition to all the classwork, and reading to the children every day—I think she read *The Hobbit*—she put on "The Wizard of Oz." Lanky Jimmy played the scarecrow. Arthur was the cowardly lion. A Swedish missionary who had become sort of an aunt to his family made his costume. It was fun to see him running around before the performance asking, "Where are my paws? Where are my paws?" The tin woodsman did fine in rehearsal, but just before the performance he was struck by stage fright and vomited all over the yellow brick road. Fortunately it was made of leaves and could easily be swept away and replaced. Replacing the actor was something else again; as luck would have it the MAF boy who played Dorothy's uncle was able to take over the role. Of course he had to use a script, and that posed a problem because tin arms don't bend at the elbow. But the performance was a delight.

The IME faculty was composed of missionaries from the UK, the US, Canada, Norway, and Sweden, also that one French teacher who wasn't a missionary. And they represented different denominations. One was the Evangelical and Missionary Alliance. They had a policy that missionary wives were not to homeschool their children; children had to be sent away to school. One such couple lived in Boma, well on the way to the coast. They sent their daughter to the English language school in Kinshasa for a year, but it was very hard on all of them, as it took them two days by road to make the trip there. They asked if they could send the girl and her brother, now six, to our little MK school at Kimpese. They would have to live with one of our families. I thought it might be a good opportunity for Jimmy, who had always been the last child of the family, to have someone younger to look after. Marjorie was now living at the hostel in Kinshasa. Everyone agreed, and the two children moved in. They were very nice children. The girl was 10, very easy to deal with but homesick. The boy was a fine lad but a typical six-year-old boy. Jimmy, 11, was not used to rooming with a little brother. It wasn't always easy.

Our second year at IME Florny was gone, and a sixth grade was needed. The English missionary took first grade along with kindergarten, and a young American missionary wife was invited to teach the other five grades. Unfortunately, she developed a serious disease and had to leave the country. We resident missionaries divided up the various subjects. Annabelle, a single missionary, taught science; MAF wife Evie took math and read novels to the children. I was responsible for social studies and English. One day two fourth-grade girls came to my desk for help. They were studying adjectives. They'd been given a list of nouns and were to think of two adjectives to go with each noun. They were doing well until they came to "grandmother." "All we can think of is old," they complained.

"Well, I'm a grandmother," I informed them, a bit proudly. I was in my late 40's. "Am I old?"

"Ah, middle-aged grandmother!" What else?

Later I thought I should have asked, "Do you have two grandmothers? How are they different?"

But they might have answered something like, "One lives in California and the other in Tennessee."

As you know, I loved directing Christmas pageants. I always liked to include Simeon. One of our committed nursing students was playing Simeon, but he made people laugh at his trembling gait. I told the fellow, "You're *pretending* to be an old man. *Be* old." He was able to do it.

Another year I tried to reproduce a Christmas pageant Agnes Sanford described in one of her books. She probably would not have recognized it. Our fine Dr. Mwimba had a great baritone voice and agreed to sing an appropriate hymn to begin the drama. To my surprise he sang one stanza only. Afterward I asked him, "Why didn't you sing the rest of the song?"

He explained, "I was kept at the hospital and had to run to the church to get there in time. I had just enough breath for one stanza!" How wonderful of him to make it in the midst of his busy doctor's life!

The pageant included some lighting changes, which I managed simply by turning on or off the switch at the back of the sanctuary. However, as the pageant progressed, more and more people crowded in, and sometimes someone's back would change the lighting inadvertently. Afterward one of my students asked me, "Was that you playing with the lights?"

That was such a beautiful little church. Once an African-American tour group visited Kimpese. When they entered the church, they spontaneously sat down and worshiped.

Directly across the road from us lived the Mpia family—father, mother, and three children. Relatives criticized them because there weren't more children coming along. Mr. Mpia taught math, but his heart was in music. Now if I want to learn a new hymn or song, I play it on the piano and then sing along with it. Mr. Mpia would sing it from the notes; then he could play it. He had named his firstborn Mozart,

Beautiful church at IME

and the boy was living up to his expectations. The year we went to the States on home assignment I left my little Irish harp with the Mpias. Mr. Mpia's fingers weren't quite slender enough to manage the strings easily, but his four-year-old daughter found she could pick out a favorite song on the harp. After we came back and the harp was back at our house, we invited the Mpias over for an evening. The little girl tried to play the harp, but oh dear! I had tuned it to a different key, and it didn't sound right at all. Many years later when visiting a Congolese church in the US, I was amused to be introduced as "the woman who taught Mozart to play the piano"!

It was Mr. Mpia who told us about the charismatic group that met in the next town. The church there had been founded through the efforts of British Baptists, but some of its members came from the Manianga, the area that had been evangelized by Swedes. When Simon Kimbangu had been preaching and healing in that area, these people's parents had discovered the gifts of the Holy Spirit, and their descendants, biological or spiritual, continued to operate in them. Kimbangu was so popular that the Belgian government, and perhaps the British Baptist mission, considered him a threat. Apparently the Swedish missionaries and the church they founded were not troubled by the remarkable healing that characterized Kimbangu's ministry.

Tata Butedi, the leader of this present group, told us, "When times were hard, when we were being persecuted, we heard the Holy Spirit speaking to us more often." These people were now leaders in the local church, which did not appreciate their charismatic form of worship, so they attended the traditional church service in the morning, and were loyal workers in the church. Then in the afternoon they met in another place to worship in their own way. At first that would have been in or outside someone's home, but by the time we visited them they had built their own small building.

We enjoyed worshiping with them and trying to conform. Everyone took off any jewelry and removed pens from pockets, also shed shoes. There was a small room at one end of the building where people could confess to one of the leaders before the service started. There were no pews or chairs; the men stood on one side of the room; the women mostly sat on the floor on the other side. All the leaders were men, but all the prophets were women. If one of the prophets had a message from the Lord, she would go on her knees (because that's the way Manianga women did) to one of the leaders, who would bend down and listen to her. A woman on her knees can have dignity and be respected and listened to.

Every woman had one or two rattles. Some are made of gourds with seeds inside; others are metal with pebbles. On the men's side were drums and a metal instrument that was hit like a gong. I found the noise deafening until I learned to get inside it.

At one point in the service, while singing was going on, individuals would go one by one to the end of the room opposite the leader and then dance the length of the room to the leader, who would grab the person's hand. I think you might call it testing the spirits. I tried to do it too, but I never felt comfortable or thought that it was accomplishing what it should. It was just a form for me. (Norm never tried.) One day I was explaining this to one of the women, and she asked me, "Don't you ever dream that you're dancing down the room to be tested?"

"No, Mama, I never have."

These people practiced healing and casting out evil spirits. They were for real. One of the women lived at IME; her husband worked there. A person from another village who belonged to the same charismatic fellowship entered our hospital with no family member there to take care of him. Our IME friend would leave her own work to come and help that unrelated person. She had not been to school; she said God had taught her to read, that she could read only the Bible. I observed that she could read the hymnbook too; probably she could read print but not cursive writing. Congolese teachers use cursive writing from day one, so kids who go to school learn that. When this woman had a baby, she named her after me. What were my responsibilities? Treat her like my own self! I'm afraid I didn't do that. I think we had moved on by the time "Mama Abell" was ready for school, otherwise I would have paid her school fees. I should have kept in contact and fulfilled that responsibility no matter where I was.

There were failures and disappointments. Norm trained a young nurse to oversee the Rural Health Zones, replenish their stocks of medicine and advise the rural nurses. The young man learned and did his job well. He became a personal friend and even invited us to his traditional wedding. We had attended a number of church weddings during our years in Congo, in villages and in the city. They were similar to the weddings we knew in the States, with a few differences. We were surprised at the first wedding we attended, at a village near Sona Bata.

The officiant asked, "Who gives this woman to be married to this man?"

Two men stood up. "I, her father, do," announced one of them.

The other man then added, "I, her mother, do." What??

The officiant then asked, "Who gives this man to be married to this woman?"

Two other men stood up. "I, his father, do."

And "I, his mother, do."

We were invited to a colleague's wedding

Eventually we understood that in the Bakongo culture it's more important to know which side of the family a person is on than the gender of the person. Your mother and all her siblings are your mothers. If you want to be specific you have to say "the mother who bore me." Likewise, your father and all his siblings are your fathers. Yes, you can have male mothers and female fathers!

We had never attended a traditional wedding. I was under the impression that it would consist mostly of drinking and dancing. This one, at least, was not like that. The father of our friend the bridegroom took a mason's trowel and pretended to be laying stones or bricks or concrete blocks to make a wall. As he did that he chanted, "I'm building, building . . ."

Then the bride's father did something similar. He too chanted, "I'm building, building . . ." They were symbolizing the promise of each family to support the new family that was coming into being with this marriage.

But after some years Norm heard rumors that his *protégé* was prospering dishonestly from his responsibilities. Eventually Norm had incontrovertible evidence and had to let this leader go and train someone else. It was a heavy blow.

Another young graduate disappointed us. As a student he had been the one to go with Madituka to the conference in Malawi. On graduating he was hired by IME, but before long he was let go. There was some question as to what had actually happened, and we thought he was innocent. Our dear friend Marc, heading up the Medical Department of the Church of Christ in Zaïre, asked us to recommend someone to assist him, and we recommended this young man. It turned out we had been wrong; the IME authorities had been right.

Then there was a student in our nursing school who developed mental problems. We knew and esteemed his mother, and I prayed hard and tried to help the fellow, but to no avail.

Another student developed glaucoma shortly after beginning the nursing course. Although he was at a quality hospital—albeit we didn't have an ophthalmologist—and received the best treatment known there, his glaucoma developed very fast and he had to drop out of school.

The school had a good library. How it came to boast a French translation of Shakespeare I have no idea, but it had a large number of books spanning a good deal of the Dewey Decimal System. It also had a bunch of novels translated from English into French and donated to schools in the Congo. Someone meant well, but the selection of books was impressively inappropriate. I read one. At the end the immoral protagonist gets what he deserves, but how many of our students would read it to the end? In the meantime, we would certainly not want them to follow his example or to base his picture of Americans on that book. I quietly disposed of it. Unfortunately I was not the only one who took books from the library and did not return them. It was very difficult to keep a French-English dictionary in the library—too valuable, too tempting.

The years went by. Jimmy had been in fifth grade our first year there. We wanted him to keep up his Kikongo and French and have Congolese *(Zaïrois)* friends as he had had at Sona Bata, so we sent him over to the other side of Kimpese, to CECO, the Pastors' and Teachers' School, where there was a good primary school for the local children. He could go with Zaïrois kids from IME and have the first two classes there, then come back to the English-language school with the upper-grade MKs (missionary kids) from CECO. This worked well until exam time. The main subjects, French and math, were always taught first thing in the morning. However, there were extra hours of French and math at other times, and of course Jimmy missed those. On the exam he got a question about something he hadn't studied and answered it by writing, in French of course, "Why must I know about that?" To Jimmy's embarrassment the teacher thought that so funny he read it to the whole class. At that point we decided Jimmy could stay on our side of the tracks for his schooling.

In March of his fifth grade Jimmy made his decision for Christ. It took him a while; when he decided, he decided with his whole heart. The good Angolan pastor you've heard about let Jimmy study the catechism booklet by himself. I guess Jimmy didn't understand how well he needed to know it, because when the pastor questioned him he flunked and had to study the book again. After passing the test, he gave his testimony in church, in French, including the words, "I don't want to sin any more." And he was baptized in the baptismal pool behind the church. A few days later I asked him to get something at the local market. He pleaded, "Please don't send me to the market. The kids tease me, 'So you don't want to sin any more!'" (Though sincere in that initial decision to follow Jesus, he emphasizes now how much of a process it is—requiring repeated decisions to obey Him, day by day.)

Teasing was hard for Jimmy to take when he went to the hostel in Kinshasa too. Especially during his first year there, other children found that it was easy to get a reaction from him. We shuddered to think what would happen if another boy broke Jim's model plane with the 6' wing span. That did not happen. One of his roommates was David, a couple of years older, who became a good and lasting friend. And during his hostel years Jim matured until as a senior he was a boy that younger kids went to for help and counsel.

In 1978 Marjorie graduated from TASOK (The American School of Kinshasa) and we all went back to the States on furlough. Marjorie didn't go with us but with her friend Betty. We had neglected to do something connected with her passport or visa or vaccinations and it was touch and go for a bit as to whether she would be allowed on the plane, but she was.

Our son Bob and his wife gave us the Ungame. It looked like a game. It included a board, dice to throw and "men" to move and cards to draw. It was actually a device for getting people to talk and listen to each other. Almost everyone enjoyed playing it. We had fun with other missionaries and with Congolese too, and we learned some things about their culture. One of the questions on the cards was, "What was your favorite birthday present?"

Birthday present? Not in the culture.

"What's the most important quality of a mother?"

"Hospitality." That important! It was a long time before we realized that we should never let anyone leave our house without at least offering something to drink.

I remember the evening we played the Ungame with three or four interns from the medical school in Kinshasa. Their education included a lot of theory but little hands-on experience. So in their last year they were sent out to hospitals where they could get that experience, and IME was one of those hospitals. I like to think it was one of the best. These men were very intelligent, of course. They knew English, so they could read the cards in the Ungame. One of them drew the question, "If you could find the cure for one disease, what one would it be?" That intern was not the sharpest of the group, but he did seem to be the most dedicated and caring. The disease he chose was malaria.

One of the others questioned his choice. "Why didn't you choose something like cancer?"

The first man pointed out, "Malaria affects so many people. It takes so much time away from work. It weakens you. It really takes a huge toll on society." It was that young doctor who came back after graduation to work at IME and actually took over the Public Health work when we went on furlough in 1978.

That last week before our departure was pretty hectic—not so much for me. School was out, and I could devote all my energy to packing up. I do remember leaving a partly packed suitcase outside our bedroom on the screened back porch and finding some things missing before I finally closed it. But in general I was able to keep to my plan of packing up one room a day. The last room was our bedroom, which also served as Norm's home office. The rest of the room got packed, but Norm stayed at the hospital, preparing the new doctor to take over his work, until afternoon of the day we had to travel to the city and make our plane. When he came home, great activity, sorting papers, throwing some away and packing others in the right places. We became less exacting as the time flew by, until finally we were just tossing papers into foot lockers. Jim helped by toting the full containers to the attic of the house next door, where we were allowed to store them during our absence. Fellow missionary Charlie came to take us to Kinshasa and joined in the frantic filling, closing, and toting. At last we were off. Then when we got to the city, Norm had to stop and transact some final business with Marc, who had taken his place at the medical department of the Church of Christ in Zaïre. We did make the plane on time, and Charlie survived the stress of trying to pry us loose. Finally relaxing on the plane, Jim felt in his pocket and found the key to the staircase that led to the next-door attic. We mailed it back from Brussels, but of course the neighbors needed to get into that attic long before the key reached them.

There were three American Baptist churches in Kalamazoo. First Baptist kept close connections with Kalamazoo College; that was where Bob and Anna had been married. It was naturally the most intellectual of the three churches. Bethlehem Baptist was more conservative, with a number of people from the South. A third church was the most active in social justice. We attended Bethlehem because it had the most for our young people. But we parents went to Sunday School at First Baptist and occasionally our family attended the third church on special occasions.

My parents were living in a retirement community in Florida. When they first moved there they had kept their old house in New York State so we could have it to retire to, but after a year they realized 1) that it's not smart to hang on to a house when you're too far away to look after it, and 2) that we would probably not want to retire in New York State, with our children far away and no other reason to live there. So they sold the house, and in 1979, Norm and Jim went down to Florida and helped my parents choose a house for us only ten miles from where they lived.

Then came our second five years in Kimpese. Doctors from Doctors Without Borders had lived in our house while we were gone, and taken good care of it.

On our last home assignment, 1984–1985, we lived in that house in Florida, the only time we ever owned a house. It was good to be there; my dad died during that year, and Mother stayed with us while he was in the hospital.

CHAPTER EIGHTEEN

Our Children Spread Their Wings

Jimmy had a little difficulty adjusting to life at Kimpese. There were other MKs (missionary kids) his own age, but he wasn't fully one of the group at first. At one point I decided to give him his first driving lesson in order to add something positive to his life. Norm was away. He didn't itinerate like earlier, evangelistic missionaries, but he did seem to be away at several crucial times. Well, for some reason I took Jimmy over to the agricultural station (yet another mission station at Kimpese!) for our practice. He remembers very clearly backing into a palm tree. Before we left Kimpese he had developed into a very skillful driver. Come to think of it, by then he was in college.

After furlough, in the fall of 1973, we had arrived back in Zaïre just in time for school to start; we'd sort of dumped Marjorie at the hostel, and she never saw her new home till the first break, probably Thanksgiving time. That was tough. The first year, in eighth grade, she roomed with her old friend from Moanza and Kinshasa, Linda.

Everybody thought it was a good idea—Marjorie, Linda, both their parents, the hostel mother. It didn't turn out that way. They were too much alike; they ended up staying in their room a lot. They both enjoyed being with Marie and were each jealous of the other with her. They both did much better later with other roommates.

When Marjorie was 14 she and Mark became very interested in each other. Mark's parents were both doctors, Mennonites, working at Kimpese—very capable people, good friends to us. Mark was slightly older than Marjorie and had a sister slightly younger. Then there were Arthur, a classmate of Jimmy's, and seven-year-old Robby. Once I remarked to the girl, "All four of you are so smart, it doesn't seem fair!"

She replied, "But if one of us weren't, think how bad he'd feel!"

IME was administered by an outstanding Congolese man named Mandiangu. Our houses were diagonally across the road from each other. He had a son the same age as Jimmy and Arthur, who played with them and knew quite a bit of English. One day I asked one of the boys to give back a book by Munro Leaf that I had lent him. When he appeared with it, I showed it to the boys. The subject was prehistoric man, but the book began by talking about ancestors—grandparents, great-grandparents, etc. For some reason I told them, "Jimmy's great-great-great-great (26 greats)-grandfather was King John of England." Then honesty impelled me to admit, "He was probably the worst king England ever had."

Little Robby was tagging along with the bigger boys. At this he piped up, "I sure hope Mark doesn't marry Marjorie. We wouldn't want anything like that in our family."

Well, he didn't. They eventually broke up, but they remained friends all through high school. When the students put on "Our Town," Marjorie played Mark's mother—and made the wedding gown for his bride. Mark headed up the photographic staff of the yearbook his senior year. The yearbook was sent to the States for printing. It arrived back in Zaïre in time for graduation, but Mark was deeply disappointed in the quality of the photos he had worked so hard on.

He wrote in Marjorie's copy, "This book should be glued shut with the printers inside." The next year, Marjorie edited the yearbook. The staff decided to have the printing done locally.

Marjorie was a project person. At home in the dry season vacation, she might stay up all night working on a skirt for me, something for herself. Late at night in her room was a good time for a mother-daughter talk.

The first event of our year of home assignment in 1978 was Grace's wedding. She was marrying Michael, a graduate student at Western Michigan University (WMU). They were buying a house, which Grace was already living in, but they had a right to a college apartment, so they lived at the college and let the four of us have their house for the year. Bob was at WMU too; the whole family lived in Kalamazoo that year. Marjorie wanted to work for a year before she started college. She got a job at a doughnut shop, then a taco place. Jim took his sophomore year at the local high school. That fall, he initially worked for an eccentric old guy who sold and repaired bicycles, also all sorts of other things that only he could find. He promised Jim that he would teach him to spoke a bicycle wheel if he worked well, but the promise was never kept. After snowfalls made his bicycle commute to and from that job impractical, Jim made a little money delivering a weekly advertising paper. That job was also difficult until the snows had melted.

Before returning to the field we saw Marjorie enrolled at WMU. On the parents' orientation tour we found that at the noon meal she could have her choice of 30 different foods and 20 different beverages. She told us later that the food was great except that they turned off the orange juice machine at 11:00 a.m. Marjorie had said she would enjoy rooming with someone from another country; they gave her an Iranian roommate. She was in what she persistently called a four-man suite. One of the other two girls became her roommate the next year.

In 1981 it was Jim's turn to graduate from TASOK. Earlier that year he and Gary had climbed the cliff at the coast and inscribed on it in large letters "Class of '81." Jim was valedictorian of his class, as Grace had been. Foreseeing that, I had encouraged Jim to take public speaking. He followed my advice and did himself proud at graduation.

Marv and Bob, MAF pilots at Kimpese, had given Jim his first flight lessons at IME. Jim found it wasn't as thrilling to be actually flying a plane, as straight and level as possible, as making a model one soar and dip! But he did want to be a pilot, and eventually he decided that yes, he did want to be a missionary. He followed David (his good friend at the hostel) to LeTourneau College, which was tops in training mechanics. An MAF pilot had to be a mechanic too. When Jim graduated from LeTourneau, John, our first MAF pilot in Congo, was marshal of the graduation procession!

It was during that second term at Kimpese that Bob and family came to visit us. Bob was in his final year of med school and was able to take one of his clerkships in the Congo, at our hospital at Kimpese. Bob and Anna now had four children. Anna let me homeschool Kiesi and Theresa. Tim had reached the inquisitive age of two, and Serenity was just learning to talk. I played ball with her, singing, "Roll the ball" as I sent it between her legs.

She didn't learn the whole sentence, but it was a thrill to hear her say, "Baw."

Someone must have come around with a chameleon for sale. Bob bought it, and his big girls had a great time with Sam, ugly as he was. Anna did not like him so well.

One day Anna saw a mouse. She did just what a woman is supposed to do—she jumped up on the dining room table.

Jim had had an encounter with a mouse some time before. He opened his desk drawer, and a mouse looked up at him. He quickly shut the drawer, and while we were at the Sunday evening picnic at the guest house, he enlisted aid in getting the mouse. We looked for a cat. Someone offered an adolescent kitten, not guaranteeing it would be a mouser. Two Dutch boys came over. So, after the picnic, three tall high school boys, one tall man, one medium woman, and one small cat came into Jim's room and shut the door. The kitten headed for the window, but Jim was sure he knew where the mouse was. He opened the drawer—and naturally the mouse had left the same way it had entered. So where was it? The kitten had been right; the mouse was hiding between the curtain and the window. But by now a very intimidated little cat was hiding under the bed. Not so the mouse. It amazed us by its athletic feats, leaping to the top of the chest of drawers

Bob and Anna's family visiting Congo ... what a joy for us!

and then to the top of a picture on the wall. But none of the large humans in the room could catch it. Finally everyone left but Jim. He kept it for several days and then inadvertently crushed it in the door trying to keep it from escaping.

While Bob's family was there they lived in our house. Our neighbors, two single ladies, were going to be away, so they let us stay in their house. They had a dog and advised us, "Just go in as if you belong there." We did and had no trouble. Later we learned that that dog had occasionally bitten a stranger. Just as well we didn't know that at first.

When the clerkship was finished, Bob and family and I went down to the coast for a week. Norm wasn't able to get away. Tim took all his Little People (tiny wooden figures) with him. Next door there was a boy maybe seven years old who took the time to play with Tim. The beach house had a porch in the back, high off the ground as it sloped down toward the water. Tim's new friend helped him fish off the porch, making a fishing pole for him and tying a rock to the line for Tim to pull up. Tim loved his rockfish and took it back to Kimpese with him. Much later, back in the States, we were all looking at photos taken on that trip and were amazed to see how many Little People had gone on vacation with Tim. The number was much reduced when we left the beach house. But Tim was delighted with his rockfish.

Bob's last excursion in Congo was to be a trip way up-country to Vanga to show Anna where he had lived and to observe the hospital there. They were set to start out one morning, but the vehicle wouldn't budge; it was dead as a doornail. Both knowledgeable men, father and son, exerted their brains to find the problem. Garage staff was called in. Finally, after some hours, it was discovered that little Tim had found a bolt and stuck it in an inviting slot which turned out to be the cigarette lighter. That was what had happened to the battery. The departure was delayed till the next day.

After two years at Western Michigan, Marjorie had transferred to Oral Roberts University, where Bob was in Medical School. ORU did a wonderful job of preparing students for summer mission trips. After her sophomore year she went with a group to Burkina Faso (formerly Upper Volta), and the next summer she led a group of five to the Congo. We met them at the airport and brought them to Kimpese, where Marjorie stayed with us, the other young woman lived with a Congolese family, and the young men went to the leprosarium a mile away and made their home with missionaries there. The first evening they were there, the group visited the Scripture Union and prayed for the leaders. Later they participated in a youth retreat. The other young woman declined the fish heads that supplied the protein for one meal.

The ORU students had several other opportunities to talk to groups and to pray with people. At one point the young women went to the other station (where Jim had gone to French school) and the fellows stayed with us. Then two of the men went up on the Bangu and

ORU Summer Missions team, in the home of a pastor and his wife

itinerated with the pastor there. When they came back from a grueling hike to another village, Rory looked at the hill on which the pastor lived and thought, "I can never walk up that." So he ran!

All three fellows had secured international drivers' licenses, but none of them had had experience with a stick shift, so Marjorie and Jim, who was visiting that summer, did the driving. After several weeks with us, the team traveled to Kinshasa for ministry there. Marjorie learned to be decisive and confident through that experience. When they arrived at the airport to go back via Paris to the States, one fellow's name was missing from the passenger list. Marjorie had re-confirmed all of them at the right time, but somehow he had slipped through the cracks. Marjorie stuck to her guns, and finally the agent gave them the five boarding passes they needed.

Jim stayed on a few more weeks. When we took him to Kinshasa for his flight back to the States, there was a letter from Marjorie. We read it on the way to the airport. Rory, the student on her team who was the most gung-ho about using French, the one she considered her co-captain, had told her on the plane to Paris, where he was staying for his junior year abroad, that she meant a lot to him and he wished she was coming to Paris too. Marjorie had had no idea. Pairing off was forbidden during summer mission, as it would break up the team. Marjorie had already done her junior year, and you can't take your senior year abroad. Now she wrote, "I won't do it if you don't want me to, but everything has fallen into place for me to take a second junior year in Paris." We had the rest of the trip to the airport to decide what we would write to Marjorie.

While Jim waited for his flight to be called, I wrote something to the effect of, "Wow! Well, it looks as if God is arranging this for you. Follow his guidance, and God bless you." And before we retired from the Congo we made a trip to the States to attend Marjorie and Rory's wedding.

CHAPTER NINETEEN

Kikongo Is Not So Bad

When we first arrived in the Congo in 1956, there were eight American Baptist mission stations, four down-country (downriver from the capital) and four up-country (east of the capital, in the interior). We were assigned first to Sona Bata, later to Kinshasa and eventually to Kimpese, a union station with several denominations working together. The one down-country station we never lived at was Nsona Mpangu, the successor to Banza Manteke, our oldest station. The up-country posts included Kikongo, Moanza, Vanga, and Boko. Norm made surgical visits to Boko from Sona Bata, and once the children and I went with him. (Grace remembers sleeping in a crib at Boko, even though she was seven years old, because it was screened in to protect her from mosquitoes. She also remembers the delight of being offered her choice from several individually packaged cold cereals, her first time ever! At home we ate oatmeal.) We had three short stints at Moanza and two years at Vanga. Now in 1985 Norm was invited to join a Congolese doctor in starting Public Health work at the Kikongo hospital.

I had never wanted to go to Kikongo. I'd heard that people there were ornery, and I had a theory that it was because it didn't cool off there, even at night. However, Kikongo had changed. Our dear friends Cliff and Joy, whom we'd worked with at Moanza, had gone there to direct the pastors' school, and I think Joy in particular had been able to unite the women so there was no longer unfriendly rivalry between the pastors' school and the rest of the station. It was easy to see how the station people would be jealous. Pastoral students, although poor as church mice, got a lot of attention from missionaries. The wives were trained as well as the husbands; there was even a three-year kindergarten for their children.

In 1985 we went to Kikongo and spent some happy years there. There was no house for us, so Pierre-François built one. It took a while, longer than expected; Cliff and Joy invited us to live with them until our little house was completed.

Pierre-François? Where did he come from? Well, he came from France, as you might think from his name. His father had vineyards there; P-F had gone to college and become an architect, but now he was at loose ends and didn't know what to do with himself. He would have liked to go to Canada but didn't have the money. So he hitchhiked to Zaïre! He must have flown or gone by ship across the Mediterranean, but from North Africa on he made his way by land, arriving finally in the capital city of Kinshasa, where an architect and his wife whom P-F knew were living. He turned up at their door one day, and they welcomed him.

Mrs. Müller was attending Bible studies led by a dynamic Swiss missionary named Jacques Vernaud. She took Pierre-François with her. It changed his life. I asked him once, "Pif, did you grow up in the Catholic church? Did you have faith as a child?"

He replied, "Anything I had had was all gone by the time I came here." Now in this strange city he gave his life to Christ. Here comes a confession. We had heard of this Swiss missionary and privately thought of him as a sheep stealer. That is, some members from our churches were leaving to join his church. When we came to know Jacques Vernaud and his delightful Dutch wife, we realized that church members were changing churches because they hadn't found dynamic, life-changing faith in their old church and they did find it in his. Instead of feeling jealous, we should be learning from him.

Mr. Müller put Pierre-François in touch with John, our American Baptist builder stationed at Vanga. P-F told us about the promise the Lord had made to him in a vision. He saw misty light and heard God assure him, "You've left your parents, but I'm giving you new parents." Jacques Vernaud became his spiritual father. Then when he arrived at Vanga one morning at dawn, mist was rising from the river—his vision! And at Vanga Miriam, Dr. Dan's wife and a gifted, dynamic, deeply committed missionary nurse and teacher of nurses, became his spiritual mother.

Now John sent the young Frenchman to Kikongo to supervise building there. P-F testified once, "When I accepted Christ, he changed some things in my life right away. I stopped drinking and womanizing. Later on I learned other things, like how to treat my workers." We found him a delight to know and a stimulus to our faith and practice.

Pierre Francois in a Congolese home

During his time at Kikongo he met a Canadian Mennonite missionary and traveled quite a distance by motorcycle to visit her at her station. Their backgrounds were very different; P-F reported they "had a lot of brush to clear away." One thing they had in common: both their fathers had vineyards! They eventually married and settled down in Canada, where P-F continued architectural work and they raised a family of boys.

The house Pierre-François built contained interesting contrasts. There was no hot running water, of course, but the enclosure around the bathtub was made of mahogany. It did turn out that there was a nest of snakes inside that enclosure, but that got taken care of. Kikongo was hot, as we had heard. I wrote one day that the temperature in our bedroom was 96 degrees, although it was only 90 in the living room. I was consulted about the color of paint and indulged my fancy in deciding what color I would like for each room. It turned out they would all be the same color, probably cream. It was a good little, two-bedroom house—little by our standards, big to a Congolese. Once at another station a visitor from America, speaking from the pulpit, said he had been born in a little five-room house. In Congo those two terms are contradictory.

In all our years in the country our cook had usually been a man, but now we had a mature woman as cook. She was a good worker. Once when we had bought a fish someone had caught in the river, she asked, "Can I have the head?"

"Why, yes, Mama, sure you can have the head." When she cut off the head it seemed to me that fish's neck must have extended well down into its chest.

"That's a really large head, Mama."

She replied, "No, it's small," meaning that her portion was definitely smaller than the part of the fish left for us. That was true.

Her teen-age son had frequent, heavy nosebleeds. She talked about buying a guinea pig so he could drink the blood. Unfortunately, we never found out the cause of his hemorrhages, and he eventually died.

The pastoral students were all married. A few of the wives had a high school education, with some teacher training. Some came not knowing how to read. The rest fell somewhere in between. It must have been a challenge to plan a program so that each woman could receive education appropriate to her needs. Joy and her staff accomplished that. Then, because their mothers were in class, the children had to be taken care of too. School age boys and girls went to the local school with the children of doctors, nurses, professors, workmen, all the other folk on the station. For the three- to five-year-olds Joy ran a kindergarten. Now that I was there and wanting to teach, Joy asked if I would teach an experimental first grade for those who had just graduated from her kindergarten, to see how they would do in comparison with the other local children who had not had the benefit of kindergarten.

Never having taught first grade, except for my own children, I jumped at the chance. I limited myself to what the other first grade teachers had—a textbook for the teacher, none for the children. A blackboard and chalk. In our early years in the country, first graders used slates and slate pencils. Now they used little notebooks. What a waste! The six- or seven-year-olds scribbled in their notebooks, thinking they were copying what the teacher wrote on the blackboard. I went back to slates. I furnished the slates; all the kids' parents had to buy was the slate pencils. If they didn't even do that, I'm afraid I provided them. I made experience charts; writing on large sheets of paper something the class had done or talked about, or a simplified version of the Bible story we were studying. I don't know where I found the paper for that or the easel. I also did something the local teachers never would have had the time to do. Every day I took home all the slates and put an exercise on each slate for the child to do the following day. I used ideas from American workbooks and adapted them to Kituba, the language the children were learning to read and write. The lessons, handed down by the government, used the Laubach method, with a picture for each letter sound. The first week we learned the vowels. *"A"* was represented by an open mouth in profile, saying *"ah."* If you work at it, you can make that mouth into the letter *"a,"* which in Kituba says *"ah."* Learning vowels was frustrating because vowels by themselves have no meaning. The second week we used a woman's breasts (clothed) to illustrate *"m,"* and we learned the word *mama,* like the English word but including any woman. Since we had studied all the vowels, we could then learn *meme,* which means "sheep," and so on.

Teaching reading was great fun. As they learned a new letter, the kids started writing it, both in manuscript and in cursive, because from second grade on they would be copying their teacher's cursive writing.

One day during the first week of school I was heading for a house I hadn't been to before, looking at the way ahead, not at the ground underneath my feet. I came to a little drop-off and managed to chip an ankle bone. First we thought it was just a sprain, but when it remained painful Norm put a cast on it. After a few days he heeded my pleas and gave me a walking cast. Then I could hobble to class on crutches. The cast turned out to be quite advantageous. The children were just learning to write their names. When one could write his or hers to my satisfaction, the child could write it on my cast.

Our most memorable letter that year turned out to be "Y." The Laubach-inspired reader had a picture for every letter. The word yuyu was excellent for "Y"; it means "spider." The book had a picture of a spider in a spider web, with a few lines darkened to make the "y." We did better, through no initiative of mine. It never occurred to me until just now to thank God for it, but I suppose he must have sent that nice large garden spider to the back wall of our unpainted concrete classroom. I gratefully marched to the back of the room with my chalk and wrote *yuyu* under the spider. I wonder if my children remember that as well as I do?

Then of course we had arithmetic. They brought in bottle caps or sticks for counting and seeing addition and subtraction facts. And the curriculum included practical education, like sewing on buttons. The youngest little girl sewed her first button from the center holes to the edge all around. Of course, then you can't put it through the buttonhole.

And there was Show and Tell. We went to see some things, and the children were encouraged to bring in objects. They had to be taught to ask questions. One girl brought in the framework of an umbrella. Classmate's question: "Where did you get it?"

My question: "What do you suppose an umbrella is made of?"

One girl's delightful suggestion: "Bat wings?"

Another advantage my class had—there were only 20 pupils. There were 21 the first day, but one little boy died that afternoon. The second day we went to his funeral. He had been so weakened by repeated malaria that his little body couldn't take a worm cure.

Thank God there were no more fatalities during the year. One charming little boy fell into an outhouse hole (outhouses in Congo have no seats), but he was pulled out, disgusting but safe.

Classes in the regular schools would start out with 50 or 60 children. Then when the first exam time came, those who had not been able to pay their school fees (although their parents had bought those notebooks) were weeded out. The oldest boy in my class was ten. He had started school several times but never been able to pay the fees. It was a big help to have such a mature and knowledgeable child in the class.

In the latter part of the school year we studied the story of Joseph (omitting Potiphar's wife). These children had the advantage that there were books in their small homes, including the Bible. As they advanced in reading, occasionally one would slip in beside me in church and read the Bible along with me. They learned the sounds of all the letters in first grade, but consonant blends (two consonants together) didn't come till second grade. That meant I had to limit the vocabulary. I couldn't use the very common word *yandi,* which means "he" or "she." (If we had it in English it would make gender inclusiveness so much simpler!) When I wrote the daily episode of Joseph on my chart I had to repeat Yosefi every time. We enjoyed the story of Joseph, and I decided to try creative drama, the children figuring out how to act out the various scenes. I thought it went well, except that, since the Joseph story includes so many men and almost no women, some male roles had to be played by girls; Jacob and Joseph were not willing to embrace when they met in Egypt. Well, Joy suggested we enact the play for the parents. Since the geography of the story is so wide ranging, I had the bright idea of having the children perform on tables placed around the perimeter of the room, with the audience in the middle. Guess what. Only the people on the outside chairs could see the action. I guess you probably figured that out without having to see it demonstrated. Also, when we actually did the play in practice, it fell completely flat. I was ready to scrap it, but Joy suggested I narrate it as the children played it, and that worked pretty well.

At Christmas time I gave each child a present—a piece of paper with a story typed on it that they could read. Remember, they had no book; up till now they had read only from the blackboard, the easel, and their slates. Now they had a story they could hold in their hands, take home with them, read to their parents.

The curriculum also called for a little French. The children learned to answer *"Qu'est-ce que c'est?"* (What is it?) with the names of common classroom objects. From there we started a little very basic conversation. Occasionally they were also exposed to a little poem or song in French. One of them was *"Escargot,"* about a snail. The children knew what snails were. We didn't discuss eating them. One day one little girl begged, "Let's do *Escargot.* Let's not do *Qu'est-ce que c'est.*"

Came the close of the school year and exam time. For their reading test, I wrote an exercise on each child's slate—a slightly different one for each child, so there was no temptation to peek at someone else's work.

Everybody passed! One little boy made just 50 in every subject—and I didn't cheat. Now 50 is passing in the Congo, as in France and Belgium. This fellow's mother was the weakest student among the wives, and his dad had been moved from the upper level to the lower, so I guess heredity was showing up. He did make 50. The little boy who could not learn the letter "K" still read *"me"* for *"ke,"* but otherwise he did all right. Some were reading their daddies' Bibles!

After graduating to public health work—the exciting job of developing a new Rural Health Zone, training nurses to run Health Centers, not just dispensaries, and recruiting mature, knowledgeable women to oversee health concerns in the villages—after ten years of that, Norm was back in general medical practice, assisting the Congolese doctor at Kikongo with patient care, and also doing some informal training of nurses and auxiliaries, at the hospital and at the rural health centers which Dr. Kwata had

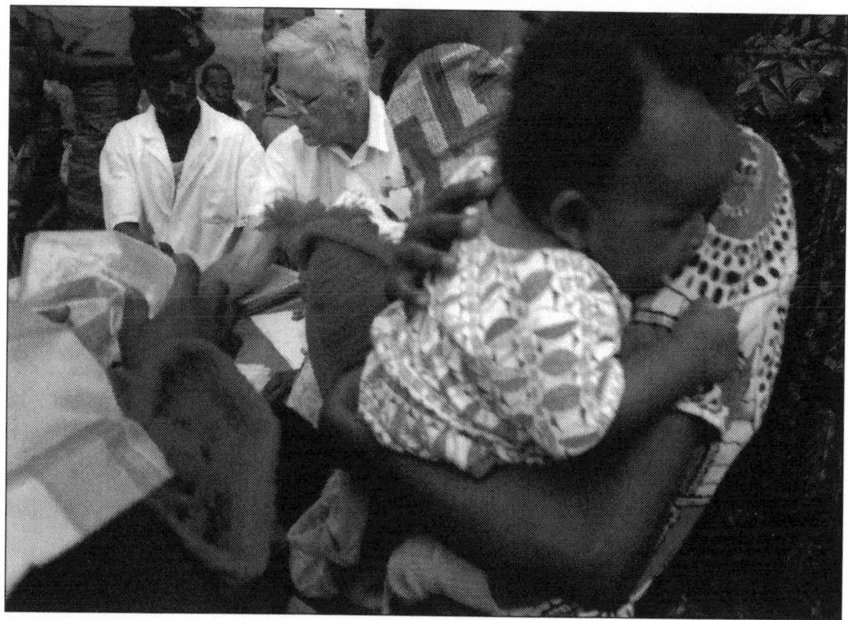

Well baby clinic

established. Norm had worked under a Congolese hospital administrator at Kimpese and under another missionary doctor at Vanga, but this was his first time to work under a Congolese doctor. It was easy, because Norm respected him and they worked together well, each appreciating the other's strengths. The doctors were pleased to see results of their baby vaccination program—only a few scattered cases of measles, rather than the yearly epidemic that had usually occurred. After nine months at Kikongo Norm saw the first case of newborn tetanus. That baby had been born at a nearby Catholic mission and had not been vaccinated. Kikongo hospital quickly invited that mission to come receive supplies of vaccine. What a change from the early days, when Catholics and Protestants were at each other's throats, each thinking the other's converts were lost forever!

Norm appreciated contact with patients—praying for them, encouraging them, helping them forgive their relatives and be forgiven. Some Congolese were surprised and gratified that he, a white man, understood that need. He found opportunities too to share Christ, and a deeper understanding of Christ, with members of the hospital staff.

Tuberculosis, a disease of malnutrition, was rampant. With modern TB medicines, Norm was able to send patients back to their villages where food was available, the health center nurse giving daily injections and follow-up. The next step was to train the rural nurses to diagnose TB and start treatment promptly, sending complicated cases to the hospital. In 1986, at age 60, Norm wrote, "We have just sent out three nurses with whom I spent two or three hours a day over a two-month period retraining them for rural health work. This has given me new ideas." He and Dr. Kwata were to give an intensive three-week course—including 120 class hours and practical training in community health work—to ten nurses, over half of them from the old government medical service.

Our second year at Kikongo I went from first grade to the pastors' school! I was asked to teach psychology and pedagogy. In college I had taken only one beginning class in psychology, but I was given a good textbook and I chose topics that were relevant to my students. The different kinds of freedom, or liberty, for instance. There's personal freedom—you're not a slave; civil freedom—you're not in prison; national freedom—your country is independent. It was good for them to make a distinction. Another topic was lying. What is lying, and what isn't?

Figurative language—the use of metaphor—is not lying. When Song of Solomon says, "Your lips are a red ribbon," it's not meant to be taken literally. If I say something untrue but I think it's true, that's a mistake, not a lie. African fables in which animals talk and cook are not lies; they're not meant to be taken literally. A lie is intended to deceive. When you lie to your toddler, what are you teaching him? Mama is far away, working in her garden. You're home with the kid, he's crying, and you say, "Stop crying, or that goat out there will eat you."

Maybe the kid believes you and stops. But someday he's going to realize that goats don't eat children, and he will have learned not to trust Daddy.

"Well, what are we to do when the child cries?"

"Why is he crying?"

"He's hungry."

"Give him something to eat."

"Nothing in the house."

"Then when you get your rations, be sure there are some bananas he can eat when he's hungry."

That may not sound like a psychology course, but it's what seemed useful to me.

I figured pastors would probably need pedagogy primarily for teaching Sunday School. I suggested that when they taught the creation story to children who had heard it for several years before, they have a new objective, perhaps to show that God wanted good for his people. I asked, "Don't some of your parishioners think of God as an angry man in the sky waiting to punish them when they do wrong?"

One student answered, "Why, yes, that's what we all believe."

Really?! I don't believe they all did, but at least he did.

I don't believe they all did, because the Scripture Union was very strong. One missionary colleague called it the cutting edge of Christianity in the Congo at that time. The Holy Spirit was working. Scripture Union members were concerned about evangelism, discipling, and prayer. One man told Norm, "I felt I needed preparation for this work, so I've spent the last 24 hours fasting and praying."

One day in class one of the students expressed a concern. Speaking of another student, he said, "When we joyfully raise our hands in prayer, he doesn't. Do you suppose he has a demon?"

I answered, "It seems to me the Holy Spirit gives us the freedom to raise our hands or not raise our hands." I thought but fortunately refrained from saying, "If a demon is involved, it seems more likely that he's influencing the one who criticizes his brother."

At Kikongo we enjoyed the help of two volunteers who became our first Catholic Baptists. One was a Peace Corps young woman who went back to Vermont both Christmases she was there, returning with real maple syrup each time. The other was a mature woman, a doctor from Cook County Hospital in Chicago. They both helped a great deal with the work, and both these Catholic women joined in the missionaries' Bible study.

That second year I was more involved with the dynamic women's group at Kikongo. In fact, I served as leader of one of the twelve groups into which the large fellowship was divided. We were using a book on James, designed for Theological Education by Extension. One day some women who could read were going over the lesson at my house before meeting in the large group. Included was our excellent hospital chaplain's wife, who served as a chaplain too. In one of the Bible verses printed in the book there was a misprint, a zero that did not belong there. This woman thought of it as an "O" and found two spiritual meanings for that misprint!

The women in Jean's small group

One day in the large group the women were discussing what to do when your child is sick and not improving with medical care. Animist family members are urging you to go to the sorcerer. (We used to say witch doctor.) It's a real problem. The lovely wife of the administrator of the pastors' school testified, "I'm so blessed I don't have that problem. All of our family on both sides are Christian."

That year it was decided that the Christmas pageant would be given by the women. "Mama Abell, you'll be Simeon."

"What will I do for a beard?"

"Make one from a coconut."

Norm had once taken a course in Addis Ababa, Ethiopia. He had brought back one of the large, thin, white cotton cloths Ethiopians use to keep off the sun and the flies. This made a fine prayer shawl. That church had choir benches on the platform perpendicular to the pews, so when we actors sat there waiting for our turn the congregation saw us in profile, and saw only the end person very well. When I stood up and went center stage, there was an audible gasp. Here was this man in prayer shawl and beard, with a white face! Is it a ghost? Then I started speaking. What a relief! It's just Mama Abell.

Marjorie and Rory were in France where Rory was completing his Master's. When he achieved that, they were able to spend a summer with us at Kikongo. Rory taught in the Pastor's school and Marjorie helped Norm at the hospital. She also found an opportunity to help one of the women with sewing. While they were there, this dear couple stayed in another missionary's house. The usual occupants had to leave for medical reasons. Here our daughter and her husband met an inconvenience we had never encountered. Oh, we had seen spiders, but this house was spider heaven! Rory remembers combatting the spider plague with a can of Baygon (insecticide) in one hand and a broom in the other. Fortunately this experience didn't keep Rory from subsequent visits to Africa. It was an unexpected delight to have them with us. It's wonderful that all of our children are grateful for their experiences in the Congo, both in growing up years and later visits. Marjorie says, "I wouldn't trade it for anything!"

Kikongo had been selected for a mission station partly because it boasted seven springs where people could get water and bathe. There could be one for men, one for women, one for schoolboys and one for girls—and three to spare! Norm, being a doctor and the son of a sanitary engineer, was interested in springs. One day he visited three of them, climbing down into the valley and back up again each time, since they were in different valleys. Then he made another trip down to the ram, which used water pressure to pump water up to our houses and the hospital. Back at home, his legs cramped excruciatingly. He'd had leg cramps from time to time ever since he had polio; he would stand up and the cramp would go away. This time there was no possibility of being able to stand. After some time I thought of filling the solar shower bag with hot water. The shower bag was meant to hang from a tree branch where the tropical sun would heat the water. It hadn't been solar heated that day, so I filled it with hot water from the stove. Norm was able to slide down from his chair so his legs were on the floor, and I put the heated bag between them. Gradually the cramps eased. That was the first indication we had of post-polio syndrome, although we didn't recognize it at the time. People who've had polio and recovered enough to live active lives often overuse the muscles they have left to make up for those that don't work any more. Then, 20 or 30 years later, post-polio will attack those weary muscles, gradually depriving the person of his strength. Some time after that episode at Kikongo, on our way back to Zaïre from the States, we spent the night in a hotel in downtown Zurich. In the morning we walked around to see some of Zurich before making our way back to the train station to return to the airport. After some walking, Norm's legs just gave out. He had to sit and rest a while before we could head for the station. That was the second indication.

CHAPTER TWENTY

Moanza Again

After two years at Kikongo, in 1987, we were asked to move to Moanza. This would be our fourth short stay at that beautiful church center. We'd spent the last year of our first term there, everyone rejoicing that now that small hospital had its own doctor. Norm had turned the work over to Frank, who stayed there barely a month before being evacuated after the army revolt following independence. We had returned to Moanza as soon as possible, Norm cutting his furlough short and the rest of the family following later. Norm hadn't been there a year when polio sent him back to the States. After our polio furlough we'd worked two years at Vanga, under another doctor, and then gone back to Moanza to replace the head nurse going to the States for further training, much as our friend Kimpiatu from Sona Bata had done. That was to be only a three-year term, Norm coming back after polio, so again we were at Moanza only one year.

Now again it was a case of further training. Our second year at Kikongo, Dr. Kwata was free to study Public Health in Kinshasa since Norm was there to supervise the hospital and the Rural Health Zone. In mid-1987 Dr. Kwata was back at Kikongo, but the doctor at Moanza had been chosen to attend that same Public Health School. So back we went.

As you saw, we loved Moanza, but we had never stayed there longer than a year. In a sense we'd had three honeymoons there. This time we were there two years, and the honeymoon ended.

Problems were apparent from our arrival. Norm was immediately handed a letter making accusations against someone who was leaving. It was obvious that tension and jealousy were rampant, not just between tribes but even between villages. There was quite a bit of epilepsy, and the number of people suffering from river blindness had increased. Poverty was more evident. The road to Moanza was in worse shape than before. Our average speed coming in on that road was 20 kilometers (12½ miles) per hour. No wonder commercial truck drivers did not vie with each other for the Moanza market. Moanza women produced quantities of peanuts, but where could they sell them?

In the face of such poverty, Moanza was third in the Congo Baptist Convention in giving. At the weekly women's meeting the offering ran around 90 zaïres, about two zaïres per woman. At Kikongo most of the women gave nothing at the weekly meeting. After the meeting the Moanza women would sing and dance their way to the hospital to give food to the patients from their own meager stocks. Once I asked the school principal's wife, "What do you do when someone comes to your door begging for food?" There were so many!

She replied simply, "If I have it, I give it." I tried that solution. A boy came to the door asking for tomato paste. I had a carton of the tiny cans. I gave him one. Another boy came. I gave him one. The word spread, and before the afternoon was over the carton was empty. Then the boys who had not received tomato paste overpowered the smaller ones and took theirs away. Obviously it wasn't going to be that simple for me.

People were praying. At Kikongo the Scripture Union had been strong. Here at Moanza there were four Scripture groups, for men, for women, boys, and girls. One of the hospital nurses spent part of his vacation joining in an evangelistic campaign. Another asked us to pray for him as he set out to vaccinate a thousand village children who were not yet protected against measles. People came individually for prayer and counsel.

An especially bright spot was getting to know the Congolese area pastor and his wife, Jacques and Rose. When we got there Rose was beginning a literacy class. Years later she was chosen to head up the literacy program for the whole Convention.

The first of those two years at Moanza we lived in the house at the top of the airstrip, because Jack and Trissie were on home assignment. Bob and Anelise lived in the other missionary house next door. The house Cliff and Joy had occupied so long before was now Jacques and Rose's.

While we were there our daughter Grace and her family came to visit. Grace and Michael now had four children: Monique, Daniel, Marjorie, and five-month-old Matthew. Grace had wanted her family to see the country she'd grown up in, but Michael hadn't been interested. Now Michael, a professor of behavioral and biological psychology, had an opportunity for some summer study at St. Andrews in Scotland (where golf originated). It made sense to combine that trip with a visit to Moanza. Michael decided to do it before Scotland. Plenty of culture shock either way.

Michael brought along materials to test Congolese children, materials that did not depend on language. There were various wooden shapes to be fitted into holes, blindfolded I believe. And there were other tests. Michael found differences between Congolese and American children. Americans tend to name things in their minds, at least, before doing anything with them. These children would deal with the object in question without bothering to name it. "What do you suppose makes the difference, Michael?"

"Well, there could be differences in brain development from the environment in which they learn and adapt from very early childhood into their school years."

Monique celebrated her seventh birthday at Moanza, as her mother had done. The difference was that Grace had been there a while and could talk with the Congolese girls who came to her party. Monique had to manage without a common language. She was fascinated by insects, so for a birthday present we gave her a rhinoceros beetle, a large and fearsome looking insect. She was delighted. She kept it in a glass jar on the little divider that separated one side of the living room from the dining room. She wanted to be sure no one swept it off onto the floor by mistake, so she made a sign warning people to be CAREFUL, BEETLE. Remember, Monique had just turned seven. The sign actually read CARFUL, BEDDLE.

Monique had a creative mind and decided to produce a play. Granted, we were in Africa, but the play involved Native Americans. She draped blankets over a corner of the fenced-in yard to create a tepee. Five-year-old Daniel was not interested but agreed to play the fearless hunter. Twice he went out with bow and arrow and shot the same log, which he dragged home, Monique prepared, and they ate. Afterwards Monique scrubbed the dishes with sand.

Marjorie was only two and did most of her traveling on Daddy's back. Some of the women, concerned, asked if she was crippled. No, it was just a lot quicker to pick her up and carry her.

Michael discovered a boy in the workmen's village who had never been able to use his legs. He just sat on the ground all the time, crawling and dragging his useless legs when he needed to move. But his parents could tell he was intelligent; if he heard a plane overhead he would draw it in the sand. Michael took the initiative to have a special chair built so the boy could sit in school. His sister agreed to carry him on her back. And the boy started first grade. Later I gave a sample lesson in that class, and that boy caught on better than any of the others. He excelled in school, and he must have felt some satisfaction in being able to read and learn with other children, but he never smiled.

From that visit on, Michael was determined to come back to Africa and do something to help those children. While continuing to teach at his college, he earned a Master of Public Health degree at the University of Michigan and eventually became an adjunct professor there.

During that Moanza term our son Jim came. He had graduated from LeTourneau College with various pilot's and mechanic's licenses and got some flying experience on Cape Cod and was hoping to take over our colleague Jack's aviation ministry when Jack retired. Now he had come to learn to fly Jack's Short Takeoff and Landing (STOL) plane and to do the flying and maintenance of that plane while Jack and Trissie would be on furlough. He occupied the guest house where we had lived our last month at Moanza in 1960. He hadn't, of course. He wasn't born till '63. Jim in French is Jacques. Pastor Jacques was pleased that our son had the same name as he.

There was another young American around, David, a Peace Corps volunteer working on water supply. He lived in a very simple house in the village at the top of the hill above us. He was a fine young man, and he and Jim enjoyed each other's company. David did not want to be called Davidi, so he used his middle name, Sabin, with the French pronunciation. We missionaries (and the young men) got together on Sunday evenings. We read a biography of Jonathan Goforth together, and then *The Great Mission Advance,* an account of a large number of Baptist missionaries who sailed together from the States to the Far East in 1835, some to Burma, some to Thailand, some to China. While discussing the book someone remarked how sad it was that just ten years later the Southern Baptists split off from the Northern ones. The Northerners felt that slave owners could not be appointed as missionaries; how could they relate to people of color as brothers when they owned people of color? But the Southerners felt it was a great loss to exclude all slave owners. They pointed out that some Southerners inherited slaves, when they themselves might be against slavery. So the split came. When Sabin heard about this, he was shocked. The son of a Southern Baptist minister, he had always believed that Southern Baptists were directly descended from John the Baptist.

Remember the junior high I had directed back in '65–'66, two whole classes? It was now part of a secondary school of ten classes. With all these students in residence, the beautiful church, built of local pink and purplish stone, had become too small. The plan was to extend it on both sides. So we all took part, all who were able, in going down to the stream and bringing up rocks. The women carried them in baskets on their heads. I'm afraid I brought up only a couple of rocks each time.

One day on my way to church I was appalled at the litter covering all the area in front of the church. Students would freely rip pages or parts of pages out of their notebooks to write letters on or whatever, and freely throw papers on the ground. In front of people's homes the wives would sweep, but no one took the responsibility for cleaning up in front of God's house. Nor was there any bin or other place to put the litter. Well, approaching the church I picked up as much as my two hands would hold. Then what to do with it? When we went forward for the offering, I deposited my trash in an empty one of the little wooden offering boxes, explaining to the usher holding another box for the offering, "I picked this up in front of God's house. There's no place to put it." But the choir was singing loudly and he had no idea what I said.

Well! Great indignation! Mama Abell had committed sacrilege! She had put trash in the offering! After the offering Pastor Jacques called me forward. "Mama Abell, you may not take communion."

Later we talked in his office. I explained, "The courtyard in front of God's house looked so terrible, covered with trash. I brought some in to protest. Then there was no place to put it. I didn't realize the empty wooden box was sacred." When I finally used the word "sorry," the pastor decided I could be forgiven. The next Sunday he explained my side of the story to the congregation, called me forward, had me kneel, and restored me to fellowship. It's nice that a missionary can be disciplined by her African pastor.

When Jim had been flying with Jack for six months, it was time for a six-month checkup with an MAF (Mission Aviation Fellowship) pilot. The pilot came, and he and Jim went up in Jack's plane. Jack's wife, Trissie, was flight following. After a while she could not make contact with the plane. Of course she didn't tell us about that until later. Another MAF pilot was at Moanza, and he and Jack took off in the MAF plane to head towards a village airstrip where Jim and the other pilot had been planning to land. Shortly after they were airborne, they heard the signal of an emergency locator transmitter (ELT)!

Here's what had happened. The flight had gone well until Jim was to land at a certain airstrip. The plane was a tail dragger—no nose wheel but a tail wheel. Jim had landed the two main wheels, but the tail wheel had not yet come down to the ground when a goat ran onto the strip in front of the plane. Jim slammed on the brakes. The goat escaped scot free, but the plane did a somersault and landed on its back. It is not good for a plane to land on its back.

The two pilots, hanging upside down from their seat belts, asked each other, "Are you all right?" They each had a scrape down the front of their leg. That was all. Great relief. They got out of the plane, removed the ELT (which had not been activated by the relatively slow forward deceleration before the plane flipped over and made a rapid "backward" deceleration), and turned it on. They prayed a prayer of thanksgiving, then got help from the local villagers to drag the upside-down plane to the side of the airstrip to make room for the other plane to land. About that time their rescuers arrived.

The plane was trucked to Kinshasa, where Jim spent the next 15 months repairing it. MAF let him use their hangar space, gave him valuable advice, and shared their maintenance expertise. Our colleagues Willard and Norma—Norma had given Jim his first haircut at Vanga all those years before—invited Jim to live with them in the city. Their own son, a little older, had also graduated from LeTourneau and was on his own. What a boon for Jim! Part of the time he lived at the hostel, where he had been a school kid, helping the hostel parents when he wasn't working at the hangar.

The plane flew again, and Jim flew it a little more, but he did not replace Jack while he and Trissie were on furlough. They were back from furlough before the plane's repairs had been completed. However, the MAF people in Kinshasa had been favorably impressed with Jim during those 15 months of working side by side. They needed a pilot right away in the northwest part of the Congo and asked if he would serve temporarily. Jim began receiving a little financial support from US churches and friends through MAF, which the organization supplemented with a small salary. He went up to the northern border and flew for MAF for a little over a year.

Back in the US he got a degree in Missiology from Fuller Theological Seminary to prepare himself for appointment by American Baptists, but the board was not willing to appoint a missionary for aviation work. We already had one missionary seconded to MAF, and a teaching doctor for Vanga was seen as the greater need. So Jim did not fly for American Baptists, but he was accepted as a career missionary with MAF and is still with them.

His time at Fuller was not wasted. Oh, he learned a lot from his creative profs. In one January term the students were told, "Pick one of the 200 languages spoken in Pasadena and see how much you can learn by contacting people on the street and saying, 'I want to learn your language.'" They were required to spend six weeks learning a language completely different from any that they already knew. Jim chose Armenian. He found that people had varied reactions when he learned to say in their language something like, "I am like a baby learning your language." But more important, he met Candace, an active American Baptist from Terre Haute, Indiana, a Fuller student working on her Master of Divinity and also a crackerjack secondary school math teacher. Shortly after our retirement Jim and Candy were married, to their delight and ours.

Now Moanza received a wonderful gift. While we were still at Kikongo, Moanza had invited a brand-new doctor to come work there, first taking a two-year residency at Vanga. Prime (Preem) came from a village about 40 miles from Moanza. Although he had lived in cities almost all his life, he had kept in touch with his extended family and now felt a strong call to work at Moanza. With a rocky start and some difficulties along the way, Prime did follow the program at Vanga, marry a physiotherapist, and become the proud father of twin girls. In 1989 he arrived at Moanza. He and Melanie were delightful people, deeply committed Christians, and dedicated medical workers. Norm and Prime enjoyed working together very much.

The year is 1989. School is out for what we would call summer vacation. In that part of the Congo it's dry season. The high school principal asks me, "Will you teach English next school year?"

"Yes, I'll be glad to."

Then Norm is called back to Kikongo. They're starting a little school for auxiliary nurses, and he's needed. "Sorry, Mr. Principal, I won't be teaching here after all." He was not happy.

CHAPTER TWENTY-ONE

The Last Year

Back to Kikongo. Back to our good little house and our Kikongo friends. We don't know whether Purpose was happy or not. Oh, you don't know Purpose. When we lived at Kikongo before, we had been given a silver tabby kitten. She did not appreciate moving to Moanza. She did a lot of meowing, and we made several unnecessary stops along the way, trying to understand her needs. Norm stopped halfway to talk with the nurse at a Health Center. Purpose was glad to get out and stretch her legs. When we were ready to continue our journey, Purpose was nowhere to be found. We called. No kitty. We looked all around the vehicle and underneath it. No cat to be seen. Finally someone discovered her. She had found some projection under the car that she could lie on. We hadn't seen her on the ground; she was a little higher. OK, cat, back to purgatory. When we opened the car door at Moanza she immediately fled to Jack and Trissie's roof. She didn't come down for some time. Jack thought he could bring her down with a broom. That just intensified her desire to remain inaccessible. Eventually she did descend and decided to make Moanza her home. Why Purpose?

Because she purred more than any other puss I had known. When she reached the age of six months she produced her first litter, asking me to hold her paw (figuratively) for that first experience of labor. Only one kitten survived from that first litter. It was so soft I named it Whisper, and every subsequent kitten received a name that had either "per" or "puss" in it. All those Moanza kittens were silver tabbies like Mama. Now at Kikongo she had a new mate and produced black and white kittens. One had a black circle about the size of a penny on the back of its neck, so it was named Per Cent. Another got stepped on but managed to survive; we named it Perseverance. We gave one kitten to the chaplain's wife, who named it Nkundi, which means "friend." That was unusual; Congolese don't ordinarily think of animals as friends.

Norm's principal job this year was directing (and teaching in) the new nursing school. Mr. Nsiny, the head nurse, also taught. A lovely female nurse named Itey (ee-tay-ee) had been working at Kikongo since she graduated from the Vanga nursing school in 1987. Now she supervised

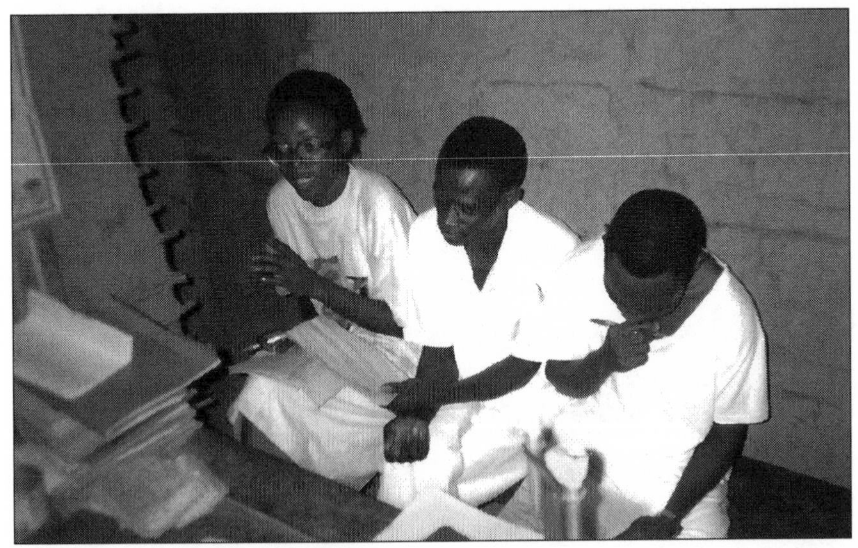

Nurse Itey and two of her students

the students' work on the wards and in the Rural Health Centers. She also taught nursing technique in the classroom and supervised the girls' dorms. Busy lady. We had 17 students that first year.

I taught a class that I suppose was called *séminaire.* One boy was a Jehovah's Witness. I asked him what differences he saw between their way of doing things and ours. The only difference he could think of was that Jehovah's Witnesses celebrate communion only once a year!

Another day we talked about AIDS, called SIDA in French. Young people in particular liked to pooh-pooh the existence of AIDS, calling it *Syndrome Imaginaire pour Décourager les Amants* (Imaginary Syndrome to Discourage Lovers). I asked them, "Have any of you seen someone die of AIDS?"

One girl had lived in Kinshasa and replied sadly, "I have." No one mentioned "Imaginary Syndrome" in my presence again. Norm saw his first case of AIDS at that hospital. We had previously heard about a man on the staff at IME who had died of AIDS. He had been a generous blood donor. How many others had he infected?!

One of the students developed rheumatoid arthritis and had to be assigned easy tasks like dealing with linens instead of the regular ward work the others had to do. All the students passed at the end of the year, and a new first-year class of 15 was added. We stayed for the first months of that second year, departing at the end of October.

It was hard to leave all the work in the hands of Dr. Kwata, Mr. Nsiny, and Miss Itey. We had hoped to be there until another doctor arrived. We weren't able to do that, but there was one on the way.

Doctors at IME recommended Dr. Ibi. Medical students in Kinshasa have only classroom work at the medical school; their last year they are farmed out to various hospitals. You read about that when we were at IME. Dr. Ibi had done that last year at IME and become known for his Christian character as well as his medical ability. His home was in the Bandundu Region but not very close to Kikongo. Would he be willing to work at this new place? Yes, he would! He answered Norm's letter enthusiastically and humbly. (Not all new doctors are humble!) He came to Kikongo for a visit, stayed with the Kwata family, and bonded with them almost immediately. When we left in October of 1990, he was in Kinshasa patiently pushing his assignment to Kikongo through the various government offices.

Remember our son-in-law Michael's visit to Moanza? His determination to return to Africa to help? Now he had learned of a Fulbright grant to enable an anthropologist or an economist to do research in Africa for a school year. Michael, of course, was a behavioral and developmental psychologist, but he applied anyway, did a great deal of work making the necessary contacts and getting the necessary recommendations—and was awarded the grant. He came with the family to Kikongo shortly before school started in 1990 and stayed till the summer of 1991. He enlisted several Congolese helpers and tested school children at our church center and also at a Catholic mission, checking, among other things, what difference medical treatment (against worms, malaria, and the like) made in their cognitive ability and educational performance. When the year was over he recorded his and his family's experience in a delightful and impressive book entitled *The Accidental Anthropologist.* And he continued his interest in Africa and ways to help.

Michael was now under the umbrella of the US State Department at the embassy in Kinshasa (which administered the Fulbright program in Zaire) and eligible to patronize the US commissariat. When the rest of the family boarded an MAF plane for Kikongo, he stayed in Kinshasa for a few days, following up with the people he had enlisted to support his project and doing various errands. That first evening at Kikongo, Grace, Monique, Daniel, Marjorie, and little Matthew were gathered around the dining room table with us when flying ants decided to swarm. They came out from between the bricks of the walls and flew around. The children were naturally frightened. Monique

Uncle Jim brings goodies for Grace and Michael's children

particularly ducked whenever an ant flew by. Much later I reminded her, "Remember how scared you were of the flying ants your very first evening at Kikongo?"

And she confessed, "Oh, I was scared at first, but then I enjoyed dramatizing it."

Daniel had a birthday, with presents to unwrap. One looked especially inviting, a toy car. His dad exclaimed, "You're going to be the envy of all the Congolese boys." Alas! As he opened it we remembered that we had packed medicines in that empty box. Daniel's focus that year was soccer. If he wasn't playing soccer with other boys, he was standing on the sidelines watching the men play.

Marjorie found a playmate in the missionary girl next door. Their favorite activity was running down the slope in front of our house. The joys of a simple life! Three of our grandchildren joined the children's choir Mama Thérèse was leading. They sang well in French! They may even have understood what they were singing.

Dr. Grandpa and Grandma taking care of little Matthew

Norm had gone back to the States in January to be with his sister, who was dying of cancer. When he returned he brought a camcorder. I took some videos of him and of the other medical personnel. When we returned to the States we left the camcorder with Michael, who made very good use of it. Eventually Norm looked at a video of himself teaching and remarked in some surprise, "In January I was able to reach the top of the blackboard!" In the meantime post-polio had been taking its toll.

We came to the last week. The local people put on a feast in our honor in the largest classroom, with lots of food and speeches. Then the last Sunday. Formal farewells in church. At the end people followed us home and sang and sang in front of our little house. Finally we clapped our hands in appreciation and went inside. I wonder whether there was something else we should have done.

We left household stuff with Grace. When that family returned to the States they would give it away. We made boxes for a few special pieces, like my portable Irish harp and a chief's chair that came apart as two pieces of wood.

And then our 34 years in the Congo were over. Our other three children and their children were in the States. Our Congolese friends we would never see again. We would keep in touch by mail for a while. We left each other in God's hands.

CHAPTER TWENTY-TWO

If We Had It To Do Over

We would listen. Listen more and talk less. Ask more questions. Find out where other people are coming from before we judge. Try not to judge! If other people aren't doing what we want, it may be they don't understand us. Try to understand them.

Michael understood so much in the short year he was in Zaïre, some things we had never learned in all our years. And he did it without knowing much of the language. Of course he's a psychologist, but no doubt we could have tried harder.

I remember trying to teach religion to a second-year nursing class at IME. I was very discouraged with that class. They did not seem to care about the patients they should have been learning to serve. And I tried to change them by scolding and punishing. If I could do it over, I would throw away the textbook I was trying to follow and devote all my efforts and prayers to helping them realize God loved them. Surely that's the prerequisite for extending love to others.

Once the national soccer team, the *Léopards,* won the Africa Cup. The President declared a national holiday. At the time I regretted one more day lost to teaching, but now I have a better appreciation for what a feat that must have been.

One thing we never understood until we read about it after we retired. We would occasionally invite Congolese over for a meal and were disappointed that they never invited us. When Norm was back at Moanza for five months without the family, he invited himself to Congolese homes, taking along a can of corned beef to make his visit less of a burden. That was certainly not in the culture. The article we read pointed out that Congolese hospitality is different. If anyone comes to a Congolese home for any reason, he is always offered at least a soft drink. If he comes at mealtime, he's invited to share the meal. If someone came to our house at mealtime, I would say, "We're eating now. Could you come back later?" How gross! How impolite! And I never realized.

This should have clued me in. One day at Vanga I was feeling frustrated and just started walking on a path, not knowing where I was

Remembering

going. Eventually I came to a little village, at least a cluster of houses. A woman came to a door, greeted me, and brought out two chairs for us to sit on, and we talked a little. After a while I went home, refreshed. The next day the woman showed up at our house at Vanga, bearing a chicken! She hadn't been able to show me hospitality when I was there so now she was making up for it.

There's a verse in Psalm 37 that says, "Don't give in to worry or anger; it only leads to trouble." Knowing that is one thing; doing it is another. If we could do it over again, we would plead with the Father, or the Holy Spirit, to deliver us from anger, which spoiled our witness so many times, and to give us understanding and wisdom as we talked with people. No matter how hot it was, how tired we were, or if we had malaria, speaking in anger was never the right response.

One thing we did do right was inviting people over to pray. We did it only once or twice at Vanga, regularly one year at Moanza, once in Kinshasa. We would do it much more. And I would remember that women like to pray with other women, men with men.

I would make sure to write our parents every week. I started out that way, but there were (many) times when I neglected that pleasant duty. When we talked with other members of their retirement community, we would hear how Dad went to the post office every single day and Mother never failed to ask, "Is there a letter from Jean?"

At least 11 days out of 12 Dad had to reply, "No, dear, not today."

I would also try much harder to write to our supporters regularly. That was one thing that too often got neglected. But I found time to read fiction. Our missionary children, and present missionaries with our board, are required to communicate regularly with their network of support. We were requested to.

We would also pray more in our home. We always planned to have daily devotions with our children but somehow it never became a regular practice. Our kids remember reading books together on the veranda at Sona Bata in the evening, and it was good, but we should have been reading the Bible too, and other books that would help us grow spiritually.

And I would pay more attention to our children. Back before we ever left the States, a neighbor had remarked, "She forgets she has children." She was right! When Grace found her daddy with the whole surgical team kneeling around a patient on our living room floor; when the man with a gun came through my bedroom window and I yelled at the top of my voice; and when we left a teenager in the city and got absorbed in our work down-country—I forgot I had children. When they didn't write I assumed they were all right. It wasn't until after our retirement, when Grace shared a book called *Letters Never Sent,* that I began to realize how different the adjustment is for missionaries' children—third culture kids—than for missionaries.

How good God is! He guided our children's growth, with the help of other Christians, and molded each one into such a great person, in spite of our neglect. Thank you, Father.

In any of these areas, we can't go back and do it over, can we? In the days when we showed slides to church groups, we liked to close with a picture taken inside the little church at Songololo, one of several churches built by our colleague Elmer. In the wall behind the platform is a lighted cross. We would ask people, "Where does the light come from?" It was not electricity. The wall was made of concrete blocks, and holes had been pierced in the blocks that formed the cross. The light was sunlight. We could say, "We went to the Congo to pierce holes in walls so the light of God's love could shine through." Did we do that? Sometimes. Sometimes not. We thank God for the times we did listen to his wisdom and his will, and for bringing good even out of our mistakes. And I think of the names of some of our Congo friends, and the faces of others, many gone on now—it's been 29 years since we said those good-bys at Kikongo—and pray his blessing on them and their children and grandchildren, and on that country, now called the Congo again, with all its problems and promise, and every person in it loved and cherished by the Father.

Made in the USA
Middletown, DE
29 December 2019